STUDIES IN MODERN ART   7

Imagining the Future of
The Museum of Modern Art

THE MUSEUM OF MODERN ART, NEW YORK

Distributed by Harry N. Abrams, Inc., New York

Studies in Modern Art is prepared by the Research and Scholarly Publications Program of The Museum of Modern Art, which was initiated with the support of a grant from the Andrew W. Mellon Foundation. Publication is made possible by an endowment fund established by the Andrew W. Mellon Foundation, the Edward John Noble Foundation, Mr. and Mrs. Perry R. Bass, and the National Endowment for the Humanities' Challenge Grant Program.

Produced by the Department of Publications,
The Museum of Modern Art, New York
Edited by Barbara Ross
Design and typography by Antony Drobinski, Emsworth Design, New York
Production by Chris Zichello
Printed by Meridian Printing, East Greenwich, Rhode Island
Bound by Acme Bookbinding Company, Inc., Charlestown, Massachusetts

Frontispiece: Yoshio Taniguchi. Competition Proposal for the Expansion and Renovation of The Museum of Modern Art, New York. Model (detail). 1997. Paper and plastic, 38 x 19⅝ x 69¾" (96.5 x 49.8 x 177.2 cm)

Contents

Preface

This is the seventh volume in the series *Studies in Modern Art,* which was instituted to encourage the study of The Museum of Modern Art's collections and programs. (The purposes of the series are more fully described in the Preface to the first issue, published in 1991.) The fourth through sixth volumes were devoted to the Museum's own history. Therefore, it seemed particularly fitting that this subsequent issue should be devoted to the Museum's future. *Studies in Modern Art 7* documents the lengthy process that led to the selection, in December 1997, of an architect for the Museum's imminent major expansion, and was planned to accompany the exhibition, to be held at the Museum from March 3 through April 28, 1998, of the design proposals submitted by the three finalists in the architectural competition for the expansion project.

The process that led to the selection of an architect is described, and its logic explained, in the overview by Glenn D. Lowry, Director of The Museum of Modern Art, that appears on pp. 11–19. The essay's main points deserve summation here, since it effectively explains the shape of the volume itself. The chronology, in brief, is as follows:

1. Extended discussions among the senior staff and trustees of the Museum over the need for, and the desired functions and venue of, an expanded Museum took place throughout the early 1990s, ultimately leading to the creation of two trustee committees: the Expansion Committee, chaired by Jerry I. Speyer, and the Architect Selection Committee, chaired by Sid R. Bass.
2. The decision to attempt to expand on a site adjacent to the present Museum led to negotiations to purchase the Dorset Hotel, on West Fifty-fourth Street, and adjacent properties, all of which were finally acquired on February 2, 1996.
3. A detailed analysis of the Museum's needs was begun in September 1996 under the direction of the architectural firm Cooper, Robertson and Partners, which also organized the preparation of the Architectural Competition, in its various stages, and the Final Expansion Program, completed in December 1997.
4. From September 1995 through January 1996, Mr. Bass presided as chairman of the Imagining the Future Committee, which met with senior staff of the Museum to discuss institutional aims for the future. These discussions led to the drafting of a Mission Statement and an Executive Statement, describing, respectively, the Museum's broad aims and the rationale for its expansion. The Board of Trustees approved these documents on October 2, 1996.

The preceding four stages, being either too extended or detailed to record properly, or involving confidential materials, are not documented in this volume (the Mission and Executive statements are, however, included on pp. 20–26). Therefore, the contents of the volume, following Mr. Lowry's overview, effectively begin with what happened next:

5. From October 4 through October 6, 1996, the Museum convened a weekend retreat at the Pocantico Center of the Rockefeller Brothers Fund in Westchester County, New York, the theme of which was "Building the Future: Museums of Modern Art in the Twenty-first Century" (see pp. 30–73).

6. From October 22 through December 12, 1996, a series of public lectures and panel discussions devoted to the theme "Imagining The Museum of Modern Art in the Twenty-first Century" was held at the Museum under the auspices of this publication (see pp. 74–141).

7. In the period January 8–13, 1997, a broad group of architects was reviewed by the Architect Selection Committee; with the approval of the Board of Trustees, ten architects from this group were invited to participate in the Charette, a design exercise that would lead to the final Architectural Competition. (This review process is not recorded herein.)

8. From February 17 through March 24, 1997, the Charette took place. It is recorded here on pp. 142–265. Within the period April 2–8, the Charette submissions were reviewed and three finalists chosen by the Architect Selection Committee; the finalists were approved by the Board of Trustees on April 9.

9. From June 4 through September 26, 1997, the three finalists engaged in the Architectural Competition proper (see pp. 266–339). The submissions were reviewed for compliance with the overall Architectural Program, and then evaluated by the Selection Committee. The committee made its recommendations to the Board of Trustees on December 8, 1997, at which time the architect named on p. 11 was declared the winner of the Competition.

The Museum had not only chosen an architect, but the design proposal submitted by that architect. This proposal will, of course, be revised and adjusted in light of the Museum's Final Expansion Program (as established in December 1997) and discussions held with staff, as the design is transformed into detailed plans for the expanded building. All that is for a future publication.

This has been an enormously complicated volume to assemble, edit, and produce. Including the proposals submitted by the architects themselves, it contains contributions by nearly fifty people. To all of them, both the Museum and I are deeply indebted for their involvement, not only in the realization of this volume, but also, and more importantly, in the process it documents.

Insofar as the volume itself is concerned, particular thanks are owed to Mr. Lowry and to Terence Riley, Chief Curator, Department of Architecture and Design, for their guiding support and the texts they contributed. Furthermore, both I and the readers of this volume are indebted to four individuals who played crucial roles in its realization: Beatrice Kernan, Executive Editor of *Studies in Modern Art,* who skillfully supervised the detailed scholarly and editorial processes that brought it into being; Patterson Sims, Deputy Director for Education and Research Support, who offered counsel in the shaping of the Pocantico Conference and the Studies in Modern Art Lecture Series, and in the orchestration of the volume's publication; Matilda McQuaid, Associate Curator, Department of Architecture and Design, who, with Mr. Riley, co-directed *Toward the New Museum of Modern Art: Sketchbooks by Ten Architects,* the exhibition from which our Charette documentation is derived; and Barbara Ross, Associate Editor, Department of Publications, who accomplished the demanding task of editing this volume with both dedication and skill.

A debt of thanks is also owed to Karen Davidson, Assistant Director for Policy and Strategic Planning; Alex Cooper, Scott Newman, and William MacIntosh, of Cooper, Robertson and Partners; and Marnie Pillsbury and Ethel Shein. Crucial research and editorial support was provided by project researcher Meisha Hunter, as well as by Museum staff members Christel Hollevoet, Bevin Howard, Jasmine Moorhead, Sarah Newman, Charles Rockefeller, and Dale Tucker. Chief Archivist Rona Roob, with the assistance of Claire Dienes and Michelle Elligott in the Museum Archives, provided important archival information and documentation. Thanks are also due to Harriet Schoenholz Bee and Nancy Kranz of the Department of Publications; Mikki Carpenter, Jeffrey Ryan, and Rosa Laster of the Department of Photographic Services and Permissions; Ramona Bannayan, Jennifer Culvert, and Cheryl Horwitt of the Department of Registration; Janis Ekdahl and Eumie Imm Stroukoff, of the Museum Library; and Charles Silver, Charles Kalinowski, and Anthony Tavolacci of the Department of Film and Video. Administrative support for this volume required involvement in a myriad of realms; it was ably provided by Amy Romesburg, with additional assistance from Curbie Oestreich, Deanna Caceres, Bonnie Weill, Deborah Dewees, Marcie Año, Amy Horschak, and Sharon Dec. The volume was designed by Antony Drobinski of Emsworth Design, and its complex production overseen by Chris Zichello in the Museum's Department of Publications.

My colleagues at the Museum and I are grateful to the numerous people outside the institution who contributed in many ways: David Hinkel, for special assistance in facilitating our research efforts; Yoshio Amika, Geraldine Aramanda, Cecilia C. Arca, Laura Brioschi, Betty Chen, Estella M. Chung, Clay Conley, Susan Davidson, Elisabetta de Simone, Martha Graves, Alice Gray, Nicole Haeren, Frenziske Heindl, Philip and Frances Huscher, Madame Annie Jacques, Eileen M. Kennedy, David Margolis, Geoffrey P. Moussas, Carina Pernia, Gaelle Lavnot Prevost, Naomi Pritchard, Encarnita Rivera, Natasha Roach, Jean Paul Robert, Hilda Rodriguez, Joan Rykoff, Andrea Saemann, Jennifer Small, Linda Strauss, Jacquelyn Thomas, Evelyne Trehin, Akiko Tsurusaki, Alice Uebe, Bettina Ungerecht, and Marja van der Burgh, for responding to our various research inquiries; and David Allison, Robert M. Damora, Marta Falkowska, Ludwig Glaeser, Dr. Paulhans Peters, Steven Rosenthal, and Michael Slade, for providing valuable visual documentation.

Finally, we are pleased once again to acknowledge, with deep gratitude, the Andrew W. Mellon Foundation, the Edward J. Noble Foundation, Mr. and Mrs. Perry R. Bass, and the National Endowment for the Humanities' Challenge Grant Program for making this series of publications possible.

John Elderfield
Editor-in-Chief, *Studies in Modern Art*

The New Museum of Modern Art Expansion: A Process of Discovery

Glenn D. Lowry

At its meeting of December 8, 1997, the Board of Trustees appointed Yoshio Taniguchi as the architect of an expanded Museum of Modern Art, reconceived to meet the needs of the institution, and its broad public, in the twenty-first century.[1]

This decision culminated a process that had begun in the early 1990s, when the Museum began contemplating a major expansion. Motivated at first by the need to accommodate its growing collections of contemporary art, the project rapidly evolved into an institution-wide initiative to explore the intellectual, programmatic, and physical possibilities for the Museum in the next century. The initiatives described below have thus been part of a still-continuing process of discovery, one that is designed to insure that The Museum of Modern Art remains a venue of debate and discovery, of enjoyment and engagement, in the next century. And it is from a desire to encourage debate that we offer herein various observations about issues that were often private in nature, if not at times highly confidential.[2] They are discussed here not only because these efforts to plan for the Museum's future now form an integral part of the Museum's history, but also because the Museum knows that it must raise as many questions as it answers if its process of expansion, when ultimately complete, is to be successful.

A Single, Integrated Entity

The Museum of Modern Art occupies a unique location for a museum in New York City, six blocks south of Central Park and roughly centered between the Hudson and East rivers. The greater site area is surrounded by several major arteries: Fifty-seventh Street to the north (as well as Fifty-ninth Street, which borders Central Park), Forty-second Street to the south, the Avenue of the Americas (Sixth Avenue) to the west, and Fifth Avenue to the east. The presence of Rockefeller Center a few blocks to the south, the Theater District beginning one block to the west, and cultural institutions near the Museum and on adjacent blocks further characterize the area.[3]

The Museum's midblock location distinguishes it from other major New York City museums, most of which are located on the wider avenues and farther to the north. As a "street museum," it is not identified as an object surrounded by space, but as a part of the streetscape, which it has occupied since it moved into the townhouse at 11 West Fifty-third Street in 1932. Even as the Museum has grown to occupy

353 feet of frontage on Fifty-third Street and 387 feet on Fifty-fourth Street, its urban identity is still defined by the streets that border it; it is not close enough to engage the avenues, nor is the building itself readily visible either from Fifth Avenue or the Avenue of the Americas.[4] (For block plans showing the historical development of the Museum site, see pp. 96–97 of the present volume.)

The character of the Museum's bordering streets is quite distinct. The south side of Fifty-third Street, opposite the Museum, is occupied by only four buildings: 666 Fifth Avenue (the Tishman Building), the Donnell Branch of the New York Public Library, 31 West Fifty-second Street (which includes the American Craft Museum and the MoMA Design Store), and the CBS headquarters building. In contrast, the north side of Fifty-fourth Street, opposite the Museum, is occupied by seventeen buildings, and consequently retains much of its original residential scale and character. The six buildings that occupy the eastern half of the block, extending 450 feet from Fifth Avenue to a point opposite the North Wing of the Museum, are all designated New York City landmarks;[5] St. Thomas' Church, immediately to the east of the Museum on West Fifty-third Street, is landmarked as well.

At the time that The Museum of Modern Art began thinking about a new expansion, several options theoretically were available to it. These included the purchase of a second site elsewhere in the city; excavating under The Abby Aldrich Rockefeller Sculpture Garden; building on top of the Donnell Library across Fifty-third Street; and moving the entire Museum to a new location elsewhere in Manhattan. The Board of Trustees, however, rejected these possibilities in favor of acquiring the Dorset Hotel, located to the north and west of the Museum on Fifty-fourth Street, and two brownstone buildings adjacent to the hotel, one on Fifty-fourth Street and the other on Fifty-third Street (see fig. 2, p. 75). The Dorset site appealed to the trustees because it provided the only coherent way to expand, while retaining the sense of the Museum as a single, integrated entity located in Midtown Manhattan. At the same time, the trustees recognized that this was an extremely expensive option, and they committed themselves to a major capital initiative to raise the necessary funds to enable the Museum to fulfill it.

The sequence of initiatives and events summarized in the following pages (and discussed in greater detail elsewhere in this volume) was set in motion by the Museum's acquisition, on February 2, 1996, of the Dorset Hotel and its adjacent properties. But even before this happened, the Museum had realized that it could embark on an expansion only if it reviewed all of its goals and aspirations for the next twenty-five to thirty years. This period of time was chosen because it stretched far enough into the future to insure that the project would not be obsolete upon completion, yet it was finite enough for a set of reasonable assumptions to be made about institutional needs and priorities during this time.

As the Museum began examining its future needs, it quickly realized it required not merely new spaces but fundamentally different spaces from its existing ones. Or, put differently, The Museum of Modern Art could not afford to enlarge itself by simply *expanding,* as it had done in the past; if it wanted to meet the challenges of the future, it had to create a *new* Museum, one that could provide the kinds of spaces and spatial relationships that would allow it to realize its intellectual and programmatic goals.

Given the complexity of the issues involved in this task, the Museum determined, first, to explore the range of ideas open to it; second, to outline and articulate its mission and goals and to define its needs; and third and finally, to select an architect for the project. Each stage and aspect of this process, however, should be seen as interconnected and interdependent. Thus, the selection of an architect followed from, and responded to, discussions among the Museum's trustees, senior staff, chief curators, and friends about the institution's mission and goals, as well as from its analysis of its needs. Three trustee committees were established to help guide these initiatives: the Imagining the Future Committee, chaired by Sid R. Bass;[6] the Expansion Committee, chaired by Jerry I. Speyer;[7] and the Architect Selection Committee, also chaired by Mr. Bass.[8] Terence Riley, Chief Curator, Department of Architecture and Design, served as the advisor to the Selection Committee and helped in the shaping of the process outlined below.

Conceptualizing the New Museum of Modern Art

From September 1995 through January 1996, Mr. Bass presided over several meetings of the Imagining the Future Committee, which comprised selected trustees, the Museum's director and seven chief curators, and other members of the senior staff. These meetings were devoted to consideration of what kind of institution the Museum wanted to be in the next century, and discussion of the qualities most admired in other museums. Their purpose was not to arrive at a concrete set of conclusions, but, rather, to establish a common vocabulary and set of aspirations for the institution. Among the issues raised during these discussions was how the Museum could balance its debt to tradition and history with its commitment to the present and the future. Other issues raised by the committee included: the significance of the Museum as a resource, in the twenty-first century, for the study of the art of this century; the scope and appropriate form of its educational mission, including the importance of insuring that it maintain a vigorous artistic and intellectual presence worldwide; and the challenge of making the best use of new technologies. Several discussions centered on physical growth, and the role that architecture could play in reinforcing the Museum's mission: how best to organize the galleries in order to tell the story, or, rather, stories, of modern and contemporary art; how the spaces of the Museum may be used to encourage, among its audience, engagement and dialogue with the collection; and how the Museum must retain a sense of intimacy, even when dramatically enlarged.

In February 1996, the process of imagining the future was expanded to include the Museum's six acquisitions committees,[9] and its conservation and education committees, each of which is composed of trustees and friends of the Museum. From these meetings evolved both a Mission Statement and an Executive Statement outlining the rationale for the Museum's expansion; these documents (see appendix, pp. 20–26 for the full texts) were approved by the Board of Trustees on October 2, 1996. Together, they articulate the Museum's commitment to remaining a forward-looking institution engaged in the collection, study, and display of contemporary art as well as the art of the recent past. The trustees recognized that, to sustain this level of activity, The Museum of Modern Art must not only foster an outstanding professional staff, but also periodically reevaluate itself, responding to new ideas and initiatives with both insight and imagination. Or, to put it differently, the Museum must commit itself to the consequences of its belief that modern art remains a vital and dynamic tradition, based on a continuing series of arguments and counter-arguments that need to be explored through exhibitions, installations, and publications.

Among the many goals set for the expansion by the Board of Trustees was the stimulation of discussion among various audiences about the future role of museums of modern art, and how architecture can contribute to fulfilling that role. The Museum, therefore, convened a weekend retreat at the Pocantico Conference Center of the Rockefeller Brothers Fund from October 4 to 6, 1996. Participants at the conference included the Museum's seven chief curators, various museum directors, critics, scholars, artists, and architects, and the trustees on the Architect Selection Committee. The discussions that took place were broadcast at the Museum for members of the staff and Board of Trustees unable to attend the retreat because of space limitations at the conference center. The theme of the Pocantico Conference was "Building the Future: Museums of Modern Art in the Twenty-first Century," and discussions were organized around four conversations, each designed to raise a group of related questions about art, architecture, and museums of modern art. Each discussion, moderated by a chief curator of the Museum, included an artist, an architect, a critic, and a museum director. (For an edited transcript of the entire Pocantico Conference, see pp. 30–73.)

Several issues emerged at Pocantico that have subsequently had a bearing on the selection process for the Museum's architect. These included the realization that the Museum needed to find a way to theorize its space rather than simply to plan its architecture; that the Dorset site accentuated the urbanistic challenge of the Museum to mediate between the experience of the city and of looking at art; and that, in order to stay "modern," the Museum had to avoid becoming merely a treasure house or safety deposit box.[10] Additionally, there was agreement that the Museum needed to diversify and complicate the experience of looking at modern art for that experience of art to remain startling and compelling. From these observations, a number of intriguing metaphors were developed to characterize the museum of modern art in general as a venue of storytelling or narration in a novel way. (Some of these metaphors are described on pp. 41–52, 93–99.)

The Pocantico Conference was limited to the thirty-two participants, and to the audience who heard the live audio broadcasts at the Museum. In order to expand the discussion about the Museum's future, a series of public lectures and discussions titled "Imagining The Museum of Modern Art in the Twenty-first Century" was presented at the Museum from October 22 to December 12, 1996, under the auspices of this publication. The series encompassed two lectures, one on the programmatic implications of the Museum's periodic expansions, the other on the architectural context of the new expansion; and two panel discussions, the first addressing the very idea of modern museums, the second centered on museums and society. The full Studies in Modern Art Lecture Series did more than merely widen the audience, beyond that at Pocantico, for the discussion about the Museum's future; it propelled the discussion in a more specifically architectural direction. (The series is published here, in a slightly revised form, on pp. 74–141).

Both the Pocantico Conference and the Studies in Modern Art Lecture Series were meant to sharpen, and to challenge, the Museum's own thinking about its requirements for the future, as well as to explore, first with an audience of scholars, critics, architects, museum directors, and artists, and then with a larger public, ideas pertinent to its expansion. The result of these exercises was the refinement of many of the ideas generated during the discussions within the Imagining the Future Committee, as well as in internal curatorial and senior staff meetings, that had been brought together in the institution's Mission and Executive statements. This led to the creation of a common set of goals for the project among the Museum's senior curators, staff, and trustees.

Needs Analysis

At roughly the same time that these initiatives were being undertaken, the Museum embarked on a detailed Needs Analysis. Cooper, Robertson and Partners, an architectural firm with extensive planning experience, conducted the analysis under the direction of Alex Cooper.[11] Karen Davidson, Assistant Director for Policy and Strategic Planning at the Museum, coordinated and oversaw the project. In order to insure that the expanded Museum would accommodate anticipated future needs, each department was asked to outline its current requirements; its needs for the year 2005, the projected completion date for the expansion; and its anticipated needs for the year 2025. Several assumptions were made to facilitate this exercise, including the following:

1. The number of temporary exhibitions, approximately twenty-five per year, should not increase, despite the growth in the size of the Museum, and the amount of space available for such exhibitions should remain at approximately 30,000 square feet.
2. The maximum amount of space possible should be allocated for the display of the permanent collections.
3. The building should anticipate the need for, and use of, new technologies.
4. Works of art as well as books and other materials could be stored off-site, but should be within easy access of Fifty-third Street.
5. A substantial increase in personnel would be needed to staff the new facility.

Questionnaires were prepared by Cooper, Robertson in conjunction with the chief curators and senior staff of the Museum, and distributed on September 16, 1996, to all thirty-five department heads for completion. Department heads were encouraged to review the questionnaire with everyone in their departments, and individual departmental interviews were conducted by Cooper, Robertson. On the basis of the responses to these questionnaires and interviews, a preliminary tabulation of needs was made by January 1997. This information was then reviewed in detail and refined by the chief curators and senior managers of the Museum over an eight-week period. After redundancies had been eliminated and consideration given to how space could either be shared, reduced, or more efficiently used, the departmental requests for space were prioritized and the beginning outlines of a spatial program for the new Museum were established.

The process of conducting the Needs Analysis became, effectively, a way of further rethinking the organization of the Museum, its physical layout, and its particular requirements for the next twenty to thirty years. The results of the analysis were indispensable to shaping the design programs given to the architects during the two-part selection process. However, these results continued to be analyzed and refined even as the selection process was taking place, until a final expansion program was established in December 1997.

The Selection of an Architect

On November 14, 1996, the Architect Selection Committee held its first meeting, the purpose of which was to establish both a process and the criteria for the selection of the architects to be invited to design the expanded Museum. Noting the complexity of the site and its many constraints, ranging from the existing buildings of the Museum to the restrictive zoning regulations of the city, the committee determined that the best way to identify the right architect for this project would be to begin by exploring the possibilities of the site with a group of architects. Consequently, the committee decided to use a two-stage selection process. First, a number of architects would be invited to participate in a Charette, or design exercise, whose aim was to provide the committee members with a means of evaluating how each architect would approach the unique problems of the Museum's site, rather than how they would actually design the expanded Museum. Second, a smaller group of architects, chosen on the bases of the Charette results, would be invited to take part in a limited Architectural Competition that asked for a specific design proposal.

The Architect Selection Committee met on January 8 and 9, 1997, to review a broad field of architects for invitation to the Charette. Prior to these meetings, the members of the committee had studied portfolios and other documentation that had been requested from the architects under consideration, who included relatively young members of the profession as well as more established practitioners, and who together represented a wide variety of approaches to architecture. After the two days of deliberations, the committee had narrowed the field to ten architects, who were issued an invitation to participate in the Charette. They were Wiel Arets, Jacques Herzog and Pierre de Meuron, Steven Holl, Toyo Ito, Rem Koolhaas, Dominique Perrault, Yoshio Taniguchi, Bernard Tschumi, Rafael Viñoly, and Tod Williams and Billie Tsien. Each of these architects, the committee felt, explored the possibilities of modern architecture in new and interesting ways that expanded and challenged the parameters of modern architecture.

The ten architects were announced to the Museum's Board of Trustees at a special meeting of the board held on January 13, 1997. Subsequently, meetings were held for the staff of the Museum as well as for its Committee on Architecture and Design to familiarize them with the architects and their work. A workshop for the architects was then held at the Museum from February 17 to 19, 1997, during which they were introduced to key members of the staff and trustees and taken on several tours of the existing building and the new site, and were provided with detailed plans and drawings of both. Meetings were held with the Museum's chief curators and senior staff, and with the staff of Cooper, Robertson, who outlined for the architects New York City zoning regulations and then reviewed the requirements of the Charette Program.

The Charette Program was designed to elicit from each architect a variety of urbanistic and schematic proposals for an expanded Museum of Modern Art. Since the exercise was not meant to be a design competition, the architects were asked to consider the range of possibilities available to the Museum within the constraints of its site, existing zoning regulations, and the Museum's conceptual and programmatic needs. Each architect was urged to generate multiple proposals and responses to these requirements, and each was asked to document his thinking through sketches, drawings, plans, and a written statement. At the end of the final day of the workshop, the participants were given an 11-by-17-by-3-inch green Solander-like box in which to submit their charettes, which were due on March 24, 1997.[12]

The only stipulation to the architects about their submissions was that they had to fit within the Charette boxes. (A detailed description of the Charette Program can be found on pp. 142–159, and excerpts from the submissions of all ten architects on pp. 160–265.)

On April 7 and 8, 1997, the Architect Selection Committee met to decide which of the ten architects should be invited to participate in the limited competition. The committee had already decided, after a great deal of deliberation, on three basic criteria as a means of assessing the Charette submissions: first and foremost, a clear demonstration of design leadership, combined with the capacity both to challenge the Museum and to remain sympathetic to its mission; second, a demonstration of the ability to think in large, bold terms while remaining able to resolve small details; and third, a clear demonstration of a sensitivity to art, in particular, to modern and contemporary art.

Prior to making the final selection, the committee discussed at length how many architects should be asked to participate in the competition and settled upon a minimum of two and a maximum of four. This led to an intense debate over two days, as the committee narrowed its choices to three: Herzog and de Meuron, Taniguchi, and Tschumi. The architects were chosen on the merits of their charettes and the degree to which they had met the criteria established by the Selection Committee. In choosing them, the committee cited Herzog and de Meuron, for their thoughtful and provocative ideas, which reflected a keen awareness of the evolving role of museum architecture in shaping the appreciation of art; Taniguchi, for the elegance and clarity of his design concepts as well as his sensitivity to light and space; and Tschumi, for his profound understanding of curatorial issues, the Museum's mission, and his exciting reconception of the site.

The three finalists were announced to the Board of Trustees at the April 9 meeting of the board. Four weeks later, on May 5, 1997, a special exhibition devoted to the charettes, including work by all ten architects, opened to the public. The title of this exhibition, *Toward the New Museum of Modern Art: Sketchbooks by Ten Architects*,[13] alluded to the 1959 Museum exhibition *Toward the "New" Museum of Modern Art: A Bid for Space*, which had been held in anticipation of the Museum's 1964 expansion,[14] as well as to Le Corbusier's modernist manifesto of 1923, "Toward a New Architecture."[15] Through these allusions, the exhibition sought not only to present the charettes in the context of the Museum's aspirations for the future, but also to situate them within the Museum's extensive architectural history, and to affirm its commitment to the rich tradition of modernism.

Herzog and de Meuron, Taniguchi, and Tschumi returned to the Museum on June 4–6, 1997, for a briefing on the Architectural Competition. This briefing included a review and discussion of all of the Charette submissions, and meetings with the chief curators, the senior staff, and the Architect Selection Committee and its advisors, as well as an extensive tour of the Museum. Members of the staff of Cooper, Robertson were available throughout the three days to answer questions about the site, its existing conditions, and zoning restraints. The briefing concluded with a review of the Competition Program and its requirements, which had been established by the Architect Selection Committee.

The committee had decided to relax the zoning restrictions used for the Charette, and to allow the architects to consider merging lots and redistributing the mass of the expanded building across the entire site. In order to give the architects the maximum degree of flexibility, the Charette "Design Program" identified 580,000 square feet of programmable space, to be realized within a maximum envelope of 630,000 square feet. The architects were asked to pay special attention to the galleries, public spaces, and circulation required of the new Museum, and to produce proposals that were boldly conceived and that creatively defined an aesthetic vision above and beyond the programmatic, technical, and financial requirements of the institution. Although the architects had not been asked to work to a budget in the Charette, they were given a maximum budget figure of $150 million for the Architectural Competition. Furthermore, they were asked to insure that there was a reasonable balance between new architecture on the Dorset Hotel site and renovations of the existing buildings.[16] (A detailed description of the Competition Brief can be found on pp. 266–297, and excerpts from the submissions of all three architects on pp. 298–339.)

In late July and early August, William Maloney, Project Director for the Expansion, Glenn D. Lowry, Director of the Museum, and Mr. Riley traveled to each of the architects' offices for a midcourse review. The purpose of this review was to provide the architects with the opportunity to query the Museum about possible directions, and for the Museum to respond to any thoughts or ideas that the architects wanted to test before committing them to paper.

The last stage of the architect selection process began on September 26, 1997, when the submissions from the three architects were posted to the Museum. They were immediately sent out for two forms of review. The review of their compliance with the given budget was undertaken by Wolf and Company, and Cooper, Robertson and Partners undertook the review of the proposals involving other aspects of the Competition program. The Architect Selection Committee then met beginning December 2, 1997. After an intense review of the submissions, the committee unanimously recommended the appointment of Yoshio Taniguchi as the architect of the Museum expansion. The Board of Trustees confirmed this recommendation at its December 8 meeting, and on that same day, a public announcement of the architect was made.

The Next Stage

As soon as the appointment was made, this publication (which was delayed in production in order that the name of the selected architect could be included herein and the winning design featured on the volume's cover) went to press, so that it might appear in time for the exhibition, planned to open at the Museum on March 3, 1998, of the proposals submitted for the Architectural Competition. The publication therefore cannot include details of related events planned for early 1998, among them: discussions with Mr. Taniguchi concerning the final expansion program; and, owing to the shape of the final program and to the opportunities that now exist for the architect to have detailed discussions about his design with senior members of the Museum's staff, preparation for the inevitable revisions and refinements in the winning design. Nor can details of the continuing institutional and public debates about The Museum of Modern Art in the next century be included here. But these debates do continue, and must, if the Museum is to build an intelligent, effective, and vital building for its future. The shape of that building and the content of the debates that help mold it will unquestionably be subjects of further publications.[17]

Notes

1. I am grateful to Karen Davidson for her assistance in the planning of this essay, and to John Elderfield for his editorial suggestions.

2. Examples of such issues include the discussions held by the Imagining the Future Committee (see p. 13, above) and the deliberations about which architects should be invited to participate in the Charette (see p. 16).

3. The Museum is also included in the Special Midtown District and the Preservation Sub District, which encompass the midblock areas from Fifty-third to Fifty-sixth Street between Fifth Avenue and the Avenue of the Americas.

4. As the Museum expands westward to include an additional 43¾ feet of frontage on Fifty-third Street and an additional 210 feet on Fifty-fourth Street, this will still be the case.

5. These buildings are the University Club, at the corner of Fifth Avenue; and numbers 5, 7, 9/11, 13, and 17 West Fifty-fourth Street (the Rockefeller Apartments).

6. In addition to Mr. Bass, the Imagining the Future Committee included Vartan Gregorian, Donald B. Marron, and S. I. Newhouse, Jr.

7. Other trustee members of the Expansion Committee included David Rockefeller, Chairman Emeritus of the Board; Ronald S. Lauder, Chairman of the Board; Richard Salomon, Vice Chairman of the Board; Agnes Gund, President of the Board; Lewis B. Cullman; Mrs. Frank Y. Larkin; Robert B. Menschel; and John Parkinson III.

8. In addition to Mr. Bass, the Architect Selection Committee included Mr. Rockefeller, Mr. Lauder, Ms. Gund, Jerry I. Speyer, Marshall S. Cogan, and Glenn D. Lowry. Three other trustees, Edward Larrabee Barnes, Barbara Jakobson, and Philip Johnson, served as advisors to the committee. In addition to Mr. Riley, staff advisors included Mr. Elderfield.

9. These committees are Architecture and Design, Drawings, Film and Video, Painting and Sculpture, Photography, and Prints and Illustrated Books.

10. These issues were proposed by Peter Eisenman, Rem Koolhaas, and Richard Serra, respectively.

11. Several members of his staff, including Scott Newman, Donald Clinton, and William MacIntosh, assisted Alex Cooper in conducting the analysis.

12. The European architects were given an additional two days for receipt of their submission (due March 26), and the Japanese architects an additional four days (due March 28).

13. Mr. Riley and Matilda McQuaid, Associate Curator, Department of Architecture and Design, organized the exhibition, which was shown at the Museum April 30–September 2, 1997.

14. MoMA exh. #654, directed by Alfred H. Barr, Jr.; this special installation, in four parts, was shown at the Museum November 18, 1959–c. December 1, 1963.

15. Charles-Edouard Jeanneret [Le Corbusier], *Toward a New Architecture* (London: John Rodko, Publisher, 1927); reprinted London: Architectural Press, 1946, 1970, 1987. Translated by Frederick Etchells. Originally published in French as *Vers une architecture* (Paris: Crès, 1923).

16. For the purposes of the Competition, the following per-square-foot allowances were given to help calculate costs: $320–345 for new construction, $270–300 for renovation, and $325–360 for excavation.

17. Thus, the next issue of this publication will contain the Fall 1997 Studies in Modern Art Lecture Series, "Modern Stories," in which W. J. T. Mitchell, Richard Wollheim, Susan Stewart, and Homi Bhabha offered views on modernist narratives and their relationship to the museum experience. Additionally, once the winning design becomes the design of the building that will be constructed, a publication will be issued to record it.

Appendix

These documents were prepared in early 1997 for inclusion in the briefs submitted to the architects participating in the Charette and the Architectural Competition.

Mission Statement

Founded in 1929 as an educational institution, The Museum of Modern Art is dedicated to being the foremost museum of modern art in the world.

Through the leadership of its trustees and staff, The Museum of Modern Art manifests this commitment by establishing, preserving, and documenting a permanent collection of the highest order, which reflects the vitality, complexity, and unfolding patterns of modern and contemporary art; by presenting exhibitions and educational programs of unparalleled significance; by sustaining a library, archives, and conservation laboratory that are recognized as international centers of research; and by supporting scholarship and publications of preeminent intellectual merit.

Central to The Museum of Modern Art's mission is the encouragement of an ever deeper understanding and enjoyment of modern and contemporary art by the diverse local, national, and international audiences that it serves.

To achieve its goals The Museum of Modern Art recognizes:

• That modern and contemporary art originated in the exploration of the ideals and interests generated in the new artistic traditions that began in the late nineteenth century and continue today.
• That modern and contemporary art transcend national boundaries and involve all forms of visual expression, including painting and sculpture, drawings, prints and illustrated books, photography, architecture and design, and film and video, as well as new forms yet to be developed or understood, which reflect and explore the artistic issues of the era.
• That these forms of visual expression are an open-ended series of arguments and counter arguments that can be explored through exhibitions and installations and that are reflected in the Museum's varied collection.
• That it is essential to affirm the importance of contemporary art and artists if the Museum is to honor the ideals with which it was founded and to remain vital and engaged with the present.
• That this commitment to contemporary art enlivens and informs our evolving understanding of the traditions of modern art.
• That to remain at the forefront of its field, the Museum must have an outstanding professional staff and must periodically reevaluate itself, responding to new ideas and initiatives with insight, imagination, and intelligence. This process of reevaluation is mandated by the Museum's tradition, which encourages openness and a willingness to evolve and change.

In sum, The Museum of Modern Art seeks to create a dialogue between the established and the experimental, and the past and the present, in an environment that is responsive to the issues of modern and contemporary art, while being accessible to a public that ranges from scholars to young children.

Executive Statement

A WILLINGNESS TO GROW AND CHANGE

Since its founding in 1929, The Museum of Modern Art has grown from a small institution located in rented space at 730 Fifth Avenue, with 4,600 square feet and a staff of four, to the foremost museum of modern art in the world, with a staff of more than five hundred, a collection of almost one hundred thousand objects, and a physical plant of approximately 352,000 square feet. Over the sixty-nine years of its existence, the Museum has been instrumental in fostering and shaping the public's interest—an interest still growing in intensity and breadth—in the arts of our times.

On the cusp of a new century, The Museum of Modern Art is now engaged in an important dialogue about its future direction. The trustees of the Museum have concluded that it should not be a shrine to the twentieth century but rather a vital, forward-looking institution committed to the art of the present as well as to the great achievements of the modern tradition. To continue to fulfill this mission, the Museum needs to expand its facilities and fundamentally alter its space. The rationale for expansion lies in the historical development of the institution and in its building program over the years.

LESSONS FROM THE PAST

The challenges the Museum faces today have their antecedents in its history. The Museum has grown over the decades not simply for the sake of change, but in response to challenges inherent in its evolving mission.

In 1932, the Museum moved from its rented space on Fifth Avenue to a townhouse at 11 West Fifty-third Street, doubling its size for exhibitions and staff, and giving the institution a more permanent public presence and identity. Perhaps more importantly, the move represented a tentative but critical step toward affirming the Museum as a permanent institution rather than an experimental enterprise.

In 1939, ten years after the Museum was founded, a new structure designed by Philip L. Goodwin and Edward Durell Stone was completed, replacing the townhouse and three adjacent lots. The new building provided not only more space for the Museum's burgeoning collection of important works (Picasso's *Les Demoiselles d'Avignon* had just been acquired), but also for facilities which would establish the Museum's unique character: an auditorium and film center, a library for the study of modern art, a members' lounge, and a large outdoor space for displaying sculpture. Furthermore, the Goodwin–Stone building demonstrated the Museum's belief in its own future, and was a clear statement of its commitment to modern architecture and design as part of its identity and overall program.

Throughout the 1950s and 1960s, Philip Johnson was commissioned to design additions to the Museum on adjacent properties, providing not only additional gallery space but new spaces to accommodate the institution's mission: the People's Art Center (1951), and the Lillie P. Bliss International Study Center (1968), among others. A vital achievement of the 1964 expansion was that for the first time it provided permanent galleries for Architecture and Design, Photography, and a shared gallery for Prints and Drawings, then one curatorial department. Additionally, access to works of art not on display was increased: The Photography Center opened in 1964; the Abby Aldrich Rockefeller Print Room, established in 1949, opened in expanded quarters in 1965; and other mediums in the Museum's collection, as well as books and reference materials, were made accessible in open storage/study spaces in 1968. In the same time period, Johnson also directed the remodeling of many of the Museum's existing spaces—the garden (1953) and the Goodwin–Stone building, to which a new East Wing was added (1964)—further demonstrating the Museum's commitment to its growing collection and to the environment and context in which the collection was to be experienced.

Despite the regularity with which the Museum undertook its expansions and renovations, in its first fifty-five years the institution's physical growth remained disproportionately small in relation to the dramatic growth of its collection and programs. By 1960, the Museum had established itself as one of the pre-eminent museums in the world despite its relatively small size. To bridge the gap between its actual size and the scope of its collections and programs, the Museum adopted the habit of regularly reconfiguring its galleries to suit its immediate needs; the permanent collection (formally known as the Museum Collections) was frequently relocated to allow for temporary exhibitions; with limited space, masterpieces would often be in storage or on loan; and staff frequently carried out their duties in inappropriate and cramped spaces, many times located off-site. As early as 1959–60, the Museum considered proposals to address the growing disparity between the Museum's mission and its available space, including Johnson's design for a 56,500-square-foot East Wing addition that would double the amount of space available for the exhibition of the permanent collection.

By 1980, the problems evident twenty years earlier had become acute. The Museum's inadequacies of space were made more problematic by a precarious financial position: it was in jeopardy of losing its place of preeminence, so hard won in the previous decades. After some delay, in 1984 the institution at last decisively addressed both issues in a unique way with the opening of the expanded and remodeled building designed by Cesar Pelli. The doubling of the available gallery space substantially addressed needs identified two decades earlier. Moreover, the galleries were configured to provide separate entrances to galleries devoted to art other than Painting and Sculpture. Prior to 1984, the other departmental galleries were cul-de-sacs off the Painting and Sculpture circuit. In addition, the expansion provided larger study centers including the Celeste Bartos Film Center and a second theater, as well as the Edward John Noble Education Center. Furthermore, the Trust for Cultural Resources was created as a vehicle to help finance the project, while a highly successful capital campaign raised approximately $78 million. The Museum's financial management was also realigned. The result of these initiatives was an endowment of $240 million, multiple sources of revenue totaling more than $60 million a year, a balanced budget, a collection that grew substantially, especially in works of contemporary art, a membership base of 40,000, and an annual admissions base of 1.5 million visitors. As newly re-created, the Museum stood as an institution better able to address the large audiences it had fostered.

While the Museum can and should consider the 1984 expansion a success in many ways, it should not dismiss a common assessment of that project: In several of its aspects, that expansion was more tied to the past of the institution than to its future and did not fully seize for the Museum the bold leadership role it most needed to assert as the culture of art museums worldwide began moving in fundamentally new directions.

LOOKING TOWARD THE FUTURE

The success of the 1984 expansion in addressing the Museum's most pressing space and financial problems provides a stable platform from which the Museum can now face the challenges of the next century. If, instead, the Museum again delays addressing the challenges before it, it will risk establishing for itself an unwanted reputation for reacting to, rather than leading, developments in its field. Other new opportunities that have arisen over the last 20 years have helped define new standards of excellence to which the Museum must aspire now and in the future. As such, the Museum recognizes it cannot expand by simply enlarging the model that has guided it during past decades. It is too complex an institution, and the history of modern art is now too long and too varied to be told within the intimate, domestic-scale galleries and buildings that currently characterize the Museum. This does not mean abandoning the sense of intimacy that makes the Museum such an enjoyable place to visit; but it does mean realizing that intimacy is both a function of scale and perception, and that in the future we will have to rely on the clarity and intelligence of the architecture to provide a variety of spaces, which in and of themselves retain a feeling of intimacy, even if the whole is no longer of modest scale. Simply put, the Museum needs more and better-designed space to accommodate its various existing functions as well as new and different kinds of space to meet the challenges of the future and better articulate its programs.

Having considered a number of options for expansion since the early 1990s, including moving all or part of the Museum to a new location, the Museum determined that it was vital to remain on Fifty-third Street but essential to alter the narrow footprint of the current building. The Dorset Hotel properties will allow us to create a larger, square-shaped footprint that will permit a fundamentally different configuration of galleries and offices structured around a central core. The Museum's commitment to undertake such a project was not taken lightly; rather, this decision was made in order to redress critical problems within the current facility and to address specific issues that will figure largely in the culture of museums in the next century:

• The Museum of Modern Art has the ability to preserve and present an incomparable collection of the art of our times, beginning in the late nineteenth century and continuing until today. Interest in the art forms represented in our collection will increase as we enter the twenty-first century. While experience has shown that it is possible to maintain a program that continuously requires the removal and reinstallation of the collection, a great museum's masterpieces should be permanently accessible to the public that wants to see them, and see them often under varying circumstances. Additional space will insure that the Museum's collection is, indeed, permanently accessible and, furthermore, that its collection galleries can be designed so as to reflect the institution's commitment to the enduring values these works represent. Key to the design of these galleries is the recognition of the diversity of the works in the collection. Variations in the types of spaces, responding to the scale of works of art, their mediums, and the artists' intentions, will dignify the presentation of those works.

• The installation of these works can reveal the most meaningful history of modern art in the world. In 1944, the Museum's founding director, Alfred H.

Barr, Jr., spoke of the mission of the institution: "The primary purpose of the Museum is to help people enjoy, understand and use the visual arts of our time." Barr expanded on his succinct statement with the following definition: "By *helping to understand* I mean answering the questions raised by works of art such as why? how? who? when? where? what for?—but not so much to add to the questioner's store of information as to increase his comprehension." To reach Barr's goal of helping people understand the complexities of modern art, the Museum must have spaces capable of suggesting such complexities. Since the 1950s, when René d'Harnoncourt spoke of a "core and satellite" structure for the Museum (a central spine of the greatest works in the collection with ancillary spaces filling out the history in depth), a more meaningful way of presenting the diversity of the collection has been paramount in the curators' minds. The ability to achieve a new configuration has always been limited by the Museum's midtown, midblock site: heretofore all of the opportunities for expansion have entailed growing to the east and west along Fifty-third Street, creating a narrow, linear configuration of galleries that may be appropriate for a narrow, linear chronology of modern art but that provides very limited possibilities to address Barr's and d'Harnoncourt's loftier goal of making clear the broader meanings and diversity of modern art. This problem—further exacerbated by the structural and mechanical needs of the residential tower built above the Museum's 1984 expansion—can be resolved by the physical opportunities created by the purchase of the Dorset Hotel. For this first time in its history, the Museum's galleries can extend the full 200-foot width of the midtown block, allowing for a rich series of spaces representative of the diverse developments in the history of art contained within the collection.

• The Museum was chartered as an educational institution and has always seen education as integral to all its programs. Barr's interest in providing information that might assist the museum visitor in understanding modern art could be seen in the Museum's very earliest galleries. Today, the Museum's libraries, archives, and study centers are largely invisible to the public; nor does the Museum take advantage of the developments in electronic media to make this wealth of important information available to an interested public. Rarely is even the most basic equipment, or a comfortable and appropriate place to sit and reflect, available. An expanded Museum would insure the possibility for the visitor to move easily from spaces dedicated to the firsthand experience of the art to educational spaces, such as seminar rooms, lecture halls, and multimedia areas dedicated to enhancing and enriching that experience.

• Furthermore, an expanded Museum can fulfill its potential as the primary center for scholarly research on the history of modern art by offering significantly increased access to the vast holdings of its archives, libraries, and study centers. Additional space is also needed for the conservation laboratories if the Museum is to properly care for its collection and maintain its position as the leading center for the study and analysis of modern materials and how to preserve them.

• The Museum is committed to collecting and showing contemporary art and to being a center for contemporary artists. In many ways it has the unique opportunity of placing contemporary artworks in the most meaningful context, within immediate proximity to the works of the preceding generations. In planning the new and larger spaces required for contemporary works, however, the Museum must be particularly sensitive to the nature of contemporary art and the direction in which it is headed, and provide space that is flexible enough to properly display whatever new forms of contemporary art arise.

• The chronic inadequacy in the amount of space available for the collection galleries has also created a mediocre quality in those spaces. As all of the galleries had to be flexible enough for near-continuous change, a generic quality has overtaken the experience of those spaces, which is incompatible with the unique works of art within them. Furthermore, the demands for maximization of wall space have severely limited spatial and architectural variety within the Museum. Great rooms, which combine a spatial and architectural experience with the encounter with a work of art—such as the Goodwin–Stone staircase and the Florene May Schoenborn Gallery—are woefully few. With additional space devoted to galleries and public areas, the experience of the Museum visitor could be greatly enhanced by the creation of more spaces like The Abby Aldrich Rockefeller Sculpture Garden, which creates an environment equal to the quality of works presented, but not in competition with them.

• To insure that the collection remains permanently installed, the Museum requires temporary exhibition galleries of sufficient flexibility and dignity befitting the important programs it generates. While the René d'Harnoncourt Galleries have hosted an outstanding group of temporary exhibitions over the twelve years of their existence, the quality of the shows has not been enough to overcome the antipathy that artists, critics, the public, and many of the curators feel toward this space. To optimize the visitor's experience at the Museum, all galleries, for both temporary exhibitions as well as collections, should have a presence within the Museum that is visible, accessible, and dignified.

• To meet the standards set by the founders of the Museum, the institution must strive toward an environment of excellence and aspire to the highest standards. Long ago, such facilities as the design and book stores, restaurants, and spaces for social events were recognized as fundamental, rather than ancillary, to the Museum's success as an art center, as well as key to its financial stability. Increased space will allow these functions to be worthy of their association with the Museum and allow for their development as appropriate elements of an overall environment for art, one that recognizes a truly diverse audience, which uses the Museum's spaces for a variety of reasons at a variety of times throughout the day and evening.

• In the years since the 1984 expansion, the changes in the way people work have been as dramatic as the changes in the world of art. As the institution becomes a more complex entity, the staff finds itself with few of the tools necessary to work effectively: no dedicated conference rooms, only minimal audio-visual support, and rudimentary use of standard office technologies, and, for a large portion of the staff, inadequate space for highly trained professionals to carry out their work in an appropriate manner. As with all other institutions, public, private, and corporate, the Museum must rethink its work environment to optimize the capabilities of its staff.

Although each of these needs in and of itself justifies the reconfiguration of the Museum's spaces, not to mention an expansion of them, MoMA requires a fundamentally new architecture to express the changes that have occurred in its thinking about itself. In providing more space to accommodate various existing functions, as well as new and different kinds of space to allow the Museum to meet the challenges of the future and better articulate its programs, the project must create a building, or complex of buildings, that demonstrates a sensitivity to the history and culture of the institution. The project's architect must bring dynamic and thoughtful leadership to the design process in order to insure that the Museum is able to show the best of modern art in the most compelling way, while dignifying the work of a diverse professional staff and making judicious use of the institution's resources (financial and otherwise), both in terms of initial construction and subsequent operation. The goal of the project is to be recognized as a great achievement in architectural design that is subtle yet polemical, substantial, and enduring.

Throughout its history, The Museum of Modern Art has used architecture as a vehicle of self-renewal and regeneration, articulating and rearticulating its evolving understanding of modern art in concrete form. At no time since its founding, however, has the Museum had such a unique opportunity to undertake such an extensive redefinition of itself. That the Museum is doing so at the birth of a new millennium could not be more appropriate, for the Museum's mission demands that we traverse the twenty-first century with the same confidence and boldness that we did the twentieth.

Conference and Lecture Series

Introduction
John Elderfield

The success of the Imagining the Future Committee, which engaged key trustees and senior members of the curatorial staff in broad discussions about future directions available to the Museum, led naturally to the suggestion of opening these discussions to representative members of the artistic community, from museum directors to architects, critics, and artists. The result was "Building the Future: Museums of Modern Art in the Twenty-first Century," a retreat held October 4 through 6, 1996, at the Pocantico Conference Center of the Rockefeller Brothers Fund, located on the Rockefeller family estate in Westchester County, just outside New York City.

The Pocantico Conference took as its overall theme the discussion of the potential roles of museums, in general, in contemporary society, and how The Museum of Modern Art, specifically, might respond to current and future developments within the art world. It was organized in the form of four panel discussions, each moderated by one of the Museum's chief curators and initiated by two or three key questions pertaining to the function of museums of modern art. In the edited transcripts, which follow, these questions are given before the names of the moderator and panelists for each discussion. Also recorded here, again in edited form, are the introductory remarks made at the dinner marking the opening of the conference, and the proceedings of the summary session that closed the conference and to which the Museum's trustees and senior staff members were invited.

In the interests of both clarity and brevity, repetitive materials, including introductory remarks and some questions asked of the panelists, have been deleted (as indicated by ellipses); necessary editorial interpolations have been made (as indicated by brackets); and some necessary annotations provided. Otherwise, though, everything is printed as delivered; in the interests of providing something very close to a recording of what occurred, no authorial revisions have been made.

Although the panel discussions held at Pocantico were broadcast at the Museum for the benefit of staff members, the conference was designed to be a small-scale, nonpublic forum in order to encourage the maximum candor on the part of the discussants and to avoid the potential theatricality of a large public event. The second annual Studies in Modern Art Lecture Series, which followed shortly after the conference in the period from October 22 through December 12, 1996, had a different aim. Its title, "Imagining The Museum of Modern Art in the Twenty-first Century," was meant to encourage public debate about the future of the Museum from philosophical, historical, and architectural points of view. The series comprised two lectures and two panel discussions, and was designed to proceed from an historical survey of how art and architecture intersected throughout the history of the Museum (which has always, effectively, been "building the future"), through broad discussions of "The Idea of a Modern Museum" and "The Museum and Society," to a consideration of "Rethinking the Modern" in specifically architectural terms. As with the Pocantico Conference, a balance among the participants, between Museum of Modern Art staff and outside contributors from varying disciplines, was sought. The names of the participants appear before the transcripts of the events to which they contributed.

As with the Pocantico transcripts, some editorial revisions and annotations have been made to these texts. In this case, however, each lecturer, moderator, and panelist was afforded the opportunity to review and make limited revisions, and, in the case of the lecturers, annotations to the record of what was said. (For this reason, these texts appear without ellipses or brackets.) With the agreement of the participants, two presentations made within the context of the panel discussion on "The Museum and Society" were eliminated from the record, as indicated in the place of their elimination, owing to the difficulty of illustrating them adequately in an already large volume.

"Building the Future: Museums of Modern Art in the Twenty-first Century"

Opening remarks by Glenn D. Lowry, Director, The Museum of Modern Art;
Kirk Varnedoe, Chief Curator, Department of Painting and Sculpture.
October 4, 1996

GLENN D. LOWRY: . . . Most of you probably know that over the last five or ten years The Museum of Modern Art has thought about expanding, driven in large part by the requirement of space for our contemporary collection. A number of possibilities were examined: off-site, on-site, an amalgam of the two. When . . . I became the director of the Museum, a . . . decision had been made that . . . an expansion that was on-site was infinitely more preferable to one that essentially cleaved the Museum into two or more parts, one of which would be at Fifty-third Street but another of which could have been on Tenth Avenue or anywhere else in the city. [Additionally,] the Museum had been in extensive discussions over the acquisition of the Dorset Hotel . . . , and that affords . . . about 250,000 square feet [for] potential expansion. We [have since been] able to acquire that space. In fact, it is the Dorset, plus a series of adjacent brownstones, all of which interlock with our current site very nicely, that [provides] the optimal footprint for the [expanded] Museum.

Along the way, we started thinking about what we wanted to achieve, and to what extent was the need for space for contemporary art the driving force of an expansion, or was it to be a consequence of that expansion but not necessarily the principal element of it. As I started thinking about it and began discussing it with all of the chief curators of the Museum . . . and the various trustees, it became very clear to me that the issue for The Museum of Modern Art was not about more space, because ultimately we would always need more space. Our collection has grown so dramatically, and continues to grow so dramatically, that . . . we could always argue that we would need more space. But . . . the real issue was about the kinds of spaces we needed. I mean by kinds of spaces something much more complex than simply gallery spaces, but public spaces, office spaces, private spaces—the whole nexus of physical relationships that actually create an environment that we call a museum. . . .

This led us over the course of the last year to an exercise that Sid Bass, . . . one of our trustees, chaired that . . . we've called "imagining the future." It was an exercise that involved all of the chief curators, most of the senior staff of the Museum, and many of the different committees of the Museum, and it's still going on. Its principal goal was to . . . create within the [institution] a dialogue about pertinent issues: what worked, what didn't work, what should be involved in any reconsideration of The Museum of Modern Art. As that process emerged over the course of the last year, a number of ideas began to crystallize. . . . So we began to think that we had to provoke a conversation that took us outside of ourselves, that allowed us to engage with a group of individuals whose thoughts about the Museum and/or about modern art would help us amplify and reconsider our own thoughts. And hence, this evening and this weekend. . . .

Rethinking the Museum is at the heart of everything we are doing. Not because we are dissatisfied with it—on the contrary. The strength of The Museum of Modern Art has been its ability over the years to reinvent itself. In fact, I think we have already undergone six substantial renovations in our sixty-seven-odd years of history. So a quick calculation suggests that just about every ten years, The Museum of Modern Art embarked on an architectural project as a need of renovation and renewal. Architecture is a catalyst for the Museum. In part, I think that's because, unlike many other museums, architecture is not only an object for us—a shell, a space, an environment in which to articulate a program—it is also a subject. We collect architecture and design: it is a field of study, and anything we build, by definition, becomes one of the principal proponents of our larger collection. . . .

Having gotten to the point of convening this weekend, we also realized that . . . we're going to ultimately have to hire an architect and that, in fact, [since] it's going to be a very important commission, we needed to have an awful lot of information at hand, and so we have already begun a needs analysis that will lead . . . to a fairly detailed program of requirements. This is an internally-driven process. We are working with an outside [architectural firm, Cooper, Robertson and Partners, that] will not be the architect of [the] expansion. . . . We hope that we can develop simultaneously two threads. One is a series of quantitative data that will inform any architectural solution, and at the same time, a series of intellectual issues that will fuel and power our architecture. . . . Over the course of this fall and winter we will begin to do so, and we will do so through the process of a limited invitational competition that will probably have several phases and won't conclude until sometime in the fall of 1997. . . .

RONALD S. LAUDER: . . . I'd like to give you some of the thoughts of the trustees. . . . The first [subject we discussed] was intimacy. . . . The second . . . was the garden, [and] the importance of the garden and to see the garden from many of the galleries. The third [was the idea of] a street museum as opposed to an avenue or a place in the park. . . . There was discussion about materials and [about] warm materials as opposed to big concrete areas. There was discussion about . . . familiarity, the sense that . . . [Picasso's] *Demoiselles d'Avignon* or the Cézanne *Bather* or various [other "classical" modern works] were where they always [had been], so that when you came into the Museum you would not have a sense . . . that things were hidden away. At the same time, there was a question about having [the] feeling of a room as opposed to large open areas. . . .

There was a very strong feeling that . . . the architecture [should] be as exciting as possible. As opposed to something that was safe, they want something that will really reflect modern architecture. There was some discussion about using one architect . . . or multiple architects, in the sense of different architects [designing] different rooms, in different parts of the Museum. There was [also] a question of how the departments are related to each other. I think everyone felt very strongly that the idea of mixing photography with painting, with drawing, with prints, with architecture, was something they were very interested in. . . .

KIRK VARNEDOE: . . . One of the things that arrived out of the process that Glenn described, when we started looking for a space for contemporary art and then gradually rethought the needs of the Museum, was that we felt that in some sense we'd already . . . [exceeded] a model that really began in the brownstone galleries that we were first born in. In the last expansion, in 1984, we squeezed the last juice you could get out of that

model and maybe killed it in the process. There's something about twelve small galleries in a row which is fine and intimate and something about twenty-four in a row which [is] claustrophobic, monotonous, and oppressive. So you can't get what you want by just doing more of it. We realized that, if we were going to change the Museum this time, if we were going to look to a new century, have a new Museum, it took some fundamental rethinking of how to deal with our original values in new terms.

. . . Just to be parochial, I'll start with the Cézanne *Bather,* which is, I think, the entry point when one goes into the painting and sculpture galleries now. . . . When I look at that *Bather* . . . [I] think about that remark [made by Emile Bernard,] that Cézanne . . . wanted to redo Poussin after nature. . . .[1] The ideal was that he . . . could make something of contemporary art that had more charge to it and more power [to it] if he measured himself against a great tradition. . . . At the same time, he realized that you never get back the greatness of that tradition by just replicating it, but that you have to reinvent it in the terms of your own time. . . . That's the basic, fundamental challenge that's in front of us now.

One of the fundamental points to make is that we believe this Museum makes sense. That is, we believe that there is such a thing as a continuity of modern art. . . . We're not a universal museum. We don't collect salon paintings of the late nineteenth century, we collect what we think is modern art of the late nineteenth century. And we don't collect everything that's made in contemporary art. We collect that part of contemporary art which we think honors the ideals or the ambitions and achievements of the founders of modern art. So we believe that there was a revolution, a fundamental change in the questions, debates, audiences, and social contexts of making art that happened—pick your date—between 1880 and 1920, between 1900 and 1910, between 1906 and 1917, and that we have not passed a similar watershed since. Therefore, . . . it makes sense to have a Museum of Modern Art that is both committed to the Cézanne *Bather* and to contemporary art. . . . We believe there's an integrity and a wholeness to what we do.

I don't think that this is necessarily accepted by other people. It's a point of debate, and we may hear [in] debate today [the argument] that is such a thing as Postmodernism and that what we're living with is a dead tradition. We simply don't believe it. . . . I don't believe we're a museum of modernism in a closed sense. I don't believe that we're the museum that we're always made out to be, of answers and absolutes, . . . we're a museum of constant argument, debate, questioning, and disagreement on lots of things, as much as Picasso and Duchamp disagree when you put the [former's] sheet-metal *Guitar* next to the [latter's] *Bicycle Wheel*. There are fundamental differences and rifts and arguments that form the paradigm of modern art at the beginning. We believe those arguments, the questions that were raised there, are still being debated and still produce the fallout that fuels the best of contemporary creativity today. If we didn't believe that, I believe we'd close the doors and not be expanding. . . .

We have a story to tell. We always, in a sense, told a story. When you walk in at that Cézanne *Bather* on any given day in the painting and sculpture collection you can walk out the other end with a synoptic overview of developments in the history of art from Post-Impressionism to roughly the present. . . . Up to now we've tended to tell the story in pockets. . . . One of the great premises that [Alfred] Barr had when he [became founding director of] the Museum was that there was something called the modern spirit, or that there was a common story that united ball bearings and paintings and made them both belong in the same museum with film and photography. That potential is yet to be exploited by this Museum in its fullest fashion, the great synergy that might happen from our collections if we put them together is yet to be realized. . . .

The other thing is that it would allow telling something other than just one main-line story. The march of the permanent collection galleries in painting and sculpture now leaves you virtually no choices. . . . One of the hopes we would have is not only would the story we're telling get more complex and more diverse and more of our collection would be visible in different contexts, but that we would not lose the sense of a main thread, the sense of a graspable parade of what we feel are some of the greatest achievements of modern art; that there would be some sense of mainstream, but that it would be punctuated, adumbrated, expanded, by a series of alternatives in which one might go into greater depth in a particular period. . . .

Ronald has brought up a question of intimacy and staying intimate, and I think John Elderfield made a wonderful point in that trustee discussion where he said, "Smallness is not to be equated with intimacy." Being in a too-small room with too many people trying to look at a picture is not what we mean by "an intimate experience," that there's something about the Museum, which was founded in a brownstone gallery and has kept the brownstone model, in part because it's an ideology, that our little white boxes are the ghosts of bourgeois apartments because Barr firmly believed that that sense of

private, subjective experience in modern bourgeois life was radical, that when they stopped making big salon paintings to hang in specific halls and judge things in huge art fairs and started making small, spontaneous, portable pictures in Impressionism or even more subjectively determined pictures in Post-Impressionism, that this was the beginning point of the different idea of individuals' relationship to a work of art. . . . [This] had to do with the kind of privacy which for him was symbolized by the nature of the private apartment and the mobile window of the picture—[it] meant something, and he wanted Cézanne and van Gogh to be seen in that context.

Obviously, the private subjectivity of bourgeois life, as I've said, has as its concomitant the possibility for stultifying monotony and entrapment, and you don't want the galleries to have that aspect of it. At the same time, you want to preserve the ability to communicate with that picture on a private basis. There's something about an eighteen-foot ceiling that Cézanne doesn't need, and in fact, won't prosper under. On the other hand, our Richard Serra [*Intersection II*; see fig. 3, p.76] needs not only eighteen feet but more to communicate. We have to have a flexible building which deals with a variety of experiences. . . .

But there's an issue about subjective communication with that art which is particular to our problem as a museum, . . . which relates to, again, how we tell the story or what the story is we're telling. And that is, if you have a painting of a person with wings looking at a kneeling woman in a gown, the viewer could understand that this is the Virgin and that's the angel and this is an Annunciation, and that makes a big difference. If you have Miró's *Birth of the World* in front of you, what is it that the viewer needs to understand in order to get at that picture? Do you want to tell him or her what the content of that picture is? The art that the Museum was founded on was truculently difficult, . . . and in that sense was inherently elitist, but in a particular way. It defied the traditional leaps of academic knowledge. It didn't make a damn whether you knew your Greek or Latin or your mythology when you were looking at one of these pictures. It reinvented the notion of what the commitment to thinking about pictures meant; it took away all the inherited baggage and opened up the possibility of what Peter [Galassi] once called a "self-elected elite"—that is, that people who really wanted to get into it could get into it.

I think that our question as a museum is, How much do you shape people's experiences, how do you give a new and different audience for modern art what they need to know. I think one of the keys to that is, How do you . . . take the authoritarian aspect of the museum away and give people permission to say that this is open-ended, that there is no right answer to this, without at the same time confusing them or condescending to them? . . . How do we do that? And that dovetails with the idea of how does the Museum address a much broader and more diverse audience than it has in the past without trying to ignore the fact that modern art is born in a specific, limited set of circumstances, that it has its roots primarily in a Western European background. How do the ideals of universalism and individualism that modern art seems to function with at the beginning come out of something other than a sort of enlightenment trap which is really about a narrow audience rather than a broad one? What is the whole idea of the so-called universalism of modern art or its appeal to so-called universal values or formal values? How does that translate? How should that be worked, in a field in which modern art has expanded to have a whole different grasp, with nationalism today, for example, with ethnic identity? What is The Museum of Modern Art's responsibility in this world and how does it deal with it? How does it preserve its identity, deal with its history, such as it's been, and at the same time keep itself open to the expanded audience that it wants to attract? That's a key issue for all of our futures. Finally, what part does architecture play in making all of that happen?

GLENN D. LOWRY: . . . We need to come up with a means of articulating our history, or our multiple histories, that's much more synthetic. . . . Ronald brought up three general issues that are still sufficiently general to be goals. We want an intimate building, but what is that going to mean? We recognize that we are a museum locked into being on a street, as opposed to an avenue, and much as we would love to have a presence on Fifth Avenue, we don't. But we should think about what that means in terms of playing to our strengths. And we have a garden. Our garden has grown and shrank and changed, but has been a focal point of definition for the Museum. We've come to realize that it is a unique space. What's important to remember about the garden—and this is a great location in which to talk about it—is it used to be a gravel pit with small bamboo screens in which you could put up a house by Marcel Breuer [see fig. 22, p. 83] . . . , and when Philip [Johnson] redesigned it in the early '50s and gave it more-or-less its current configuration, it was still a space where you could show cars, if you wanted to, as well as sculpture, that it has had an elasticity of use, that, in recent years—what, since [the 1984 expansion], I guess—has been relatively fixed. But that doesn't mean we couldn't have more gardens, or different gardens, or rethink the current garden. . . .

Conversation I

- *What are your most memorable modern art museum experiences?*
- *Is there a difference in kind between the architecture of a museum of modern art and art museums of another kind?*
- *How can architecture shape the experience of the visitor or influence the visitor's experience with art?*

Panelists: Peter Eisenman, architect; Lars Nittve, Director, Louisiana Museum of Modern Art; Richard Serra, artist; Mark Taylor, Professor of Religion, Williams College. Moderated by Margit Rowell, Chief Curator, Department of Drawings, The Museum of Modern Art. October 5, 1996

AGNES GUND: We do indeed need to shape our future space, so that our public understands the many complexities of today's art in a very accessible, serene, provocative, and hospitable setting. . . . The content of the Museum must be of the best quality, . . . graspable, and still retain the sense of a private environment. . . . We want to build a passion to see in our public; we want to have an audience that comes because they are inspired to do so, not because we have lured them through skillful marketing. . . . [We want to] meet Alfred Barr's criterion for MoMA: to help [people] enjoy, understand, and use the visual arts of our time. . . .

In 1929, the Museum was an idea. Today, it is a reality that has been built to international proportions. It cannot now afford to permit its future to be less than its past. Most of you recall the great educator Paul Sachs. I believe he summed up the wish of all today's trustees and staff in a speech he delivered to MoMA's trustees [in] 1939: "There is another, [and] even greater, danger as The Museum of Modern Art grows older: the danger of timidity. The Museum must continue to take risks. It has taken risks, with its eyes open, from the very start. It must not stop taking risks. For the reputation of The Museum of Modern Art will rest more upon its successes more than on its mistakes. In the field of modern art, chances must be taken. The Museum should continue to be a pioneer—bold and uncompromising. . . ."

MARK TAYLOR: . . . Kirk [Varnedoe] said last night that . . . at the end of the nineteenth, beginning of the twentieth century a significant transformation took place that continues to have ramifications for art and culture and, indeed, our lives as a whole today. . . . [He] identified what seemed to be four guiding

or, indeed, foundational principles: continuity, intimacy, privacy, and this notion of a seamless whole. . . . I think these notions, as framed, have less to do with imagining the future than they have to do with remembering the past. Indeed, I think they border, as framed, on the nostalgic, in a way that is really at odds with much of the very art with which you are associated that you want to honor and display. Let me briefly . . . indicate some of the ways in which I would reconfigure some of these notions.

Continuity . . . influences the notion of narrativity, . . . [and] involves the way in which art is shown. Even within modernism that notion is rendered problematic. But certainly as we move into the new century, rather than continuity, what I see emerging is something like a layered convolution of the discontinuous. . . .

Secondly, intimacy. Intimacy is, of course, always culturally mediated. . . . I think that, as has already become evident, experience has less and less to do with proximity and intimacy than it does with, if I can rephrase Freud, contact at a distance, [which is] a very, very different notion than that of intimacy.

Privacy . . . is becoming increasingly problematic in the culture in which we live. If privacy continues to be possible—and I think we really need to confront whether it continues to be possible—it will be less a matter of physical presence or absence and more a matter of cryptic coding. In these processes I would want to insist, because privacy and subjectivity go together in important ways, in the way in which I heard . . . the relationship of the viewer to the work of art gets construed, I think given the changes that are now occurring the very structures of subjectivity are themselves undergoing significant transformation that will influence the way in which culture is produced and appropriated.

Finally, and perhaps most importantly, the notion of the seamless whole, which evokes in certain ways, at least for me, memories of the whole notion of the organic. . . . I think seamless wholeness is giving way to complexity. . . . I mean by complexity much more than I think [Robert] Venturi meant, because Venturi still thought of complexity in terms of wholeness.[2] I don't. As these shifts take place, it seems to me [that] two fundamental aspects of current cultural or sociocultural developments are crucial, and will be crucial for what you're trying to do: globalization and virtualization.

By globalization I don't mean a universalization which erases or reduces or represses differences or localizations. To the contrary, globalization is quite different from a universalization which is in any way homogenization. Secondly, virtualization is a much, much broader category than its particular technological embodiment in virtual reality. . . . Virtualization is a process that is taking place throughout culture in everything from the economic to the communications domains of experience. It's not the negation of the real, it's a reconfiguration of it. With both the processes of globalization and virtualization, what is happening here is some kind of a quasi-dialectical reconfiguration of opposites that is psychologically, socially, and culturally transformative. . . .

What will some of these transformations mean for the Museum? . . . What will be the conditions of cultural production and consumption in the twenty-first century? What will be the status of the object? What will be the relationship between the material and the immaterial, on all kinds of levels? How will one relate to this object or nonobject, depending on production? Will viewing be the primary mode of relating to the object, and what will viewing become? Will viewing be primarily the kind of intimate and private experience between a subject standing in front of an object in the object's presence? Will the consumer/producer relation still be able to be understood in terms of activity/passivity, or will that polarity itself have to be reconfigured? What will be the relationship of the Museum to other institutions? . . .

In other words, what will globalization mean for interinstitutional cooperation. As universities downsize, as they are doing, will they outsource certain of their educational mission to the museum, and therefore, will the museum have to reconfigure? Will it have the opportunity to rethink its educational mission in relationship to universities in a heretofore unthinkable way? What will be the relationship of the museum to the communications and entertainment industries? With five hundred channels, will most people visit the museum televisually? That is to say, should the museum be thinking about one of the ways of fulfilling its educational mission as being involved in this kind of dissemination of information—that is, through televisual means. By televisual, I don't mean simply television. . . . If the museum is to remain financially viable as well as competitive, can its exhibitions remain single-venue, or will it be necessary to create networks for real-time multiple-venue programs? . . . I think it's important to think of the museum not only as the site for the display of products but also as a site for production, something like a frame, a stage perhaps, or even a terminal for productive processes. To do this, space must be thought not merely physically but also virtually. The success of the museum, or your Museum, might have as much to do with the architecture of your softwares, understood in the broad sense of that term, as it does with the architecture of your hardware, understood in the broadest sense of that term. I know, especially as presented so briefly, that these reflections complicate things, and the whole issue of complexity and simplicity is at the heart of the problem of modernism, but I firmly believe that complexity will be the shape of the twenty-first century.

MARGIT ROWELL: How can we plan the museum of the twenty-first century in terms of how can we think about the art of the twenty-first century, or something in those terms?

LARS NITTVE: We can both think and we can plan, but we can't really say much about the art of the twenty-first century, . . . without knowing what will happen. One thing that I think we've all noticed is that, [whenever we project what a] new generation of artists will be doing in ten years, they do something else, . . . [or] many very different things. . . . But still, we have to confront this question, because we have to plan for the future.

I think for me the starting point has to be the artists. . . . Then, you must start thinking about the meeting between the artist, the artwork, and the audience. . . . The museum is there in order to create a kind of ideal meeting point between an audience and an artist's work. This means that I think we have to actually engage . . . with artists in discussion about what space they would prefer, what situation they would like, [that] they kind of have in their mind when they work, when they make their artworks.

I think this was, for example, done in the planning for the new Tate at Bankside, where . . . the Tate asked about a hundred artists about their preference about space, their experiences of exhibition spaces, and what they would prefer. . . . The main tendency in these . . . was that they preferred . . . a converted industrial space to a newly built space. I think some of the reasons that were given were that they said that they had the experience that, if you convert a space, you spend less energy on facade and shape of the building and put much more energy into the interior. The interior is the focal point, and that turns out to be a good thing. . . . Industrial buildings are, in a certain sense . . . are more neutral. The word "neutral" . . . can't be used, really, but I think we all understand what they mean if they say that an industrial space is more neutral. . . .

What is also important [to] take into account [is] that, whatever the new art of the twenty-first century will be, it [will] also change the old art. As we all know, Cézanne is not the same painter before Picasso and after Picasso: he's a different painter. . . . And this process goes on all the way through, and continues. It's not only art that changes art, but also, we change; we are different people. We see a different Picasso than the audience did in the '30s, and this means that we can't be sure that the presentation of a collection, of the works from the 1910s, '20s, and so forth, will be or has to be the same forever, because our reading, our understanding of these works do[es] change over time. . . . [If] you look around in Europe and see what the main tendency—I would almost say a fashion—in displaying the collection right now is, it's like breaking up the chronology, showing Georg Baselitz together with, for example, Picasso and Lucio Fontana in the same room. . . . One may very well conceive in ten years or twenty years from now that you may see a video work or a computer work or who knows what in the same room as a Cézanne painting. . . .

PETER EISENMAN: . . . Unlike Mark Taylor, I am not a futurologist; I do not know what the . . . space in the twenty-first century will be, nor do I want to even hazard a guess. And, unlike Lars Nittve, I do not believe that the museum is an ideal meeting point between art and the audience, if "ideal" is still an operative word. Where is architecture in that mix? Where [are Karl Friedrich] Schinkel, and [James] Stirling? And why should art, which confronts always society, also have to confront architecture, which is also a critique of society? I always think that the best museums are those places of confrontation between art and the society and architecture. . . .

The three issues that I think are before us today is, What is a museum? I will not hazard a guess, since I don't know anything about museums. Number two, What is a museum in the city, which I think is the second issue that is before us, particularly in one of the world capitals. Again, I want to dodge

that for now. And the third is, What is architecture and how might it mediate the relationship between the museum and the city. . . .

Architecture has, traditionally, from the time of Vetruvius to the present, been an embodiment of value and meaning that . . . a pope, a prince, a king, or a revolutionary society has put forward. I believe that those reflections, those embodiments, have constantly changed throughout time. The first embodiment was in the Gothic cathedral, where the embodiment of the relationship between God and man was important. In the Renaissance it was the embodiment of the ideal subject. Architecture was always that place of embodiment, that mediates between nature, man, man and power, science and man. What I believe is that today architecture as an embodying agent faces an enormous crisis. . . . I do not any longer think that architecture is the place of embodiment, i.e., the museum as an embodied space. Because one, we have a different kind of mediated world, where media certainly embodies the value of society much more readily and easily than, in fact, architecture does, because in fact architecture is very weak media. . . . The second thing, as media also threatens the iconic capacity or the embodying capacity of architecture I think it also threatens the notion of place and space. I think today we are all urban nomads, and because of the Web and the Net, we live in a very different kind of space—not merely Postmodern nor post-Freudian, I think, but postreal. I think that we need to consider what that means in terms of the relationship of an active subject in space. This is the thing that I believe that architecture has always done, has been an affective place for the human body/mind/eye relationship. I think that media tends to cut off the eye and the mind from the body. So I'm convinced that architecture must in fact restore that affective dimension to the world; therefore [it] must not be merely a neutral, virtual condition but an active and an affective condition.

I believe that to do this, I want to turn to a phrase by Rosalind Krauss and Yve-Alain Bois in their catalogue on the *L'Informe*.[3] I believe that what they say about art is, to me, also at stake in architecture and also in this particular project for a museum. They say that what is at stake in art, architecture, museums, is the preservation of the singularity of objects, and in order to preserve the singularity of objects they argue that they must be cut off from their conventional modes of legitimation. Now, the conventional modes for architecture means the notion of function, of meaning, of comfort, of interiority, and all of the kinds of things that legitimated architecture. I'm not suggesting that architecture shouldn't be comfortable, functional, mediating, etc. I'm saying that it should no longer be legitimated by those issues. Therefore, what architecture needs to do in order to maintain its singularity is to ask how it can function, it can mediate, and embody without using these as sources of legitimation. Therefore, what we're asking is, How can it engender a new sequence of conventions necessary to deal with the conditions of the present? I'm saying, therefore, that I'm very much waving a flag—not a nostalgic flag, but a flag for the future of the singular, cut off from their conventional modes of legitimation.

RICHARD SERRA: . . . We . . . become something other than what we are by the places we construct and inhabit to view works of art. Having said that, there lies the contradiction, because if you asked me what's the difference between Schinkel and Stirling, none. It's another line of the treasure house and the safety-deposit box.

The treasure house and the safety-deposit box, in terms of the linearity of presenting some sort of index reading of art, seems to be not only encyclopedic but boring. . . . [It] doesn't deal with how art has transformed the context where it was made but kind of drops it into a new context that pacifies it and reduces it to historical reading that has nothing to do with its relation to the context in which it was first seen or first made. . . . In terms of building a museum here, what I've always found is that you can't identify what unexpected youth is going to do, no matter what the technological innovation is. . . . I think the architecture has to be a kind of possibility out of the impossible. It has to think in ways that we haven't thought before because we can't foresee the time and place that we're going to be in, let alone what the technological advancements are going to be. . . . [Like Taylor,] I also believe that fragmentation has to occur. I think that things have to open up. I think the box, the industrial space, came out of kind of artists building a loft and the loft was transformed into the industrial box; now they take the industrial box and they can sell it between New York and Spain. They move the whole box. Now that, to me, doesn't seem a very interesting way of turning the product into a consumer-transportable installation; that seems to be robbing the initial impetus of challenging the site.

I think a lot of ways have to open up to allow the engagement between the infrastructure, the art, what's built, what the potential is, what the critical analysis is, so that the place can become one of, not function, but the tension with function. So I think [one] has to deal with the tension of function in relation to the spaces and places where it's exhibited. I think that people who come into contact with the art have to be aware that the tension with function is one of the contents of the work of art, and you don't go back to the same place in the same way each time. . . . Rather than Schinkel and Stirling and that continuous treasure house/safety-deposit box, there has to be created a condition where the works of art in relation to the container is somewhat startling. . . . I think the whole thing has to be rethought. I think, right off, possibly [Philip] Johnson's garden [The Abby Aldrich Rockefeller Sculpture Garden] has to go. It has nothing to do with the way sculpture is going to be seen in the next century. That seems to be a really conventional idea. I think it was great for what it was; I think you got a lot of people out there very happy. I think when they rebuilt the Modern, in effect, that the only place that didn't have any columns was the cafeteria, and [that] they gave that space over to dishing out food was a big mistake. I think you have a whole possibility there of using the entire block and passing through the entire block. . . . I [also] think the situation has to be kept very, very open and very fluid, and I also think that there probably has to be space set aside for growth, because if this Museum is going to go on through the century, don't complete it now. Build it and leave it open, like some kind of centipede structure that can mutate, because [the] spaces you're going to need in 2050 aren't the spaces you can anticipate in 2010. So I think there has to be a certain kind of open definition to these spaces and places that are being designed. . . . I think there has to be a fracture. This thing has to be split apart. The notion of these big boxes for a museum, that ought to be over. Forget about Schinkel and forget about Stirling: that's finished, that can't go on in the next century. . . .

MARK TAYLOR: The model of intimacy that was being suggested was the intimate relationship of the viewer . . . the presence of the viewer in the presence of the work of art, and that kind of communication that presupposes that kind of presence. . . . I don't think there's anything such as immediacy—I think it's always mediated—but what you begin to have, it seems to me, because of complex structures of mediation is that physical proximity becomes distinguished from intimacy, so that you can have something like a distant proximity. That's a weird kind of notion that begins to emerge, so that there's an intimacy at a distance that doesn't presuppose the physicality of the presence. . . . The notion of the private gets scrambled with all of this, because it's not just that interiority and exteriority somehow come to be, and where privacy really does become a matter of access rather than presence. Those are two different ways of thinking about privacy. Increasingly, what constitutes our privacy is preventing access. Now, you can say that that's physical access, but it's much more than that now.

RICHARD SERRA: . . . It comes back down to something that's very common-sense, [to] these objects in the museum, whether material or immaterial. Is the relationship going to be mediated, . . . [is] the relationship . . . going to change to the point that . . . it's not going to be a one-on-one experience?

MARK TAYLOR: In some instances I think that will be the case.

RICHARD SERRA: Aren't you saying that that seems to be the driving force, that intimacy and privacy are going to change in that way in relation to objects?

MARK TAYLOR: I don't know, obviously, but I think certainly that should be a possibility that's entertained as you're trying to imagine the spaces in which you're going to. . . .

RICHARD SERRA: It leaves sculpture in a very weird place, I'll tell you.

MARGIT ROWELL: This doesn't mean that we're going to discard the old experience. It doesn't mean that, if I want to experience a Richard Serra sculpture, I can bring it up on the Internet and think that I'm going to get the same thrill that I get when I walk through it.

RICHARD SERRA: No, but we're already doing it. We have computer models projected and people walk through them, and I can tell you right now, they have nothing to do with the experience of space and place. . . .

MARK TAYLOR: It's not substitution, it's a layering. One thing's not going to replace the other.

RICHARD SERRA: But isn't it a contradiction?

LARS NITTVE: There was a slogan already, I think in the '80s, that you couldn't distinguish anymore between public and private. Private is really a function of the public, and intimacy is a function of another dichotomy. The problem is that these are blurring through mediation, and it's happening basically in our head.

MARK TAYLOR: I wouldn't say it's blurring; they're becoming complicated. Complication and blurring aren't the same thing. . . .

RICHARD SERRA: I think Peter's questions about singularity and embodiment are also really important, and that we should talk about them a bit more.

PETER EISENMAN: I wanted to make one clarification about Schinkel and Stirling. I was not suggesting that we . . . should reify again in a palace or a temple as a sacred space. I was merely pointing to those sacred spaces as having functioned quite well in society . . . during their time, [and] . . . suggesting that we needed to have an architecture that was up to the critical role of the art and the institution, the three of them. I also believe in . . . cutting, the notion of cutting [off] and the operation of cutting [off] is a really key issue. Cutting off is the notion of the transgressive activity, and I always believe that at any moment in time great art and institutions and architecture in a sense transgress the existing conditions and boundaries that they find themselves within. That's why when Richard says to think the possible with the impossible I couldn't agree more. When he [compares] Philip's garden [to] a sacred space in a temple, it may have had its time. . . .

RICHARD SERRA: I think everything kind of has to be up for grabs, even though there's going to be a program, there are going to be certain functional aspects. What I'm asking for is a tension within that function, and however that tension is programmed in, I have no idea. . . .

TERENCE RILEY: . . . When you talk about contemporary art, all of a sudden the issue of the reused industrial building pops up on the screen. . . . I've never completely understood this relationship. It occurred to me that if I was to take the Dia building [the Dia Center for the Arts in New York City] and rebuild that building in exactly the same dimensions . . . it would be considered a bad museum. . . . But somehow, it is considered a great museum through its reuse. I really am kind of befuddled by this. . . . Is there a distrust of artists, of their contemporary fellows in architecture? Is there a dissatisfaction with contemporary architecture . . . ?

RICHARD SERRA: I think it's something else. I think Dia's done this string of great shows. [Robert] Ryman never looked better. I don't think it really matters that the Prado is poorly lit. . . . I think what Dia's been able to do is have a string of shows that made you *think* the architecture was interesting. It may not be, but it allows you to have an experience with works of art that you want to see. . . .

I don't think the impetus for people to do large-scale

works in loft spaces which became industrial spaces was to challenge the museum. I think it was to kind of reinvent the work that they were dealing with on that scale. . . . I don't think it was "Let's challenge the museum." I don't think [Dan] Flavin thought, "Let's challenge the museum." I'm not interested in challenging the museum; I'm interested in following the language of my work. . . . I think probably the museum is going to have to adjust to a particular time and circumstance where thoughts converge to say these particular works that are being done in terms of the experience of a lot of people are more interesting and challenging than others. Now, how do you keep the museum flexible enough to incorporate what those people are doing. . . .

LARS NITTVE: I also think it's important that the museum doesn't only think . . . about physical space. . . . Dia at a certain point could [accommodate] *The Lightning Field*. . . . I think it [the 1977 New Mexico earthwork by Walter de Maria, commissioned and overseen by the Dia Art Foundation] should be in the program of a museum to be able to handle these kinds of artistic initiatives as well, as well as things that are virtual, electronic, whatever, and don't require real physical space but a different kind of space. . . .

GLENN D. LOWRY: I think there is an issue at play, whether a museum has to be a physical space. Clearly, there is a model of a museum that is a physical space, but there are other models of museums that exist simultaneously that may be virtual. This word has been so linked to a particular reading at the moment that it's probably not the right word to describe it, but I was thinking, Richard, of what you were saying, that in theory, the experience of one of your works cannot be done virtually; it's a completely different experience. And yet, there are going to be very large numbers of people whose only experience of your work is that way.

RICHARD SERRA: They'll be in defiance of my contract.

GLENN D. LOWRY: If not your work, someone else's work. There is the legality of it, that ever-larger numbers of people are creating, if you wish, what Malraux thought about—an imaginary museum, or at least a museum without walls. At what point does that get layered onto one's understanding of the physical space?

RICHARD SERRA: I think what happens, then, is really that works of art are robbed of their intention. If you take even a

Giacometti—Giacometti can deal with the continuousness of the space with one fragmented figure. . . . As soon as you transpose that to some electronic media, it's gone.

LARS NITTVE: Absolutely. But there are two major ideas in play when people speculate about art and the future, and one is that art, future art, will be kind of dematerialized and it will be virtual and you will only see it on screens and so forth and 3-D and so on. And the other is, of course, that the materiality, the presence, the physicality, and so forth will be more important than ever because of the direction the world is going. Of course, it's not either or: it's both, most likely. We have the same thinking in relationship to museums, that there is this, on the one hand, when people predict the future of the museum it is the theme park, that it's a kind of cultural theme park, where the masses will go to a larger and larger extent. And the other is as a kind of a continuation of a major trend in society. Or the museum is seen as—and people think that it may be—a counterculture thing, where it's against the general tendency. Of course it will be both. And that's the problem.

PETER EISENMAN: Terry [Riley] mentioned the idea of a typology of museums. What's interesting about museums is, some of the best museums that I know were never designed as museums. The Frick [Collection, in New York City] is one of my favorite museums, [as is] the Palazzo Rosso in Genoa, and on and on. They weren't thought of as museums. The museum, like the house, is one of the most easy typologies to be malleable with, number one. So maybe the . . . Museum should start out not to design a museum but in fact to have a work of architecture that deals with the world today. . . . Maybe the program should be a program of ideas and concepts that lead to spaces where startling and tension-filled relationships between the art and the spaces and the audience can be created. Because clearly, the subject that we're talking about is a subject that still needs to come face-to-face, to confront a Richard Serra piece or other artworks. These other artworks are not only sculptural pieces, they're not only wall art in frames, they are laser art, they are performance art, they are all new kinds of mixed-media art that we have to think of spaces for. We cannot just think of a specific genre of art, because we're talking about a heterogeneous mixture, not only of the people who see this art but the artists themselves. So maybe the only program that one can make, because you don't want infinitely flexible space, is . . . to say how does one make architecture today rather than how does one make a museum.

MARK TAYLOR: I want to come back to . . . the educational mission of the museum and try to approach it through what I do in terms of teaching. We all know that to teach well you have to meet the student where the student is. . . . They see differently, they think differently, they read differently, they attend differently. Now, that doesn't mean I don't teach Hegel, but it means that I also have to rethink how I do some of the things . . . it means I'm going to have to rethink some of the ways in which I write as well as think. It's also going to be the case for the museum. That's what I mean when I say you have to ask what viewing will be like in the twenty-first century. It won't be the same, because they process things differently. Don't think of virtual reality as a particular technology; think of it as glasses, goggles as wide as the cultural forms of mediation that we have, and the way in which those glasses are modulated affect the ways in which you see. One has to attend to that, because your audience is going to be different. They're going to think, see, be different.

JAMES CUNO: . . . I think what one is feeling is the point of being dragged into the future by the future itself rather than seeing the future as something one contributes to and makes, and that one of the most transgressive acts that maybe can be done is to [move] it backward, to find—to, in fact, explore—the possibilities of nostalgia in many different ways. I think some of the places in which Richard's work has been most arresting has been in very old places, whether those old places be volcanic or romanesque or early medieval. It ruptures what's interesting. Rupture needn't always be in terms of what's not yet known, what's new to be created, as it is to move back and see again what's been done. . . .

PETER EISENMAN: . . . I just want to say two things. One is, perhaps one of the problems with museums is that we in architecture are in fact stuck with a tradition which I would call theorizing form, from Michelangelo to [Andrew] Palladio to Schinkel to [Claude-Nicolas] Ledoux to Le Corbusier to Frank Gehry, Peter Eisenman, Jim Stirling, etcetera. We are the end of a dying line. That line is a line that has always thought that form took care of everything and that space really was what happened. What I think I hear us talking about is that we're looking not to form these architectures but to create space. It's interesting to me that the line of my generation and back five hundred years never theorized space, and I think one of the few architects that I find interesting to look at today, because he's one of the only architects that did theorize space as opposed to form, in other words, and thought about not the object but the void, was Adolph Loos, somebody that has been long overlooked. That's one point I want to make, and maybe this Museum will be a place to begin to theorize space and the void rather than this antiquated history of which I am one.

The second thing was about this idea of nostalgia. . . . I'm reminded of . . . Gottfried Semper, who built the opera house in Dresden in 1834. [Semper] was exiled from Dresden with Richard Wagner in [1849] for being a revolutionary at the barricades. But there was this great opera house that Semper had built that people loved in Dresden. In 1869, the opera house burned down, and [Semper] was recalled from [Vienna] . . . and [told] "We love your old opera house; couldn't you put it back together the way it was for us?" And [Semper]—I'm not quoting from the German, but literally translating into English—said, "Hell, no. I'm an architect. You want me, I'm going to give you something new." Of course, the opera house that we are rebuilding today, as it were, in Dresden is the new opera house that Semper put up [after] 1869. I think these issues continually dog institutions that are [continually] changing and revising themselves. . . .

Conversation II

- *How do we best tell the story of modern art?*
- *How do we balance our debt to history while pursuing our commitment to the present and future?*

Panelists: Adam Gopnik, writer, *The New Yorker*; Robert Irwin, artist; Susanna Torruella Leval, Director, El Museo del Barrio; Bernard Tschumi, architect. Moderated by John Elderfield, Deputy Director for Curatorial Affairs and Chief Curator at Large, The Museum of Modern Art. October 5, 1996

JOHN ELDERFIELD: The first question that we were asked to begin to consider during this session is: How do we best tell the story of modern art? We heard in the last session that narrativity is one of the signs of a kind of hopeless nostalgia, and I think that, perhaps, before getting on to how do we best tell the story of modern art we should be asking ourselves do we want to be telling the story of modern art? Obviously, this is a complicated thing, and as Mark Taylor said in the first session, we don't want to be setting up polarities which really make things more difficult for us to get to the issues we're talking about. Obviously, in this case we are talking about continuities and discontinuities, but is our framing it in this way in fact one of our problems? Bernard, do you want to start?

BERNARD TSCHUMI: I'll try. . . . The previous panel talked about a number of issues in outlining the issue of form or of space, but they really talked about time, and if you talk about how to tell the story of modern art, which immediately makes everybody feel uneasy, it immediately addresses this question of time, because a story suggests a narrative—not always, but most of the time—and a narrative suggests a sequence. A narrative sequence feels awfully close to a spatial sequence to us architects. . . . But then, of course, which sequence? Is it the sequence of public experience. . . . We need a sequence from the street to the lobby to the grand stairs to the elevators to the garden to the bookstore or the printshop—all these new functions, or these functions that accompany a museum today. Or are we talking about the sequence of private experience, the one that directly involves the work of art, the viewing and reviewing of an artwork or a series of artworks? The . . . sequence of public experience will be crucial to the new Museum, because it will bring together all these different parts in an extraordinary global experience of the senses, and that may achieve that seamless whole that was mentioned by

Glenn Lowry last night. But the theme of the panel now seems to be of the other sequence, of the private sequence, insomuch as they are constructed as a separate one. In other words, how do we tell that story of modern art?

Again, I have to state at the onset my enormous uneasiness about this, namely, whether the architecture can or should tell a story, whether there can be a cause-and-effect relationship between the sequence of spaces and the narrative that it contains. Of course, it also raises other questions. First, the question of the continuum of history as perceived as the normative view of modernism. Secondly, the question of whether we are dealing with the modern or with modernist or with the contemporary period, all of which have specific historical features—spatial features. Art after 1960—does it call for the same type of spaces as art before 1960? Thirdly, the question—and this is the one I want to go more into—the question of ascribing to the architecture [of] the exhibition, the function of configuring a spatial unfolding of a story.

If we touch upon this last point, namely, that gallery spaces are helping that story . . . of course we have two excellent examples that were mentioned this morning, which are embodied in both the classical museum and the museum of the modern period, whether it is in the MoMA collection galleries as they were put together by Bill Rubin [William Rubin, former director emeritus, Department of Painting and Sculpture], or in Jim Stirling's Stuttgart museum [the New State Gallery and Chamber Theater, 1977–84]—in other words, a particular sequence where the spatial movement of the observer's body through the progression . . . [of] gallery spaces has its analogue in the unfolding of time, of the narrative of art, as an unbroken story of interlinked movements, or moments, that culminate in the denouement of the present, something that I could call the dichroic.

I know that many curators, and I would count among

them the distinguished curators at The Museum of Modern Art, have tried to disrupt that assumed sequence, imposing counter-narratives to the process suggesting eruptions to the continuum, and new or different articulations among artworks, period movements, and even media. I think the discussion early on about electronic media is the ultimate disruption. This is particularly the case in the field of modern art, however, because possibly you could say that modern art started by being a contested field filled with misfits, discontinuities, alternative perspectives, all which require attention. So, back to the space of the museum, the question becomes, How do you stage these misfits, how do you stage this contested field, how do you convoke it, put it together through the architecture or the design of the Museum?

Should it be done literally, through confrontation and conflagration, an explosion of spaces? Or through the creation of a void, a void where everything is possible, an ultimately pliable nonspace. Or should it be through infinitely changeable moving walls and suspended partitions. . . . Many years ago, we all remember that when MoMA first embarked on discussion on its expansion plans there was a series of very interesting statements made by Bill Rubin, in an entirely different register. They talked about some of the questions which are being addressed today. Some of them had to do with the audience, some of them had to do with the spatial arrangement of the galleries, but some of them also had to do with intimacy. In other words, the question of the observer's relationship to the surrounding space—a question of scale as well as a relationship to the individual artwork.

What interests me here is not so much the intimacy itself but the sequence of intimacy. You don't view things only in turn but you view it in space. A museum is really the place of staging that time. Think of the collection of spaces when they are being taken over by a blockbuster show, like the recent Picasso show.[4] The question of the intimacy of the sort of isolated perceptual communion is radically modified. The question is not anymore a homogeneous perception but a completely heterogeneous one, with people of different backgrounds and histories. Susanna Leval might talk about this. In other words, through the sequence and through the occupation of the space the spaces themselves are never neutral. There's no such thing as a general space, no such thing as a neutral space, no nineteenth-century neutral space, no neutral white box, no neutral private home, no neutral factory-like space.

That question of the qualifying of each one of these spaces quite often happens through the sequence, the time.

That notion of the time, which of course is that perception as it unfolds over a period of minutes or hours, however long you last, you stay in the Museum, has also an implication in terms of the relationship between, let's say, the different departments of the Museum. What I mean, really, is the different media. Are the different spaces of the Museum related to the different media that it displays? Is there a sort of cause-and-effect relationship between the space of photography and the photography? Is that space a different one from the one of painting and sculpture? This question of that time element which allows what was mentioned here last night, the bouncing back and forth—in other words, you never perceive something in isolation but always in a timeframe—makes the question of the sequence completely irrelevant but not necessarily the sequence as a spine.

A friend of mine once was sort of saying that the museum should never be a spine, but it might have to be a sponge. What's interesting about this analogy of the sponge is that it suggests the autonomy and the specificity of each of its cells, and also, an endless combination of linkages and of configurations. In a sense, a sponge is a seamless whole of sorts that preserves the possibility of heterogeneity: whether it's small or large, you have a coherence—not necessarily a linear coherence, but one of unexpected relation, both in a relation of intimacy and relations. Here, I think, a crucial discussion which we should have is the one of estrangement, because, as we know, again, much of contemporary artwork has to do with strategies of disruption, of distancing. They are part of this story, a story in time—a movement of a body through space.

JOHN ELDERFIELD: The reference to modern art as the place of discontinuities means, of course, that the idea of cutting oneself off from traditional legitimation is itself a traditional legitimation. But how, then, can we have the freedom to rethink the stories that we tell? I actually once did see an installation of contemporary art which was organized in [a] sequence determined by the alphabetical order of the artists' names. Are there other ways of doing it than this? Susanna?

SUSANNA TORRUELLA LEVAL: I was struck by the way the question was framed: how do we best tell the story of modern art, and of course, . . . the story, one story is no longer enough to tell. We must tell very complex, multiple stories and their complex junctures and intersections, and tell them in a way that will be relevant to contemporary life and that will strike a chord with our audiences, because it's from the audiences that the next generation of artists, critics, museum professionals, trustees, architects will come that will replace all of us around this table. So the relationship to the audience seems to me a crucial one. To whom we are telling these stories, again, is therefore crucial, and I am always struck and amazed how very recently museums and institutions have begun to ask themselves who their audiences are. Are their audiences the same as their communities? What is the relationship between their communities and their neighborhoods? Tom Krens [director of the Solomon R. Guggenheim Museum] and I share a neighborhood. We share some parts of our audiences; we certainly do not share a community. So those are questions that are very important as we go forward to ask in terms of retheorizing the spaces. I'm also struck by how seldom institutions ask themselves questions like this collectively; for instance, Museum Mile institutions, which are nine within one mile [along upper Fifth Avenue in New York City], have never done any collective studies of audiences and how these can be used to affect installation practices or spatial configurations.[5] How we tell these stories is, of course, crucial, and hand-in-hand with the fascinating opening-up of possibilities in terms of what viewing will mean in the twenty-first century and the theorizing of spaces that we heard earlier, I think those of us who concern ourselves with the institutional vision and programming must . . . rethink our exhibition and collection installation models and practices, which really we have been using for two hundred years without really enough creativity and change in their rethinking. . . .

In thinking, of course, of different models, coming from different communities, the museum that I direct, and of course that is why I am interested in the telling of multiple stories, is a museum that comes from very much of a model of artmaking coming out of collective experience very often, and so the experience of the collective in the galleries is very, very different, and the use of the gallery as a workshop and a studio is much closer to the way the galleries were conceived in the beginning of the museum.

In terms of a balance of the debt to history and to the present and the future, MoMA's challenge, which is unique, . . . from its inception has always been to provide a very exciting and yet fragile transition between the modern and the contemporary, between the international and the national. . . . It's certainly not a question of resolving those unresolvable creative tensions, but rather of advancing and understanding their parameters in terms of space and, again, installation and curatorial practices that will be relevant to the next century. That challenge, no matter where our institutions

start from or their difference in sizes or orientations, is the same challenge for all of us.

It seems to me that one of the ways of considering meeting those challenges is bridging certain age-old gaps that have existed in the teaching of art history, and within our institutions, of bridging those gaps between, for instance, curators as traditionally the holders of the cultural memory, and educators, who are basically the bridges to the audience and the audiences who are our future. I think the new generation of museum professionals is keenly aware of that gap, and obviously MoMA, with the creation of a deputy directorship for education, has taken a major, major step in bridging those gaps that have existed and that are so harmful and destructive to a holistic view of what a museum can do. Basically, the other gap is that of between contemporary artists and the institution and/or the staff, which then gets translated onto the audience. Kirk said that artists reinvent tradition, and so they are key to the continuity between past and present that we in institutions are attempting to hold together. We must make contemporary artists active collaborators with the staff, so that the staff in turn can bridge that collaboration to the audience. Contemporary artists really must be assigned spaces that are commensurate to their importance as creators and appropriate to the ways that they create, which are ever-changing and surprising. That way, I hope that in that sense the spaces . . . might be reconceived as a huge laboratory or a studiolike atmosphere for creative interaction between the artist, the institution, and the audiences that are our future.

JOHN ELDERFIELD: Thank you. As most people here know, The Museum of Modern Art was in fact founded and chartered as an educational institution, and the idea of the institution being an educator and in fact teaching lessons has existed in very different ways right through its history.[6] Adam, I wonder whether you want to pick up on modern or contemporary or whether you'd like to talk more about audience.

ADAM GOPNIK: Sure. I prepared for this conference by going around to various museums, to as many museums as I could go to in Paris and in London, and in Italy, with a two-year-old in tow. One of the things I learned was, to paraphrase Peter, that we wanted to defend the singularity of the object without the conventional means of legitimation, and we also want to be sure that there are diaper-changing tables in the men's rooms, because there aren't enough of those.

I don't mean that as a joke, really. I think that that will be an important part of the plan of any new building, because it represents a new reality, which is that, just as there are more women artists in the galleries, there are going to be more dads changing diapers downstairs. I think that if we try and build a program, not out of vast abstract generalizations about what the future may or may not be, but out of those particulars of what we know in fact the present demands, we're going to be, or the Museum may be, much closer to something. It may lift a certain fog of unreality that tends to settle over general conversations.

One of the things that struck me as I went around, and this speaks to the first question we were given today, is about the necessity for art in art museums. That may seem like the single most obvious thing one can possibly say, but one of the things that I think one is struck by in most museums that have been built in the last ten years is how hard it is to get to the art. This is particularly true at the Louvre, where I go two or three times a week, and I spent a long time trying to think about why is that such a terrible experience, going down into the pyramid and all the rest of that, and I realized because it takes you about twenty minutes before you're actually dealing with a work of art. . . . It feels like a mall, as everybody says, because it's like a mall, because you're not dealing with works of art. How much it would change if you simply put all the bad Roman statuary in that space, because at least then you'd be dealing with works of art.

I think that was a problem in the last expansion, and I think that dealing with works of art in a somewhat indiscriminate way is one of the things that museums are very good at. When we talk about the kind of story, how to tell the story of modern art, the one thing I wanted to say is that it seems to me that the storytelling powers of museums are generally overestimated. They're overestimated, I think, because storytelling powers in general are overestimated, and you know this again if you have a two-year-old; you know that if you tell a story, like the story of Peter Rabbit, that's trying to teach a norm of good behavior, what the child learns is transgression and the beauty and excitement of transgression. On the opposite side, if you're trying to teach a story as the Museum has tried to teach it, about transgression, the virtue of transgression, what people learn are the comforting norms, that is, that it's a pleasure to come back into the Museum and be reintroduced to these kinds of transgressions. So in my experience, generally, whatever story you're trying to tell or trying to teach you can pretty much count that your audience will learn the opposite story, or they will make up their own story and create their own story out of it.

I think in that sense I've always been sort of benumbed and bewildered when people talk about the dangers and the power, the entrapment, of the single-minded story that Bill's installation, or less consciously so, Kirk's installation, would tell. . . . Maybe I'm just too dense to get it, but it seemed to me that, in fact, your experience of walking through the Museum was that you made up your own story and you did it simply by not paying attention to the things that didn't interest you. It seems to me that the notion that there's a kind of strange, occult, coercive power in the way that pictures are lined up one after another is simply false to all of our experiences of museums and going to look at pictures. So it seems to me that it's almost more important, as we think about this new building, to worry less about the kind of story we're going to tell than the notion that the story should begin immediately, that is, that it's terribly important that whatever this building does that the singularity of it has got to be that it's a place that's devoted to . . . looking at things, and it seems to me that there's no more grander or more necessary conception that one needs of a museum except that it's a place to go and look at things. I think it's certainly true, as we were talking about in the last panel, that it may very well be that the activity of going to look at things will be less important in 2045 than it was in 1945. Nonetheless, the Museum is going to be a place where you go to look at things. There will be other kinds of activities in the world; they will not be the activities that you go to a museum to pursue. . . .

JOHN ELDERFIELD: I absolutely agree with you in terms of how we do in fact make our own stories, whatever the story being told to us. However, it is a characteristic of stories that their coherence depends not only on what got in but what's left out, and I think that this was one of the issues that Susanna was addressing, and maybe this is something that we can come back to.

ADAM GOPNIK: I think there's no question that any story depends on what's left out, but the class of things, the set of things left out will always be infinite. You cannot possibly include everything, and that will finally depend, then, on the judgments of curators like Susanna, like yourself, about what left, what should come in. But I think that, inescapably, something's going to come in and something's going to be left out. The Museum can't be a place where every imaginable story gets told—not because there's no virtue in telling every imaginable story, but because this simply isn't the kind of place where that can happen.

JOHN ELDERFIELD: Bob?

ROBERT IRWIN: . . . Somehow, for me the whole idea of communication as a purpose for art is something that mystifies me. . . . Communication is a normal result of . . . two other activities—one, the activity of knowing something, and the second, of being able to put that into some kind of intersubjective form. . . . There is another myth, like this myth of communication, the idea that expression is an issue in modern art. . . . When you stop and think about it, everything is an expression. There's nothing that's not an expression. In fact, even further, they are equal: Whether I do something or don't do something, they're equal. So it strikes me that the positing of a question is probably the most critical act that you can make in this kind of inquiry we're having here, this kind of discussion we're having. . . .

It begins somewhere in the philosophic realm, . . . not in the architectural realm and not in the [realm of] "How are we going to make the building?" or "How are we going to communicate?" or "What's going to happen in the future?" Maybe more of a discussion about the source, which is the third myth that bothers me the most in terms of what I . . . [have been] hearing, which is the mix-up between the object and the subject—a lot of conversation about the object, as if the object has somehow become the subject, or that the communication has become the subject, or that the audience has become the subject, or that who's going to come and why are they going to come or what are they going to do has become the subject.

It seems to me we are all, in a sense, brought together by the fact that there is an [already overriding] subject. . . . [The subject is not the Museum's architecture or its relations to technology or the public; the subject is modern art, and how that should inform and determine the shape of the Museum]. There is a quote by Cézanne that I like a lot . . . which [bears on my point]: "[One] must make an optic; [one] must see [nature as no one has seen it] before."[7] [In the] . . . discussion earlier about the artists, Richard Serra's response was appropriate. [Responding to] the idea that artists are making things to change or alter museums as just kind of a gameplan, that they make 'em bigger because the museum is bigger and so on and so forth, I think his point was well taken: artists don't do things for that reason. There's something more complex involved here, and there's something more fundamental here. . . . Some of the things that were discussed here . . . are implicit in the work itself. The work isn't just a picture, it's not just an image; it is actually, in a sense, a restructuring of the consciousness of the artist as

such. He reexamines the world and thinks about it and puts it together in a way which is unique. There is an infinite [art] subject, and this goes on continuously, but it's not disconnected, it's not sort of wandering around. I don't know if they're hold up now, but last night in the middle of the night, after hearing everything, I wrote down a series of questions which sort of look in the opposite direction [from what has been previously discussed].

What is The Museum of Modern Art's role and its relationship to the pure subject of art? In what critical ways should the modern art museum rethink its organizational structure—how it makes decisions, forms its programs, and modifies its facilities from an understanding of the structural changes implicit in modern art, past and present? Since one of the key principles implicit in modern art has been its break from a nonhierarchical ordering and all that that implies—which is like about as big a revolution as you're ever going to get—a) what would a nonhierarchical order look like and how would it work and how would it affect any of this kind of structuring that we do when we talk about a museum as such? How should this development in art inform and change The Museum of Modern Art as an institution? How does The Museum of Modern Art affect the social innovation of such complex ideas? By example as well as by exhibition . . . that is, each example in terms of how it orders itself. If modern art should question or break the traditional boundaries of frame and object, as it has, what would be the extended frame of reference for the critical process of recognition, understanding, and orderly assimilation? How does this need for an extended frame of reference affect the shape of the Museum, its mindset, and its facilities? How does a modern museum facilitate the innovation of an art practice which now manifests itself in both pictorial and phenomenal form, . . . [as both object and as nonobject, permanent and impermanent]?

[What is the impact of these concepts on the existing methodologies of historians and institutions? What kind of history or institution is it that fails to examine its most cherished methods and practices in the light of its own evolving pure subject? We have a highly developed pictorial perception, and we also have now developed a phenomenal perception; artists now entertain things which are nonobjects, impermanent and transient—things which are principally phenomenal in character.] What should the responsibility of the institution committed to the principles as well as the objects of modern art be in its use of [architecture and] technology? My one question is, [isn't] there an inherent conflict of interest that [first] needs to be examined?

JOHN ELDERFIELD: Perhaps we could . . . talk more about the relationship of contemporary art, of a wide variety of kinds, to the stories which we tell about things historical and how we present them. We know, of course, that when the '84 building was opened, we could tell what was historical and what was contemporary by the fact that the carpet stopped at the end of the historical [section], and everything that was contemporary was on wooden floors. Are there other ways of doing it?

BERNARD TSCHUMI: When Adam Gopnik said that he wanted to go quicker to the art, I thought of what an editor once told me in front of a text I had written. The editor said that she always [took out]. . . the first paragraph and the last paragraph.

ADAM GOPNIK: Absolutely.

BERNARD TSCHUMI: So I thought, yes, that's what happens in a building: You take off the first paragraph and the last paragraph. If you take all these things that lead you into the building, that lead you into the experience, and you get right to the experience. . . . I think there's an extraordinary power to that. At the same time, it goes totally against the notion of staging. The question is then, who does the editing? Is it the viewer who does the editing himself or herself, or is it the curator who prepares it? I'm not forgetting your carpet and the floor. This is a form of editing; it's a form of staging. It's not the same experience, and we architects know extremely well that sometimes we resist someone saying put a carpet inside of that concrete floor, because we know it's not the same story, the same framing. But the question is, again, who is empowered to frame? Is it the architect? Is it the viewer? Is it the curator? Is it the museum? And here, I think your question whether it is about the floor, which would mean that maybe it's the museum that determines what you put on the floor, or whether you take shortcuts, which is the power of the viewer, is crucial, and I think the power to take shortcuts is something that is very often missing in museums, that the moment when you can start to establish those relationships yourself, that you can make that relationship between photography and painting, because somehow, somewhere there you have those crossovers, those cross relationships. Maybe it's perhaps a good idea not to have some rooms with carpets and not to have rooms with the wooden floor, and try to leave it as, not neutral, but as conducive to the shortcuts as possible.

ADAM GOPNIK: In response to something Bob was saying,

it strikes me in general in everything we've been saying that we all have a tendency, I think, to sort of romantically expand that conceivable domain of the Museum, what the Museum can do, what a museum can do, what it can include—all of that too. So I think what Bob was saying about the vast number of hugely important works of art which are ephemeral in some way, have passed, have gone away, it's obviously and it seems to me importantly true, and that's what historians do. Historians try to write books and talk and give lectures about things that are no longer there, whether they're works that Bob has done or they're battles that were fought a long time ago. There are some very, very important human constructions that are ephemeral in their nature, and that's one of the jobs for an historian. I think that any historian who didn't want to do that job wouldn't be doing his job. But for a museum to try and re-create the ephemeral in perpetuity strikes me as unreal as the attempt of the historian to pretend that anything that isn't still around doesn't count. So that it seems to me that the question of what history is, which is endlessly interesting, is not the same question as the question of what a museum can do or what the museum should do. . . . [A museum] has a much more limited role to play. A museum isn't a history machine. It is a place where you go to look at objects, and it seems that to try to overload the Museum, either ideally or as a practical matter of the kind of thing you build, with tasks and jobs that are of huge importance but that a museum is not well constituted to solve or to do, is unreal in some way.

ROBERT IRWIN: Especially if you shift the emphasis and you start out with the idea that that is its role.

BERNARD TSCHUMI: Go on.

ROBERT IRWIN: In other words, I'm agreeing with you completely, but it even goes further, because it's not only due to the attempt to do some of these things which maybe they should not be doing but that actually may be made the subject.

BERNARD TSCHUMI: Yes, I see.

SUSANNA TORRUELLA LEVAL: But isn't it by virtue of the fact that those objects are on the wall in a particular configuration chosen by someone, as you say, and a very complex series of decisions have gone into those objects in that order, and doesn't the museum just buy those choices or have already attempted and pretend to make some kind of mystery?

ROBERT IRWIN: They also corrupt.

KIRK VARNEDOE: We've talked a lot at the Museum about the idea of a kind of core installation and then things that intersect it. One of the suggestions [made earlier was,] Why not invert the order and have a spongelike structure where the spine exists only on an audioguide or on Inform [The Museum of Modern Art Artphone], so that if you want a spinal structure, if you want to follow a step-by-step history as the Museum presents it, you have the option of following that order through a structure which in itself doesn't present it or determine it as the necessary mainstream of work. So you just turn the thing upside-down that way.

ADAM GOPNIK: Kirk, what would this look like?

KIRK VARNEDOE: For example, the core and satellite, the spine idea, one [can] imagine as a grand avenue and a series of side streets to go up. Suppose there is no grand avenue, suppose there is a kind of set of plazas that one wanders around. It's not a grid city, it's a city of episodic things laid together.

ADAM GOPNIK: It's Venice rather than Philadelphia.

KIRK VARNEDOE: One has no idea of what the grand boulevard is, and where one's going to hit the monument. One has a series of experiences. If you then say, Well, I'm here for four hours and I really would like to see the parade of Cubism unfold I'm going to grab a guide that's going to show me how to navigate this space in a way that I can see it. If you go to Paris and the guide says today I'm going to look at eighteenth-century architecture, and you know that it's all over the city, you want to unfold eighteenth-century architecture. You take that guide and you go that way, as opposed to having a city that's built with an entire eighteenth-century street.

BERNARD TSCHUMI: Your question—What would it look like?—I think is crucial, because your example of the spine intersecting the sponge doesn't need to look like something; it can take a variety of forms. I think one of the difficulties that we have with the idea of the museum is, it doesn't have an archetypal form. . . . That's why we can so easily talk about the adaptive reuse of industrial buildings or the salon, because there is no strong archetype of the museum. If you think of those [Michel] Foucault categories of the prison, the asylum, the clinic, and so on, what is the one?[8] The prison is for the criminal and the asylum is for the ones who are mad. What is

the museum for? What does it enclose? You don't have that easy. . . . It doesn't enclose art history; it's something else. So the question of what does it look like I think it's probably one of the central ones to this whole discussion, and at the same time is the one that we should perhaps not address or we should say it is not a question of what it looks like but how do we, instead of conditioning or preparing a design, is how we can design those conditions. That's why I think that the notion of rather providing an infinite variety, an edited variety, of roots is probably one of the ways to go about it. It's about movement rather than about form; it's about movement rather than about space.

JOHN ELDERFIELD: Jim, you wanted to say something?

JAMES CUNO: I think one of the dangers of getting people like us together in a room is that we do take ourselves far too seriously, and that's why I agree entirely with Adam, that we exaggerate our influence or the importance of what we do. . . . So we do exaggerate the role of the curator or of the museum in telling the story, but we also exaggerate . . . the importance of the story, or that is a kind of a tyranny of history. We've talked about history, the history implied in storytelling, but there's still so much more that the Museum can do than tell about the history or to present a certain history. . . . It just strikes me that a philosopher, for example, would have a whole different take on how one would install things in a museum than would an historian. . . . [Like] Adam, I think we are in danger of taking this too seriously, when we forget that the thing we mean most to do is to present that object so that it can be seen and experienced.

ADAM GOPNIK: Just to add, when I say "too serious" I don't mean in any sense that it's not of profound importance, but I just mean that its profound importance is, like most profoundly important things, of a limited kind, that it gets its importance from being modest and particular rather than from being overarching and capable of doing everything. The only thing I would say here is that one of the things that's obviously very attractive to everybody thinking about a new Museum is that it could do a lot of things. . . . In a certain sense it's also unreal to think that it will be endlessly flexible and at the same time a museum could then also have the kind of allegiance and affection that The Museum of Modern Art, quite remarkably, does in New York.

JOHN ELDERFIELD: So would you argue that, because most

people are going once or twice a year, that a very clear story should be available for people who are not used to going to art museums?

ADAM GOPNIK: Yes.

JOHN ELDERFIELD: Then what is it?

ADAM GOPNIK: The story as it's told right now. Two cheers for the status quo. I think obviously the story could change depending on who's telling the story. I just mean that it seems to me that the . . . power, the coercive, manipulative power of any one story as it's told is easily overrated. Secondly, that the human appetite for a story being told is a palatable and inevitable one.

JOHN ELDERFIELD: But Susanna is saying that we should be finding structures to tell a lot of stories.

SUSANNA TORRUELLA LEVAL: Yes, and it's not just about multiplicity and inclusion. That's only the beginning. It's about layering and a complexity of the same phenomenon necessarily. The story of modernism cannot be told, the same assumptions don't apply in the same sequence to different countries at the same time, so the layering and in that sense a centrifugal kind of construct would be much more possible. It's not just about exclusion; it's about layering of complexity in the installation.

ADAM GOPNIK: Could you make that more particular for me? Give me an example of what a layered installation would . . . give me an example of one that exists now.

SUSANNA TORRUELLA LEVAL: For instance, to me the story of the U.S. vis-à-vis modernism is something that I would like to see more . . . more strongly included within the MoMA installation, . . . particularly at a time when the importance of the arts in this country is being so intensely challenged. It's so dangerous. That challenge plays into this country's insecurity about its own cultural production. . . .

JEAN-LOUIS COHEN: I wanted to return very briefly to one of Adam's comments about going to the Museum with his kid. Kids like hearing always the same books, always the same stories, and I think there's also at the Museum something about the compulsion of repetition. People return to see the same statues, to see the same pictures in the same place, and

they will return forever, and this is something which we have to deal with in a positive way, that is, trying to keep that quality of clarity and at the same time introduce other types of stories that people would be attracted to.

ADAM GOPNIK: I agree. I think that that's a need. It's easy to make light of that need, or to see it as being in some sense vulgar or inappropriate, and I think you're right that it has to be honored as well.

RICHARD SERRA: I'd like to ask Bernard about the sponge, but I'm not sure if I know how it works. Is it equally perforated, or are the connections in the core in closer proximity and the ones in the periphery further apart? Or if you unroll it, is it equally punched? I don't know how sponges work.

BERNARD TSCHUMI: People make a [distinction] between a synthetic sponge and an actual sponge. One has an infinite variety of sizes, the other one may have repetitive ones and repetitive relationships.

RICHARD SERRA: But we're thinking of it in terms of the structure of the Museum. Were you thinking of a core structure where rooms are in closer proximity and the ones on the outside were in further proximity, or was it just a form. . . ?

BERNARD TSCHUMI: In the previous panel there was an interesting moment when the question of hierarchy was brought up, and I think you said yourself that we'd arrive at the moment of nonhierarchy. The sponge is not dissimilar. It doesn't have a hierarchy, but there are bubbles or cells that are bigger than others. In other words, introducing a form of selection and saying, hey, something different is happening—not necessarily hierarchical, not better, but of another nature. That sort of set of differences that are being brought in and that also, because the tissue is porous, there's an infinite sort of passing of information from one cell to another, is a possible model. But I'm by no means advocating that the Museum is taking it literally.

RICHARD SERRA: But it's interesting to pose, because it implies multiple entrances, it implies multiple connections, it implies spaces closer together or possibly further apart. It flies in the face of modern architecture in some ways: okay, let's think of this big block as a sponge. And right away, architects are going to have to start thinking in a different way about connecting to the passages, the tie between one and another, the closer proximity. We could also set that up historically. You could have a spine in the center of a sponge. There are lots of ways of thinking about that, but as soon as you set it out, it kind of takes Schinkel looking out the window, right?

BERNARD TSCHUMI: That might be the idea, yes.

JOHN ELDERFIELD: But isn't it also true that the more articulated the structure is, the more you are organizing the viewer through it?

BERNARD TSCHUMI: Yes, but this is why, again, I think that what has been interesting in a part of the discussion also involving the audience is that the emphasis was not anymore on the object, or even possibly on the space—after all, you can say that an object, a space maybe is an object turned inside-out—but rather, placing it in a dynamic sense, in other words, again the emphasis of the movement through. Much of the architecture of discussion is always about the static object. You can instead of taking it from the static you can take it from the movement that begins. Then the question is, of course, does that movement, does it have to go through an archetype or through something very definite, like the sponge, like the spine. Take the Guggenheim, for example. The spiral is something that forces the movement through, but forces it in such a way that there is nothing else but that. It's a wonderful building, but there is nothing else. Or the Stirling museum [the New State Gallery], which is a classic *enfilade* or sequence of rooms. It works pretty well, but at the same time there is nothing else, except it opens up to all the central space in a different way than the Guggenheim. So here the question is, to which extent the movement can become a way to articulate an experience in time. . . .

JOHN ELDERFIELD: Jim?

JAMES CUNO: I'm still troubled slightly by this ancient premise that museums need to tell stories, and I'm wondering how we know that museum visitors experience museums as telling stories, other than what's included and what's not, which people may or not be conscious of. Are they really conscious of the museum telling stories in a sequence of installations? Certainly, critics consider it; we know that they and we are conscious of that, or conscious of looking for that, but do all people who come to look at works of art take the story away with them, and how do we know that they do . . . ?

ADAM GOPNIK: . . . The point I [had] wanted to make was not that you shouldn't worry about what story you're telling, but you shouldn't be afraid to tell a story that you think has a great deal of authority out of fear that this will somehow have some kind of hypnotic power over the masses entering your museum, who will then exit, repeating to themselves, "Cézanne, Cubism, Richard Serra." They'll be imprinted with some notion about the development of twentieth-century art, which then they will be victims of or prisoners of for the rest of their lives. That's what I think is foolish. . . . I think what we should take from that understanding is exactly to be emboldened to tell the story that we think has truth and authority without being apologetic for it. . . . I hear very often when people talk about the story The Museum of Modern Art tells right now that one need apologize for it in some way, that it's a thing that one does only in extremis, it's a thing that one should be very careful about and clearly post as one possible story in a multiplicity of stories. The point I'm trying to make is just that it seems to me that some story or other will be told by the curator, some story or other will be taken away by the visitor, that that relationship or that interchange is not, in fact, a coercive or manipulative one, but it's a natural part of the interchange of human beings who tell stories and come away with other stories. It seems to me, in fact, that the lesson to learn is that you can be emboldened to tell the story that the curator wants to tell, without dealing with the small print of fear.

JOHN ELDERFIELD: Isn't it . . . not only the story [and] how it's told, but [also] whether it's coercive or not.

ADAM GOPNIK: Give me an example.

JOHN ELDERFIELD: If you enter a sequence of galleries and aren't allowed to leave.

ADAM GOPNIK: Absolutely. But doesn't it have as much to do with, I was going to say that it seems to me that probably at some simple, practical level, when the building gets built it will be seen to be successful if there's a lot of art in it that's easy to get to, there are windows so that there's light and people know where they are, and if it's comfortable in that simple sense: you can get in and out without feeling that you're trapped. On some very basic, primal level, that's what will matter. But it seems to me that that has as much to do with the simple fact of being able to exit, of being given the choice, as it does with the way that the story's hung up. You want to be able to get out, you want to get to Matisse quicker or get out before Futurism, but that isn't necessarily so. This reflects the story I would tell if given the chance to tell it. But that doesn't mean that you couldn't keep that same story or spine, to use Bernard's nice metaphor, intact, provided that you could get out. I wonder if in some sense—I'm just thinking out loud—if in some way that the sponge isn't simply the apertures of the Museum, the capacity you have to get in and out of the spine; that the sponge is what we bring with us, in effect, if we're allowed to have it.

BERNARD TSCHUMI: The spine can be endlessly reconfigured.

JOHN ELDERFIELD: Mark, you wanted to say something?

MARK TAYLOR: I'm bothered by the privileging of this category of story. In a certain sense, stories are over.

ADAM GOPNIK: In what imaginable sense is that the case?

MARK TAYLOR: . . . Just as spatiality is not hardwired, neither is temporality. That there are different modalities of temporality; that those modalities of temporality are in part culturally constructed, and that those cultural fabrications of spatiality, contemporality—and they are enfolded within each other, spatiality and contemporality—are tied to modalities of production and reproduction in which any given society operates at a particular time. If one were to think through, and again, when you think this through in artistic terms, some of the differences between narrativity and association, or the kinds of associative logics that might have a different kind of reader than one that privileges narrativity. I think the notion of the sponge is very, very interesting, and one of the things I try to think about a lot and I don't think has been thought [of] enough, [that there is] a certain kind of logic to webs. The image of a web is what I think of more than of a sponge. There's a logic to these emergent structures, but it's not a narrative and it's not a . . . it doesn't conform to the same kind of logic that some of these others conform to. Story, narrativity, all of that, I mean, Guston got it, that's where he was thinking about it all began in a certain way. But there are different temporal modalities that are emerging which bring problems for privileging too much narrativity, it seems to me, and it's not just a question of juxtaposing anything. How are our experiences of temporality changing and how does that affect the way in which the experience is mediated, and does it render problematic a privileging of narrativity. . . ?

REM KOOLHAAS: Isn't it the unique condition of MoMA that it is actually based on a particular narrative, and it is to a certain extent a prisoner of this narrative, and that each of us and each of you can only tinker with the narrative within a very limited sense?

KIRK VARNEDOE: We can tell the story that our collection allows us to tell. You can expand and tinker with the collection, but we're also . . . I wouldn't say we're prisoners of our history, we have the *advantage* of our history. Barr bought certain things and didn't buy others, and the story that we have to tell is going to be determined by the elements with which we have to tell it. So that immediately puts a constraint on what we do. But also, the Museum has a tradition that on any given day you should be able to walk in and have some coherent, synoptic overview of how history happened, and in fact, the *Demoiselles d'Avignon* was painted before Mondrian, and that is an interesting fact in history, that one doubts in some sense that . . . you know, one doubts that Mondrian could have painted what he painted unless the *Demoiselles d'Avignon* had been painted in 1907. There's endless speculation, but there are lots of things that couldn't have happened unless those things happened before them, and because they seem peculiar things to have happened, the viewer may get some insight into them if he understands all the things that happened that, that gave permission for that to happen. So we lay out with that first step of the Cézanne *Bather* a set of permissions given for new things to happen that in some sense should make more intelligible what the quality of innovation is. On any given day you feel that when the viewer walks in and has the opportunity to follow that sequence; whatever story you want to make up about it, that's the sequence in which it happened. In fact, that Cézanne was painted before that Picasso was painted, and that Picasso was painted before that Mondrian was painted, and that's not an insignificant fact to know about history, and it's one of those things that we pride ourselves on being able to present with a greater density and thoroughness than other museums present it.

REM KOOLHAAS: But that's precisely the point. The narrative is there, the sequence is there, the story is there, the research is there, and the coherence is there. So why are we kind of having this discussion, then? There's nothing modest about it and there's nothing apologetic about it. It's fairly linear, strong. . . .

KIRK VARNEDOE: But it wasn't. When I inherited the

installation from Rubin, it was essentially what happened with Barr: you hit the *Demoiselles d'Avignon* and for three straight rooms you learned Cubism inside-out and backwards, up to [Picasso's] *Three Musicians*, at which point you then suddenly were reminded that German Expressionism happened, then you backed up and backtracked and went through Cubism. So, having gone from 1907 to 1924, you then went back and started again in 1908 and went back to 1913, and then when you got through to Picasso and Surrealism at the end, suddenly you were at the *Bicycle Wheel* and you're back in 1913 and in a rationalist tradition in which Dada has appended to Surrealism. And that was the canonical, linear presentation, and it wasn't chronological at all. It was a very different kind of story. It was a story about a rationalist tradition and an irrationalist tradition; it was a story about a dominant stream and a minor stream. The new installation brings Duchamp and de Chirico back to butt up against Futurism and Picasso, breaks apart Cubism, and is more governed by a sense that World War I was a greater fissure in that landscape than the previous installation allowed. In five years somebody else is going to juggle those cards again and do it again. We're not prisoner to it. Because we believe that there's a story to be told doesn't mean we believe that there's one story graven in stone that one will always understand. One of the points of being involved in contemporary art, one of the reasons we feel—and somebody said this—the point is not to resolve the tension, the point is to exacerbate the tension and keep it alive. The point of being involved in contemporary art is that it constantly reminds us about the arguments and potentials and origins. So if I put Duchamp together with Picasso, it's in part because Jasper Johns is not understandable unless Duchamp and Picasso coexist as a set of possibilities for creativity, as a permanent argument built into the foundations of modern art. So looking at Johns changes my notion of how I ought to install 1913, and that will continue to happen all the time.

LARS NITTVE: But of course there are so many different kinds of historical narrative. At the Walker Art Center . . . [curator Gary Garrel's reinstallation of the permanent collection in 1992 addressed] . . . how artists from different generations have been dealing with color. Of course that is also a story that can be told, and you can go right through history. Or you can work like Rudi Fuchs in the Stedlijk, where he combines . . . odd things, but having this idea that there is . . . an undercurrent, that is really interesting to decipher or to see. Or I was trying for a very short moment in our collection, which is basically displayed as a kind of narrative, as in MoMA, . . . where I created two or three galleries that dealt with undercurrents that had to do with silence and violence, and we combined works by, let's say, Yves Klein and Paul Klee and artists who would never be seen in the galleries beside basically being used as kind of one thing follows on the other or comes from the other, but there is an undercurrent, and of course this adds to the understanding of these works and you see something different in familiar works, the audience that come there. And then you think of that as, I wouldn't call it a master narrative but it always seemed like that.

GLENN D. LOWRY: That's where the issue of the sponge or the web as a metaphor, because it's not at all clear that it's a metaphor that can be translated into comprehensible space, in fact provides a variety of opportunities to think about what a museum should be. The notion of the web, particularly as one understands it now, is that it is incomprehensible. There is an infinite number of possibilities that are constantly recombining themselves, just as the organic sponge, at least on the surface or at least partly, seems incomprehensible. We are limited, perhaps always, by the objects in our collection, but they can be combined or recombined in a multiplicity of ways, each one of which has its own narrative. I was reminded of Elizabeth Murray's recent installation at the Museum,[9] where she took the issue of gender as a narrative, which is virtually absent from our current installations, and it is as legitimate. History, of course, demands that something couldn't have happened before something else happened, but from the perspective of today, everything that's happened before can be realigned by what is of interest at the moment.

BARBARA JAKOBSON: I think the subject of the narrative is very apropos, because I see the narrative as an impulse that the curators have followed for as long as I've known this Museum, and I see the Museum more as a Swiss cheese because the word lacunae is about the favorite word that constantly gets invoked because this narrative is an imperative. It seems to me that all along there has been this overweening desire to fill in the chapters of the story which are not there, to make it more complete, to make it more comprehensible, and it seems to me the excitement and the drive in the entire sort of spirit, the way the Museum goes forward, is exactly by going backward, exactly by keeping this story, however this story is told, with as many words, with as many phrases as is possible, so that the audience gets more on which to chew each time they come to the Museum. . . .

PETER EISENMAN: . . . In the nineteenth century, the French beaux-arts thought of the *marche*. It was an axis, and [one would proceed through the axis in a sequence]. Le Corbusier reacted against that and . . . made a thing [he] called the *promenade architecturale*, [or swirling motion through space]. If we say that our children conceptualize these spaces in various different ways now, Bernard's sponge, no matter how it is configured, may be more accurate, or a network, a neural network or a plasma, may be more of allowing this multiplicity of narratives to be reconfigured by the individual that Adam is talking about, and that architecture is the only impediment— not the curator, not the artist, but in fact the limitations of us as architects to conceptualize other ways of deploying space.

ADAM GOPNIK: It . . . seems to me that in certain ways we're talking . . . about a master narrative and alternative narratives. In a very commonsensical sense, that's the difference between the permanent collection and the special exhibition. When Kirk and Bill did *Primitivism*,[10] a lot of it was from the permanent collection, but he told a different story that would have been easily overlooked about a cultural clash. When Kirk and I did *High and Low*,[11] the same thing was true: many, many familiar things told in a different way, and [also] when Elizabeth did her show, which I didn't get to see. Just following a point, Peter's saying that in a certain sense the pain of it is, the reason one doesn't feel that as a natural thing, is because you have to go down, as things stand right now, into the inferno in order to get the alternative story, which no longer has the sense of being a kind of natural, alternative and natural part of the thing that you're doing; rather, it has the sense of being homework that you're assigned to descend into.

SHEILA LEVRANT DE BRETTEVILLE: I thought what I was hearing in your sponge [concept] is that you've given up the master narrative, so I'm really surprised to hear you say this. . . .

ADAM GOPNIK: . . . I don't think master narratives exist, because I think the notion of mastery, when it comes to storytelling, is misapplied. My kid, as long as we're talking about kids and space, . . . tries to control reality whenever anything unpleasant is happening, by looking at it and saying "pause," because he's had the experience of having the pause button in his hand since he was born. So when he doesn't like it, pause. . . . So the notion, it seems to me, of the fact that, as the world goes on, our ideas about narrative change, that doesn't discredit the idea that it can be an appetite for a story at the same time.

JAMES CUNO: And there's not necessarily the conflict, and Bernard put his finger on it. You can have the master narrative and the sponge, as long as you got a lot of potential short circuits. It's the Museum's job not to be absolutely right but to be clear, so that the people who want to argue against the Museum have something clear to argue against. If it's chaos, it's pointless. . . .

Conversation III

- *What role will technology play?*
- *How will visitors' perceptions of the world be conditioned by their exposure to technology and how should we respond?*
- *What kind of relationship will technology allow among space, ideas, and the collections?*

Panelists: Jean-Louis Cohen, architect, architectural historian, and Professor of Art History, Institute of Fine Arts, New York University; Arata Isozaki, architect; Elizabeth Murray, artist; John Walsh, Director, The J. Paul Getty Museum. Moderated by Peter Galassi, Chief Curator, Department of Photography, The Museum of Modern Art. October 5, 1996

PETER GALASSI: Our charge . . . is to raise issues concerning the role that technology will play, or should play, in the future of the Museum. . . . Clearly, one of the key issues here is the role of the new digital technologies. . . . Technology has been playing a big role in our lives for a long time. It is to technology that we owe Mr. Isozaki's presence here today. (He [arrived] from Japan yesterday.) This was not possible at the time when the Museum was founded. . . . I can remember a good fifteen years ago having a wonderful time looking at some of Bill Wegman's videotapes, and [yet] . . . feeling uncomfortable [when it] occurred to me that here, finally, was an artistic medium where there was absolutely no reason whatsoever that people had to come to the Museum to see it; that everybody had [a] television sitting right in their own living room; and that in fact it was an artificial situation to watch . . . video in a museum. I [have discussed] . . . with our video curator at the Museum . . . the idea of distributing artists' videos . . . as opposed to video installations, which obviously can only exist in a big space. . . .

ARATA ISOZAKI: . . . I think there are three generations [of art museums]. The first generation is a classic type of museum, [seen] . . . everywhere and based on the concept of nation-states (most are converted old palaces). . . . The second generation . . . [is typified by] MoMA. After the first-generation museum [was] very much established in society, artists started to escape [these] museum[s and] to produce something not exactly [like that housed] in . . . the first-generation [museum]. [This phenomenon] probably started in the middle of the nineteenth century, [and is] basic [to the] concept of modern art. The . . . second-generation museum [houses art that has become] . . . a com-

modity. Because most of the clients for that [art] are basically [among the] bourgeoisie, [the] art pieces have to be moveable. . . . Second-generation [museum] architecture [is often] . . . based on the building type of the loft or the small factory. . . . All objects are [either] . . . two-dimensional (hung on the wall) [or] three-dimensional [displayed] on the floor. . . . This is the prototyp[ical] museum [for art from] . . . the mid-nineteenth [to the] mid-twentieth century. After the '60s, as the artist again started to escape [from] or protest the second-generation museum, . . . [with] installation works and . . . multimedia [works]. . . . To contain these new types of art, museum buildings [confront] difficulty, because . . . artists want to create not only their own objects, but the environment or the space itself. . . . [These] artists want many kinds or different kinds of spaces. . . . Media artists, [for instance], need blackout rooms, [which can be fixed or moveable]. . . . The problem [is] the relation of . . . container and contained. . . . [With] the third generation, we have to focus . . . on this very dedicated relation[ship]. . . . For example, I designed MoCA [the Museum of Contemporary Art] in Los Angeles, and [there] I tried to define each gallery as a different type—[in its] sides and proportions and also, at the same time, [its lighting conditions]. . . I tried not to hurt or to disturb the art itself, but when Robert Irwin had the huge show in this museum he made holes in the existing walls.[12] Even though I [had] tried to make each room as[discrete] as possible, he made a hole connecting the second room [to] the other rooms in such a way[as to try] . . . to break the container from the inside to the out[side]. If Gordon Matta-Clark were still alive, surely he would make a hole in the floor or the ceiling. . . The relation between contained and container. . . [is] very problematic at the moment.

At the same time, many artists do not want to stay inside of this frame of the existing museum; they like to go out, to establish something completely different. Donald Judd built his own things, not connected to any museum of art. I think . . . we have to focus on this relation[ship between the] architects who design [museum] buildings [and] the artists who work inside [them]. Most of the artists—I have the feeling when I work with them in many cases—want to be architects, . . . and sometimes [the] architects want to be artists, to eliminate any artworks inside. In such a way there are psychological struggles between architects and artists. This is my view. If we stay as a profession, as architects, constant conflict may happen with artists. . . . The architect's role has to be a little bit different from today, [to be both] . . . construct[or] and at the same time [the intellectual mediator with the artists]. . . . I think the third generation may need to create this new type of museum. . . . Tomorrow's *New York Times* [covers] . . . a small museum that I designed in Japan . . . called the Nagi [the Nagi Museum of Contemporary Art, 1991–94]. . . . Working on this small, small museum for a little town (they had no important collections), I asked that maybe one-quarter of the budget could be direct[ed toward] commissions for the permanent installation inside of the shell of the building. The other three-quarters could [cover] supporting elements and the building itself. I selected three artists, each with a completely different way of installation. I tried to design, working with artists—not dictating or forcing them into the architect's frame—[in] . . . a [more responsive] process. . . .

[Simultaneously], we have new situations [in] developing technology, [and] a new type of art which is called multimedia art. . . . [All the] information which a museum has [is] digitalized, [and that] information is very easy to transport, or to transplace. You can get all the information as an art from any distance, if it is connected with wires and so on. In such a way this digitalization of the information makes museums maybe shrink into one single computer floppy [disk], or disperse everywhere, so [there is] no real place to meet with real art in the museum. . . . But at the same time we have to have the audience, who has a body and has a perception of the body. The media of perception is facing the objects as an art in the space itself—real space, not a virtual [space]. . . . I'm not sure whether in the next century museums could have this kind of type of audience or not. . . .

JOHN WALSH: My little contribution will be in the form of five hopes—two high-tech, three low-tech hopes—for MoMA. The first has to do with technology as tools, and I'm mostly talking about information technology. I'm mostly talking about digital information. Like Iso, I hope, really expect, that MoMA will more than make room for, in a passive way, but make active plans to give artists ways of making and showing new art using these technologies. I regard this obligation, well, anticipating something analogous to the creation of photography, right now when we can see it happen, and when we have a very good, clear, strong instinct of its coming importance. As a tool for documentation of the work of artists of the twentieth century and its consequences it goes without saying that MoMA's going to be expected to lead the way, I think, both in terms of compilation and recording [and] also in publication and dissemination. Publication and dissemination are no longer the same thing, because we don't have to think in terms of books any longer, solely. And finally, [as a tool for] public education, both inside and outside the Museum. I go to Peter Galassi's . . . exhibition of New York Times photographs[13] and watch people gravitate to the little monitor—an interesting use of technology, a computer program to explain something about digital technology as it applies to the use of images in newspapers. We have a long, hard debate about the exact role, the physical placement of these devices within museums, and the relative primacy of the one-to-one experience with works of art versus the implied interference/competition from information-giving devices. I don't want to get into it, but it's simply to say that we know that there's a huge area of unfilled potential for all of [our] museums, and I think MoMA will be expected, and can, in fact, make a huge contribution here.

My second hope has to do with technology, and this means information technology, computers. . . . We know that this experience, conditioned by the Web and multimedia in general, deals in nonlinear progressions: one moves in, one moves back again, one moves sideways with alarming ease between bodies of information. We know the information is increasingly nonproprietary: You can't own it. Maybe you did once, but you don't anymore. . . . We know that this information is practically infinitely connectable to other kinds of information. That doesn't say that we'll understand it. In fact, now the World Wide Web resembles nothing so much as a sort of bazaar of brochures, little one-shot hits that look glamorous and are very thin. But that's going to change. It's a world that is naturally anarchic. Its sources are more grass-roots than institutional, not centrally sanctioned or guided, not top-down but generally bottom-up, and increasingly threatening to, if not actually subverting, the distinction between the real and the virtual. I think above all we need to understand what will happen, how the minds of our audiences will be changing, are changing and will be, and it is amazing to me how little is really understood and written about this area. . . . I have a sense we'd do very well to make some links with universities and perhaps with computer manufacturers and software developers and see if we can learn more about this sector of our audience, which is going to grow. So that's a hope, that MoMA will be an active participant in something that will bring it benefit, not just to its own audiences but to all of us [in] museums who are dealing with the same issues.

I have just three sort of low-tech hopes for MoMA. I hope that the Museum [that] emerges when it's rebuilt and reconfigured in the ways you're discussing makes a great effort to induce a receptive state of mind in the visitor, and that to do that is a first. . . . I mean, there are obviously issues of comfort and such that we've talked about already, but I wish that in the process it were possible for MoMA more actively to question and listen to visitors, to learn as much as you can from the daily experiences, . . . about visitors' reactions to what you do in the way of exhibitions, the use of space, the planning, or not planning, of the various amenities, all aimed at trying to see how well you are sustaining the attention and engaging people's minds and hearts in what they do in the galleries. . . . It is for all of us, I think, vitally important that we understand the kind of interaction that we're creating through our buildings and installations, and I think there's a lot to be learned from our relatively small experience with this, a lot that's very direct and useful. I suspect that one thing you will learn is the benefit of variety in spaces, installations, types of places, that your galleries will probably, as I heard this morning's discussion, run a gamut between what we could call period rooms—at least in my world we call period rooms, and that's probably the way to see Alfred Barr's sequence of bourgeois living rooms, whatever we think today's version of that [is]—all the way to the quasi-industrial space that we heard more about this morning. I suspect there's no need to make a direct choice, that this Museum should be heterogeneous enough to accommodate very many styles of presentation and spaces.

I hope one of those styles includes small, highly focused pods of material and information, allowing all kinds of interesting combinations, juxtapositions, questions asked, thematic connections, and I hope that you can somehow introduce a greater variety of the voices heard and read in what you say and publish about the collection by way of interpretation, and that those voices are identified. You do this sometimes, but you don't learn much about who these people are, and in fact I think all of [our] museums will be progressing towards a greater level of honesty and usefulness to our visitors,

if we come out from behind the anonymity, the sort of godlike voice of authority that we have traditionally adopted. It seems to me it's fair for someone you ask to read your stuff or listen to your voice to disclose a line or two about who you are.

I have a last hope, and this is a big one, but at this junction I can't not say it to you all. We have come through and are still in a fairly terrible time so far as the national view of modern art and contemporary art in particular is concerned. I don't have to tell you this, but I will, that we have been through a time in which some contemporary art and by extension a lot of contemporary art has been smeared with the accusation of obscenity and a ludicrous waste of money, foolishness, elitism, all of this, and all of us had a kind of bitter discovery that the kind of tacit assumptions we've been working on a long time, that we were somehow honored or at least given space and money by the government and by implication at least a fair proportion of the populace, those assumptions weren't holding up anymore. I think that broad consensus we discovered rather bitterly has been deeply weakened, and I think we discovered it's our fault in part, not just the fault of Southern yahoos and media manipulation, but in good part the fault of us in not having made a clearer, stronger, more lucid, more heartfelt case for the importance, the value interest, of the work of living artists to a broad public. I know that's hardly easy to do and the irony of it is, of course, it's exactly those transgressive acts that get taken to characterize us all and it's exactly those that we have to defend—have to defend. We have to make the case, not for the fact that they're really inoffensive and not really a problem but that they are a problem and that it's good and healthy for society that they are.

So I look to MoMA, I have to say, since there really isn't any other national leader than yourselves, for the same kind of role as an advocate and as an educator in the broadest sense for modern art and its value for society. I can see many ways in which you could be doing that more aggressively than you are, if you're willing to take on that role. . . .

ELIZABETH MURRAY: . . . But first of all, I have to say that my first reaction when I found out I'd landed in this particular panel or conversation was how does somebody who spends [her] days extruding paint out of a tube and dabbing it up through the air onto a canvas have any interest, really, or anything [to say] about how . . . the museum should . . . attend to [technology]. I can only really address it in a really personal way. First of all, as a painter I'm a Luddite, in a certain sense, in terms of artmaking, but . . . [I also] don't even know how to turn a computer on. I forget every time I'm shown by my kids, who are complete whizzes. . . . In my own work . . . I want to use my mind, I want to be visceral. . . . [All] I know about it is that the Museum, as it develops, is going to use all these technologies. In a sense, it's like preaching to the converted. You're going to do these things, you're going to do it intensively because you have to, because of our kids. . . . It's there and it's with us and we can't fight it. . . . Actually, I think, what I love about it is that technologies create these conflicts that are wonderful. . . . There's so much conflict, and technology is part of it, and the Museum is going to have to deal with these conflicting things. You're going to have a space, you're going to make these spaces, with or without the deck for the aliens to land on, and yet in twenty years nobody may come to it. As Isozaki said, there may be no need to come to this space anymore. However, in my mind it's incredibly important that the space be there, and how the space is formed actually interests me more than anything, the combination—and it's going to be a combination, of a spinal column and a sponge. There's going to be a sponge with a spinal column, in a web shape with a spinal column imbedded in the center somehow—all those ideas are going to be in there, because what has to happen is that there has to be enormous flexibility towards all of these things.

The reality is that time to make a museum that will function in ways that we can't even predict is like being an artist now, in a very, very, I think, impossible art-world situation, trying to make art, trying to be a parent. It's like a ride down an icy hill on the seat of your pants. You really, really don't know what's going to happen next, and I think that's where the Museum has to focus and think about all these things.

Yesterday, . . . I pulled out of my bookshelf . . . the *Machine* show catalogue [of 1968]. . . .[14] I realize that the Museum was doing [with that exhibition] what it's got to do now and must do in the future, [to] hold a mirror up to these technologies, that it's not just something that you ingest and accept. You have to let people see themselves inside of it somehow. I don't know how one does it. It can't always be through exhibitions, . . . but there has to be . . . a critique there of what's going on around us. . . . There is such enormous conflict, and the Museum is part of it. . . .

JEAN-LOUIS COHEN: . . . Of course, technology has been present always in the history of The Museum of Modern Art. It has been present in modern art itself; in Impressionism it is an issue. It has been an issue in a field of discussion for The Museum of Modern Art even before . . . Pontus Hulten['s exhibition]. I'm just remembering the *Machine Art* show of 1934.[15]

This institution, MoMA, has always been open to issues connected with art and technology, and I think that today we should not abandon, drop, issues of art and issues connected with the objects in front of the emerging technological challenge.

I don't think that the aura of the object of art is completely lost in the age of technological reproduction. People still go to the museums to enjoy, to have the delight of looking, of seeing, of visiting objects. Of course, this desire, this delight, is articulated with historical understanding, with knowledge, but [there is a] compunction to touch a sculpture, to look at the materiality of Meret Oppenheim's cup,[16] to touch the rest of the sculpture or to look with great detail at the brushstrokes on a painting—to resist the digital age. In that sense, the museum experience still remains an important feast of the senses as well as of the intellect.

Then, of course, the question . . . of what are the useable metaphors. It has to be asked: Is the metaphor a biological one—a sponge or a vertebrate or an invertebrate organism? I think we should probably use metaphors that have also to do with meaning, with emotion, with understanding, with more complex experiences. I would use here the metaphor of attraction—not in the physical sense, not magnetic attraction, but attraction as it is performed in the realm of the circus, the realm of show business, to which also museums belong today. When . . . [issues of] the temporality of the history of art and the temporality of the visit to The Museum of Modern Art are articulated, . . . a concept developed in the movies by Sergei Eisenstein seventy years ago when he discussed the notion of the montage of attraction remains very interesting. John Walsh was talking about heterogeneity, we were talking about the predicted or master narratives.

I think that a visit to the museum is facing a montage of attraction, of attractions, with major performances, side stories, intermissions, enclosed or encapsulated episodes. Here, I think that the problem and the challenge is to probably look for, maybe not for different narratives but different montages, to alert people to their own montage in front of attractions that have to be constructed—rooms, clusters of objects—the question being then to open the gate to other types of montage. Here, of course, we require . . . specific talents from the curators there, who must not only be storytellers but also *métiers-en-scène,* and the technology there should serve them.

Here, also, I think we should be careful not to dream too much about the potential of digital technology today in the museum rooms. In the world it is happening, it will happen, it will develop. We have the experience of how obnoxious the audioguides can be for people who are not wearing the device, and so I think that although providing the data in the exhibition rooms can be very important it has to remain rather quiet. Providing the data, that is in a way using the information technology to produce what I would call superlabels—hyperlabels that would allow visitors to go beyond the object, to have access to similar objects in the collection, to have access probably to information about context. I remember a very interesting show in the basement of the Louvre—the Louvre is very much now about basements, unfortunately—a show about Egyptian art with very efficient liquid-crystal screens telling a small story about the context, in a mute way, about the context the specific work of art, without disturbing your first-level tactile and visual perception. So here, I think, in this there is a potential for integration, for what I would call the paradigmatic development of certain works of art in relationship with other of the same kind or of the same artist.

There is a great potential which should not, however, disturb the calm, the repose, of the Museum, which is also a purpose, especially in the heart of Manhattan. So I think what could be designed here is probably a new concept in the relationship of main galleries and study centers or study galleries. I think MoMA has an incredible potential for providing all sorts of information, for putting people in contact with study, with a deepening understanding of the works and their context. Therefore, I think that spatially this could be part of the program of the future Museum, a new pattern of integration which could also take the form of information blocks, of the superlabels I was mentioning but which would rather be on the side of rearticulating delight and study in space.

Of course, there is another dimension to the technology called factoring. It has been mentioned to some extent before—[that] is, providing useful technology in the Museum, not only to construct the reception and the relationship with the works but also providing the possibility of producing works in the Museum, and producing, of course, the potential for change in the Museum.

Here, I think that we should not overestimate this potential and dream of a constantly changing Museum. This has been the dream of the "toolbox" museum. Richard Serra was mentioning the treasure [house], disenchanting himself from the treasure [house], but we have to disenchant ourselves from the toolbox museum like the [Centre Georges] Pompidou, which again becomes extremely costly to operate and doesn't operate and is probably much less flexible than a nineteenth-century hospital converted into a museum, where the loftiness of space allows for a very easy and inexpensive flexibility. So I think here technology should remain a rather obedient servant

for experimentation and in particular for full-scale experimentation, which should return to MoMA. MoMA had a tradition of building full-scale models of houses as well as full-scale works of art, and I think this should be returned to on an extended site. MoMA should become or return to being a playground for architects as well as for artists.

I would return, as a conclusion, and this is not purely technology, to the condition of the Museum in midtown Manhattan. This is of course a very challenging situation which should lead not only to inclusion but also to exclusion. A museum in Manhattan can't be like a museum in open land. It should out-contract or out-produce some activities in order to give more space to its primary goal, showing art and information about art. At the same time, and this is probably contradictory, it should be a hospitable place, and here I would insist on this notion of hospitality. In midtown Manhattan MoMA functions sometimes, and this is for instance the role that the garden and cafeteria take, as a refuge, as a peaceful place in the middle of a metropolis. But this peaceful place should not be turned into a microcosm where shopping, food services, etcetera, would at the end eat the primary goal of the Museum, which is showing art. Here I think our challenge is in order to build a building which from the outset should be thought of as a museum and not simply as a work of art to be distorted or hijacked into a museum. Museums in the past, including modern museums, have been conceived as *gesamtkunstwerken,* as global works of art, integrating not only art shown but also all sorts of art in the making. I think that today this temptation should be resisted and that the Museum should return or should become an architectural statement per se, leaving at a certain distance the relationship of architecture to art to be a specific architectural statement—providing it integrates all of these dimensions, of course.

PETER GALASSI: Thank you. There really obviously are two issues which may not be completely separate but it's possible to think of them as separate. One is the opportunity created by new digital technologies for the Museum to better serve its educational mission, both to people onsite at the Museum and people around the world. The other issue has to do with the technological evolution of the art itself, and in that case we do have someone in the room who has some particular experience. Bill, I wonder if you might want to say something to this.

BILL VIOLA: I think one of the things that's interesting in hearing the discussion break down between showing the art and presenting information about the art . . . [concerns] the technologies of artificial imagemaking—machines that make images such as some photography, film, video, and now computer. It was Hollis Frampton, the American avant-garde filmmaker, who called film "the last machine."[17] In other words, it has the gears and pulleys that are familiar to us of the machine age but it represents the end of the evolutionary line, because its product is what we today would call software or information. I've known this very strongly in my own work that we're in a situation now at the end of the century where these artforms that I've mentioned, which now have healthy histories, are in fact the same media that is being used to discuss art with (and that's not true of painting and sculpture at all).

PETER GALASSI: If I can interrupt you for a second. . . . Of course, one of the huge effects on our collective life that photography had was that it meant that the same person could have a photograph of a painting in London or Paris or Tokyo, and that revolutionized art history.

BILL VIOLA: Exactly, and that means that a tremendous number of people [are now affected], via the Internet and the Web and cable TV. . . . The Department of Education is going to take on really a new meaning, because this is not only going to be educating the public about art, but it's going to be the way that people are going to be experiencing art, or it's going to be talking to a public who increasingly is not going to distinguish between the representation or the information about something and the thing itself.

PETER GALASSI: Except that some people would say that exactly the opposite is true, that the more common becomes the reproduction, the more easily available, . . . [the deeper the] curiosity about the thing that can only be experienced by standing in front of it. Intellectually, I don't think it's possible to decide which one. I think you have to see what actually happens. . . .

BILL VIOLA: . . . You all know more about . . . the details of art than I do, the stories of these objects—but what remains in the end is a fundamental kind of inner feeling, soul or whatever you want to call it, spirit, that's in these works, that speaks to us throughout history, through time. It's got us all interested in the stuff, when we started on our career it wasn't some strategy about changing the way art is talked about. It's a real passion, and that is what the essences of these things are. We live in the apex of the material development of history, the two

great voices in history that changed people's lives being revelation and technology. . . . So we're at this pinnacle of technological evolution, to the detriment of our inner lives, as many would say, in this century. . . . You go to the Met and you go to the wonderful collection they have of Melanesian art, . . . these incredible masks and images that are there; but they're there as material objects, presented as things in a museum, and that is not the reality of what those things were. The reality of what those things were was spiritual energy objects which happened to have physical form, . . . but on another level whatever is in that thing is portable, is transportable, and can go out. I've been very moved by reproductions in artbooks of paintings. I know I'm not looking at the painting, but I've been very moved by those things, and some of them I confess to having never seen in real life. So it's not something to be discounted. . . .

PETER GALASSI: Can I ask you a really mundane question? . . . What kind of practical, physical things, like wiring in the Museum, should there be to accommodate the kind of art that you make . . . ?

BILL VIOLA: A flexible space is obviously one. The wiring is usually important. I think to make a building at the close of this century and not put computer, video, and audio, any kind of electronic wiring through the walls, is like making a place without plumbing. One of the best experiences I had recently was at the Musée d'Art Contemporain in Montreal. . . . They have this multipurpose kind of room downstairs . . . a theater— you can have seats or it [can] just be a big cube—and they have [a] control room next to it with thirty channels of video playback. It's not that . . . this room [is seen] in conjunction with what goes on in the theater just outside it, but the room is wired out to the rest of the building, so they can send anything from that room out to any other room. . . . Every gallery [has] . . . six audio lines, two computer lines, and four video lines. . . . It was the only place in the world I've ever showed my work where they had electronic preparators. . . .

TERENCE RILEY: The range of issues that kind of fell into this slot, under technology, are so broad this probably should have been a double session or even a whole weekend. It's pretty clear that when it comes to technology, there are artworks based on newer technologies. In many ways that's another issue than information technologies. I think as John Elderfield has argued, one of the things that we have to do in programming the Museum is allow for the fact that in certain instances artists produce works that were not meant to be understood in the way that these . . . information systems attempt to provide facts. . . . John, maybe you could jump in here.

JOHN ELDERFIELD: It was a very broad point, but I think this is less to do with technology than with education in general. . . . I think there's always this tendency to try to be more specific than the work of art itself, not to allow for the kind of mysteries that we're talking about, which again are specified and given particularized meanings. . . . [Preparing] Acoustiguides [and] wall labels are among the most difficult things that any curator has to do, because [there is] the inevitable tendency to want to provide single descriptive interpretations of works of art. But I think it also is . . . the issue to what extent can one be true to the conditions of the creation of the work, in one sense it gets one into very difficult territory because obviously one can't know. . . . It becomes a kind of idealism of sources, . . . we can't know these, but there are certain things we can know. We can know, and decide whether or not we want to use this information, whether the work was created in natural light or under artificial light, and we can decide whether this is important to us in the installation.

TERENCE RILEY: The issue of the role of technology—by the way, I think the Museum has a particular reputation because of its attitude about art and . . . education . . . . From the very beginning there's been this implication that in addition to the experience of looking at works of art there is another dimension, another level of enjoyment, that has to do with knowing what other people have thought about the same work, how it might appear next to predecessors, etcetera, etcetera, and I see all of this discussion about technology as a way of delivering information, as a kind of downstream version of that attitude. In and of itself, as far as MoMA's concerned, from day one there was a way of looking at the art and then also learning about the art. . . .

JAMES CUNO: While we're talking so enthusiastically about the benefits of technologies, I wanted to introduce a skepticism about it. . . . One must educate rather than simplify or reduce. But technology tends to encourage expectations of instant gratification: they all want it now. One of the great things about museums, and one of the things that I think the Modern has got to insure, is that museums are a slowing-down experience, as opposed to most of life, which is about speeding up experience. . . . Also, the illusion of the transfer of power in technology, that is, that it's going to be transferred

from the work of art itself, say, to the beholder, who can now interact with it and begin to manipulate it. One of the great things about works of art is the humbling experience of being powerless before them. . . . While there are so many benefits there, I'm just skeptical of some of the more profound aspects of how [technology] alters the relationship between the beholder and the work of art. . . .

RICHARD SERRA: How is the Museum . . . going to be a political advocate, is it going to be an aspect of public relations, or is it really going to be politically active in defending art, and ought that be their role, and if it is the role, is it contradictory to the people who are supporting it, namely, corporations and where they are politically aligned. So isn't there some enormous conundrum of agitation that's going to be immediately established between the trustees, the people who put up the money, the fact that the art is critical of both and yet the institution asks you to defend it. Don't you run headlong into that problem right away?

JOHN WALSH: I would say so.

RICHARD SERRA: I can say that the Modern is very, very "helpful. . . ." I think museums ought to lead in that fight, but I don't know that they can, given the way they're instituted, constructed, paid for. . . . You brought up that you all should do more, [and] I really think we should all do more now because we were all guilty of censorship of every kind, but how is it that, as a group of people we come together to figure out what to do. I'll make my poster [promoting Bill Clinton], but what do we do? What does the institution do? How does the institution lead that charge? Can the technology help the institution lead that charge . . . ?

JOHN WALSH: I think we have a couple of things going here. One is preparing the ground, . . . [so] there isn't the gap that Bill was talking about, the . . . stereotype that comes up when the notion of contemporary art is brought to mind. That's what all museums can and should be doing, MoMA out front, so far as modern art is concerned, it seems to me. That's preventative, you could say. The reactive, the defensive, the advocate and defender role, is, granted, a difficult one for some museums to handle when the shooting starts and when the offense is given by the transgressive, whatever it is, especially if it's sociopolitical critique that's involved, and the Museum's supporters tend to be equivocal at best. . . . I'd like to say I have personal experience as an institutional person, but I don't. But some of you do.

RICHARD SERRA: This is going to be a recurring dilemma, and as far as I see it, we lose battle after battle, and I fear that we're losing the war; the gap between what we do and the community out there is getting larger and larger. I work with low-tech industries, so if you're working with bikers and whoever they are in steel mills and shipyards and you say you're an artist, they have no relation to museums. It would be interesting to take The Museum of Modern Art and see what the level is of income that comes in there, what the level of education is that comes in there, what the level of multicultural distribution is that comes in there, because could it be that the technology is affirming the gap, that when you employ the new technology you're going to disassociate yourself [to an even greater degree] . . . from the people you want to bring in.

JOHN WALSH: I'm afraid it's not a very encouraging picture, as far as one knows about the demographics of users of these technologies. The people who study this have been the marketing people who sell CD-ROMs, and the demographics of cyberspace must roughly follow the demographics of CD-ROM buyers, and it's very discouraging. It's male, it's young, it's educated, and it's white. . . .

MARY LEA BANDY: I think [the Museum] has to be fairly self-critical in terms of use of new technologies for educational purposes. Back in the '50s, . . . we had an educational program [that] actively commissioned filmmakers at that time to make films about events at the Museum, whether it's the Japanese house constructed in the garden[18] or interviews—Frank O'Hara talking to Barney Newman. . . .[19] The Museum recognized that they had to [take] creative approaches to providing materials for television, for outreach. I'm oversimplifying it, but in the time I've been at the Museum it's tended to be . . . up to the sponsor [to] create the biographical film or the educational film or whatever. The resources of the Museum have all gone into books and the exhibition, presentations, which have gotten very complex and expensive. So I think that we haven't sat down ourselves and recognized the potential we all have to produce materials. . . . We haven't begun to recognize the potential of television, of video, because we haven't made the materials ourselves, we haven't produced, we haven't committed ourselves to producing materials.

MARGIT ROWELL: Actually, I wanted to address myself to [the fact that] the Centre Pompidou has just started a program where they archive all their exhibitions, and I was thinking in terms of Robert Irwin, for instance. If these exhibitions had been documented on video or in some other way I think we'd all be a lot happier today. . . . Most of the collections of the Centre Pompidou and most of the collections of museums in France are on videodisc and can be brought up in a few seconds' or a few moments' notice, and this is an incredible inside professional tool which as far as I know very few American museums have. . . .

Conversation IV

- *What values of contemporary society should be reflected in art museums and, in particular, museums of modern art?*
- *Who will the audience of the future be, and what will they expect from an art museum?*

Panelists: Sheila Levrant de Bretteville, artist, and Director of Studies in Graphic Design, The School of Art, Yale University; James Cuno, Elizabeth and John Moors Cabot Director, The Fogg Art Museum, Harvard University; Rem Koolhaas, architect; Bill Viola, artist. Moderated by Deborah Wye, Chief Curator, Department of Prints and Illustrated Books, The Museum of Modern Art.
October 6, 1997

DEBORAH WYE: . . . The subject today is the future audience of the Museum, and . . . the values of contemporary society that are reflected in the Museum, or should be reflected in the Museum. Speaking as a curator, I know that I'm always baffled at how to present things for the heterogeneous audience that's not monolithic [but] multigenerational, it's got people with all kinds of varied experiences and levels of sophistication. . . .

SHEILA LEVRANT DE BRETTEVILLE: . . . For me there are three notions that have coalesced over these two days.

One is the notion of the street museum. . . . The [second] is the notion of comfort, because when you talk about intimacy and even continuity, . . . there is a desire for things that we know. . . . [The third is the notion of] metaphor . . . of a crazy quilt. . . .

For me, the street museum is the difference between what I heard and what you said, and therefore there's a difference between what is shown and what is seen. . . . We must stay attentive to that difference and . . . , allow for it and . . . in no way try to close it down by telling so much. I really have a great resistance to the overinterpreted museum. I prefer the unfathomable in art and the confrontation with that, then you need the unfathomable, that which is explained, because the explanation is always more linear and more specific than I ever want. . . . In terms of the street museum, the city was always, as far as I can tell, a critical part of modernism, so a critical engagement with the city seems to be an appropriate agenda for The Museum of Modern Art and certainly one for right now. . . . Modernism is a multivoiced discourse and [has] always changed position. . . . You have been mining those dif-

ferent voices, and I would like to remind you to keep mining them, so that [the story of modernism] stays multifaceted. The modernism that I tend to remember . . . is the modernism of Europe and not of America, the modernism that had a social agenda and was not embarrassed, even though it was arrogant in its internationalism. . . .

In the '80s, I used [the notion of the crazy quilt] to help me remember radical heterogeneity, because from my own modernist background I find it ugly. It's hard for me to engage with it. It's not ordered enough; I can't find the order. You can go back and do an aesthetic analysis of it and find all the reds and where they go, but in fact, the order of a crazy quilt is one which accepts the parts the way they are; it doesn't try to change them. It has a structure that holds it together, but you can hardly find that structure. I think there are things about looking at the metaphor of the crazy quilt that might have some paths for notions of [the Museum's] built form, that I'm not the one to give form to. So I'd like to run through some of my crazy quilt associations.

One, that it doesn't try to resolve the difficulties. . . . There's a lot of modernist thinking that would want unity, and [I think it's important] to resist it and to stay with the notion of community without unity. . . . I think that we often want to trap people through space and teach them how to come in, teach them where to go. I think that myself I've learned . . . not to need quite so much direction, that I'd rather wander. . . . Getting lost provides much more [opportunity] for chance encounters than knowing things. . . . The kind of nonlinear occlusiveness that . . . exists in the crazy quilt can also be transformed into a lived space and a working space. . . . If you compare a crazy quilt to, say, an Amish quilt, which is far more modernist in its abstraction and its reduction, you know where to look and you know what the patterns are. You cannot see the patterns in a crazy quilt, and I like that. I like not seeing the patterns. . . .

I also like the crazy quilt because it reminds me of how it's made and the fact that this is probably true of all quilts, that the pieces in the quilt actually come from leftovers, the leftovers of other kinds of fabrics, of fabrics and things that people have associations with. I think that's some of what's being talked to when different pieces of art in a museum are remembered, because they remind us of something. I think there's something very, very different to be embraced when you embrace the meaning of memory as opposed to nostalgia, that memory has much more to render up to us than nostalgia does, in that it's in pieces. We all remember differently, we all choose different things to remember, and remembering has longing in it and has a sense of ourselves in it. . . .

The . . . crazy quilt also is essentially American in many ways, but because it is American, it's from somewhere else also. It comes from Africa, it's made by people other than the people sitting around this room, and it's often made by women, or most often made by women, so that we remember where things come from as well as where they are. That actually reminds me again of a different way to think of globalization. . . . I heard from Peter Galassi this morning . . . that a very large majority of [the] population [that] comes to the Modern [is] actually coming only twice a year or five times a year, and comes from elsewhere than New York City. How do you then engage the people who are here in New York City who don't ever come downtown or into town, who don't even know there's a Museum. If they don't come down your street, how will they know you are a street museum, and what do you do to reach out to those populations so that they feel that they are, not given voice, but actually are listened to. . . .

DEBORAH WYE: Sheila, in terms of . . . bringing the street in or the museum going out into the street, could you say anything about projects in which you've gone out into the community? . . .

SHEILA LEVRANT DE BRETTEVILLE: . . . I go out into the street . . . to talk to people . . . because I can't make the work without knowing what they think. So I have to devise questions . . . [that] are truly open-ended, so that I can hear when they speak back to me. . . . I know when the Whitney [Museum of American Art] did *Black Male*[20] and every single subway had *Black Male* [posters] in it . . . people looked at those

posters . . . because they saw something that they recognized, and they may have—I don't know—gone to the museum to see what that was because it said something familiar to them, whereas, if you have a show of Roy DeCarava [photographs], how do they know that Roy DeCarava is going to deliver this fabulous work that they can see?[21] What is it that you could say in the setting where somebody actually is that would let them know that that work is going to resonate with them if they saw it? That's harder to do. I think, perhaps, you might think of outposts . . . in different parts of the city, . . . [with] some of the interpretative stuff outside where people can actually access it, outposts . . . that are disconnected from each other, and connect either electronically, connect personally, connect on every kind of level that you can imagine, so that people don't only have to come to you but you go out to them where they live.

REM KOOLHAAS: I've made a number of points, about value and also about the question of audiences and the different audiences that the Modern is missing. . . . If the Museum has proved anything, it is that you can be a successful institution in mediocre architecture, and that you can develop the importance of architecture to the success and even triumph of MoMA, so that this is a very important point to begin with. If I look at the Modern, as a frequent visitor and as somebody who's occasionally been involved, if I look at its history, then I would say that the most impressive thing about MoMA is its production of aura, and I think that, in fact, that is an important thing to discuss in terms of value, and in terms [not only] of the past value but also the future value. I think that this aura has been achieved through operations of exclusion, operations of selection, operations of propaganda and, from a very early age, from study in the 1930s, operations of media manipulation. You only have to look at the incredible artificiality of some of the photographs in the Museum's early catalogues to see that the art of the retoucher was always a very important part of its repertoire, and therefore I find it slightly bizarre that you see now such reluctance to address the issue of artificiality, the synthetic, and the manipulated, because the Museum in a very serious way was always involved in manipulation.

Of course, the strength of its aura is in direct proportion to its efficiency of manipulation. For me, the issue is for MoMA how to manage its aura and how to modernize its aura, and I think that these two issues are to a large extent independent of architecture. By coincidence, I've recently been involved in an American corporation, where I also had to confront the issue of aura. I've been fascinated with this, how they address aura as a kind of separate issue and how they then think systematically what they could do with an aura, how they could manipulate the historic development of aura, how they could exploit the aura, increase the aura for branding.

In other words, I think that the issue of aura is the whole thing, and that therefore the focus on architecture is slightly misguided in that, more so than a new museum, MoMA might need headquarters, and in those headquarters it could study what to do with its aura. This is one issue I want to introduce and maybe discuss later. Then there is the issue of Museum members and the issue of the public. If a key experience MoMA offers is an intimate encounter with authentic work, can you really talk about intimacy if you have one and a half million visitors a year, or is it intimacy of the American kind, namely, a million and a half of my best friends. . . .

It is very clear that the success of museums and their enormous and overwhelming and frankly inexplicable popularity is actually threatening the very experience that is the supposedly key moment in the value system of a museum system, the authentic work. But what I find also surprising is that this kind of resistance to artificializing, and to disseminating of the work through other means. The skepticism that I've kind of registered here vis-à-vis this artificiality is surprising to me because I think in my view anyone who is willing to settle for the artificial is somebody who saves a part of the authentic, and therefore I think it would be very important, when you're confronted in numbers in millions, to actually create equal but separate systems, whereby those absolutely adamant about the authentic can actually enjoy that experience, while all of those who have other agendas or other needs or other interests that could be dealt with via the new media . . . should also be treated equally seriously. Therefore, for me there is a very direct relation, that is, that basically all these artificial media are the ultimate redemption of the authentic.

I think that it is also very important and, in terms of the discussion of the sponge and the trajectory or the spine, that we devise separate trajectories, and that maybe we have a slow, a medium, and a fast sequence that recognizes that being in a museum need not necessarily be the same experience for everybody anymore.

Another thing which has been very noticeable to me as an outsider is the critical use of "the." I've heard the Museum, the story, the extension, and even the architect. I think implied in the word "the" there is an anxiety, namely, that the anxiety seems to be that the new Museum will all somehow compromise or belittle MoMA's past. I think also when I heard Kirk Varnedoe's demand for a seamless whole, that also seems to me a sign that there is an expectation of and an insis-

tence on, but at the same time a fear of, a new homogeneity or consistency, by which the demands for the new will somehow compromise the needs of the old. Therefore, I would say it is very important to acknowledge [this emphasis on] "the" and to say "a" or to somehow de-escalate the intensity and the singularity of what is looked for or searched for, because I think it is very easy to predict that it will never be a single element that will satisfy the [fluctuating] demands [of the viewers].

For me there is a paradox—and actually, I think it's a very beautiful paradox at this moment—in that MoMA knows everything about the twentieth century and nothing about the twenty-first century. I would say that that in itself produces a very rare and interesting moment, that perhaps it would be liberating for everyone concerned and involved to accept the arbitrary division of the new millennium as a break between knowing and unknowing, between product and process; where, in the twentieth century, MoMA could be the aura machine (which guarantees its eternal life), it would [in the twenty-first century] sponsor the experimentation, the research, that would actually [bring about a new view of art]. So in that sense, again, it's interesting to note that there is always a degree of continuity, but I think that the word "seamless" puts a burden, both in retrospect and in prospect, that actually creates a kind of pallor over the . . . entire discussion, and I think that to explore a deep knowledge, on the one hand, and a deep ignorance, on the other, could in fact be a very profound position.

I would also say—and this is my last point—that there is the skeptical problem of the diversity of the [Museum's] present components, but of course that is only going to increase. Their divergent interests, the necessity of new components, the differentiation of the publics, combined with the enormity of the site, makes this most urgently an issue of urbanity rather than one of architecture. . . . I think, rather than architecture, which always induces enormous anxiety in its either/or logic—since architecture is, just like MoMA, but so far, about exclusion—the urban is the ideal medium, combining the unpredictable with a degree of organization. Because of course a city never preempts what is going to happen; rather, it offers the latent potentials for things to happen, to happen in a kind of a related way. So I think that, again, seeing this issue as an issue of urbanization in the first place and only then eventually and partly an architectural [one] would perhaps . . . remove some of the sense of anxiety that I've felt here more than an eagerness to embark on an unpredictable adventure. I think it is interesting to note that the entire [J. Paul Getty Museum] program is more or less identical to the sum of existing and future MoMA, and you could say that, where [the] Getty has dismantled its entire volume for reasons of architectural interest and diversification, maybe the Modern should dismantle its entire program in the first instance for programmatic interests. These are basically the points I wanted to make. . . .

BILL VIOLA: . . . The passage of time happens by itself, but history is written by people. We talked about the sort of narratives that are found in the Museum, and I think everybody in this room knows, of course, that the overnarrative represented in the collection of the Museum is not the only history: the modern history in the collection is not the only history of art in this century. I think [that], if you look at what Elizabeth Murray did with her [exhibition], taking the objects out of the collection and tracing from a feminist perspective . . . I think a lot of us had wished, of course, that that had [come] from within the Museum itself instead of from an outsider. But it's important, nonetheless, it happened, and it showed that there are other histories . . . in that collection. The collection itself then gets viewed as a kind of a creative object in and of itself, [as] a vast creative pool of resource that can be used and interpreted in different ways, and that the way it has been interpreted up till now is one way of many ways. And that's how it will always be contemporary, no matter how historical it is. . . .

There are two things here we're talking about, and they're [both] represented by the idea of the Museum wanting to be contemporary and modern. The modern side is, you have these objects that, when they were originally brought into the collection, were contemporary, and now, all of a sudden we wake up at the end of the twentieth century and there is a major, almost Metropolitan Museum–like aspect to The Museum of Modern Art, which has all these historical objects in it that are looking period and very old. And then on the other side you're talking about wanting to always be contemporary, which involves us, the living artists . . . the connection between those two things . . . [is] the material objects themselves. And we shouldn't forget that, no matter what happens, no matter what technology gives us, no matter how the society changes, the Museum will always remain a place for communing with objects. That's absolutely essential. You have to understand an object in an extended sense. It's not necessarily going to be a Ming Dynasty vase. It could be a room with light in it, or it could be an idea even on the Internet, but it will be some thing that you engage. . . .

I made a little list here of thinking about this opportunity you have of restructuring the Museum. First of all, I have

administrative structure. Restructuring is just as important as physical structuring. The current structure of museums that we have, with the various departments, has its origins in [the] eighteen- and nineteenth-century scientific worldview, the thing that gave us zoology, the thing that separated giraffes from zebras, and that [is the] current structure [that] we have. So I think we have to include in this physical structuring of the Museum the nonphysical structuring of the organization, and therefore the thought processes within the Museum. We have to include the mechanisms of change and tension in that structure. I think interdepartmental curating is extremely important, cross-fertilization. We have to put the zebras with the hyenas, with the hawks, [and] together into an ecology, because it's not about looking at these things differently, it's not about works on paper and works made of metal and works made of video; it's about what these works do and how they interact with each other in the world of art and with the large world of culture. . . .

The idea of outsiders as curators is also very important, what Elizabeth gave us from her access to the collection. I know that that's [part of a continuing] program at the Museum, and I think that's really wonderful. Expand that to other fields; get philosophers in there, get religious figures in there. . . . Don't shy away from the Internet and try to get rid of this adversarial . . . oppositional way that we have of thinking about the world and engaging the world. Technology's not going to kill material objects; material objects are not going to come back and kill ethereal technology. It's just part of a larger process, part of a larger river that we're all floating in. I think [it's] important that the Museum should recognize the power of its institution. It's a very powerful place, and what you do makes a statement that does matter and does resonate on a number of levels.

There was a little bit of a discussion yesterday [about] the social and political responsibility of the Museum. Does it have a social and political responsibility? Yes, it does, and I want to point out also that this is not your choice: it exists whether you want to acknowledge it or not. You're doing it right now and you have been doing it for a good part of the twentieth century, so why not think about it in an open and conscious way, because it's happening anyway. I think the opportunity there is incredible. . . . Art is under siege today, there's no question about it, and if that could be brought out again, the work that that could do, no matter how great or small, I think can not only, from a more selfish standpoint, place MoMA more in the forefront of the national discussion (and it's certainly good for the institution), but it can also affect the whole community. . . .

Finally, in terms of the architecture and the building, I think, first of all, to be contemporary—if you really want to be contemporary—. . . I think you should also involve artists in the next stage, too, when it really gets down to the nitty-gritty of talking with the architects [about the] spaces and things like that, keep the artists as part of the process; that's the contemporary part of the "modern and contemporary" we've been talking about. In terms of the architects, I just want to say that, no matter what the hype about the Internet, physical space is never going to go away. People need to be in a room together, we know that, and [in the future] we're going to have works of art that we can't now imagine, . . . but, please, give us simple spaces, just simple, wonderful, beautiful, elegant spaces. They can have a character—nothing like a good dialogue between a work of art and a space; there's no such thing as a neutral space—but give us nice, simple, wonderful, beautiful spaces, and leave . . . a place for the passion in those spaces, because that's the thing that holds everything together.

JAMES CUNO: The question facing us about what values of contemporary society should be reflected in art museums, especially modern art museums, leaves me a little uneasy, I have to say, if only in terms of the word "reflect," which sounds to me too passive. It seems to me that the Museum has a role to play in shaping . . . and confronting these values. In fact, if the Museum has a vital role to play, then it should engage and address the intent to change these values. And from what position might it do so?

As I recall from this weekend a couple of remarks, one was Aggie Gund's, quoting from Paul Sachs's report of 1939 to the trustees, [in which he said] that the Modern must take risks, it must not stop taking risks. I also recall Kirk Varnedoe's remarks from the first evening, saying that the Modern's founders stood against inherited values and for the truculently difficult in modern art. That is, I think the Modern should engage, address, and intend to change the values of contemporary society, from a set of defined values, institutional values, which were its founders' values. It should take risks, stand against inherited values, and stand for the truculently difficult in modern art. What contemporary values might the Modern then address? . . . [One] is fear of the different, the unknown, the unknowable, in a conventional sense, the nonverbal, the complex, and the complicated; a tendency to value the familiar and the self-confirming, whether that be an individual self or a collective self; and a tendency to violence and suspicion, if not even paranoia. These values have social consequences, that has to be said, and they're being acted out in our city streets

today and in the wilds of Montana and Idaho. The real question is, what can the Modern or any art museum do to address the social consequences of these values? The answer is, I think, we don't know. We don't know enough about how art effects social change to answer that question. We may want to; we may want to know that it does in specific kinds of ways effect social change. But I don't think we do know that. Well, what do we know?

I think we know that the Modern as an art museum stands a pretty good chance of effecting changes in values with regard to the apprehension of and regard for works of art, more so than those with regard to social structures and personal behavior. If the Modern were to limit itself to what I think it can do, it would be doing radical work of a most original and important kind. It is when museums in this country today talk about effecting change through public education, often they're really talking about political and social change of a very direct kind, . . . about increasing access to the collections, diversifying the collections and exhibition programs in terms of the social, political, ethnic, or any other identity category we choose, of the museums' constituencies. They're talking about empowering those constituencies, saying that they have a place in the museum too. But they aren't really saying that, once they're there, once they are so empowered and have a place in the museum, that they're going to be helped to think and experience things in a fundamentally new way. In fact, often there's a contradiction.

The museum stands for disrupting people's expectations. . . . The museum is also about providing confirming opportunities for people who have been left out of the museum itself. . . . [Having invited them in], this place that is thought about as a radical place of rupture is meant to at the same time confirm, to confirm the new-familiar and . . . the self that seeks confirmation, and those two things, those attitudes, those positions, seem to be in contradiction. . . . I'm wary of asking art museums to do too much, and here I agree with some of the things that Glenn Lowry was suggesting at the end of yesterday's session. We hear people asking of art museums to heal social wounds and to raise individual and group self-esteem. . . . The history of western civilization is to suggest that, for all of the great art that has been produced over so many centuries, the world is not a markedly better place on those individual terms, that wounds still need to be healed and violence has to stop. So I don't know that art in and of itself is capable of what we are wishing it to be capable of.

I think at least that's certainly true of art museums and what art museums do, which is provide people an opportunity to look at and engage with works of art. Tim Rollins [who organized the group of young inner-city artists known as Kids of Survival, or K.O.S.] is often persuasive about the role that making art plays in the lives of individuals, perhaps even particularly troubled individuals, and certainly the work that Aggie [Gund] has encouraged in schools in New York [through The Studio in a School Association, of which she is founder] is also very positive and very persuasive, but that's a very different thing, and I think we can't confuse the benefits of learning to make art at a certain age in one's life and what can be accomplished by helping people to look at works of art.

I think museums often, in an effort to simplify the complexities of the lives we live, confuse the evidence of those two different categories of experience. So the question is, does looking at or experiencing art make better people? I don't know that we have the evidence on which we can say yes to that question. At least some people say that art museums can enhance self-esteem, by empowering people, inviting them in to the center from the periphery and showing them images of themselves once they're there. But again, doesn't that run counter to the other ambition of the museum, which is to complicate, to cause rupture in the lives of people and help them see the beauty of complexities, the beauty of things that cannot be explained, the beauty of things that are not necessarily affirming in the literal. . . . So I think the most radical thing that art museums can do . . . , and what they and we should be challenged to do, and what we should be supported in doing is to help people appreciate and then refine their visual and haptic modes of cognition or whatever these things are, or to explain . . . ways of thinking and apprehending the world that are nonverbal, that are distinctly what it is that we deal with and what is not being dealt with in other institutions through other means, that cannot be reduced to words and they cannot be quantified for consideration by foundations or government agencies. . . .

SUSANNA TORRUELLA LEVAL: I was struck by the question of what values should be reflected. I think in a way the values will be reflected, and it's out of the institution's hands in [this] sense that those values are going to arise from the artists and the artists' works that reflect those values. Of course, this will all assume the particular rate or sensitivity that good curators have to find and see those values in the artists' work and transmit them.

I'm not sure I'd go as far as Jim in saying that institutions should shape values, but certainly to transmit them is one of our highest missions in terms of contemporary art and artists.

We are not social service agencies and never should turn into that. I think our role is to choose artists wisely and then support them one hundred percent in the transmission of those values, however difficult that may be. I'm assuming that there will be a consistency over time in those values that are reflected by any institution, because obviously those values are going to be tied, or the choice of artists, I should say, over time the values that will surface are clearly going to be reflective of what that institution's sense of its own mission, and we've not talked about mission here and of course obviously an in-house discussion for MoMA, but this mission is completely different and obviously it seems to me that plays a major role in how the institution interprets the values and words it chooses and the values it will transmit.

Yesterday, there was some mention about the elitism, that in some cases we're working with art that is difficult and the elitism of art. . . . There has to be made a distinction between the difficulty of the work and the elitism of an institution; those are two very different things. Of course, related to that is the idea of diversity. . . . But diversity is a relative concept, and diversity in Burlington, Vermont, is different from diversity in Little Rock and in New York City, and so all those concepts have to be played in. For instance, at the Museo del Barrio we found out that we weren't diverse enough because our whole board was Latino, our whole staff was Latino, and if we wanted to communicate to anyone who wasn't Latino, [we would have to change]. We made some very hard decisions; we look very different in our board and in our staff today, and forty percent of our audience is non-Latino. But we had to think about where we were and whether we [wanted] to think [as we did] in '69 when we were founded or not. . . .

JOHN ELDERFIELD: Could I ask a question of Rem Koolhaas? When he said that the popularity of museums is threatening their very reason for being, it obviously strikes a chord in anyone who's been to a very crowded exhibition. When you then said, wonderfully, that anyone who settles for the artificial saves part of the organic, I think we all enjoyed the sentence, and I think conservators, particularly, would be very happy to hear it; but are you talking about two audiences, an audience for the artificial and an audience for the authentic?

REM KOOLHAAS: No, it wouldn't be a kind of classification or, let's say, a division of the audience into those good enough, presumably a minority, and those crude enough, presumably the majority. . . . What is important to realize about that is that it implies an equality, an equivalence, and so what I find fatal in the whole [concept] is that the artificial is still seen as a substitute or a condensation, but never as an authentic and entirely legitimate experience in itself.

JOHN ELDERFIELD: But didn't you imply a priority when you talked about the two?

REM KOOLHAAS: I was, in that particular sentence, just throwing a kind of bomb at the [curators and administrators] of MoMA. . . .

RICHARD SERRA: Are you saving the aura [of a work of art] by synthesizing what you're calling part of the authenticity, or is that a big contradiction? You're not redeeming or really saving the aura of the original, you're changing it for [mass] consumption, but the artificiality doesn't save the aura. And there's the big dilemma. It's a different category. . . .

JOHN WALSH: . . . Of all the artists you could have chosen whose aura involves contact with the original object, you couldn't have chosen better than Vermeer. I wonder, your idea is that for only a part of the audience was that aura of contact with the original the critical element, and for a segment of that audience something else might have done; perhaps a succession of beautiful images with some explanation might have satisfied. They didn't have to stand in line to deal with the crush of the Mauritshuis.[22] I think in the case of Vermeer and many other artists there's a real impoverishment, and an unrealistic expectation that that substitution really can be made. I agree with you that this was completely idiotic at the Mauritshuis. They didn't have to have the catastrophe they had. . . . They could have been realistic about what it takes to put a very large number of people in front of original objects. There's a lesson for exhibition organizers here, but it is not necessarily that cloning the original by artificial means is the remedy.

REM KOOLHAAS: . . . I think an absolutely critical issue is to address the issue of quantity, and I haven't heard it addressed. . . . I think that's a very important exclusion, that once again MoMA has prepared, not for us, but those who are actually engaged in the production of "credible" . . . alternatives for real experiences. . . .

KIRK VARNEDOE: Isn't one of the paradoxes that the more synthetic alternatives you generate, the greater you increase the hunger for the original object? The Vermeer show would not have been so well attended were it not for mechanical reproduction. . . . Vermeer wouldn't exist without photography, in a certain sense. The ability to constitute Vermeer in the middle of the nineteenth century had in part to do with the ability to assemble reproductions of his work and look at them on a table, but that there was no Vermeer before that, and the more Vermeer got reproduced, the more precious those original objects have become. So, increasing the one only increases the other. It's not like this compensates for or reduces the pressure on the other. . . . My absolutely favorite example is [that of the artist] Jim Turrell. He told me he grew up seeing art history courses in California. He used to sit in dark rooms in front of huge white screens, and these big, luminous Rothkos would come on the screen, veils of color. . . . And when he went to New York and he looked at one of these paintings [he thought], "I don't want to make art like that, I want to make art like the big luminous projections." They generate their own aura.

PETER GALASSI: This is the core of what Rem was talking about, or one of the cores of it, that the experiences of many of the people who went to see the Vermeer exhibition, whether it was in The Hague or in Washington or elsewhere, was that the conditions under which they saw the authentic "real thing" rendered the experience false. That's the problem. That was a true problem in our Picasso show recently. The reasons so many people wanted to go to that show were underlyingly false. I don't mean that some of them . . . [would not] have [had] a real sense of discovery in front of the real work they couldn't otherwise have; I'm sure that that's true. But I'm also sure that it's true that many of the people were more distanced from what Bill's calling "the authentic spark" by the hoopla of this show and the actual experience of it. . . .

PETER EISENMAN: Can I speak to this issue of the authentic experience being hampered by crowds, which seems to be on the table. I would imagine that the trustees of The Museum of Modern Art would be very disturbed if this million-and-a-half number started to skyrocket downward at an active rate in order that the authentic experience would be in some way embellished and made better. Glenn Lowry would also be a short-lived director. . . .

So therefore, are we facing a true problem of consumption and media hype, because it is precisely the media that is created by this aura machine that Rem is talking about that lessens the aura of the objects' capacity to be seen. . . .

GLENN D. LOWRY: I think there's something inherently paradoxical in museums. . . . One of those paradoxes is the different kinds of experiences that they provide, from the unique moment of an individual engaged with a work of art, to a more complicated social environment in which engagement with a work of art or works of art is complicated by an engagement with other people. But the reality of museums is that they are social constructs; they are about people as much as they are about art, and that intersection provides a multiplicity of experiences. There may be a difference. There may be a threshold where it becomes reckless, moving a lot of people in single file through an aged house in conditions that literally put works of art at risk has crossed a social threshold. We all know because we feel we are privileged by that unique engagement with the object alone, that that is a different experience than the social experience. But it seems to me that museums paradoxically provide all of those experiences, and have to.

PETER EISENMAN: But Glenn, if we go back to the architectural, which I really like to return to always, isn't the issue that the notion of quantity of people, which could go into an *en-suite* set of galleries to see original works, was one thing in the nineteenth century and it's another thing in the twenty-first century, and to continue to insist on this *en-suite* ensemble of rooms that might have been wonderful for the Uffizi [Florence] doesn't any longer work for quantity, and we have to rethink the typology in order to deal with that?

GLENN D. LOWRY: I couldn't agree more. I don't believe the current typology, to the degree that there is a typology, is effective. What I do think is very important is to recognize that museums provide a multiplicity of experiences.

REM KOOLHAAS: Except that that would allow you also to organize different trajectories, and to address those different social roles?

GLENN D. LOWRY: Yes.

JAMES CUNO: Isn't there another contradiction? Yesterday, I think it was mentioned that one of the benefits of developing a large audience and a more diverse audience is that these are the people who are going to vote, these are the people who are going to be able to support the museum. But we now, I think, have evidence, at least from a National Endowment for the Arts survey, that says that more people attend art museums than attend all sporting events combined in this country. Yet this is precisely at a time when support and understanding of works of art [are] declining. So you've got increased audience in numbers and kinds, you've got less understanding and less support. . . .

Summary Session

Panelists: Mary Lea Bandy, Chief Curator, Department of Film and Video, The Museum of Modern Art; Terence Riley, Chief Curator, Department of Architecture and Design; Patterson Sims, Deputy Director for Education and Research Support. Moderated by Glenn D. Lowry. October 6, 1996

GLENN D. LOWRY: . . . The purpose of this weekend's discussion was to raise questions about art, architecture, and, in particular, The Museum of Modern Art as we contemplate building our future, . . . and I want to underscore that the goal was not to find answers, but rather, to posit questions that over the course of time would provide answers for us.

It seems to me that the two categories of questions or issues that emerged were in the first instance ontological. What is a museum, and how does a museum structure and operate itself? The second category of questions was experiential. What happens inside a museum? How does it affect the way in which we engage with art, and what can The Museum of Modern Art do to nurture, articulate, expand, and inflect that set of experiences? A number of . . . important ideas emerged very quickly in the category of ontology. Peter Eisenman raised the issue of not looking for a theorizing of architecture but looking for a theorizing of space—that is, the particular problem of The Museum of Modern Art may not be a purely architectural one, but may, in fact, be one of space. Rem Koolhaas later picked up on this by suggesting that the Museum's first issue, its first order of address, was urbanistic, about a site in midtown Manhattan; that architecture comes into play, but in a secondary fashion, not a primary fashion. Richard Serra brought up a point which resonates, I think, with all of us who think about the museum, and that is whether or not the model of the museum as a treasure house or safety-deposit box is a pertinent model in the late twentieth century, and whether or not there are other models . . . that create a different kind of engagement with, not only the works of art we show, but with the public we so willingly seek to engage with our art. It also emerged, and . . . it was Richard who said this, that we need to create a context where the experience of art can be startling. It's something we forget, that the encounter with art, whatever way in which that happens, needs to have that ability to startle and surprise. . . .

I found particularly interesting that a number of metaphors seemed to emerge [in the effort to] describe the Museum. . . . We talked about the museum as being a crazy quilt, a random patchwork of assembled possibilities, or the museum as a storyteller or narrator that creates histories and experiences, not one history or experience but multiple histories and experiences. The two metaphors that struck me as perhaps most resonant were the metaphors of the museum as a skeletal structure—as a spine off of which different pieces could be adjusted, articulated, and framed—or the museum as a sponge, something that is expandable and compressible and that is layered with different sets of possibilities held together by seemingly infinite webbed relationships. . . .

There was a further metaphor or notion of the museum that on its own, I think, was perhaps the most complicated but an equally interesting one, and that is the museum as a montage, as a series of layered and, at times, related and, at times, disjunctive experiences that have led to the museum as attraction—that is, attraction as in a circus, a multiringed environment where different possibilities and different experiences could occur. It was Jean-Louis Cohen who articulated that reading of the museum. Underneath it all was a continued affirmation, . . . that the singular purpose of the museum is [to provide] a place where people go to look at art. . . . Museums require a physical space, works of art, and people, and all three have to exist in some kind of dynamic relationship to each other. I think, finally, [that] the most intriguing aspect of this weekend . . . is how do the different conceptual readings that we have of a museum ultimately translate themselves into specific architectural solutions. . . .

PATTERSON SIMS: . . . Let me say that this notion of education being key was reiterated by the whole group of individuals who were here. . . . One thing that we discovered was that technology is going to play a key role in all of this. What kind of role, it became increasingly clear, is completely unclear, . . . but I think it's going to be very key for the Museum actually to get involved with an extremely young generation of people if we're going to have any clue about what we're really going to do in ten years' time. . . . I just want to say that we do have an extraordinary challenge ahead of us. We're going to be telling the sort of über-narrative of modern art in very different ways than we have in the past. It's going to be based on a kind of dialogue that will be, I think, even richer than it's ever been in the past. . . . Bill Viola spoke of the "spark." Sheila de Bretteville spoke of social hope. So, somewhere between a spark, the very spark that we experience as we look at a work of art and have that kind of satori which sustains our visits to museums, even within the sometime excruciating circumstances of the Museum at the end of the twentieth century, with its extraordinary popular success, with the buzzing of the earphones which I feel are so mandatory for understanding exhibitions and can be such an extraordinary tool, with the bustle of our lives in the late twentieth century, that spark, combined with social [hope], are the two ingredients, so appropriately given to us by artists, that may provide the key for why the great Museum of Modern Art will become an even greater institution with its new building and expansion.

MARY LEA BANDY: I'm going to address the issues of technology. . . . In the '80s, at the Museum, in which we talked about the future but we did not talk about technology, we did not really address the issues of technology in an expanded Museum of Modern Art. . . . This time around, we cannot expand the Museum without dealing with technology issues. We cannot look into the twenty-first century without focusing on what has happened technologically since the last expansion, and where we want to go. I do think that what I've been hearing from all of the speakers this weekend is that the educational and advocacy roles of the Museum can only be served if we radically rethink our technological opportunities. . . . We have an opportunity to radically rethink our involvement with current as well as new and heretofore nonexistent technologies, which will serve a variety of purposes. We heard that our technologies could or could not replace, enhance, extend, enable us to confront or to deny our traditional function of presenting art in our galleries to individual viewers. Technology can help us create the tension, present the discontinuities, and provoke the confrontations of modern art. Bearing in mind that we have several histories, technology can further assist us in dealing with them. The first, of course, is that by the time we open in 2004, we will have a hundred and a quarter years of modern art—an extensive history. We also are valued now, and are going to be valued, I believe, as a museum of the history of the twentieth century. And then, as many of our participants pointed out, the history of the Museum itself is a vital history and an influential and important one. Technology also has to serve, not only our historical goals, but our con-

temporary art programs as well, and . . . we can only guess . . . how technology might develop in the future. We cannot hope to predict this with any certainty; we can only guess and provide. To me, this means that there are three layers or functions of the technology in our expanded Museum.

First, our galleries and public spaces. Bill Viola recommended that we . . . provide computers, video, audio—whatever electronic means we can [and] provide flexible spaces in our galleries for artists to create and present their own work, as well as for curators and artists to install works in various mediums as they analyze our own collections. It's easy to build such a "smart" museum, as Arato Isozaki pointed out, but it is much more difficult to build an intelligent museum. But we can be smart technologically. Secondly, Mark Taylor spoke of . . . our study centers and libraries, . . . the importance of globalization in the next century, we can use communications technologies to link our study centers, libraries, and archives with universities, archives, other museums and libraries around the world. We can create and broaden an institutional network, and we can experiment with ways to reproduce art, to study art, . . . to provide the information, analyze the history, and provoke a dialogue, provoke commentary. This will be our new museum without walls. Richard Serra asked us to reflect on how museums can better advocate. How can we bridge the gap in understanding between people and art, and what are the means . . . which we can consider, to reach out to young people, to students, to people all over the world. We don't have the answers, but [as] I think he pointed out, importantly, . . . we must consider our role as advocate and use our technologies accordingly. Finally, we also want to know how we can serve, very importantly, individuals in ways that may be equally important to the gallery experience. As Bill Viola and others emphasized, the primary experience is still a one-on-one experience of the viewer in a gallery, looking at the work of art, discovering the work of art, reacting to the work of art. How can we face the notion of exchange between the individual and the Museum technologically? Now that we have the Internet, the Web, the CD-ROM, these might only be the first stages of Mark's globalization, the first effort to create, as Bill said, a "community of desire."

This is not, as he said, a mass community, a mass audience, but many, many individuals around the world, each of whom wants to be able to explore and discover. New generations are finding the aura of the art object, that the aura of the art object can go into nonmaterial objects. This is possible because we are in a period of fundamental change in our society at the end of this century, and for many of our participants, technology symptomizes the changes that we can take advantage of. In this regard, Mark Taylor said that the architecture of the software is as important as the hardware, and I think that this can be applied to every aspect of our expansion. If Mark and the others here are correct, complexity will be the shape of the twenty-first century. We must not be timid; we must realize that there are new generations looking at themselves and their art and the society in radically different ways, influenced profoundly by the technologies they are growing up with. . . . Peter Eisenman said that museums are places of confrontation between art and society and architecture. They must also be places of confrontation with technology. Susanna Leval said that we should conceive of spaces in the museum as studios, or laboratories, for contemporary art. I think we should think of the Internet, our technologies, also as studios and laboratories. . . .

KIRK VARNEDOE: I think probably in honor of the upcoming Jasper Johns show,[23] Glenn concedes that the role I could best play in this dialogue this weekend was to stand up on the opening night and turn myself into a large target. I tried to do this, and it seems that the word that got stuck somehow in everyone's mind, or the thing that I can't remember saying, is I somehow uttered the words "seamless whole." . . . I'd like to go back to that notion, because I hope I was misunderstood. . . I tried to raise that question because Alfred Barr had the idea that there was a museum where it made sense to have painting from 1880 and painting from 1930, that there was some continuity there that made a museum like that make sense, and furthermore, that there was an intelligence to having a museum where film, photography, ball bearings, and paintings were all shown together, that there was some binding modern spirit that made the museum make sense. I tried to affirm that and I believe [it's] true, that we do make sense and that it makes sense for us to be a unity. But I want to insist, not on the seamlessness of it, perhaps, but on the unseamlessness of it, that we are a very fractious group. . . . I always remember Bob Hughes's phrase for this Museum, "the Kremlin of modernism,"[24] and I think of [Rem] speak[ing] about aura. . . . Before I came to the Museum I was sure that somewhere in the basement there was a vault and you opened it and there was a set of stone tablets on which there were graven instructions—which works of art to buy, which not to buy, which exhibitions to do, which not to do—that set the stone ideology of the great, monolithic Museum of Modern Art. When you get inside the cat-and-dog fight that actually constitutes The Museum of Modern Art, what you find is that the Museum got where it got not by being inhuman but being incredibly human, by being constantly fractious, constantly riven with seams, constantly self-critical.

There are two crucial things about the way our great collections were built. On the one hand is Barr's attitude toward contemporary art, which is that sins of omissions are always worse than sins of commission—take the risk, take the flier, make the gamble. Mistakes can always be corrected, opportunities never come around again. . . . But one of the other things that he did was to make the Museum great by constantly criticizing and reexamining the past to make it more radical, not to make it more comfortable. We were born as a museum of Kolbe, Maillol, and Pasquin. We got to be a museum of Tatlin, Malevich, Duchamp, and Picasso by retrospective self-criticism. We bought the *Demoiselles d'Avignon* in 1939; we bought [van Gogh's] *Starry Night* in [1941]. The point of going back into tradition is not to provide a more comfortable pillow to rest on but constantly to put spikes in our butt, so that we move forward more, we understand what the radical challenges that early modern art set before us were. . . .

If we think about that idea of the seamlessness, I also set myself up by talking a lot about the nature of the individual and how I believe so strongly in individual creativity. I was rightly called to task for the notion of the modern construct of individual subjectivity, the myth of whole personal autonomy, of complete, rational integrity of a private self. That's not true and that's not the kind of individuality I believe in. The kind of individuality I believe in, on the part of artists, on the part of our audience and viewers, is equally a fractious and divided individuality in which people can have conflicting tastes within their lives. . . . The individual is an infinite source of surprise and complexity, and it is from the resource of that fractiousness and creativity that modern art is born—not as a seamless whole, not as a monolithic modernism, but as a series of arguments and human debates, out of which amazing and wonderful things come. And it is this process that we've been going through this weekend. . . . The combination of self-criticism and deep dissatisfaction with what is and desire for what might be better, combined with the thing that makes it wonderful to work at this Museum, which is the love for . . . a certain ideal of The Museum of Modern Art, of the Museum, of the mission, whatever that is. . . . I think of the comment Bruce Morton made on television on the occasion of the Bicentennial of the American Revolution. . . . He said about a nation two hundred years old and going what I would say about a museum coming up to its seventy-fifth and going, that is, this great dream that never was and still must be.

TERENCE RILEY: . . . Bill Viola spoke of a rare moment that we're in: Something is changing. It is a great time of uncertainty. I think this is true, and that this information provokes alternately anxiety and optimism. . . . Rem Koolhaas noted that, despite the emphasis on architecture here—there are plenty of examples—and the Modern is one of them—that you don't really need great architecture to have a museum. . . . I think that upsets architects, but probably no more than curators [are upset] when they realize that the Isabella Stewart Gardner Museum and the Barnes Collection are wildly successful museums, and there is nothing for the curators to do but sort of dust the pieces and stay out of the way. Certainly the Guggenheim must outrage some artists when they realize that a lot of people think that it doesn't need any art in it, that it's a great museum yet visitors might not even remember what they saw there, they're so bowled over by the museum building itself. So there is no formula for a great museum, there is no prototype, but there is paradigm. Peter Eisenman provided what might be one of the more enduring epigrams of the weekend, and pointed out the irony in our search—and it is ironic: if you want a great museum, don't try to design a museum. I think what Peter was saying is that there is no precise model to follow, that, in fact, . . . if I could paraphrase him, if you do try to design a museum, the most you can hope for is to create a monument to a past idea. The effort is incumbent upon those who would like to create a great museum to find a new model. I, too, was struck by the number of metaphors, and actually very excited about the number of metaphors that were being used. . . .

Sheila Levrant de Bretteville's metaphor, the crazy quilt, is very powerful for a number of reasons, one of which, specific to MoMA, was her observation that in a crazy quilt there are frequently fragments of older, now disused garments that get incorporated into the quilt and assume new meanings and new usages. Certainly when you're talking about a museum that's been expanded six times, there is in fact already a bit of a crazy quilt, and as each new piece is added, it changes the meaning of the other pieces. . . . Jean-Louis Cohen cited Eisenstein's theorization of a montage of attraction. . . . The Museum *is* an attraction. It attracts people from around the world. Why it does that and how it does that is something that the architecture can complement and assist. Rem Koolhaas not only talked about urban planning as a prototypical strategy for designing a building, but I also understood him to suggest that an urbanism is indeed also a metaphor for what we're trying to do. He defined an urbanism as an unpredictable series of events with a degree of organization, something that some of us experience, of course, every day. And then, of course, Bernard Tschumi suggest[ed] the metaphor of the sponge, not a spine. It was a metaphor many people found very laden with potential meanings to be explored. . . .

One of the questions, and a very reasonable one, that it was hoped we might get to is what will the new Museum look like, and I have to report that there's no report. The conference was rather inconclusive in that regard, but I think that's also important, to realize that there wasn't a rush to talk about style and that the metaphor and the means, the strategies, were much more important. . . . Peter Eisenman proposed . . . that architects have virtually exhausted the possibility of theorizing form and must now turn to the notion or the concept of theorizing space. It would follow, if Peter's words can be considered accurate, that in fact we wouldn't be spending a lot of time talking about how the building would look—not at first, anyway, but thinking about how it would be in various other ways before thinking of how it would look. And so in that sense I think we were definitely and in a most exciting fashion on the right track. . . . This is both the risk and the opportunity. . . . So, in fact, this Museum could be something that none of us have ever seen before. . . . Arata Isozaki phrased it very interestingly. One of the problems with contemporary museums is that architects are trying to be artists and artists are trying to be architects. . . . Robert Irwin lamented the notion of complexity in the museum and the dilution, if you will, of the museum's truly, in his mind, legitimizing purpose, which is art. Adam Gopnik also felt that the self-evident function of a museum, being a place for art, was frequently being overlooked. This polarity—complexity/simplicity—remains. You have an added sort of spin to that: this is not in Iowa. Even if we built a very simple museum with nothing in it but art, it is in the middle of Manhattan, and therefore becomes part of a complex organism. Many people talked about rupture and transgression; [others] talked about refuge and reflection. . . . Again, Manhattan adds another spin to it. Even if the Museum is designed as a calm and peaceful oasis, it is again in the center of Manhattan and thus part of a complex, transgressive, and ruptured whole. . . .

Notes

1. See Jack Lindsay, *Cézanne: His Life and Art* (London: Evelyn, Adams and MacKay Ltd., and Greenwich, Conn.: New York Graphic Society, 1969), p. 325.

2. See Robert Venturi, *Complexity and Contradiction in Architecture* (New York: The Museum of Modern Art, 1966).

3. Yve-Alain Bois and Rosalind E. Krauss, *L'Informe: Mode d'emploi* (Paris: Editions du Centre Georges Pompidou, 1996).

4. MoMA Exh. #1743, *Picasso and Portraiture: Representation and Transformation,* directed by William Rubin; shown at The Museum of Modern Art April 24–September 17, 1996.

5. The nine institutions that constitute Museum Mile, extending from Eighty-second to One Hundred Fourth Street on Fifth Avenue, are: The Metropolitan Museum of Art; the Goethe Institut New York/German Cultural Center; the Solomon R. Guggenheim Museum; The National Academy Museum and School of Fine Arts; the Cooper-Hewitt, National Design Museum, Smithsonian Institution; The Jewish Museum; the International Center of Photography; the Museum of the City of New York; and El Museo del Barrio.

6. The Museum of Modern Art was chartered in 1929 by The Board of Regents, New York State Department of Education; see Provisional Charter, The Museum of Modern Art, in The Museum of Modern Art Archives: Reports and Pamphlets, Architectural Plans, By-laws, and Charters, Box 1/14. See also Alfred H. Barr, "Chronicle of the Collection of Painting and Sculpture [1940–63]," in *Studies in Modern Art no. 4. The Museum of Modern Art at Mid-Century: At Home and Abroad* (New York: The Museum of Modern Art, 1994).

7. Quoted in Emile Bernard, "Une Conversation avec Cézanne" (Mercure de France, 1921); reprinted in Herschel B. Chipp, "Postimpressionism: Individual Paths to Construction and Expression," in *Theories of Modern Art: A Source Book by Artists and Critics* (Berkeley and Los Angeles: University of California Press, 1968), p. 12.

8. See Michel Foucault, *Madness and Civilization: A History of Insanity in the Age of Reason* (New York: Pantheon, 1965), *passim.*

9. MoMA Exh. #1720, *Artist's Choice: Elizabeth Murray,* selected and installed by Murray; shown at The Museum of Modern Art June 17–August 20, 1995.

10. MoMA Exh. #1382, *Primitivism in Twentieth-century Art: Affinity of the Tribal and the Modern,* directed by William Rubin and Kirk Varnedoe; shown at The Museum of Modern Art September 19, 1984–January 15, 1985.

11. MoMA Exh. #1559, *High and Low: Modern Art and Popular Culture,* directed by Kirk Varnedoe and Adam Gopnik; shown at The Museum of Modern Art October 7, 1990–January 15, 1991.

12. As part of the retrospective *Robert Irwin,* co-organized by Kerry Brougher and Richard Koshalek, installed at the Museum of Contemporary Art, Los Angeles, June 20–August 15, 1993, the artist created the site-specific installation *Five Openings: 2 + 3,* in which holes were made in the building's interior walls.

13. MoMA Exh. #1749, *Pictures of the Times: A Century of Photography from The New York Times,* directed by Peter Galassi and Susan Kismaric; shown at The Museum of Modern Art June 26–October 8, 1996.

14. MoMA Exh. #877, *The Machine as Seen at the End of the Mechanical Age,* directed by Pontus Hulten of the Moderna Museet, Stockholm; shown at The Museum of Modern Art November 27, 1968–February 9, 1969.

15. MoMA Exh. #34, *Machine Art,* directed by Philip Johnson; shown at The Museum of Modern Art March–April 29, 1934.

16. A reference to Meret Oppenheim's "fur-lined teacup" (*Object*) of 1936, purchased by The Museum of Modern Art in 1946.

17. Hollis Frampton, "For a Metahistory of Film: Commonplace Notes and Hypotheses," *Artforum* vol.10, no. 1 (September 1971), p. 35.

18. MoMA Exh. #559, *Japanese Exhibition House,* installed in The Museum of Modern Art sculpture garden June 16–October 21, 1954, and April 26–October 16, 1955.

19. *Continuity of Vision* (1964), an interview with the artist Barnett Newman by Frank O'Hara, then an associate curator in The Museum of Modern Art International Program; directed by Bruce Minnix and produced by Colin Clark for PBS Channel 13 in New York City.

20. *Black Male: Representations of Masculinity in Contemporary American Art,* directed by Thelma Golden; shown at the Whitney Museum of American Art, New York, November 10, 1994–March 5, 1995.

21. MoMA Exh. #1736, *Roy DeCarava: A Retrospective,* directed by Peter Galassi; shown at The Museum of Modern Art January 24–May 7, 1996.

22. A reference to the exhibition *Johannes Vermeer,* co-organized by the National Gallery of Art, Washington, D.C., and the Royal Cabinet of Paintings Mauritshuis, The Hague; directed by Arthur K. Wheelock, Jr. and Frederik J. Duparc. The exhibition was installed at the National Gallery November 12, 1995–February 11, 1996, and at the Mauritshuis March 1–June 9, 1996.

23. MoMA Exh. #1754, *Jasper Johns: A Retrospective,* directed by Kirk Varnedoe; shown at The Museum of Modern Art October 15, 1996–January 21, 1997.

24. Robert Hughes, review of *The Revenge of the Philistines: Art and Culture, 1972–1984* by Hilton Kramer, in *The New Republic* 194 (April 14, 1986), p. 28.

1. The Museum of Modern Art, New York, campus viewed from the northeast, 1997. At center right is the Dorset Hotel.

Building the Future:
Some Observations on Art, Architecture, and The Museum of Modern Art

Lecture by Glenn D. Lowry. October 22, 1996

Since its founding in 1929, The Museum of Modern Art has had a long and important tradition of engaging in public discussions about modern art and architecture. Always stimulating, at times contentious, and often highly visible, these discussions have helped shape, if not actually form, our understanding of the unfolding patterns of modern art. What I hope to do here is to extend that tradition of debate and discussion by outlining a number of issues that are of concern to the Museum as we contemplate a major expansion and renovation of our building.

Until recently, the problem of the Museum's requirements for the future was an abstract one; today, it is substantially more concrete. The reason for this is that, with the acquisition of the Dorset Hotel and two adjacent properties on Fifty-third and Fifty-fourth streets (see figs. 1, 2), we have affirmed our commitment, not only to our current site, but to the notion of a single museum complex for all of our diverse functions. In addition, by virtue of the property we have purchased—which permits approximately 250,000 square feet of development—we have defined the potential scope of what we can do.

The issues that I hope will emerge from this discussion could not be more timely, for the advent of a new century, not to mention a new millennium, is less than four years away, and the Museum's seventy-fifth anniversary will occur shortly after that, in 2004. Although such dates are arbitrary, they compel us, I believe, to take stock of what we have achieved, and to focus on what we hope to accomplish in the future. Over the last few years, there has been a great deal of debate, both inside and outside the Museum, concerning what our goals should be as we move into the next century.[1] While some have argued that the Museum should cease to collect contemporary art and focus its energies and resources on what it already has, thus becoming a shrine to modern art as manifested in the twentieth century, that is not the course we intend to follow. On the contrary, we plan to continue vigorously

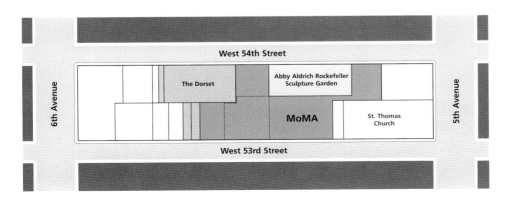

2. Existing Museum of Modern Art site and adjacent properties. Diagram prepared by Cooper, Robertson and Partners, 1996

pursuing our interests in contemporary and modern art throughout the next century. Recent acquisitions of such seminal works as Richard Serra's *Intersection II* (fig. 3), a gift of Ronald S. Lauder; Andy Warhol's *Campbell's Soup Cans* (1962); and James Rosenquist's *F-111* (fig. 4), only affirm our commitment to building a collection of unparalleled strength in the twentieth century in order to have the basis for one in the twenty-first century. Indeed, The Museum of Modern Art is dedicated to the encouragement of an ever-deeper understanding of modern and contemporary art for the diverse local, national, and international audiences that we serve, through the creation of a dialogue between the past and the present, between the established and the experimental. To that end, our Mission Statement recognizes:

- that modern and contemporary art "transcend national boundaries and involve all forms of visual expression . . . which reflect and explore the artistic issues of the era";
- that these forms of visual expression, "including painting and sculpture, drawings, prints and illustrated books, photography, architecture and design, and film and video, as well as new forms yet to be developed or understood . . . [are] an open-ended series of arguments and counter arguments that can be explored through exhibitions and installations and that are reflected in the Museum's varied collection"; and
- that it is essential for the Museum "to affirm the importance of contemporary art and artists," no matter how difficult or uncomfortable that may be, if the institution is "to remain vital and engaged with the present."[2]

One of the strengths of The Museum of Modern Art has been its ability to periodically reevaluate itself, or, in the words of Alfred H. Barr, Jr., the Museum's founding director, to remain in a constantly evolving state of self-renewal.[3] Thus, the questions for us are: What kind of museum will be required to fulfill our intellectual and programmatic needs over the next couple of decades; and, How should that be articulated in our architecture.

What follows, then, is a series of observations on museums and their architecture in general, and the specific problems of The Museum of Modern Art as it contemplates a major building program sometime in the next decade.

3. Richard Serra. *Intersection II.* 1992. Cor-Ten steel; four plates, each 13' 1½" x 55' 9⅜" x 2" (400 x 1700 x 5 cm). The Museum of Modern Art, New York. Fractional and promised gift of Ronald S. Lauder, 1993

4. James Rosenquist. *F-111.* 1964–65. Oil on canvas with aluminum, 10 x 86' (3.1 x 26.2 m). The Museum of Modern Art, New York. Purchase, 1996

Over the last twenty-five years, there has been a dramatic growth in art museums around the world—one need only look at what has been happening in the United States to realize the extent to which museums have become central to our intellectual and cultural life, not to mention the infrastructure of our cities. There are currently 1,241 art museums in the United States alone; fifty percent of these were founded since 1970.[4] Many museums devoted to modern and contemporary art have recently inaugurated new buildings, including the San Francisco Museum of Modern Art (SFMOMA), in 1995, and the Museum of Contemporary Art in Chicago, in June 1996.

Despite the number of museums that have been built in the last twenty-five years, however, no clear typology has developed for the museum of art, and, in particular, for the museum of *modern* art. As Michael Brawne has noted, "The word 'museum' will often evoke a particular character of building, rarely however, a particular space organization. This is probably the case because museums and galleries of all kinds exist in a considerable array of buildings. Some of these were specially designed for the collections which they house at present but most were, as likely as not, built for some quite other purpose."[5]

The three principal museum typologies of the nineteenth century—the temple, the palace, and the exposition hall (typified by the Altes Museum in Berlin, the Musée du Louvre, and the Grand Palais, respectively)[6]—have given birth in the twentieth century to such museums as The Cleveland Museum of Art (fig. 5), the Freer Gallery of Art (fig. 6), and the Centre Georges Pompidou (fig. 7). These models have since been joined by a variety of new types. Among these are single-purpose museums like The Museum of Modern Art, teaching museums like the Fogg Art Museum (fig. 8), and shrines to individual taste like the Isabella Stewart Gardner Museum, as well as many others.

Clockwise from top left:
9. Mario Botta. San Francisco Museum of Modern Art. 1988–95. Photograph by Richard Barnes

10. Marcel Breuer and Hamilton Smith. Whitney Museum of American Art, New York. 1963–66. Photograph by Jerry L. Thompson

11. Daniel Perry, principal architect. Sterling and Francine Clark Art Institute, Williamstown, Massachusetts. 1953–55

One of the reasons why there is at present no clearly defined typology for the art museum lies in the fact that there are so many different kinds of museums, including:

- urban museums such as SFMOMA (fig. 9) and the Whitney Museum of American Art (fig. 10);
- small, private repositories such as the Frick;
- rural museums such as the Sterling and Francine Clark Art Institute (fig. 11);
- large public institutions with local, county, or national charters, such as the Museum of Fine Arts, Boston, the Los Angeles County Museum of Art, and the National Gallery of Art (fig. 12);
- large university galleries such as the Yale University Art Gallery;
- small university galleries such as Williams College Museum of Art; and
- encyclopedic institutions such as The Metropolitan Museum of Art (fig. 13).

There are many more categories that could be isolated here, but what is more striking is that even within any one of these museum types there is no clearly identifiable architectural typology. It is as if, once the great nineteenth-century models were modified and superseded, no single architectural model was possible, and no subsequent models were able to assert themselves for any one type of museum. "What any such catalogue would therefore seem to indicate," according to Brawne, "is that the museum as a building type is distinguished, not by well defined and characteristic spatial arrangements which we may associate with particular uses, but by attributes which are able to exist within a number of different architectural enclosures."[7]

Above, left to right:
12. National Gallery of Art, Washington, D.C. West Wing: John Russell Pope, architect. 1935–41. East Wing: I. M. Pei, architect. 1968–78

13. Richard Morris Hunt and Richard Howland Hunt, principal architects. The Metropolitan Museum of Art, New York. Begun 1895–1902

If museums are institutions whose spatial organization is adaptable to a wide variety of architectural enclosures, as Brawne suggests, the reason for this undoubtedly resides in the fact that even the simplest museums have become extremely complex institutions engaged in a wide variety of functions. While each function may require a specific kind of space, no one function is so dominant that it can determine the overall spatial or architectural characteristics of the institution. Moreover, the primary spaces of most museums, galleries, and lobbies are sufficiently supple that they can be articulated and elaborated in a number of different ways—with or without natural light, extensive details, regular shapes, and clearly defined spatial relationships to other parts of the museum—while still retaining all of the elements required to fulfill their function. Just as the parts of a museum are malleable, so, too, is the whole. Albert Ten Eyck Gardner, a curator at The Metropolitan Museum of Art from 1956 to 1967, recognized this chameleon-like aspect of museums when he observed:

[The museum] is in fact a modern hybrid, bred with mingled characteristics of the cathedral, the royal palace, the theater, the school, the library, and according to some critics, the department store. As the emphasis or activity shifts, the character of the organization changes. Thus when the museum serves as a place of entertainment it takes on the dramatic quality of the theater, when it is used for scholarly purposes it can become an ivory tower, when its educational activities are stressed it becomes a school. For the scientist or professor it may seem to be merely a series of specimens illustrating a seductive theory, or a library of artifacts filed in chronological order. In the family of social institutions invented by man, the place of the museum is not rigidly fixed. It is pliant and can develop in many directions, or sometimes move simultaneously in several directions.[8]

Museums of modern and contemporary art are perhaps the most open of all museums to an evolving typology. There are a number of reasons for this, the most important being that, by definition, museums of modern and contemporary art seek to reflect the new, and so set themselves as a goal a break with the past. At the same time, precisely because there is no fixed typology, architects have seen in museums unique opportunities to create buildings that will reflect their own ideas and interests,

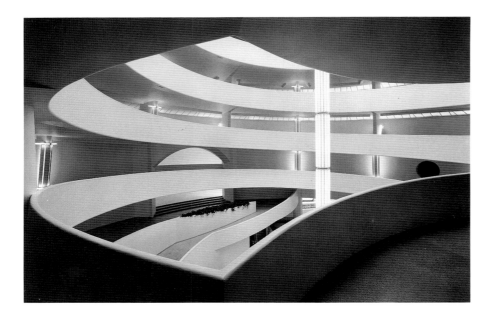

14. Frank Lloyd Wright. Solomon R. Guggenheim Museum, New York. 1943–46, 1956–59. View of main circulation ramp and upper galleries. At right: *Dan Flavin. Untitled (To Tracy, to celebrate the love of a lifetime).* Fluorescent light, various dimensions. Solomon R. Guggenheim Museum, partial gift of the artist in honor of Ward Jackson. Installed as part of the exhibition *Dan Flavin,* June 22–August 27, 1992. Photograph by David Heald © The Solomon R. Guggenheim Foundation, New York

15. Richard Meier and Partners. Museu d'Art Contemporani, Barcelona. View of main circulation ramp, with galleries at left. 1987–94. © Scott Frances/Esto

and be in and of themselves understood as works of art. The degree to which contemporary museums can differ, at times in fundamentally antithetical ways, is evident in even the most cursory comparisons. Both Frank Lloyd Wright's Solomon R. Guggenheim Museum and Richard Meier's Museu d'Art Contemporani in Barcelona (MACBA), for example, are structured around monumental ramps that provide a centralized means of circulation in each building. At the Guggenheim, the ramp was designed to fuse movement with display, as it also forms the main galleries of the museum (fig. 14). At MACBA, however, the ramp was designed to separate circulation from exhibition, forming a barrier between the monumental public spaces of the museum and the more intimate and private spaces of the galleries (fig. 15). Like almost all museums of modern and contemporary art, each is an idiosyncratic building, designed to be unique rather than typical.

A second reason why it may be impossible to develop a clearly defined typology for museums, and especially for museums of contemporary art, is that the nature of contemporary artistic practice is to constantly challenge preconceived notions of art. Museums that wish to engage with contemporary artists must, therefore, continually seek to create spaces that can support rapidly changing notions of art. In this context, typology must be understood as a flexible means of realizing certain functional goals rather than as a standard set of criteria. Over the course of the twentieth century, artists have become increasingly aware of the fact that museums are not simply repositories of their work, but important sites of their practice. This transfer of activity from the privacy of the studio to the public arena of the gallery has meant that the container, or the museum building, has become in and of itself a catalyst that transforms the contents of the institution into events, so that the contemporary museum is no longer simply a place of contemplation and study, but a venue of provocation and debate.[9] In order to accommodate the needs of contemporary artists, many museums have sought to modify their spaces to reflect the studios of artists—thus the bare, industrial loft, which is to a certain degree the antithesis of the elaborate and detailed museum gallery, has become the norm in many museums

16. Postcard view of the Heckscher Building, 730 Fifth Avenue (left), and the Plaza Hotel, New York, 1923.

of contemporary art. Once integrated into the museum, however, these spaces are no longer spare and neutral; rather, they are facsimiles of those spaces. They remind us in an almost romantic way of the purity, if that is the right word, of the artist's studio; yet, because they have been sanctioned and sanitized by the museum, they are anything but pure.

What does all of this mean for The Museum of Modern Art, which gave birth to the whole notion, at least in North America, of an urban museum housed in its own specially designed building, open to the street and the beat of the city? In the first instance this means, I think, that the Museum cannot rely upon either its past history or that of any other museum in terms of establishing a model for its future. Secondly, and somewhat paradoxically, given the importance of its collections and history, it means that the Museum has an obligation to create an architecture that argues for a particular understanding of what it means to be a museum of modern art at the beginning of the twenty-first century. I will return to this issue of polemics later, but before I do, I want to review, if only cursorily, the Museum's architectural history, for it is against the backdrop of this history that The Museum of Modern Art must create its future.

Established in 1929, the Museum began its existence in rented quarters at 730 Fifth Avenue (fig. 16), where its opening exhibition attracted 47,000 visitors in its first month.[10] The approximately 4500 square feet of the new Museum was organized into six rooms, accommodating temporary exhibition galleries, library shelving, and office space for the staff of four. By the end of its first year of operation, the Museum's success was such that it was clear that it was soon going to need more space, as well as a permanent home. In 1932, the Museum relocated to a five-story townhouse at 11 West Fifty-third Street (fig. 17), leased from John D. Rockefeller, Jr., husband of Museum cofounder Abby Aldrich Rockefeller. Within three years, however, it had outgrown this space, and in May 1935, William S. Paley (head of CBS and a Museum trustee) donated space in the CBS Building, at 485 Madison Avenue, to store the Museum's burgeoning film library. In 1936, the Museum formally

17. The Museum of Modern Art building at 11 West Fifty-third Street, New York, 1932

Above, left to right:
18. Philip L. Goodwin and Edward D. Stone. The
Museum of Modern Art, New York. Aerial view. 1939.
Photograph by Andreas Feininger

19. Philip Johnson. The Museum of Modern Art, New
York: Grace Rainey Rogers Annex (left foreground).
1949–51

20. Philip Johnson. The Museum of Modern Art, New
York: The Abby Aldrich Rockefeller Sculpture Garden.
1950–53

acquired both its 11 West Fifty-third Street headquarters and three adjacent town-houses.[11] It then commissioned Philip L. Goodwin and Edward Durell Stone to design a building for its newly expanded site. (For the architectural "footprint" of the 1936–39 site, as well as subsequent Museum expansions, see appendix, pp. 96-97.) The Goodwin–Stone building (fig. 18), which occupied 109,100 square feet, 23,200 of which were devoted to galleries, opened to the public on May 10, 1939. By that time, the Museum had mounted 112 temporary exhibitions and accommodated one-and-a-half million visitors.[12] A. Conger Goodyear, the Museum's president, noted in the catalogue to the tenth-anniversary exhibition, *Art in Our Time,* that the Museum had finally reached a certain level of maturity, with a home of its own in a building designed specifically for its unique mission. He proudly stated that:

The exhibition galleries provide three times the space available heretofore. In the offices the Museum staff for the first time has space to carry on its work properly and all of the Museum's activities are now housed under one roof. The library emerges from its state of crowded confusion and is at last equipped for public use. An auditorium makes possible lectures, moving pictures and other developments. A final touch of completion is to be found in the garden which provides an outdoor display space as well as a setting for the building.[13]

In celebrating the new Museum building, Goodyear's words outline what was, and continues to be, an unrealized dream of The Museum of Modern Art: to have ample galleries for all of its collections under one roof, adequate spaces for its library and archives, dignified offices and research centers for its staff, effective theaters for its film program and public programs, and a multipurpose garden. For the simple reality of the Museum is that its collections have continued to grow and expand with such rapidity that its spatial requirements have not been able to keep up with its pro-grammatic needs.

Throughout the 1950s and 1960s, the Museum's architecture underwent a num-ber of changes under the supervision of Philip Johnson.[14] In 1950–51, Johnson designed an annex to the Museum's west at 21 West Fifty-third Street, named in honor of Grace Rainey Rogers (fig. 19). This seven-story addition provided much-needed space for the People's Art Center (the site of a program of children's and adult's art classes), storage areas, additional stacks for the library, and offices.[15] In 1953, Johnson completed work on The Abby Aldrich Rockefeller Sculpture Garden (fig. 20).

Far left:
21. Installation view, *Ten Automobiles,* The Museum of Modern Art, New York, September 15–October 4, 1953. Exhibition directed by Arthur Drexler

Left:
22. Installation view, *House in the Museum Garden,* The Museum of Modern Art, New York, April 14–October 30, 1949. House and landscape design by Marcel Breuer; exhibition directed by Peter Blake. Ezra Stoller © Esto

Although the garden has now come to be associated almost uniquely with sculpture, it has, in fact, been used for a variety of installations, including cars (fig. 21) and houses, most notably, a reconstructed Japanese pavilion. (The 1954 installation of the pavilion continued a tradition begun in 1949, when the then-garden—really a large, gravel-filled open space—was used to display a model home designed by Marcel Breuer; see fig. 22.)

In celebration of its thirty-fifth anniversary, in 1964, the Museum expanded again. Philip Johnson designed a wing immediately to the east of 11 West Fifty-third Street (fig. 23), redesigned the existing lobby (fig. 24), created a Founders' Room in which trustees and the director could entertain, and increased the garden by one third.[16] Gallery spaces were more than doubled and the lobby reshaped to accommodate larger crowds, a bookstore, an information center, and two small exhibition rooms. The galleries on the first three floors of the new East Wing were fifty feet wide and one hundred feet deep, and were designed to be as flexible as possible. With long, clear spans, they reflected Barr's interest in anonymous, loftlike spaces.[17]

The second phase of Johnson's 1964 scheme proposed a new West Wing to replace the Rogers Annex. This addition ultimately would have provided several

Below, left to right:
23. Philip C. Johnson Associates. The Museum of Modern Art, New York: East Wing (at right). 1962–64

24. Philip C. Johnson Associates. The Museum of Modern Art, New York: Entrance Lobby. 1964

floors of galleries, yet another new library and archives, and much-needed offices (fig. 25).[18] Plans for expansion, however, were delayed until 1968, when the former Whitney Museum of American Art (fig. 26), located to the immediate northwest of The Museum of Modern Art and purchased by the Museum in 1966, was converted into the Lillie P. Bliss International Study Center. In 1968–70, Johnson, working with John Burgee, did a series of expansion studies for an office tower, a new West Wing, and permanent and temporary galleries to be sited below The Abby Aldrich Rockefeller Sculpture Garden (figs. 27, 28). The tower was to be used as a means of financing the rest of the project. Although this scheme was never realized, the concept of a major expansion of the Museum to the west, financed by the sale of air rights for a commercially developed tower, became the basis of Cesar Pelli's 1984 project[19] (fig. 29). The Pelli project celebrated the Museum's fifty-fifth anniversary and resulted in a reconfigured museum, enlarging its gallery space to 87,000 square feet, approximately 20,000 of which is devoted to temporary exhibitions in the René d'Harnoncourt and International Council Galleries, and the Projects space; and increasing its facilities to include four study centers for the departments of architecture and design, photography, prints and illustrated books, drawings, and film and video; a vastly expanded library and archives; new offices; a restaurant and café; and an enhanced bookstore.[20]

To a large extent, however, the Pelli expansion responded to issues identified in Johnson's proposal of 1969, addressing the acute space problems of the past—total gallery space having shrunk to less than fifteen percent of the overall building—rather than positioning the Museum for the future. In an environment of constant and rapid growth, this may have been inevitable, but it is clear that as the Museum looks toward the twenty-first century, it cannot be reactive in its development. Or,

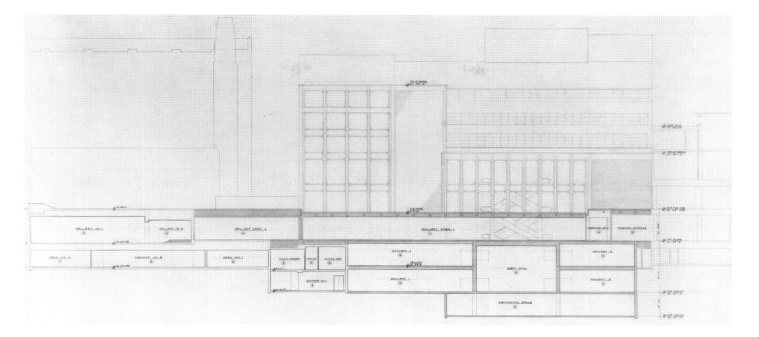

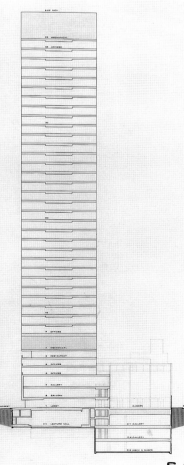

Above:
27. Philip Johnson and John Burgee, Architects. The Museum of Modern Art, New York: Expansion Proposal. Sectional elevation (longitudinal) through the garden. April 10, 1970, with later revisions. Pencil and colored pencil with Letraset on mylar, 35½ x 48" (90.5 x 122 cm). Philip Johnson archive (165.163), Department of Architecture and Design, The Museum of Modern Art, New York

Far left:
28. Philip Johnson and John Burgee, Architects. The Museum of Modern Art, New York: Expansion Proposal. Cross-section. October 20, 1969. Pencil with Letraline and Zipatone on vellum, 45 x 18" (114.3 x 45.7 cm). Philip Johnson archive (165.75), Department of Architecture and Design, The Museum of Modern Art, New York

Left:
29. Cesar Pelli and Associates, Edward Durell Stone Associates, and Gruen Associates. The Museum of Modern Art, New York: West Wing (at left) and Museum Tower. 1980–84

put somewhat differently, the Museum's architecture must state clearly and effectively the goals of the institution as it wishes to be, not as it should have been.

The degree to which The Museum of Modern Art has changed since its founding in 1929 is made clear by examining a number of photographs of exhibitions and installations taken at the Museum over the course of its history. In *Cézanne, Gauguin, Seurat, van Gogh,* the Museum's inaugural exhibition at 730 Fifth Avenue (fig. 30), the walls were covered by a light-colored fabric, and every available space was used, a point that is made even clearer in photographs of the 1931 display of the Bliss Collection, where works are even hung on doors (fig. 31). Photographs of exhibitions installed in the Heckscher Building consistently show works displayed in long, axial sequences (like Old Master paintings, they are hung from moldings on picture wires, a practice abandoned in 1932, when the Museum moved to West Fifty-third Street). These early photographs also show the extent to which the architecture of the building and its fixtures intruded on the space of the galleries; note the many beams of the ceilings, the awkwardly placed lights, and the extensive air returns that mar almost every wall. By the time the Museum moved to West Fifty-third Street, installations had become more complex, involving elaborate pedestals and partitions, and the insertion of numerous false walls to divide the space of the townhouse into more effective galleries (figs. 32–34). These insertions, often minimally detailed, contrast with the elaborate moldings, beaux-arts plasterwork, banisters, and baseboards of the townhouse. Evident in the installations of this time is the use of dark curtains both to screen off windows and to create counterpoints to the white partitions and false walls. Lighting was provided by long banks of pentagonal-shaped lights suspended

Above, left to right:

30. Installation view, *Cézanne, Gauguin, Seurat, van Gogh,* The Museum of Modern Art, New York, November 7–December 7, 1929. Exhibition directed by Alfred H. Barr, Jr.

31. Installation view, *Memorial Exhibition: The Collection of the Late Miss Lizzie [sic] P. Bliss,* The Museum of Modern Art, New York, May 17–September 27, 1931. Exhibition directed by Alfred H. Barr, Jr.

Below, left to right:

32. Installation view, *Vincent van Gogh,* The Museum of Modern Art, New York, November 4, 1935–January 5, 1936. Exhibition directed by Alfred H. Barr, Jr.

33. Installation view, *Modern Works of Art: Fifth Anniversary Exhibition,* The Museum of Modern Art, New York, November 20, 1934–January 20, 1935. Exhibition directed by Alfred H. Barr, Jr.

34. Installation view, *Cubism and Abstract Art,* The Museum of Modern Art, New York, March 3–April 19, 1936. Exhibition directed by Alfred H. Barr, Jr.

from ceilings by short posts and angled to wash the walls. Works of art, and paintings in particular, were displayed in relatively generous installations with ample room between objects, but, like the installations in the Fifth Avenue building, every available space was used.

The completion of the Goodwin–Stone building in 1939 provided the Museum with custom-built spaces for the first time (figs. 35–37). Yet many of the features of the old townhouse continued to be present, including the extensive use of curtains, finely detailed baseboards, albeit narrower and more streamlined than the ones of

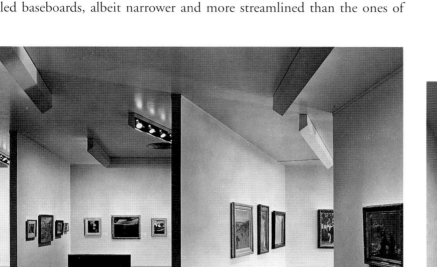

35–37. Installation views, *Art in Our Time: Tenth Anniversary Exhibition,* The Museum of Modern Art, New York, May 10–September 30, 1939. Exhibition directed by Alfred H. Barr, Jr.

the townhouse, and long banks of lights. Now, however, the lights are mounted flush to the ceilings and covered by plain baffles, and the ceilings are devoid of the beaux-arts details that marked the townhouse. Despite the Museum's vastly increased spaces, installation photographs of the inaugural exhibition reveal small, domestic-scale galleries echoing the rooms of the townhouse, and densely hung installations suggesting that space was already tight for the burgeoning collection. Present as well is the extensive use of seating, an amenity that is generally absent from earlier installations.

Barr recognized from the outset that the new building was not a fixed entity but a frame in which to explore a variety of possibilities. In the introduction to *Art in Our Time,* he wrote:

After the close of the exhibition the various departments, those already in existence and those in formation, will gradually be established in more or less permanent exhibition galleries on the second and third floors of the new building. Just how these galleries will be arranged will depend to a considerable degree upon the public's response to the present exhibition. Nothing that the visitors will see in the exhibition galleries, neither the works of art, nor the lighting fixtures, nor even the partitions, is at present permanent.

The Museum of Modern Art is a laboratory: in its experiments the public is invited to participate.[21]

This sense of experimentation is clearly visible in the photographs of exhibitions from the 1940s, where color and lighting were used to create dramatic environments for the Museum's displays. Look, for instance, at the way dark walls are deployed in *Modern Primitives* (fig. 38) to offset the white expanses of the main walls of the galleries, or how pin point lighting is used in *Art in Progress: 15th Anniversary Exhibition* (fig. 39) to highlight sculpture set otherwise in a dark room.

By the 1970s, the bold use of color and dramatic lighting, highlighted by discrete but important architectural details such as baseboards, has given way to a more consistently minimalist approach (fig. 40). Walls are uniformly white; all details are suppressed except for those required by the engineering of the building, such as air returns. Lighting is provided by the same long baffles that marked the 1939 building.

Above, left to right:
38. Installation view, *Modern Primitives: Artists of the People,* The Museum of Modern Art, New York, October 21, 1941–April 30, 1944. Exhibition directed by Alfred H. Barr, Jr.

39. Installation view, *Art in Progress: Fifteenth Anniversary Exhibition,* The Museum of Modern Art, New York, May 24–October 15, 1944. Painting and sculpture section selected and installed by James Thrall Soby and Dorothy C. Miller

40. Painting and sculpture galleries, The Museum of Modern Art, New York, 1973

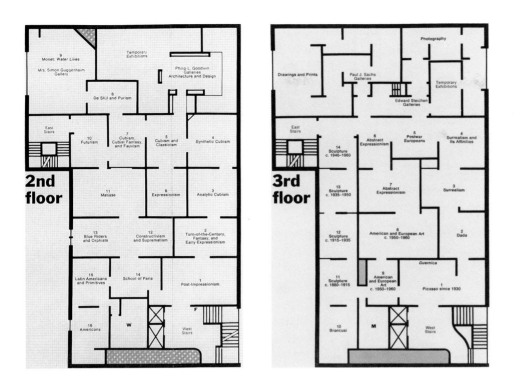

41–42. Second and third floor information plans, The Museum of Modern Art, New York, 1978–79

Seating is more limited, and the upholstered benches with supporting backs of 1939 have given way to unupholstered benches designed by Arthur Drexler, director of the Department of Architecture and Design, that are as spare and lean as the rooms in which they are set. The domestic scale galleries of the townhouse and 1939 building were maintained in the 1970s, creating an extensive series of relatively small galleries that read like a maze in the installation photographs and floor plans of the period (figs. 41–42). This is particularly evident in the painting and sculpture galleries, where the staggering of thresholds makes it impossible to anticipate the relationship of one space to the next.

Although the 1984 expansion provided the Museum with an opportunity to rethink the display of its collection, few formal changes were made. The same spare white walls, minimal details, and small, domestic-scale galleries continue. Even the lighting system of long, ceiling-mounted baffles, first introduced in the 1930s, is again deployed. Now, however, the number of galleries has expanded dramatically, so that the mazelike qualities of the earlier building have become exaggerated, to the point that it is extremely difficult to navigate through many of the Museum's spaces without feeling either claustrophobic or disoriented. This feeling is accentuated by the Museum's current long, narrow footprint and suites of galleries (fig. 43) that force visitors to follow an uninterrupted sequence of spaces with virtually no option to change course. Even the most recent attempts to ameliorate this in the painting and sculpture galleries—by cutting a door through the central spine of the sequence —has not fundamentally changed the nature of these spaces. In an effort to provide at least some form of orientation in the painting and sculpture galleries, carpet has been used in the spaces devoted to art before 1960, while wood floors have been used to denote the areas devoted to more recent work. This, however, has created a formal

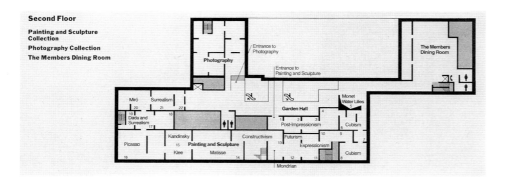

43. Second floor information plan, The Museum of Modern Art, New York, 1986

break in the presentation of the collection, albeit a subtle one, that ruptures the flow of the galleries and suggests that the art after 1960 is different in kind from that of the first half of the century. This rupture in the presentation of the painting and sculpture galleries led Hilton Kramer, one of the Museum's most outspoken critics, to observe that:

What is really new in the new MoMA is not so much the added space the museum has acquired—important as that may be—as the way it has utilized that space as a means of institutionalizing this categorical separation of the past from the present. As a result, the new MoMA is no longer a single museum with a unified purpose and outlook, but two (or more) museums which pursue vastly different objectives and uphold very different standards.[22]

This sense of the Museum as a series of museums existing under one roof is further amplified by the separation of the collection into distinct departmental galleries spread out over four floors. Although efforts have been made recently to introduce different media into some of the galleries, most notably in the painting and sculp-

44–45. Cesar Pelli and Associates, Edward Durell Stone Associates, and Gruen Associates. The Museum of Modern Art, New York: Garden Hall. Interior views. 1980–84

ture galleries, and to provide a more logical movement from one department to the other, the result remains the same. It is left to the atrium (figs. 44–45) to provide an organizing structure for unifying the experience of visiting the Museum.

With the purchase of the Dorset Hotel and its adjacent properties, The Museum of Modern Art again has an opportunity to reconfigure itself. Among the virtues of the Dorset site is that it provides the Museum with the possibility of breaking away from its narrow longitudinal axis. This will allow us to create a new, broader and deeper, footprint that should result in a fundamentally different alignment of galleries and offices structured around a central core.

The changes in the Museum's potential layout parallel changes in the institution's thinking about itself and its collections. Among the issues that the Museum must contend with as it endeavors to articulate its future are:

- how to deal with both the historical dimensions of modernity and the requirements of contemporary art;
- how to balance the allocation of space between the different functions of the museum—from the display of the collections, to the housing of library collections and archives, to the accessibility of theaters and study and educational centers;
- how to create an environment that preserves the intimacy of the Museum yet can give full scope to its breadth;
- how to build a complex that integrates the new architecture within the historical fabric of what already exists; and
- how to define the acceptable dimensions of a renovation within the context of this project.

As the twentieth century draws to an end, it has become clear that there is no single story of modern art to be told, but, rather, many stories, each imbedded and refracted to a certain degree in the others. If the Museum is to fully explore the richness of its collection—a collection that is perhaps the only truly synoptic collection of modern art in the world—it is going to have to find ways of revealing these different stories while still providing a comprehensible overview of modern art. This will inevitably mean developing a series of intersecting galleries, and strategies of presentation, that will permit the Museum to articulate a primary reading of the collection that can be interrupted at multiple points by alternative readings, or, by opportunities to delve in greater depths into the work of a given artist, period, or issue. Since each of the mediums that make up the Museum's collection have differing histories, especially photography and film and video, the need to retain departmental spaces to explore these histories will be important. Yet, if the expansion is to be a success, solutions will have to be found that allow these different histories to intersect with each other so that the whole is perceived as part of a larger continuous tradition, rather than as separate and distinct.

This layering and complicating of history must also take into account the Museum's own history, and make evident the ways in which the Museum itself has evolved over the years. By this I mean that The Museum of Modern Art, because of its success in developing a synoptic, if not comprehensive collection, of modern art in the twentieth century has become part of the very history it seeks to present and explicate to the public. The Museum's role in defining and explaining modern art thus becomes polemical. In Roger Cardinal's words, "a collection encodes an intimate narrative, tracing what Proust called *'le fil des heures, l'ordre des années et des mondes'*—the continuous thread through which selfhood is sewn into the unfolding fabric of a lifetime's experience."[23] Taken in the context of the museum this becomes a collective process of interlocking dialogues and narratives played out over a theoretically infinite number of lifetimes. Each thread, each experience, is part of an ever-expanding set of ideas and realities made concrete by the objects collected and displayed by the institution. As each of these narratives is encoded into the unfolding pattern of the Museum's history, it inflects and alters both the Museum's intellectual and its physical space.

In the case of The Museum of Modern Art, the unfolding nature of this narrative began with Alfred Barr's vision of a museum that dealt with all of the manifestations of a modern spirit in the visual arts, from painting and sculpture to photography, drawings, prints, architecture, design, and film. His seminal acquisitions of key works of art, combined with his efforts to trace the development of modern art through a series of clearly articulated and linked movements, beginning with Post-Impressionism, gave a palpable presence to his vision. In the years since Barr's retirement from the Museum, in 1967, this narrative has been expanded to include new media such as video, and works that reflect such movements as Minimalism, Conceptualism, *arte povera,* and a variety of other contemporary expressions. It has also been expanded by the ideas of William Rubin (Department of Painting and Sculpture), Philip Johnson and Arthur Drexler (Department of Architecture and Design), Riva Castleman (Department of Prints and Illustrated Books), and John Szarkowski (Department of Photography), among others; and, more recently, by the thinking and interests of Kirk Varnedoe, John Elderfield, Terence Riley, Mary Lea Bandy, Margit Rowell, Deborah Wye, Peter Galassi, and the other curators at the Museum. As each new generation assumes responsibility for the Museum's direction, there is by definition a reconsideration of earlier decisions and directions, and a realignment of focus—sometimes large, sometimes small—so that the dialogue with the past is always one of active engagement.

The challenge for the Museum is to privilege its collection and its history, while at the same time remaining free to move in new and different directions. Both of these things become increasingly difficult as the Museum's collections continue to grow and require ever more space for their display and ever-greater resources for their care and storage. The increasing needs of the collection compel the Museum to respond to those needs in a way that precludes other possibilities. It is this dilemma, in part, that prompted Gertrude Stein to comment that a museum can be either modern or a museum, but not both at the same time. For, to be modern implies the ability to be constantly engaged with the present, to be in a constant state of self-renewal and change—what Barr called "metabolic."[24]

I would like to conclude by highlighting some specific considerations about the Museum's architectural requirements. Many of the ideas that I want briefly to outline grew out of a brainstorming session that took place October 4–6, 1996, at the Pocantico Conference Center, involving the Museum's senior curators and trustees, and a number of artists, museum directors, architects, and critics.

The first and perhaps most obvious point I want to make is that given the location and potential size of the project, it poses a fundamentally urbanistic problem, in which architecture becomes a mediating force between the experience of the city (most particularly, Fifty-third and Fifty-fourth streets), and the experience of the Museum. Unlike The Metropolitan Museum of Art, the Whitney Museum of American Art, or the Solomon R. Guggenheim Museum, which are located on major avenues, The Museum of Modern Art is bound by its location on a side street. Where the Guggenheim and the Metropolitan read as integral parts of the rich urban fabric of the city, the Modern is barely visible, its presence marked only by a flat, subtly modulated facade. With the possibility of developing a north-south axis, this suddenly changes, as the north side of the Museum can be set against the garden and can be seen from Fifth Avenue, thus creating a more complex, three-dimensional, interaction with the city.

To a great degree, however, the Museum's primary requirements are not a function of architecture per se but of the articulation of space. The strength of the Museum's collections, the demands of their installation and presentation, the need to engage the street and the garden, all require spatial solutions more than purely architectural ones. What is needed is, in the words of Peter Eisenman, a "theorizing" of space,[25] where the predictable order of the Museum merges and engages with the unpredictable order of the city. Architecture within this context becomes a means of giving definition to a specific set of spatial needs that reflect the unique location and programmatic needs of the Museum, in particular, the desire of the Museum to reorganize the presentation of its collection into arrangements that would allow visitors to see a synoptic overview of the collection, while also being able to explore specific issues and artists in greater detail.

To this end, there are several different ways that the Museum can configure itself. None of these should be taken literally, but, rather, as a series of metaphors that provide different ways of thinking about the organization and structure of the institution, and its collections.

The Museum could, for instance, expand upon its present structure, creating an elaborate skeleton from which each of its departments and functions is attached. This would lead to a relatively rigid configuration of space, although it would provide for a centralized spine, giving definition and spatial clarity to the Museum's many parts. A somewhat different metaphor for the Museum is that of a sponge composed of an extensive number of monocellular parts linked to each other in a multidimensional web of spatial and visual relationships.[26] The beauty of this metaphor is that it reflects the complexity of the Museum's many functions, and the reality that the most exciting and rewarding visits to museums are those that we construct for ourselves, moving from object to object, gallery to gallery, space to space, at will, and often in an unpredictable order. Another feature of this notion of the Museum is that, like the sponge, it could contract and expand without losing the integrity of its shape and form, thus accommodating changing circumstances and unique programmatic opportunities.

A very different conception of the Museum is provided by the idea of a crazy quilt.[27] In this conception, the Museum is composed of an ever-expanding set of possibilities, each independent of the other, stitched together in a random order. The result is a structure that reveals itself through the complexity of its individual parts and so becomes a narrator or storyteller of a theoretically endless series of histories and experiences. As such, the Museum, like the crazy quilt, would be built up of disjunctive assemblages that are nonsequential and that make no attempt at a linear inclusivity. The Museum thus becomes a venue of exploration that does not endeavor to resolve difficulties or impose a hierarchy of experience.

A fourth, though somewhat related, notion of the Museum is that of a montage of attractions.[28] Here, the Museum becomes a multiringed circus with a series of related events clustered together in main and secondary stages. In this way, the visitor can compose for him- or herself different sets of interrelated experiences. The result of this vision of the Museum is a kaleidoscope of experiences that encourage the visitor to linger and explore the collections while constantly confronting new and surprising events.

While each of these metaphors offers intriguing possibilities for the Museum, three issues are central to any configuration of the institution in the future. The first is that the Museum is, above all, a place to look at and encounter the singular achievements of modern and contemporary art—a place to see and enjoy objects— and its *raison d'être* is grounded in the objects that form its collection. The second is that it is about the creation of unique experiences that are a result of the engagement of its public with the works of art that are on display, and the way in which those objects are presented within the fabric of the building. It follows from this that no matter what the Museum of the future looks like, it will have to organize itself in a way that slows down, rather than accelerates, the trajectory of its visitors through the building. In this context, new technologies like digital accoustiguides and computer-based programs need to be combined with furniture, like chairs and benches, along with spaces that encourage rest and contemplation, to create an environment that privileges a substantial engagement with the Museum's collection.

Finally, any consideration of the Museum must take into account the fact that it is a heterotopic building composed of many different parts loosely linked together. From Goodwin and Stone's work in 1939 to Philip Johnson's many additions, to Cesar Pelli's expansion in 1984, the Museum consists of a series of spaces that no one architect can fully claim as his own. Given the complexity of the Museum's site and the need to accommodate a variety of functions—from looking at art, viewing films, and conducting research, to shopping and dining—it will be essential to find singular solutions to each of these requirements. If the past is any guide, this may well mean the need to engage more than one architect in the design and realization of the new program. Such a process would, of necessity, involve a master plan and a primary architect but might include other architects who could focus on specific issues or areas of the building. This would allow the expansion to build upon the inherent heterotopicity of the existing site by emphasizing unique aspects of the project while establishing an overall organization and structure to it that gives meaning to the whole.

Notes

This paper was originally presented as a lecture at The Museum of Modern Art on October 22, 1996.

I would like to thank Charles Rockefeller, Marcie Año, Bevin Howard, Sarah Newman, Amy Romesburg, and Christel Hollevoet for their assistance in preparing this paper; Peter Reed, Associate Curator of Architecture at The Museum of Modern Art, for sharing his research on Philip Johnson's role as architect for the Museum; Rona Roob, Chief Archivist for The Museum of Modern Art, and her staff for their help in uncovering information on the Museum's past; and, above all, Karen Davidson, Assistant Director for Policy and Planning at The Museum of Modern Art, for her encouragement and advice.

1.   See, for instance, Michael Kimmelman, "A Renewed Modern: More of a Museum or More Modern?," *The New York Times,* November 22, 1994, Section C, pp. 15, 21.

2.   For the full text of the Museum's Mission Statement, see p. 20 of the present volume.

3.   See Alfred H. Barr, Jr., "Report on the Permanent Collection" (November 1933), Section III, p. 3, for an outline of the theory of basing the Museum's permanent collection "upon a metabolic principle of continual building up and tearing down" (p. 13). The Museum of Modern Art Archives, New York: Alfred H. Barr, Jr. Papers, Series 9a. Writings: Chronicles, file 7A.

4.   These figures were published by the American Association of Museums (AAM) in *Museums Count* (Washington, D.C.: AAM, 1994), p. 43.

5.   Michael Brawne, *The Museum Interior: Temporary and Permanent Display Techniques* (New York: Architectural Book Publishing Company, 1982), p. 9.

6.   These typologies are elaborated upon by Helen Searing in her "The Development of Museum Typology," in which she conflates the "template/ palace" model and opposes it to that of the "exposition hall"; in *Museum News* 65, no. 4 (April 1987), pp. 20-31.

7.   Brawne, op. cit.

8.   Quoted in William T. Alderson, Introduction to Edward P. Alexander, *Museums in Motion: An Introduction to the History and Functions of Museums* (Nashville, Tenn.: American Association for State and Local History, 1979), p. 14.

9.   This description of the museum as container and catalyst, and as a place of provocation and debate, is indebted to Ian Ritchie, "An Architect's View of Recent Developments in European Museums," in Roger Miles and Lauro Zavala, eds., *Towards the Museum of the Future: New European Perspectives* (London and New York: Routledge, 1994), p. 12.

10.   For a chronology of events prior to the opening of the Museum's first exhibition, in November 1929, see A. Conger Goodyear, *The Museum of Modern Art: The First Ten Years* (New York: The Museum of Modern Art, 1948), pp. 15-17 and 139 *ff.*

11.   For details on these transactions, see The Museum of Modern Art Archives, New York: A. Conger Goodyear Papers, V.1, pp. 36–37, 125–26.

12.   A. Conger Goodyear, Preface to *Art in Our Time: An Exhibition to Celebrate the Tenth Anniversary of The Museum of Modern Art and the Opening of Its New Building, Held at the Time of the New York World's Fair* (New York: The Museum of Modern Art, 1939), p. 11.

13.   Ibid.

14.   Philip Johnson's role as The Museum of Modern Art's de facto architect of record is the subject of a recent study by Peter Reed, "The Space and the Frame: Philip Johnson as the Museum's Architect," in *Studies in Modern Art* 6 (1998), pp. 76–103. The Grace Rainey Rogers Annex was demolished in 1979–80 to make room for the Museum Tower.

15.   Ibid., p. 76.

16.   The expansion was decided upon on the occasion of the Museum's twenty-fifth anniversary, in 1955; for the various proposals made subsequent to this decision, see Reed, "The Space and the Frame," pp. 78–92.

17.   Ibid., pp. 78–92. Johnson's 1959 proposal for a Fifty-fourth Street East Wing was abandoned when the Fifty-third Street site became available in 1962.

18.   Ibid., p. 92.

19.   A new expansion program was surveyed as early as 1968, and announced in 1976; see *The Museum of Modern Art, New York: The History and the Collection,* Introduction by Sam Hunter (New York: Harry N. Abrams, in association with The Museum of Modern Art, 1984; fifth printing, 1990), p. 33.

20.   Drawn from the press packet issued by the Museum upon the building's completion in 1984. Department of Communication, The Museum of Modern Art, New York.

21.   Alfred H. Barr, Jr., " 'Art in Our Time': The Plan of the Exhibition," in Goodyear, *Art in Our Time,* p. 15.

22.   Hilton Kramer, "MoMA Reopened: The Museum of Modern Art in the Postmodern Era," *The New Criterion,* Special Issue (Summer 1984), p. 2–3.

23.   Roger Cardinal, "Collecting and Collage-making: The Case of Kurt Schwitters," in John Elsner and Roger Cardinal, eds., *The Cultures of Collecting* (London: Reaktion Books, 1994), p. 68.

24.   See n. 3 above.

25.   Proposed by Peter Eisenman at the Pocantico Conference; see pp. 36–37, 40.

26.   This notion of the museum was first articulated at Pocantico by Bernard Tschumi; see pp. 41–42.

27.   As argued by Sheila Levrant de Bretteville at Pocantico; see pp. 61–62.

28.   This notion of the museum was presented by Jean-Louis Cohen at Pocantico; see pp. 56–57.

Appendix

All diagrams and charts prepared by the New York architectural firm of Cooper, Robertson and Partners as part of the Needs Analysis undertaken by The Museum of Modern Art in 1996–97.

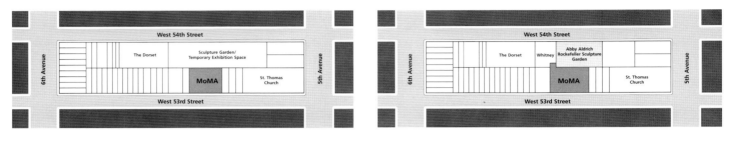

Site of the original Goodwin–Stone building, 1939

Museum site, including The Abby Aldrich Rockefeller Sculpture Garden, 1954

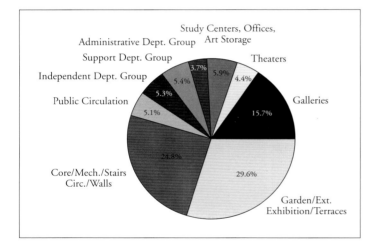

Allocation of floor space by area, 1939

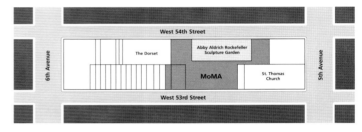

Museum site and adjacent properties, 1968

Curatorial Dept. Group		
Galleries		23,200
Theaters		6,500
Study Centers, Offices, Art Storage		8,700
Administrative Dept. Group		5,500
Support Dept. Group		8,000
Independent Dept. Group		7,800
Public Circulation		7,600
Core/Mech./Stairs/Circ./Walls		36,700
Garden/Ext. Exhibition/Terraces		43,800
Total (Gross Square Feet)		147,800

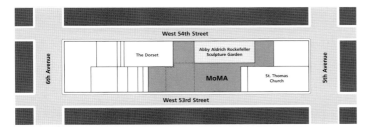

Museum site, 1984

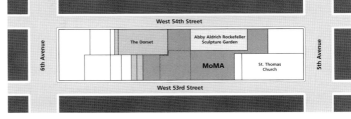

Museum site and adjacent properties, 1996

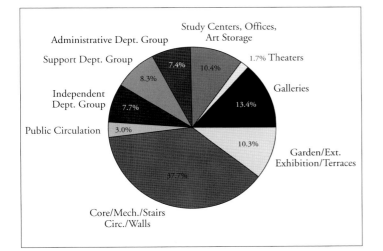

Allocation of floor space by area, pre-1984 Museum expansion

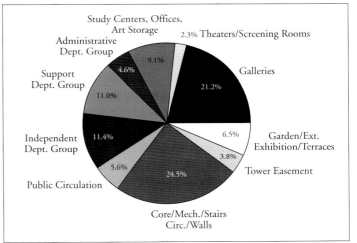

Allocation of floor space by area, 1996

Curatorial Dept. Group	
Galleries	40,500
Theaters	5,030
Study Centers, Offices, Art Storage	31,320
Administrative Dept. Group	22,260
Support Dept. Group	25,150
Independent Dept. Group	23,170
Public Circulation	9,100
Core/Mech./Stairs/Circ./Walls	113,670
Garden/Terraces	31,000
Total (Gross Square Feet)	301,200

Curatorial Dept. Group	
Galleries	85,745
Theaters/Screening Rooms	9,440
Study Centers, Offices, Art Storage	36,750
Administrative Dept. Group	18,750
Support Dept. Group	44,350
Independent Dept. Group	46,290
Public Circulation	22,605
Core/Mech./Stairs/Circ./Walls/Loading	99,000
Tower Easement	15,400
Garden/Terraces	26,330
Total (Gross Square Feet)	404,660

The Idea of a Modern Museum

A dialogue between Jorge Klor de Alva, Class of 1940 Professor of Comparative Ethnic Studies and Anthropology, University of California at Berkeley; and Henri Zerner, Professor of Fine Arts, Harvard University. Introduced by John Elderfield. November 19, 1996

JOHN ELDERFIELD: I am pleased to welcome you to the second in this series of Studies in Modern Art lectures this fall. . . . We are talking tonight about the idea of a modern museum. The way in which we thought we might do this is to begin with introductory statements, then talk among ourselves, and then, at a certain point, we will welcome questions from the audience. . . .

JORGE KLOR DE ALVA: When the three of us spoke not long ago, we decided that one way to begin was to discuss the invention of the modern museum in response to a particular set of forces, and then to address the history of the idea of a *modern* museum. Our topic is so huge that we can at best only hint at it, but I wanted to . . . speak, however briefly, about some of the forces that I think affected the rise of the modern museum in the United States and elsewhere—though the United States will be a particular focus. Without moving into particular details of museums, I want to identify and develop three forces that I think have been absolutely critical. . . . I think museums, from day one, have had to deal constantly with three different sets of internal conspiracies and their construction, three different sets of publics, and three different missions. I want to borrow the categories from my former colleague Paul Dimaggio, who speaks about all museums being *patrons' museums* and having a set of forces associated with that.[1] Generally, the conspiracy here is one composed of curators, of patrons, of collectors, art historians, artists, conservators, etcetera. The discourse is generally one of connoisseurship and of expertise, where the focus is very much on questions of acquisition and interpretation. The constituencies of these museums have, historically, at least, let's say, from the late nineteenth century through the present, . . . been made up primarily of a more elite group that frequents the museum quite extensively, but which numerically has been relatively small. It is a group that has had a sense of the museum as their own personal province and has seen authority primarily as coming from their particular position, that is, their position in relation to the object, and therefore direct experience of the object has been significantly more important than information about it and such.

Running counter to that, one begins to see in different historical moments, . . . a shift in favor of those who perceive the museum *less as a temple and more as a forum.* This certainly fits into my own . . . work at the Smithsonian Institution, where I've constantly been pushing for it to stop being the nation's attic and to become the nation's parlor. This is where the marketing forces have come to the fore. This is where the consumers, to use the language of marketing, are seen much more impersonally, where the discourse is primarily one of economics and of business, where now the visitors tend to be not those who visit museums frequently or who are the most likely to visit museums, but those who by their very nature make up a larger proportion of the population and, consequently, a larger part of the museum's constituency. Here, their sense of the museum is one of being collectively theirs rather than personally theirs, and, to continue my typology, where authority is seen more as coming from, . . . an understanding of the context of the objects—that is, obtaining information about the object is more significant than experience.

Then, very quickly, I want to add a third force in the creation of the modern museum, and that is what Dimaggio has called the *social museum.* Here, . . . instead of seeing the museum as *temple* or as *forum,* the museum is seen in part as a *tribunal.* In the so-called social museum, the focus is primarily on education and outreach. This is the context within which the linkages are neither personal nor impersonal, but what I would call redemptive; they have something to do with redemptive kinds of values and their redemptive program more than anything else, that is, they are focused to a great extent, in terms of patronage, on the poor, minorities, the elderly, children, and others who have generally identified themselves or can be identified as disenfranchised from the museum scene. Their discourse, needless to say, tends to be highly political, a discourse . . . that is dramatically different from the discourse of education, let's say, or the discourse of economics and business, and certainly different from the discourse of connoisseurship or expertise. They make up, needless to say, a very small percentage (if any percentage at all at some museums) of the visitors, but they make up for that with tremendous political visibility, and all museums feel that today. Their sense of the museum is not of "ours, personally" or "ours, collectively," but, rather, "theirs, and not ours." Therefore, for them authority is seen more as coming from representativeness, the representativeness of the museum, and therefore of the relationship between themselves and the objects.

I'll summarize . . . this typology as follows. If one looks at the history of the creation of museums, . . . I believe that all three of these forces have been there constantly. All have helped to shape the way in which museums have tended to be a totally amorphous phenomenon; they can be just about anything under the sun, and they can be one thing or another primarily on the basis of the way in which tensions among these three groups are being negotiated or resolved at any particular time. I think that the rise of the marketing museum, on the one hand, and the social museum, on the other, is probably the most significant force in the context of the creation of the modern museum—that is, the museum that has moved away from a fully patron-based institution.

HENRI ZERNER: I will talk briefly about the beginnings of modern museums, historically. I would like to point out that there is a slight ambiguity—and, I think, a voluntary ambiguity—in the title of tonight's discussion, which is the idea of a modern museum. That is, is it a modern museum or is it a museum of modern art? When it comes to the idea of a modern museum, I would argue that there is no other. It is true that there is a formation, from the sixteenth century to the eighteenth, of the notion of the museum, the *kunstkabinet*; there are collections of curiosities in palaces which are sometimes displayed, things like that. But what we call a museum in the full sense is a modern idea, and it starts, essentially, with the opening of the Louvre to the public, which is a very different thing from earlier phenomena—which do exist and which were sometimes called museums; but these were, in fact, sometimes very different. I will distinguish between the idea of the museum and then the idea of a museum of modern art, of the art of one's own period. One should also distinguish between what is modern and what is contemporary. The notion of the contemporary plays an important part here, and it is a term that has changed meaning. Up until the eighteenth century, "contemporary" was strictly a matter of chronology; that is, one would talk about the contemporaries of Queen Elizabeth, but the term was usually used in relation to the past and did not have connotations of the present. But in the nineteenth century, it became almost entirely attached to that. If you talked about "contemporaries" it was *your* contemporaries. In the middle of the nineteenth century you began to have, for example, The Gallery of Contemporaries, publications called "The Contemporaries," and that means the culture of the present. This, I think, plays a part here.

The modern museum in the sense of the fully developed museum starts with the Louvre, which was very spectacular and which was projected already in the mid–eighteenth century but was only implemented after the French Revolution. . . . Already at that point the issue arose as to whether modern art was going to be housed there or not. Initially, there was going to be modern art, and in fact one of the interesting discoveries of the recent past, Andrew McClellan's up-to-date history of the creation of the Louvre,[2] has shown something very interesting, I think, which is that when the marquis d'Angiviller, the director general of royal buildings under Louis XVI, commissioned Jacques-Louis David for a painting of the defense of Horace (ultimately realized as the *Oath of the Horatii* of 1785)—which . . . many people see as the beginning of modern art—the picture was commissioned specifically with the intention of putting it in the new Musée du Louvre. . . . That is very interesting, because this historic picture was painted *for* a museum, and this is very, very significant indeed. Obviously, at this point the idea was that "modern" art . . . should be part of the Louvre, it should be part of a great museum. However, in the 1790s, in the assembly of deputies, Emeric David, who was a major critic, said, "We want an olympic museum of the living French school." In other words, modern art—the art of our time—should not be in the Louvre, it should be in a separate place. This was a radical departure. It was an important move, and the implementation of it was not precipitated by the Revolution; a series of circumstances caused all the pictures that were in the Luxembourg Palace to be sent to the Louvre because, you may remember, the Louvre, under Napoleon, was the most spectacular museum that anybody would ever see. It had practically all the works of Raphael, which had been plundered from the churches of Italy and from private collections. It had just about all the great masterpieces, including the *Laocoon,* and all the greatest works of antiquity.

Of course, in 1815, with the fall of Napoleon, the art spoils had to be returned, and suddenly the Louvre was half-empty. So all the pictures in the king's collection, which were then publicly displayed in the Luxembourg, had to be put there—and now the Luxembourg was empty. A number of people said, "Well, here is our chance: We are going to put our museum of contemporary art there." So it was decided in 1816, and the Musée du Luxembourg, a museum of *living* artists, opened in 1818. The principle was to display works of art which were bought by the government, or occasionally given, in the Luxembourg museum until five or ten years after the artist's death, and then one would decide whether they went to the Louvre, if they were good enough, or . . . to a provincial museum, if they were good enough for that, or to some city hall, or, if they were truly bad, to the basement of some public building. In other words, the Luxembourg museum was a sort of purgatory for artists, where their ultimate fate was decided through time.

The Luxembourg museum was a very extraordinary institution, and when it opened it was truly a museum of living art. Interestingly enough, there were eight major works by David when it opened in 1818, although David was then in political exile in Belgium—and this was a state museum. Ingres was represented from the beginning, although he was extremely unpopular, and Delacroix entered the museum in 1822, when he was twenty-four. So it was truly a museum of the living art of the day. That didn't last too long, and by the middle of the nineteenth century there was a real divorce between living art (Courbet never entered the Musée du Luxembourg), so that the Luxembourg, by the second half of the nineteenth century, was, if you like, a museum of *contemporary* art in its original sense, but it was no longer a museum of *modern* art. It was in the hands of the Academy, a museum of accepted traditional art. . . . Only when the museum was closed in the 1930s, when it was clear that it was undefendable, that it was decided to open a museum of *modern* art which would really represent the art of the present. Jean Cassou was appointed as the first director, but because of the war, it only opened in 1947. The idea of this new museum was different from the Luxembourg; it was no longer this purgatory but truly a museum of modern art, where you didn't sample all the artists who were vaguely popular at the time but where you have an idea of what modern art *is*. . . . I'd like to read one sentence from the introduction by Cassou to the first catalogue, where he says, "It is the panorama of a vast and uninterrupted adventure of the human spirit that we wish to unroll to the eyes of the first visitors to the museum, an adventure which with equal power relays the movements of the nineteenth century as they are represented at the Louvre and in its continuation at the Museum of Impressionism." . . . The idea of separating Impressionism from the rest of art, that was characteristic of this concept of a modern tradition, an adventure which was not simply a sampling of whatever happened in art at a given time, but a story of the modern movement, of the development of modernism. This idea, of course, was very much present in the foundation of *this* Museum, which preceded the establishment of the Musée National d'Art Moderne in France and which was, in fact, probably very much its model. . . .

JOHN ELDERFIELD: I think, clearly, the modern/contemporary axis is something we should talk more about. Obviously, I think we've long thought about the Louvre–Luxembourg polarity as being one which in the history of MoMA was made equivalent in the relationship between the Metropolitan and the Modern. Your talking about the shift in the focus of the Luxembourg to become a museum of *contemporary* but not *modern* art reminded me that it was at the time of the rather difficult relationship between the Modern and the Metropolitan, that the Museum of Modern Art in Boston changed its name to the Museum of Contemporary Art, effectively to become, as the Luxembourg was, a museum of contemporary, but not modern, art. The other thing which crossed my mind as you were talking . . . is that when the Louvre opened it was, of course, the ten-day revolutionary week, and that during those ten days the Louvre was open, for two days to the public, three days to artists, and five days for being cleaned, which raises interesting issues in terms of audience, which Jorge in effect began with. So that it suggests, in fact, leaving aside the cleaning function, that the Louvre was, interestingly, largely a forum museum in your terms. How do you see the future of museums in terms of your three types? Do you think that we are irrevocably upon this line where we're moving more and more toward tribunal museums?

JORGE KLOR DE ALVA: I think that it's nearly impossible to generalize, . . . because we have museums and their settings, and the museums and settings are so terribly important. A museum in New York is not a museum in Washington and it's far from a museum in Los Angeles, for instance, and certainly from one in Omaha. What the future for something like a particular modern museum is, I think, greatly dependent on the context in which it exists. In the case of New York, where the museum is so much a part of the economic fiber of the society—and I hate to speak in such empiricist terms, but then that is what I do for a living—in this kind of context it's hard to imagine that the museum cannot survive the negotiation that it must in order to remain intelligible, as a museum of modern art, to the community that attends to it, especially given its importance to tourism and the kind of revenue that it . . . generates for the city. But one can easily imagine places that are far more susceptible to the third part of the triangle I am drawing here: the social museum. One can easily see museums, in more isolated contexts, not being able to resist that popular pressure, not being able to make the same kinds of arguments on behalf of, let's say, a more patron-oriented and marketing-oriented environment. And therefore we can see museums of modern art that, I don't want to say disappear, but that become dramatically transformed, and probably dramatically transformed in the sense that, the way for them to negotiate across these three tensions in the world of modern art would be for them to pay a great deal of attention to contemporary art, so that contemporary art would become the mechanism by which they, as modern art museums, would buy the social and political space needed in order to continue doing what they are doing while opening up spaces for the representation of previously unrepresented types of objects and artistic expressions. In those cases, I can see the rise of far more activity along the lines of contemporary art in places outside of the more privileged environment of New York, or, for that matter, Paris, although I would say that, even in the case of Paris, the forces that I spoke about are evident. In effect any place that has significant numbers of immigrants is going to be subject to the kinds of transformations we're speaking about. If one looks at the history of the "modern museum"—leaving that somewhat undefined for the moment—at the turn of the century in the United States, when all of a sudden the working class and immigrants and others demanded . . . to have some sort of representation in those museums, a significant change takes place in the 1920s toward more socially-conscious and popular representations. So that's one part of my answer. Very briefly, the other part of my answer has to do, obviously, with the federal environment. We tend to speak generally about museums as being funded only partly by the public sphere and to varying extents by memberships and patrons, etc., but, if I put on my lawyer's hat, museums look like they are largely supported by the federal government in one way or the other, either through the property-tax subsidies or through the deductions that one takes in one's income tax when making a gift or donation. From that perspective, one has to admit that the United States is in fact the most generous country when it comes to supporting its cultural institutions. If one does not accept this, let him or her imagine a transformation, whereby a new political majority changes the rules of the game, and that subsidized funding would be restricted. At that moment, you would see a dramatic transformation in the nature of the modern museum, as it becomes transparently recognized as subsidized by and for all taxpayers, rich and poor.

JOHN ELDERFIELD: Do you want to respond to that, Henri?

HENRI ZERNER: My point of view is very different, less concerned with . . . the social aspect, dealing more with what you might call the mandate of the museum. Of course, these are directly related, since it is the issue of who decides, who goes there, that determines the mandate and how that mandate is fulfilled. What strikes me is the importance of something that is very, very basic, which is the issue of education. Part of what one expects of the museum today is that it should teach people how to look at art. There are three views of the museum. First, the museum is basically a storeroom, where the people who are interested and educated go and look at whatever they want to look at. Basically, in its original incarnation the museum was seen as paralleling a library, and indeed, in the nineteenth century most museums were located in the same buildings as libraries. There was the museum of art and the museum of science, of natural science, usually. Then the museum of art tended to be separated, no longer seen simply as a storeroom but as a temple, as the last refuge of spirituality. The populace was supposed to go there and revere, to remain orderly and to respect the authority that put the canon of the museum in place.

The third view of the museum is still in the making. The museum as temple is not gone, but it is being challenged by another view of the museum, which is the museum as educator. The museum, to a certain extent, is more and more expected to be like a school or university. If it was decided that libraries had to teach people how to read books, everybody would think it was absolutely ludicrous, an impossible task. But the fact is, that is precisely what the museum is now being asked to do. Why? Because there is no visual arts in the education system until very, very late. You have courses on visual art in college, a little bit in high school in some places, but certainly not everywhere; even the teaching of drawing in regular schools, I think, which used to exist widely, has practically disappeared. At least my children never had anything like that. So people in their basic education have had absolutely no instruction in how to look, . . . in how to read images or how to draw them, so that the public who arrives in the museum and who is not just expected to revere has to be told how to look at the works of art, how to make sense of them. I'm just raising a question: Is such a thing possible? It seems to be a truly daunting task, and I think all of us are interested in what the educational function of the museum is, but I think that one has to realize that it is an unbelievably challenging business. There are no easy answers.

JOHN ELDERFIELD: In passing this back to Jorge, I'd like to add a rider to it, which is, given the fact that the educational role of the museum is so stressed these days, one thing which has come with it, I think, is questioning the extent to which the museum's role as telling historical stories actually functions as a sort of pacifying of objects. I know that certain artists have said that they would actually like to see a more startling relationship of objects to the viewer in museums than the one created by providing what some artists and some academics and critics see as a too-tidy history told by many museums.

JORGE KLOR DE ALVA: I think I will begin with a little anecdote about the president of the Field Museum in Chicago, Lee Webber, when he wanted to demonstrate the uplifting value of museums. He would speak about seeing all types of kids at the Field Museum, including teenagers, some of whom, when tumbling down the grand staircase, began to jostle each other, and one of them turned to the other and said, "If we weren't in a world-class museum I'd push your face in!" That's about where museums and education are for the overwhelming majority of the populace. It's the temple. One is to remain quiet there, and "I'll take care of you as soon as we get out of here" is the order of the day. I think this harks back to another age, and it's a wonderful "other age" for those who could take advantage of it, when one could really believe in high-minded things of that sort; but when you are confronted with what I would consider to be the age of the image—our age, and that's hardly a novel opinion—where what we have today are probably the most sophisticated interpreters of images, on the whole, that we have ever had, where the image has completely overshadowed the written word, where television, advertising, the internet, . . . MTV, fashion, etc., have completely overshadowed the sets of sensibilities that in some part you wisely suggest here, we are confronted with a different exercise for the museum when it comes to visual arts education. . . . Today, the museum should be far less concerned with claiming that it's going to educate visually, and more concerned with distinguishing itself from other, more popular images, and should attempt to educate folks around those other sets of images, and not necessarily the purely visual. . . . But what is it that gets left out by MTV? Once we move across the city into this Museum versus the Met, it's not so clear that the boundaries are there for one to distinguish between what belongs in *The New York Times* and what belongs in an exhibition of *New York Times* photographs at The Museum of Modern Art? How does one distinguish between the two? What was popular, what was not, what was high, what was low, what is art and what is not? Ultimately, those canonizations tend to be somewhat institutionally identified—that is, "You made it to the Modern," and that says it all. . . .

That's my first point about education. It's not clear to me that it necessarily goes beyond keeping somebody's face from being pushed in until they get out of the "world-class museum." The other part, the one about the pacifiers and the objects and such, my response to that is a highly personal one. When we know perfectly well that museums are in fact better-attended today than they have ever been before, it is difficult to avoid claiming that this is the age of the museum. In no small part, museums, particularly museums of art, have gotten a reprieve because of the baby boomers, because the very profile of the museum of art public is the profile of the mass that's moving across the demographic environment. The question is, are we producing another generation that's also going to go to the museum the way this generation has gone to the museum? Let me just stick to the pacifier of objects. It seems to me that the museum as forum, in that sense, is absolutely critical, because it really does compete . . . with a whole series of other sets and genres of images. Its capacity . . . to canonize, but, more importantly, to legitimize certain sets of images is so crucial that for museums to yield to the abrasive, to put it that way—since you used "pacifier" I'll use "abrasive"—is to yield too much. Because it is not enough to attempt to tell the story; every time you attempt to tell the story, by definition, you have to leave most of it out. As a consequence, . . . every story is a tidying-up, and to not have a location for tidied-up, gussied-up stories would be an absolute disaster, when we have an infinite number of possibilities for the abrasive to show its face. . . . Consequently, from that perspective I would say that we should let museums attend to being something different, to struggle to diversify themselves rather than to struggle to be the first to be the same as everything else.

HENRI ZERNER: . . . I have, perhaps, a slightly different point of view, though I would agree that the main thing is that the museum cannot and doesn't want to show everything. It's simply not possible. It is something to think about. The tendency is for a museum to become bigger and bigger and bigger. It is true of every museum, but it is the particular problem of museums of modern art, because of accumulation. The Luxembourg had this advantage, that what it swallowed at one end it got rid of at the other—that is, when the artist died the work went somewhere else. The museum of modern art in Paris in principle also did that, even after its re-creation. The idea was no longer five years after the death of the artist, but that once an artist had been dead a hundred years his works would be housed somewhere else. It didn't work anymore, because there was no room in the Louvre, so a nineteenth-century museum, the Musée d'Orsay, was made to solve the problem. Eventually, a new museum of modern art will have to be closed for a museum of next-generation art or post-generation art or whatever, but the problem of accumulation remains. A museum of modern art has this increased tendency to become larger and larger; it is crucial to control it, and that is what the creation of a canon is all about. Part of the problem of the present situation is that the modern canon, that is, that adventure of the spirit which went from David to Géricault to Delacroix to the Impressionists to Cézanne to Gauguin, etcetera, up to Picasso, etcetera, that story became so withered with the modernist canon in all its purity that it became a caricature of itself. In the last, let's say, quarter of a century, there has been a tendency, and a very healthy one, to explode this canon and to open the museum to different tendencies, to cater to different tastes but also to different social strata; the question, then, is how this expansion can be in some way managed and controlled. The two things are different. Managing is one thing, controlling is another. One needs to manage, but one doesn't really want to control too much, because of course controlling means the control of one class over the rest, to put it in crude political terms, so that there is that very, very sensitive issue of how you manage without controlling too much and how you keep the museum manageable. Otherwise, the museum also becomes pandemonium. If there are too many things in it to see, you can't see anything; if you have a collection of everything, then everything is reduced to nonsense.

JOHN ELDERFIELD: So would you advocate . . . the idea of a museum which deals with this by telling different stories at different parts of the year, for example?

HENRI ZERNER: Yes. I think that it's totally different. . . . There is an established canon, and it's very unlikely that the *Demoiselles d'Avignon,* Mondrian's *Broadway Boogie-Woogie,* and Jackson Pollock's *One: Number 31* [all in the collection of The Museum of Modern Art, New York] are going to become irrelevant. A museum can have a presentation of the canon but then also make it clear that this is not the only possibility, that there are other stories, which perhaps will be told not all the time but at different times in galleries that will change temporarily. That is one possibility that

I can think of. . . . The idea is to preserve the notion of a canon, be it only as a historical phenomenon, what has been considered by a given society as the icons that represent that society, and at the same time present possible alternatives.

JOHN ELDERFIELD: In effect, to fully historicize the canon and make it clear that it's being presented in that way.

HENRI ZERNER: Yes.

JOHN ELDERFIELD: Jorge, do you want to respond?

JORGE KLOR DE ALVA: Just very briefly, I agree that the question of the sharing of authority is *the* central question. That's what these tensions that I'm speaking of are about: who gets to make meaning, who gets to identify what. I tend to look at the maintenance of the canon from a slightly different perspective. The maintenance of a canon, for me, in no small part has to do with finances. It's extremely expensive to educate human beings to accept a particular canon, a canon that calls for a certain . . . we can use the language of refinement, but it's the language of education, a whole set of experiences that are extremely expensive to obtain. So I believe that the canon of, let's say, the patron's sensibilities can be maintained without any difficulty whatsoever, it's just a matter of the federal government changing its policies about the distribution of money for education, so that we have school choice, for instance, and everybody ends up in very nice private schools and is able to attend to the redefinition of proper sensibilities. I see it primarily from that perspective, but, not to be glib about it, I also see it from an even more significant perspective. It's also a matter of power; that is, those who hold the canon as we're speaking about it, without defining it too much, those who hold that canon as their own are without question significantly more powerful in the society, because it represents precisely those privileged kinds of experiences, those privileged kinds of networks, who you know and what you know. I'm a terribly different man because I happen to like Cézanne and Renoir, and can pronounce their names, from someone who has never seen them, who can't pronounce their names. I hold a different place in the society, . . . I live in a different world as a consequence of that. . . . The question about museums being able to address these kinds of tensions, surrounding canons, on the basis of specific exhibits needs to be qualified a little bit in the following sense: A permanent exhibit is not the same as a temporary exhibit. It does not have the same status. It's just not the same thing. Anybody with any degree of, let's say, social and political sense knows that. . . . Nor am I advocating that museums have this full panoply of experiences presented or represented; that's not at all my point. I just want to speak about the fact that exhibits have consequences. Exhibits held in one central part of the museum have consequences different from those located at other, more remote sites. For example,the Aztecs were around for less than a hundred years; they were the last expression of Mexico, and far from its most intelligent, most sophisticated, or anything of the sort. But they happened to be Mexico City's "home team," and there they are in the national museum, right at the center, taking up the maximum amount of space. Now that's the canon, that's the national canon. If you are a Maya, or if you are anything else, you have to go and bow in the capital to the fact that you folks are on the margins, on the sides, next to the elevator, next to the rest lounge, whatever. All these things have implications, about status, education, and the role of the canon. That's the point that I'm making. . . .

JOHN ELDERFIELD: Would anyone like to ask any questions of Henri or Jorge?

AUDIENCE MEMBER: I'm sort of flabbergasted that at the end of the twentieth century here we are discussing the broad future of the modern museum, and you're bringing out a canon that no one seems to be willing to suggest perhaps debunking slightly. But no one's talking about the role of capitalism, no one's talking about the role of elitism in this Museum. We're in this brand-new world of the new Common Market, . . . but you've already decided the canon as being totally French from the inception, with Picasso at the end. . . . No one's talking about any of the other ideas about what should be brought in, and that there should be a channeling of ideas about what created what. There's no question here, except I'm not sure I understood what you said about what's in and what's out and what should be and what isn't—no question about opening out things and saying that these channels are the product of all kinds of political, social, and economic things, and that we no longer necessarily understand them that way. So I'm really sort of surprised. I was expecting a totally different discussion rather than sort of patting each other on the back in terms of these issues.

JOHN ELDERFIELD: Who would like to take this on?

JORGE KLOR DE ALVA: All of the points that you're making are obviously the case. There are all these outside forces. . . . My understanding of a dialogue of this sort is that, assuming all these forces exist, now what about the modern museum? . . . I think, once again, that these forces are felt unequally in different settings; the way they're felt here is very different from someplace else. How that will be responded to within the context of future taxing structures, etc., all of that is going to come into play. But I would prefer not to reduce the debate to some struggle between canon and noncanon, because I'm familiar enough with the anticanons to realize that one of the fundamental struggles of the anticanon is to become a canon of its own. As anybody who's participated in curating exhibits for an ethnic audience realizes, it's the same old struggle with a slightly different accent. So the question here is whether there is a dramatic transformation or simply new players, like at the turn of the century, who wanted in.

JOHN ELDERFIELD: Anyone else?

AUDIENCE MEMBER: The point was made before, [at the first lecture in this series, that] the Museum would expand its space and continue to increase its collections. Do you have any idea or suggestion about what would be a reasonable way to deal with such an expansion?

HENRI ZERNER: I guess that comes to me. It's a very, very tricky question, because what we witness today in a way is a sort of "musefication" of the world. It's not only that the museums expand madly—and the Louvre was the most staggering example of it; this is acres of museum, and in typical French manner centralized, so that you have to go in one place and it takes you half an hour to get to see anything. So it's total madness; it's like a caricature of what is happening today. But beyond the museum proper, the entire center of the city has become sort of a tourist attraction, with the museum just one part of it, in competition with, first of all, the mall at the Louvre. . . . It's very hard at the Louvre now, as Mr. Pei [I. M. Pei, chief architect of the Louvre expansion of 1983–89] has set it up, to tell when you're leaving the museum and when you are in the shopping mall, because it's all a very aestheticized attraction. . . . Fewer and fewer people live in the center of the city. This is true of all the major cities, not just Paris; everybody moves to a suburb and the center is turned into a huge theme park, which is fundamentally a museum—not a museum of art, necessarily, but a sort of general museum, where the past, but a very sort of Disney-land past, is preserved as spectacle, as entertainment. . . . I realize this is not a direct answer, but I thought it was necessary to give a sense of the magnitude of the problem now. When it comes to a museum proper, how do you control or manage this general expansion. Obviously, first of all by trying to be really very rigorous as to what you accept into permanent museum collections as opposed to the variety of things that you might want to show in an ongoing, revolving, way, a flow of material, of visual material, which will go through the museum but will not necessarily be locked into the collection; but deaccession, that is, getting rid of things in a collection is extremely dangerous, as we know. This is one of the major problems of museums, so one way is to be more rigorous about accepting things in a permanent way, with a greater flexibility about things that go through, this flow of material through the museum. This being said, there is a problem that ultimately cannot be solved entirely, because we are a society which has what you might call a historical neurosis or compulsion. There are societies that are very well-equipped to get rid of such materials, societies that make ritual objects, for instance, and then, when they have been used, get rid of them. . . . We have this anal-retentive society that cannot get rid of anything. It's like these people who are stifled in their own houses because they don't know how to get rid of anything. This is a very, very profound cultural phenomenon that is very hard to deal with because it is completely inseparable from the values that are considered the highest values of our society. We feel that the past is what guarantees our identity. It's a problem of the social psyche, a very tricky business.

JOHN ELDERFIELD: We're also, obviously, a society who could go on talking forever. I promised that we would finish at 7:30 and we've passed that time, so thank you for being here.

Notes

1. See Paul J. Dimaggio, "The Museum and the Public," in Martin Feldstein, ed., *The Economics of Art Museums* (Chicago: University of Chicago, 1993), pp. 39–50, for a discussion of the three museum typologies referred to here by Jorge Klor de Alva.
2. Andrew McClellan, *Inventing the Louvre* (Cambridge, Mass.: Harvard University Press, 1994).

The Museum and Society

Panelists: Janet Abrams, architecture and design critic; Robert A.M. Stern, architect; and Fred Wilson, artist. Moderated by Helen Searing, Alice Pratt Brown Professor of Art History, Smith College. December 3, 1996

HELEN SEARING: Since the mid 1960s, art museums have been subjected to a blistering cultural critique—from artists, art historians, and critics, of conservative as well as Marxist persuasion; from members of the public no less than museum professionals, and finally, the U.S. Government. The searching reexamination of the role of the museum in society has resulted not only in verbal diatribes, but in acts of commission and omission that argue passionately against many of the museum practices that we have accepted as intrinsic to the institution. Recent examples include the creation of works the museum cannot embrace or coopt, as the case may be; the staging of exhibitions that bar the public from entering; and, perhaps the most eloquent and persuasive of all, the development within the gallery itself of installations that vividly demonstrate the way the institution has privileged certain groups—be they collectors, artists, consumers of culture, or dealers—and set up exclusionary value systems that stand between art and its potential audience. The spatial organization and the architectural language of museums have been seen as participants in enforcing these strategies, as has the paraphernalia that have become indispensable to the museum mandate—to educate, through publications, programs, and, increasingly now, electronic media; and to entertain, through the provision of spectacle and consumer services such as restaurants and shops.

Museology—not the history of museums but the decoding of the role those institutions have played in society, a role which goes far beyond their apparently disinterested purpose of collecting and displaying works of art and teaching the public to appreciate and value them—has become a hot academic discipline, one that addresses issues of space, viewing, and spectatorship, power and control, and the ways in which the agenda of states, classes, and groups penetrate and shape cultural practices and acts of communication. As Marcia Pointon has written, museology "offers the opportunity to understand artefacts functioning neither as isolated cultural icons or masterpieces, nor as emblems of personal wealth, but as components in a perpetually shifting language that works to create understandings of concepts such as 'the past,' 'the present,' 'art,' 'nation,' 'individual'"—concepts that allow us to recognize "structures of power in a modern world and how those powers function."[1]

Once such museum practices have been deconstructed, once they have been pointed out, however fiercely or gently, they seem fairly self-evident. Although one should not underestimate the difficulties, they are not impervious to reform and repair. Surely it is time to accept the fact that an institution born in the Enlightenment as a place for the leisured and monied classes to celebrate and cultivate Western values inevitably will manifest shortcomings in the present day. Now that these shortcomings have been revealed, we should move forward without getting mired in recrimination.

In addition to atoning for its dysfunctional past, the art museum must confront novel challenges to its future. These include the need to claim, in the face of possible resistance, new constituencies, the need to respond to the postmodernist insistence that, since every experience is filtered through the decisions and the actions of others, no collection or display can be innocent of ideology, and the demand that the museum experience be made more interactive, personal, and be ethically as well as epistemologically accountable. These challenges are compounded by new electronic technologies that some may view as a threat, offering competition to the museum that it cannot transcend, or as a promise, freeing the museum to be a more effective and inclusive institution.

The planned expansion of The Museum of Modern Art into the next century seems a fitting occasion to consider positive ways in which the institution can conduct self-analysis from within and counter criticism from without, can review its own history and posit future directions. What we talk about this evening under the broad rubric of the museum and society has resonance beyond MoMA, of course, and in our discussion we may range far from West Fifty-third and Fifty-fourth streets. But I propose that we focus the discussion on museums of modern and contemporary art. Burdened with shorter histories than encyclopedic museums, dealing with living artists, such institutions encounter the most opportunity and urgency in assessing the museum's public and social role. . . .

Before the roundtable discussion began, Fred Wilson gave a slide presentation of works he has installed in various museums throughout the United States. These installations call into question the museum's role in society, and address the issue of art's exclusivity[2] (see figs. 1, 2). Janet Abrams followed with an overview of the new digital media that museums have begun to use as means to extend the experience of art beyond the walls of the gallery, including works of art available on CD-ROM and sites maintained on the World Wide Web by arts organizations and institutions in the United States and abroad.

ROBERT A. M. STERN: I thought the purpose of this discussion was to talk about the museum and works of art, and the magical possibility that someone can come to a museum and see a work of art and be transformed by that work of art, and also see the juxtapositions. I don't want to get on a high horse, but it seems to me that, whether the book is on the machine or the book is in your library, you're not really in a museum; you're still at a remove from it. Besides that, you can't date anyone in a book. You have to come to the museum, you have to have a social venture; that's part of the culture of museumgoing, and it has been since the nineteenth century. I don't think it's quite so elitist as even Helen suggests, because I know from reading about the history of New York museums that The Metropolitan Museum of Art, when it opened on Sundays—after the ministers of the City of New York said it wasn't a sin to go to a museum on Sunday—was packed with people who could never go during the week because they worked. And so from the moment that we allowed the museum to exist, there has always been an audience for the experience of it. What is it? It's different for every different person, but I think that the heart of the museum experience is still the gallery, the works of art, how the curator . . . juxtaposes those works of art and, by doing so, illuminates them. . . . So I like Mr. Wilson's stuffing all the things together, because I think he's made some wonderful points about . . . the frozen isolation of works of art.

I was thinking as I was listening to the earlier conversations that I was born in

Top:
1. *The Museum: Mixed Metaphors* (Fred Wilson Installation: 1993 Biennial Anne Gerber Exhibition), Seattle Art Museum, January 28–June 13, 1993. Photograph by Susan Dirk

Above:
2. *OpEd: Fred Wilson*, Installation, Museum of Contemporary Art, Chicago, 1994

the year The Museum of Modern Art opened, in 1939, on this street. So, in a certain way, I feel a special affinity for this place. I came here as a teenager; I came mostly for the movies, I have to confess, because there were all these wonderful movies, beautifully presented, that I'd never seen. My parents said, "Why do you want to see those old movies?"—and mind you, this was in the early 1950s. So we always need a place to bring together those experiences. Too, I can remember exactly to this day certain ways that works of art were hung next to each other, certain characteristics of spaces, certain sandwiches served in the tea room—every little thing—and I don't think that, sitting at home, if I could have done it at that time, coasting through a Web site on my couch or in my rather untidy bedroom, with all the shades drawn and the door locked so my parents couldn't get in, would have had quite the same meaning. . . .

Although I have had, like every other person who's ever been to the Modern and thought about it, a quarrel or two with this or that, I don't think any of us have ever had a quarrel with the commitment that this Museum has had to presenting works of art in their best possible light, to as many people as possible, and to accompanying them with scholarship (and that's where the Web sites may or may not help), but, finally, to allowing the works of art to have their own life and to remain on display, often for a very long time, so one could return to them over and over again, with yet another, adjoining gallery providing a changing matrix. I think that's what a museum is about. If we're thinking of the new building, and I'm trying not to think of it as an architect seeking a job—which I'm not; I wouldn't want to do that building at all—but of course I was thinking of all these conceptual pieces, like those shown by Mr. Wilson. I was thinking that maybe the Dorset Hotel should just be left alone and each artist should be given a room, a guest bedroom, and allowed to do what he or she wants in it. . . .

Finally, this place once had an intimacy about it; it doesn't have an intimacy anymore. It was a place about what was called modern art, and I think Mr. Wilson's work makes it clear, and Helen Searing in a very good introduction makes it even clearer that we don't know exactly what modern art means anymore. It means very many different things today than it did to the canonical group that founded this place in 1929. So I don't have an answer to this question. . . . I think this is really important—the *building* is important, the setting is important, and an awareness of the danger of losing the focus on or reverence for the work of art is to me very, very important. If we're going to lose it to a Web site, then let's not build the building, let's just get better computers, and then we don't have to come to this room, we could all sit on our little couches in our little rooms and watch it. But you know, the truth of the matter is, we wouldn't watch it—we wouldn't do it. *Nobody's* going to watch it half as much as possible. People want to come together to share an experience, with panelists, they want to hear something, they want to talk, they want to meet afterward and discuss it. We are social people and we experience art, like much in our lives, on a social basis. So all of this, I think, is temporary; it won't go away—we can't be that lucky—but people will stop obsessing about it. It's like talking about plumbing in the nineteenth century. Can you imagine people talking about plumbing? It's *not* important. So I would include this slight little irreverent thing, which is that, as an architect. . . . I did a building at Stanford University, the Gates Computer Science Building. We've heard of Mr. Bill Gates [Chief Executive Officer of the Microsoft Corporation], and he's pretty up on this stuff. At the building's dedication, he said, "You know, I guess we need this building for people to come together in a room to knock heads together." And I think that's what a museum is also about. You need to see that art, you need to experience it directly, its tactile qualities; but you also need to see it *with other people seeing it.* How the work of art affects you and how it affects the other people in an environment—whether it's someone's living room, if you're privileged to see it that way, or a public place, a gallery—is very, very important, fundamental, and those experiences we must not lose sight of as we beam into the twenty-first century.

HELEN SEARING: . . . I think that the most interesting exhibition I've seen all year is the one on the late work of Degas, because it really had a point of view that was filtered through the informed sensibility of the curator.[3] It gave you completely new insights about the work, and if you don't have to have every work that the artist ever did on display, but can show that through another medium, . . . that might in some ways mitigate what has become just a spectacle.

ROBERT A. M. STERN: There are blockbusters that are excessive and there are others, it seems to me, that make a point. Last winter, for whatever reason, I was moved to go see the Chinese porcelains from . . . Taiwan.[4] It's not something I know anything about, really, but it was fabulous to be confronting, in one place at one time, that panoply of hundreds of years of beautiful stuff. So that was a blockbuster that, if somebody said, "Let's not have blockbusters," would have been a meaningful loss to me. But I agree with you, every toenail clipping of every artist is not all that important.

FRED WILSON: I just wanted to say something about cyberspace. I used to teach police officers art. . . . I brought them to The Museum of Modern Art. Basically, I told them, "Listen, it's like coming to a foreign country. You don't speak the language but you understand that there is a language, and you don't make fun of the natives." They could understand that. When they came, they really enjoyed their experience, but they were particularly taken by a painting by van Gogh. . . . They were familiar with van Gogh's work through printed material, so experiencing that painting became that much more interesting because it was the real thing. I think the cyberworld is going to in many ways enlarge the audience for the actual experience of a work of art. On the flip side, unfortunately, as museums are now opening up to invite many more people to be involved in coming to their sites and will move farther and farther in that direction, the cyberworld is creating two different sectors of society—those who are involved with computers and those who are not. So, oddly enough, I'm conflicted about its use as well. It runs along monetary lines.

JANET ABRAMS: I have to respond to that. Yes, it's obvious, even for people who have a certain level of computer equipment, . . . that accessibility is always going to be a kind of moving target; there's always a pressure to have the latest upgrade of whatever software or hardware, and the cost of that is a constant factor. I personally agree that the experience of the "real" thing is likely to remain in high demand, and I think the blockbuster phenomenon goes in tandem with these developments in cyberspace. The number of people gathering in a particular space to pay homage to a particular artist, however well curated, has to be seen as a phenomenon on its own terms, like going to see the movie *Pocahontas* in Central Park or the Pope during his visit to the United States or something like that. These are events of our time, where people feel that they want to be able to say that they were at that show. I was at The Art Institute of Chicago just the other week, and the front of the building is now emblazoned with signs saying, "Today's show is sold out. If you have your advance tickets, file in here," and it's become much more like an airport, that experience; that you're being processed through an experience, whether it's *Degas* or *Cézanne*.[5] I wonder how this Museum is planning to address that specifically, whether there are ways of understanding how people move through museum spaces. That's why I've become interested in audiotour guides, because . . . that technology . . . can be programmed to find out as much about the user as the users find out about the art while they're listening to the audiotape; the apparatus can record how long people spend in front of a particular painting, how often a particular piece of work is accessed from the CD-ROM or the digital database that is storing the narrative. That material can then be fed back to the museums that commission or rent that equipment, and provide the curatorial narrative for a particular show or to plan future exhibits. I'm very interested in what might be called flow-management through these spaces. . . . The demand for access to information can actually slow you down from getting it. When you go to a blockbuster art exhibit, you have a rather problematic time seeing the work most of the time. I don't agree with Bob, though, that the development of museum Web sites is irrelevant. At the same time, I don't want to be considered . . . a complete cyberfanatic, because I think there are a lot of problems still to contend with, such as how the hardware and software of the audiotour experience might detract from the reverential experience of art, an experience whose importance you were just emphasizing. Those problems certainly need to be addressed.

HELEN SEARING: It seems to me what both Fred and Janet are talking about, though they approach it from different standpoints, is the possibility of giving the audience more and more of a choice in the way it experiences the museum, by expanding the number of people who actually are involved with exhibits and setting up museums, and through giving people the opportunity to make the choices via the Web of what sorts of objects they're going to bring together on the site. Is there anything that you see that would enhance this greater accessibility that has to do with the space and the architecture of museums? . . .

FRED WILSON: I think some museums do engage with the new media, but I think that the conversations that I hear most often are about fear of the new media. I think once you get past that fear, . . . you can see how the new media fits within a museum context, and use it without thinking that it's going to overtake what the museum does best. At that point, then, once the fear subsides and you realize where it goes and how it fits comfortably, where it works best. Then the design of the institution, the building itself, follows suit. I think it's the same with being open to a variety of communities and their cultural practices. Once we realize that we're not going to lose everything that we know because we're allowing these "hordes" to come in, then a design that takes into account different ways of seeing can happen, and you really do have a different kind of institution.

JANET ABRAMS: It makes me think about the hierarchies of design that are involved in making successful exhibitions. I guess I'm always scanning—not just art-museum displays, but also other kinds of museums. Some of the most provocative exhibits I've seen recently have been in natural history museums. I'm thinking of the American Museum of Natural History, the dinosaur exhibit that was reinstalled by Ralph Appelbaum Associates. . . and in Paris, the Grande Galerie de l'Evolution in the Jardin des Plantes, which presents a very different approach to how you show the evolution of species. Both of those incorporate new technology in distinct ways from each other, but the Paris exhibit in particular is extremely sophisticated in its spatial design, the design of the vitrines, the ratio of your confrontation with stuffed animals, which are, in fact, arrayed as promenades of species relating to different kinds of habitats around the globe. Then the media displays which are available to you are set off discreetly behind doorways and archways—you don't have to encounter them if you don't want to. There's a kind of tiering—from the architecture of the building as a whole, down through the gallery spaces, to the actual design of the display cabinets and the interfaces of the interactive material—that needs to be incorporated to make for a really succesful exhibit. Architects, in my experience, have tremendous skills in the making of the buildings and the gallery rooms, but there are now professionals who are more involved with the actual exhibit design—the graphics, the signage, the cabinetry, the decision about how much to put on display for different levels of educational and cultural ability, let's say, the reading age (literacy) levels that one has to address—those professionals are usually *not* architects. It seems to me that there is a new breed of, not interior designers and not really exhibit designers, but *information* designers who bring under the umbrellas of their studios a lot of other skills, some of which are traditionally architectural. It's in that area of storytelling, of making material a story, that newer kinds of interdisciplinary design practices are emerging, and they may be perceived as a threat or as competition by more conventional architectural firms. Yes, I think the design of the physical experience is extremely important, and maybe underestimated in its importance. . . .

ROBERT A. M. STERN: I'm just focused on this Museum—I think it's very difficult to make generalizations about other museums, because they have so many different characteristics, histories, and locations. The Museum of Modern Art has become a huge enterprise, and is about to become a much bigger enterprise than ever before, probably doubling its size—I'm just guessing. The whole structure of the Museum and its environs has changed radically. The Metropolitan Museum's environs have basically *not* changed substantially, nor has its ambition, since the day it was conceived, or almost the day it was conceived. It was to be a grand, encyclopedic museum; in a funny way, it's just finishing up the master plan of Richard Morris Hunt as developed by the architectural firms of McKim, Mead and White, and Roche, Dinkeloo. The Museum of Modern Art, I don't think, was ever conceived to become anything like an encyclopedic institution, yet, at least with respect to the art of this century, it has become one. Moreover, it's located in a neighborhood that was once a quiet residential neighborhood, with a genteel Fifth Avenue and an undeveloped West Side. Now, you know what its context is—without a park setting, or even that of a major street like Park or Fifth Avenue, commercialism to the *nth* degree. The Museum of Modern Art lacks any of the orchestrating devices, some of which Janet was hinting at, that prepare you for a museum experience, whatever that museum experience might be. You enter—*bam*—off this noisy street. . . . Plus, it's a mob scene, with crowds of people now and many more anticipated in the future. The physical framework of the original building was not geared to lots of people. When escalators were added—well, is that the right way to experience a building, never mind prepare yourself to contemplate a work of art as opposed to making an impulse selection in a store?

This institution has a major dilemma in this place, and I also would say that most architects in their designs of new museums have been more interested—quite naturally, I suppose—in certain issues of architectural expression than in issues of gallery design. I don't agree with you that, as a profession, we've done such a good job in designing the galleries. I think we do some very exciting buildings, but the spaces in which the works of art are shown—the loss of intimacy is the thing that really is a problem, it seems to me, in museum design in the latter part of this period. That is most vividly brought home in this Museum, with the change in the sizes and the scales of the galleries from those of the Alfred Barr days—which many people here probably remember—to the reinstallations, where everything somehow got bigger and . . . the art somehow got smaller; it seemed to get smaller in relationship to this flowing space. I don't know how long the spatial ideas of the galleries now in place can be sustained without really altering the context with which the art was originally made and intended to be understood. . . . This building—and I really mean the galleries in it—reflects, more than any other museum building that I can think of, the troubling yet exciting, changing nature of the museum experience; that is, the relationship between the genuine experience of works of art and the realities of a century of mass communication, crowds, mass democracy, what-have-you. I don't have an answer. I just feel it's a very interesting question that should be part of the agenda . . . in considering this new building.

FRED WILSON: I think there's a lot of confusion. Part of the excitement and the frustration—the excitement that some things do work and the frustration that comes from our sense that some things clearly are not working in museums—is that sometimes the art is not particularly considered, as you're saying. Some of the spaces are not well considered. Not enough attention has been given to what's actually going to go into them or the variety of ways of experiencing the art, which in turn reflects the variety of reasons that we make art. Certainly, contemplative spaces are highly important in museums of contemporary and modern art, as are more frenetic spaces that include the outside world within the gallery space, within the gallery context, to make meaning of what you're actually seeing. I think a new museum needs to orient its viewers to the variety of reasons that art has for being, and that experience should happen the moment they go into the museum. I find generally that the first space, in many museums, is experienced as a party space, basically as the great hall, and art-viewing is ancillary to what has become its main purpose. Not to say that's something wrong, but it's something that should be understood, that this is the viewer's orientation to the museum; it tells them how they're supposed to think about the museum, and creates meaning in much the same way as the exterior of the building. Seeing the gift shop also tells the viewer something about how they should experience what they're going to see when they walk through the spaces. I think more concern should be given to orienting the viewer, in design terms, to the variety of experiences that they can have in an institution like the museum.

ROBERT A. M. STERN: For example, I felt your installation with the Morris Louis and the four Barcelona chairs (fig. 1) was an amazing contemporary installation. I'm sure many of us in this room have been to some collector's house on a tour and seen just such a little shrine. But the point is that, when Morris Louis painted, certainly by the end of his career, he had in mind where his work would be shown. Then, when you put it in a room that's so "other," whatever that other might be, you may be illuminating a new aspect of the work of art, but you're also compromising it. Even the art gallery scenes downtown are intimate compared to the typical gallery spaces of these large museums, which this Museum is on the threshold of perhaps becoming. When you have a tondo or something from the Renaissance you can know exactly how it fit into the architecture, and you can even have a photograph to the side, with a caption that says this is the way it was—or on the Web, whatever—but it's part of a construct, and ripping the art out of that construct is already questionable. But with the art of our century, we have lost, in a way, the sight of the room that it was made to be in. The clutter of your installation, which I love, is the way Gertrude Stein's studio *was*. It didn't have everything all on nice, white walls. But that's a whole other argument. The point is, what is the museum if it is not to somehow show us the art in some kind of context that will help us to understand the work of art, and also the intentionalities of the artist and how he or she would have imagined their works of art would be displayed.

JANET ABRAMS: But surely that's what Fred's work is all about—dismantling the idea that there is at any time a sort of fixed, correct view of what that context was.

ROBERT A. M. STERN: Yes, but when you dismantle, you also have to know what you're dismantling, so that's the postmodern game. That's fine, but I'm worried that we might dismantle without remembering what the structure of the thing was to begin with, in the process of making more space or more stuff.

JANET ABRAMS: Can I ask you what you mean by intimacy, because you've used that word repeatedly, and I'm not sure whether you mean it as a spatial thing or as a matter of solitude in front of a particular piece of work, so that you have a privileged experience . . . .

ROBERT A. M. STERN: I think it's many of those things. In this Museum, and of course we all remember the past, our own personal pasts, though slightly veiled and usually more positive than they in fact were—we think our youths were special, especially as we get older, even though we hated those youths when we had them and couldn't wait to get older—but the entrance to this Museum was a very small room. Eight or ten people could sit and wait on a little round bench, . . . and the ticket taker was a little poky person and there was a little area where you bought some postcards to take home; and then there was the gallery itself, the stair that went up, next to the Schlemmer painting.[6] That was it. The elevator was manned, usually by a guard, and there you waited. There were sometimes a lot of people in that building. It wasn't deserted by any means, but everything had a certain scale, which was still the scale of the art, the environments for which that art was produced. Much of the art that we could see in that Museum at that time is now lost in vast spaces on . . . the second floor of this building, . . . and the way we get to it is through a huge, flat, aircraft-carrier lobby. The garden itself has become a tiny postage stamp to the building it serves; that has been transformed. The garden was the *biggest* space in midtown, practically; now it seems tiny. Then you escalate up, which is hardly, in my view, a preparation for any kind of contemplation. That has changed the meaning of this institution, it has changed the way we can see these works of art, and I think people have lost a certain connection to the work of art that they could have had before. I recognize that millions of people come here now, and only hundreds of thousands did before.

Therein lies the rest of the problem: the loss of intimacy. There has been too little discussion of intimacy. So it's physical intimacy, the opportunity to get close to the work of art and somehow, if the room is designed right, get away from the hundred people walking by with the lector if you want to have that moment. I don't want to pretend that I have that moment every moment of my museum day—I'm not that dedicated—but once in a while something catches you and you want to be "alone" with a work of art. But more to the point is to create a set of environments which prepare you for the works of art on a scale that you can appreciate the works of art within, not just as so many trophies on the walls, as you move through the history of art on a kind of treadmill. Amazingly, the beaux-arts architects did it well. The Metropolitan Museum has more capacity for intimacy, strangely enough, than other, more recent museums. The reinstallation of the nineteenth-century paintings there, in a not-very-interesting faux–nineteenth-century manner but reflecting the defeat of everyone in the face of the previous installation, shows that there is something to this gallery business that we have lost sight of in our time. This place did a lot to undo the nineteenth century, but it was so small that it worked on its own terms. When you take that idea and you blow it up, I think something has been lost. Can it be recaptured? Maybe nobody else but me wants it; I don't know.

Notes

1. Marcia Pointon, Introduction to Pointon, ed., *Art Apart: Art Institutions and Ideology Across England and North America* (Manchester, England: Manchester University Press, 1994), p. 3.

2. For discussions of the work of Fred Wilson, see Martha Buskirk, "[An Interview with] Fred Wilson," *October* 70 (Fall 1994), "The Duchamp Effect: A Special Issue," pp. 109–12; Donald Garfield, "Making the Museum Mine: An Interview with Fred Wilson," *Museum News* 72 (May–June 1993), pp. 46–49; and Fred Wilson, *The Museum/Mixed Metaphors: Fred Wilson* (Seattle: Seattle Art Museum, 1993).

3. The exhibition *Degas: Beyond Impressionism* was organized by the National Gallery, London, where it was shown May 22–August 26, 1996; it was subsequently installed at The Art Institute of Chicago, September 28, 1996–January 5, 1997.

4. This is a reference to the exhibition *Splendors of Imperial China: Treasures from the National Palace Museum, Taipei,* directed by Wen Fong and James C.Y. Watt, and shown in New York at The Metropolitan Museum of Art, March 19–May 19, 1996; its subsequent national tour concluded in Washington, D.C., at the National Gallery of Art, in April 1997.

5. The exhibition *Cézanne* was organized by curator Françoise Cachin of the Galerie Nationale du Grand Palais, Paris, where it was shown September 25, 1995–January 17, 1996; a subsequent international tour in 1996 included the Tate Gallery, London, and the Philadelphia Museum of Art.

6. A reference to Oskar Schlemmer's *Bauhaus Stairway* of 1932, acquired by the Museum in 1942 and installed in the circular stairwell leading upward from the lobby to the upper-level galleries.

Rethinking the Modern

Lecture by Terence Riley. December 12, 1996

The lecture was followed by a roundtable discussion with Mary Lea Bandy, Glenn D. Lowry, John Elderfield, and Mr. Riley; the transcript begins on p.131

The title of this lecture is meant to be understood in two ways: as a reference to the rethinking of the conceptual as well as the physical structure of The Museum of Modern Art. As you are no doubt aware, the Museum has acquired in the last year the adjoining property of the Dorset Hotel and is currently in the process of deciding how to join that property to the existing Museum. The intention is not simply to increase square footage, but to reinvent—or invent again—the institution for the next century. To this end, the Museum staff and leadership have undertaken over the past twelve months a broad self-analysis, a process that has taken various forms: dialogues between the curators and Museum trustees; staff discussions and debates; a conference with the Museum's leadership and noted architects, artists, and critics; and this lecture series, along with a compilation of a detailed architectural program and more than a little soul-searching.

Shortly, this rethinking will shift from the purely conceptual to the more concrete. Sometime in the coming months, it is our intention to, first, engage a number of architects in a design exercise—a charette—to explore the urbanistic and architectural implications of the rethinking already undertaken; and secondly, to stage a lim-

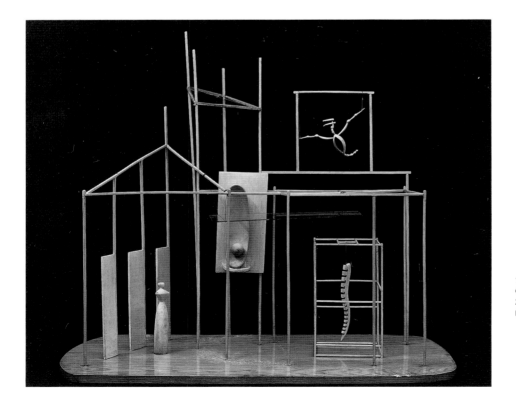

1. Alberto Giacometti. *The Palace at 4 a.m.* 1932–33. Construction in wood, glass, wire, and string, 25 x 28¼ x 15¾" (63.5 x 71.8 x 40 cm). The Museum of Modern Art, New York. Purchase

ited competition to more fully explore architectural visions of a new Museum of Modern Art. My purpose is not to recapitulate all that has preceded, although much of it will be published as part of the Museum's commitment to this process as a critical one, and will have a usefulness beyond our own project. My goal here is to present a bridge between rethinking conceptually and rethinking physically, to straddle the heretofore internal debates about our future and that time when we will look to others to give formal and spatial expression to our plans.

I should also say that this is my own personal synthesis. The five architectural concepts that I want to discuss tonight are those which I think are the most important. They represent my own way of presenting ideas whose development has involved many people. I will illustrate these concepts by using architectural images, which should be understood as just that. These are conceptual illustrations rather than clues as to what the new Museum should look like (an issue which we're trying to leave open). I will intersperse a few nonarchitectural images in order to achieve a broader, nonverbal understanding of the issues I am trying to convey. I am aware that there is a lot of interest in which architects we may be considering. For those of you interested in reading between the lines, please note that all of the architects whose work I will be illustrating tonight do have one thing in common: They are, how shall I say, *formerly living* architects.

For the first illustration: *The Palace at 4 a.m.* by Alberto Giacometti (fig. 1). The Museum of Modern Art must be a place of many places, that is, a heterotopic institution. While our primary purpose should be to provide the best-possible environment for an individual to see works of art, the Museum cannot be characterized by one single type of space or experience, nor should its diverse programs be homogenized into a singular form or space, of a kind perhaps best illustrated by A.-L.-T. Vaudoyer (fig. 2). The amount of space in the present Museum dedicated to galleries is less than thirty percent. The expansion is to address this deficiency. But people come to the Museum for many different reasons, and always have. They come to look at art and to conduct research; they also come to read about art. A good number of people, five hundred approximately, come to work. The Museum is also a social space. Many different kinds of social transactions occur within these walls. Yet it is also a place that is nonsocial: a place to be alone.

I urge you to consider that heterotopic is not the same as multifunctional, a term which has distinctly historic roots. "Multifunctional" refers to the obvious fact that a restaurant is not the same as a gallery. "Heterotopic" refers more meaningfully to the coexistence in one building of distinct kinds of spaces, characterized by subjective differences rather than utilitarian categories. Despite the neologism, a model of heterotopia can indeed be found in our status quo. A number of entirely different environments currently do exist within the Museum—galleries, traditionally styled for paintings; the garden, for sculpture; and theaters for film and video. If the galleries have been referred to as a white box, certainly the theaters are equal and opposite in their being a black box. Furthermore, the number of artists producing installation art also portends a new and more complex kind of heterotopia— multiple-art environments, each distinct in their own way, within other, larger art environments. Yet a new museum should recognize this diversity of experience in more profound ways, within the galleries and beyond as well. Ironically, the original Museum of 1939, designed by Goodwin and Stone, despite its small size,

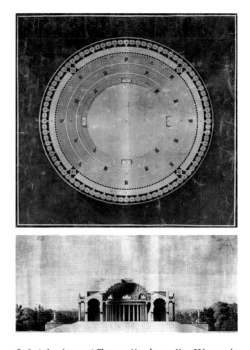

2. Antoine-Laurent-Thomas Vaudoyer. *Une Ménagerie d'un Souverain*. 1783. Ampitheater plan: India ink and wash, 36⅗ x 36⅗" (93.5 x 93.5 cm). Pantheon section: India ink with gray and pink wash enhanced by green watercolor, 17⁷/₁₀ x 36⅗" (45 x 93 cm). École Nationale Supérieure des Beaux-Arts, Paris

3. John McAndrew and Alfred H. Barr, Jr. The Museum of Modern Art, New York: Sculpture Garden. View to southeast. 1939

achieved this in ways that are no longer evident. Consider the garden of 1939 (fig. 3), with that incredible little chain-link woven-wood fence between it and Fifty-fourth Street. The Members' Lounge was also a unique kind of space (fig. 4). The library was an open, flowing space (fig. 5), and none of the galleries, although minimal in many aspects, could be described simply as a white box.

      The second point I would like to address tonight might be called "Heterotopia, Part II." There are various strategies which we might take to realize this vision of a

Below, left to right:
4. Philip Goodwin and Edward Durell Stone. The Museum of Modern Art, New York: Members' Lounge. 1939

5. Philip Goodwin and Edward Durell Stone. The Museum of Modern Art, New York: Library. 1939

place of many places, one of which would be to say that we want an entirely new series of spaces that will achieve this diversity of experience through an *ex-novo* architecture. A clip from a film on Le Corbusier illustrates the ramifications of this approach in the Marais in Paris (fig. 6). (The Marais, of course, includes the Plâce des Vosges, the Hôtel Sully, and other interesting monuments.) The text immediately preceding the clip reads, "Le Corbusier proposes to pierce Paris from west to east and to demolish the old quarters which occupy the center of the city."[1] Le Corbusier then demonstrates his approach, first penning a rectangle to identify the Marais, and then quickly infilling its perimeter to make it disappear. As brutal as this might seem, in thoroughly evaluating our institution the possibility of an entirely new Museum was considered. In fact, Philip Johnson, who has more to lose than any other architect, was one of the people most open to exploring the option of, not demolishing the Museum, but simply picking up and finding a new, unfettered site. As radical as this seems, if one is claiming to thoroughly investigate oneself, this is an option. A different strategy, in my mind equally radical, is a complete historical restoration and preservation of the existing buildings, whereby the new site, the Dorset, would become an appendage or wing to what would become the historic structures—the Goodwin–Stone building of 1939; Philip Johnson's East and North Wings; the sculpture garden, also by Johnson; and the Pelli extension and tower. However, both of these approaches, I feel, represent a distinct discomfort with history, a discomfort that, despite Le Corbusier's ancestry, has a very American flavor.

6. Still from *L'Architecture d'aujourd'hui*. 1931. Pierre Chenal, director. Le Corbusier (Charles-Édouard Jeanneret) outlining the Plan Voisin, Paris. Photograph © Fondation Le Corbusier

We have a unique tendency to try and form new societies. In describing the people who join such new societies—for example, Sun City in the Southwest, a community entirely comprised of people over sixty—Frances Fitzgerald has written that "they live in a town without any history on the edge of a social frontier, inventing a world for themselves."[2] I quote Fitzgerald cautiously, given how much we talk about reinventing the Museum these days; however, I feel her point is that of a historian, and her objections have to do with attempts to, in effect, cheat history rather than with the idea of reinvention per se. In this sense, I agree with her. Both tabula rasa demolition and blind preservation are different forms of the same institutional amnesia. The one scrapes away the past, cutting it off from the present, and the other embalms the past, making it remote and inaccessible to the present in any meaningful way. The challenge of designing a new environment without shucking off our history and traditions is much more difficult than either of these two approaches. Rather than relying on the extremes, we must theorize what is now the status quo, and make some kind of sense of the programmatic and physical diversity that now exists.

One way of illustrating this notion (and I want to say I think there are many) is to consult Carlo Scarpa's Museo di Castelvecchio in Verona as a model (figs. 7–10), wherein he alternately refurbished certain aspects of the medieval structure, bull-dozed others, and throughout the entire project threaded new material. (I should at this point repeat the caveat: These slides are not meant to suggest what I think the Museum should look like. . . .) The project manifests what I would consider to be a profound understanding of the idea of the past and the idea of the present, a profundity that goes beyond either the blank slate or the preserved artifact, a profundity beyond both the realm of the futurologist and that of the preservationist. In this instance, consider the fabric. In the foreground are the medieval foundations exposed by the removal of a baroque stair that had been added in the early seventeenth century, revealing a gap between two joints in the whole structure (fig. 7). Into the space created by removing the stair he projected a series of additions: a cantilevering concrete beam, on which rests a medieval sculpture; and a new roof covering the entire building. So in other words, it's almost impossible to separate what is the older fabric and what is the newer fabric. When you look at the galleries (fig. 8), it's almost impossible to think of them as either old or new structures. Similarly, in the patio garden (fig. 9) there is an equal mixture of the sort of found medieval portions of the Castelvecchio as well as a number of insertions and intrusions that confound the whole notion of old and new. Medieval columns support one of the openings, behind which there are steel spandrels in new openings, plus another steel spandrel to the far right supporting, again, a medieval piece of art (fig. 10). If I spoke before about a discomfort with history, we're speaking here about a profound comfort with the whole notion of history and the passage of time.

The third concept I would like to discuss is that of critical space. This is a term which has been used before by different people with, I admit, very different meanings. Here, I am using it to describe the qualities of the galleries as well as other spaces where art is exhibited. There are, of course, a variety of ways of framing this issue, such as the idea of neutral space—the white box—the issues of contemplative space, interactivity, intimacy, etcetera. Despite the importance of these issues, I think that a different kind of discussion can place them in a new context, which is precisely what I am trying to do here. Even as I might labor to do so, I realize that defining the term "critical space" requires a certain amount of subjective speculation. The concept hinges on relative scales, and on a perceived difference between other types of spaces, which I might call "monumental," a fairly recognized term, and on the other hand, for our purposes, "celebratory." Both terms, monumental and celebratory, suggest spaces that go beyond the merely functional. Yet, for me, in an institution

7–8. Carlo Scarpa, principal architect. Museo di Castelvecchio, Verona. 1956–64. Far left: Passage between the original castle wall and the museum wing, with a view of the *Cangrande* on a cantilevered concrete beam. Left: View of the galleries

Above:
9–10. Carlo Scarpa, principal architect. Museo di
Castelvecchio, Verona. 1956–64. Left: View of the central loggia. Photograph by Paolo Monti. Right: View of
the courtyard. Photograph by Antonio Martinelli

whose daily success depends on the ability of individuals to exercise critical judgment about an environment of objects and spaces that are themselves the product of
the institution's critical judgment, in such a contest the monumental becomes, for
lack of a better term, a spatial 800-pound gorilla. Monumental space is space where
skepticism is not allowed. Critical space, on the other hand—and here we're looking
at Marcel Duchamp's *L.H.O.O.Q.* (fig. 11)—is the kind of space that does just that:
It allows skepticism. It is a space where individuals feel free to exercise their own
judgment as to how they will participate within the Museum's context, how they will
approach and understand a work of art. This autonomy is particularly important in
a museum which features the art of the twentieth century. I imagine that you are trying as hard as I am to envision precisely what these spaces might look like. How does
a space look like a moustache on the Mona Lisa? I think in the end it requires an
architect's interpretation. However, I can offer a negative definition: The conveyor
belt that rolled past Michelangelo's Pietà at the 1963 World's Fair was not critical space.

If critical space addresses the need of the individual, what about the expression
of the common experience? I spoke earlier of celebratory space. Museums should
celebrate that increasingly rare event, the shared experience, in which great numbers
of strangers momentarily find themselves part of a common event. It also seems to
me that critical space can live alongside the celebratory, whereas it is difficult to
imagine the elision between the monumental and the critical. I can imagine architects responding very differently to this somewhat vague notion. To be a bit more
precise, consider two examples, both libraries. In the Bibliothèque Ste.-Geneviève in
Paris, by Henri Labrouste, the cast-iron vaults rise above a datum, below which is the
reading room and the stacks. The twin volumes of space unify and dignify the areas

where individual readers go about their tasks (figs. 12–13). Yet the aura remains one of unstructured activity. In essence, the critical space of the individual is layered over by the more celebratory. And then, when focusing slightly more downward, one sees a different world, one of individual activity, etcetera. It is this sort of autonomy that I was speaking of. In Louis Kahn's Exeter Library, the celebratory space, a central atrium, gives way in a lateral rather than a vertical direction (figs. 14, 15) whereas the Bibliothèque Ste.-Geneviève layers the two, one on top of the other, vertically. In this instance, I would say that what I am calling the critical spaces move away from the center, creating these spaces of more autonomous activities, spaces in which an individual can choose to participate or not, to be part of a group or not, spaces in which one is free to be skeptical. Whereas in the center of the building there is a focus on the group, on the common effort, as you move away from the center there are spaces at the actual perimeter of the building that are, indeed, intimate (fig. 16). Yes, we talk a lot about intimacy, we talk a lot about a certain kind of scale, but I don't think it's only an issue of scale; it's about opportunity within the building. In this case, as you move away from the center you find spaces where the individual can actually ignore the center and look out the window. The fact that these two examples are both libraries is notable. There are, however, essential differences between a library and a museum: The latter has demonstrated an ability to absorb various aspects of other building types—palaces, exhibition halls, the bourgeois apartment (in the case of the early Modern), the temple, etcetera. I don't, in fact, believe a museum should be a library or that a museum should look like a library, but if a large building aspires to any feeling of intimacy it has to first give the visitor the sense that they are participants in the creation of their own intellectual and social experience.

11. Marcel Duchamp. *L.H.O.O.Q.* (replica). From *La Boîte en valise*, 1941. Collotype handcolored with watercolor, 7⅗ x 4⅘" (19.3 x 12.2 cm). The Philadelphia Museum of Art. The Louise and Walter Arensberg Collection

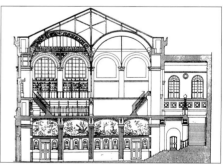

12–13. Pierre-François-Henri Labrouste. Bibliothèque Ste.-Geneviève, Paris. 1842–50. Above: Cross-section. Left: View of the reading room

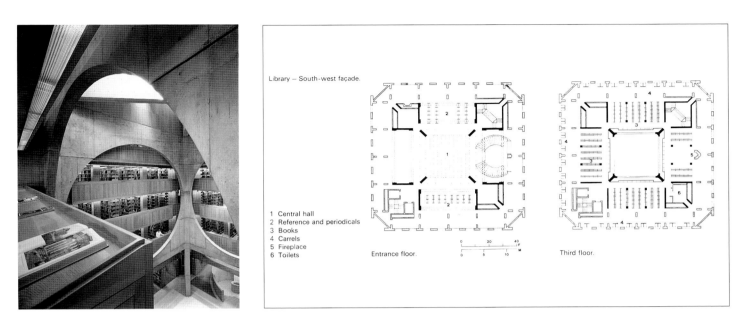

Library — South-west façade.

1 Central hall
2 Reference and periodicals
3 Books
4 Carrels
5 Fireplace
6 Toilets

Entrance floor.

Third floor.

A fourth concept to be considered is that of interiority. Referring to the many regulatory codes and ordinances, as well as the lack of vantage points from which to view a building amidst the city's density, I have heard it expressed that you cannot really have architecture in Manhattan; you can only have interiors. I would take exception to several aspects of this formula, particularly the relationship that it implies between a building's exterior and interior. True, some great architecture can be characterized as all form and no space. Consider the exterior form of the pyramids at Giza (fig. 17) and the exclusive space of the interior (fig. 18). The greatness of other architectural examples lies equally in outward and inner space. For instance, in the Hagia Sophia in Istanbul, the one (fig. 19) is virtually the inverse of the other (fig. 20): An isometric section shows that its interior space is literally a volume that inflates the balloon of the dome. In other instances, the emphasis is decidedly on the interior. Consider Michelangelo's Medici chapel (fig. 21) or the Laurentian Library (fig. 22). The architectural focus is so concentrated on the interiors that, when I first thought to include images of them, I realized that I did not really know their exteriors. The issue of interiority has, however, a more heightened meaning in the twentieth century, due in no small part to Dr. Freud—a heightened meaning that I feel works to the advantage of buildings such as museums. (An illustration of Magritte's *Vulture's Park* registers the impact of interiority in twentieth-century art; see fig. 23.) Octavio Paz, in defining the difference between the works of Picasso and those of Duchamp, described the former as being characterized by a "vertigo of acceleration" and the latter by a "vertigo of delay."[3] If I were to borrow Paz's duality, I might say that Borromini's S. Ivo in Rome expresses an architectural vertigo of acceleration (figs. 24–25). Throughout its entire composition, from the courtyard, through the façade, into the interior, to the pinnacle of the dome, there is the classical expression of seamless continuity, culminating in one precise point. In opposition, I might propose another courtyard project, Pierre Chareau and Bernard Bijovet's Maison de Verre. Both the Roman church and the Parisian house are viewed from an inner courtyard inaccessible,

14–16. Louis I. Kahn. Phillips Exeter Academy Library, Exeter, New Hampshire. 1967–72. Top, left: View of the central hall and stacks. Photograph by Steve Rosenthal. Top, right: Plan of the entrance and third floors. Courtesy Louis I. Kahn Archive, University of Pennsylvania, Philadelphia. Above: Reading area on the periphery. Photograph by John Ebstel

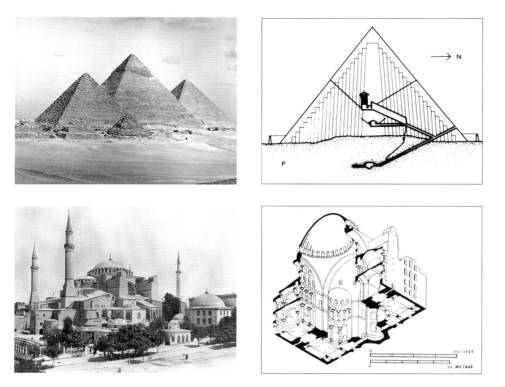

17–18. Pyramids of Khufu, Khafre, and Menkaure, Giza, Egypt. Fourth Dynasty, c. 2589–2530 B.C. Far left: View to the north. Photograph by Max Hirmer. Left: Section showing Ludwig Borchardt's conjectural internal buttress walls

19–20. Anthemius of Tralles and Isodorus of Miletus. Hagia Sophia, Istanbul. 532–537. Far left: View to the north. Left: Isometric view

or not evident, from the street, so there is a space that precedes your experience of seeing the façade (fig. 26). In the Maison de Verre, however, rather than there being a kind of continuity, a vertigo of acceleration, if you will (the movement toward a single point of resolution), there is a translucent glass façade—a filtering device—that forms a membrane (fig. 27) between the inner and outer worlds. The façade is, I think, very close to what Duchamp was talking about when he said that his works

21. Michelangelo Buonarroti. New Sacristy, Church of San Lorenzo, Florence. Sepulchral monument for Guiliano de' Medici. 1519–34

22. Michelangelo Buonarroti. Laurentian Library, Florence. View of the vestibule staircase. 1519–59

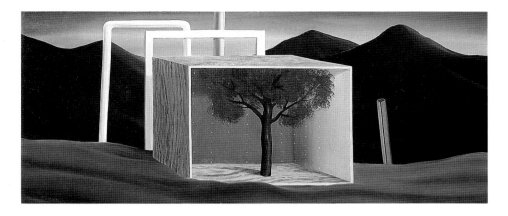

23. René Magritte. *Le Parc du vautour (The Vulture's Park)*. 1926. Oil on canvas, 25⅗ x 59" (65 x 150 cm). Private collection

weren't paintings—"Use *delay* instead of 'picture' or 'painting'," he said of the *Large Glass*. "'Picture on glass' becomes 'delay in glass.'"[4] As you can see, the world within is entirely a complete world. The light from without connects it to the real world, but this is not a world that is continuous with the outside world but a world defined from within. (If I were to offer a negative example, it might be Joseph Maria Olbrich's Sezession Exhibition building, where indeed, there is a transformation from the interior to the exterior, but the interior almost assumes a kind of sacral or ritualistic aspect, none of which you notice in the Maison de Verre.) In the 1930s, Paul Nelson designed a house called the Maison Suspendu (fig. 28)—the Suspended House—which consisted of an exterior volume, a lattice of steel and glass, in which were suspended various

Below:
24–25. Francesco Borromini. S. Ivo alla Sapienza, Rome. 1641–60. Left: Courtyard elevation. Right: Interior view of the dome

Above:
26–27. Pierre Chareau and Bernard Bijovet. Maison de
Verre, Paris. 1928–32. Left: View of the façade from
the interior court. Right: View of the living room

rooms connected by a spiraling ramp. (I should repeat the caveat that these images are
not meant to indicate what the Museum should look like; I suppose it's foregone that
we will not have spiraling ramps throughout the building.) Of the Maison Suspendu,
Nelson said that "suspension in space heightens the sense of isolation from the world."[5]
While Nelson's project implied literal and physical suspension, I feel the term "suspension" is similar in meaning to Duchamp's "delay," and might be said to characterize an
interior experience which involves a transformation, both architecturally and personally. Frank Lloyd Wright's Johnson Wax building (fig. 29), interestingly, roughly contemporary with the Maison de Verre and the Maison Suspendu, perhaps best
describes this phenomenon. There is little in the exterior of the building to prepare
you for the transformation that takes place between the blank outer walls and the
world within, a world which Philip Johnson likened to being underwater—a "sub-
aqueous" space, in his words[6] (fig. 30).

       The Museum, at least its garden, is often referred to as an oasis of peace within
Midtown's hustle-bustle. However, to be truly successful, the Museum's interior
architecture must not only represent a cessation of the random events of the city but
have a life of its own, encouraging a personal, if momentary transformation of the
individual's awareness and receptivity. I began this evening with a neologism, so
there is a certain symmetry to ending with an arcane Latin phrase, which, I realized
when I was writing this, I have not had a single opportunity to use in the two decades
since I studied logic. It's a phrase which I hope will illustrate the often-contradictory
relationship between architectural form and urban culture, particularly Manhattan's
urban culture. *Lucus a non lucendo* might be translated as "a grove from shining not,"
and recalls the fact that the Latin word *lucus,* or "grove" is derived not, as might be
logical, from the Latin word for "shade" (*umbra*) or some similar word, but paradoxically, is derived from the word for "shine" (*lucere*). In other words, it is the place
where it is shining *not.* The phrase describes the illogic that a word with a specific

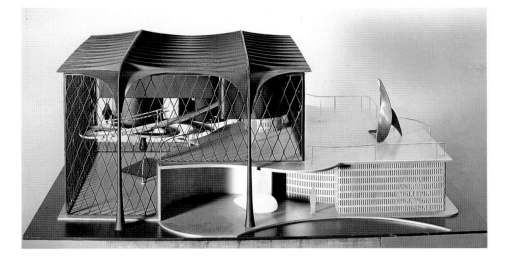

28. Paul Nelson. Project: Maison Suspendu. Model.
1938. Mixed mediums, 28½ x 36½ x 13½" (72.4 x 92.7
x 34.3 cm). The Museum of Modern Art, New York.
Gift of the Advisory Committee. Photograph by Herbert Matter

meaning might have imbedded within it the opposite meaning. Such a logic or illogic can be applied to the visual analysis of built form. Close your eyes and imagine an aerial view of a suburban landscape—winding roads with names like Forest Glen; cul-de-sacs; dozens of houses in Spanish, Colonial, French, Norman, Georgian, or whatever style—picturesquely sited amidst a varied landscape agog with freeform aqua-blue swimming pools running adjacent to a four-lane highway with a Wal-Mart. A superficial interpretation of the forms that I just described might suggest an unstructured society, a society dedicated to individual expression, more-or-less a genteel anarchy. Yet we know that this is not the case necessarily, that places like this are often characterized by extreme social conformity. A similar analysis might indicate that the endlessly repetitive pattern of uniform blocks separated by equally uniform roadways with such romantic names as Twenty-eighth, Thirty-sixth, and Fifty-third streets (figs. 31–32), and populated by endless reformulations of a very few basic building types, would be the creation of an obsessively conformist society. This is the paradox of many dense urban cultures, particularly Manhattan.

Below:
29–30. Frank Lloyd Wright. Johnson Wax Company
Administration Building, Racine, Wisconsin.
1936–39. Left: Exterior view. Right: View of the
Great Workroom

Imbedded in a restrictive formal language is the potential for the opposite, a near-infinite expressiveness as might be seen in this series of ink drawings by Agnes Martin, all uniformly 9 inches square (figs. 33–35). I believe the best architect for the new Museum of Modern Art is one who understands this paradox, one who sees the Midtown Manhattan landscape as one of inherent possibilities rather than defeating limitations, one who sees the glass as half-full rather than half-empty. Many of my favorite buildings in this city are thus conceived; even so, I concede that Manhattan may be an acquired taste. The Ford Foundation, the Columbia University campus, the Flatiron Building (fig. 36), the "Twin Towers" of the World Trade Center, the buildings along Central Park, or the Seagram Building (fig. 37) would not be nearly as interesting, I admit, along a strip mall or in a gated community. Yet within the confines of the Manhattan grid they achieve great critical distinction. I'll close with an illustration of Karl Friedrich Schinkel's design for the Altes Museum in Berlin (fig. 38). At the right is a view down the Unter der Linden. The museum is rather meekly presented on the left, its colonnade echoing the ordinance of the street façades to the right. What impresses me most about this image is Schinkel's attitude

Above:
31–32. Left: Aerial view of Midtown Manhattan, 1940. Right: Aerial view of Manhattan looking east from the Hudson River, March 30, 1978. Photograph by William Fried

Below, left to right:
33. Agnes Martin. *Untitled # 1.* 1990. Ink on paper, 9 x 9" (22.9 x 22.9 cm). Collection PaceWildenstein, New York

34. Agnes Martin. *Untitled # 3.* 1990. Ink on paper, 9 x 9" (22.9 x 22.9 cm). Collection PaceWildenstein, New York

35. Agnes Martin. *Untitled.* Late 1970s. Ink and ink wash on paper, 9 x 9" (22.9 x 22.9 cm). Collection Philip and Frances Huscher, Chicago

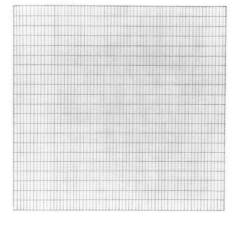

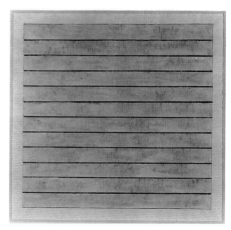

towards his own work as part of the urban scene, an attitude which, quite frankly, I feel borders on the nonchalant. For me, this image serves not so much to speak about context—a much-overused word these days—but the nature of urban culture. Not only does architecture build the city but, in the best cases, great cities build the architecture.

GLENN D. LOWRY: Let me ask Mary Lea Bandy and then John Elderfield to first respond to some of the observations Terry has made, and then to lead into issues about the Museum that are of particular concern to them.

MARY LEA BANDY: First of all, I think that the space we are now in, the Titus 1 theater, is certainly about as *interior* a space as you can find in the Museum. I've given a great deal of thought to it because it is really one of the triumphs of the 1939 construction of the Museum. Few, if any, museums of the visual arts throughout the world have a theater dedicated to the presentation of film; this is certainly a space, if we're looking into our collective memory, our Museum memory, that we're very anxious to retain. However, as I sit here in lectures and during certain films, I wonder if there's any value in retaining the rumble of the subway as it goes through; we hear it throughout our theater. Just as an aside, this theater has been a space in which many filmmakers have been inspired—filmmakers such as Charles Laughton, who studied German Expressionist films here when he was preparing *Night of the Hunter*. But François Truffaut, when he introduced his screening of *The Last Metro* at the New York Film Festival in 1980, said that he had actually thought about making a film on the subject of the subway when he was sitting in the back of this theater watching Buster Keaton in *The General*. As he watched Keaton put his ear to the railroad track to hear if the Union army was coming, a subway train apparently went by on the track that runs adjacent to the Titus theater. (This may be an apocryphal story.)

Far left:
36. Daniel H. Burnham. Flatiron Building, New York. 1902

Left:
37. Ludwig Mies van der Rohe and Philip Johnson. Seagram Building, New York. 1954–58

38. Karl Friedrich Schinkel, delineater, and Johann Friedrich Jügel, etcher. *Palace Bridge with the Altes Museum, Dome, and Palace*. 1823–33. Aquatint on paper, plate: 20¹⁵⁄₁₆ x 37⅘" (53 x 96 cm). Stadtmuseum Berlin

In general, museums do not conceive of film as one of the traditional visual arts in the sense that Alfred Barr did. Alfred specified that he wanted this Museum to deal with objects that were made as multiples—films, prints, illustrated books. Only two other museums in the United States have taken up his notion of film as something that should be collected and exhibited as art—the George Eastman House in Rochester and the Berkeley Art Museum. It is part of the integration and discontinuity that Terry and I have talked about: How do you provide both a celebratory space and a critical space for this wonderful medium? This theater, the Titus 2 theater, and a variety of spaces that we're studying will provide the celebratory space. We are looking backward very strongly to keep a traditional approach, to retain film as the original experience on the screen. We are not going to present films in galleries, we are not going to present films as objects you pass by; we're going to retain them in the most traditional sense, because we feel that that's the way the works of art were conceived and must be shown.

Alfred Barr could not and did not conceive of an artistic medium that has become extremely important and ambitious in our time, and that is video. Television was being invented and becoming commercial in the late '20s at the time this Museum was formed, but artists did not begin to experiment with video until forty and fifty years later. One of the most interesting ways for us to plan the new Museum is to determine the ways in which we can provide critical space for study of this profoundly influential and interesting medium. We are looking at, for example, not only dealing with the invention of new technologies between now and the time we will open, but the possibilities of providing galleries that will enable us to present video installations, whether on a temporary or very long-term basis, experimental galleries in which we might make available selections from the video collection that an individual user might look at on demand. We very much want to incorporate video as a major component of the new Museum, and I think we will find that it will work in different departments and in different ways. Those are some of the more practical consequences, I think, of rethinking our spaces for film and video.

I just wanted, Terry, to respond to your notion of the urban museum and the courtyard, which has nothing to do with film and video but I think it's a terribly interesting notion. This Museum is not on a river or a plaza or a park. It's a museum that is now totally surrounded by skyscrapers, by an urban fabric, that includes Rockefeller Center. I think that the great challenge to the architect, of course, is to architecturally respond to this very dense urban fabric, which has changed since this building opened in 1939—an enormously complex situation for design today. On that point, I turn to John to comment, perhaps, on the notions of lighting in our Museum.

JOHN ELDERFIELD: I should begin by saying that my profound disappointment upon learning that the Museum will not look like a wonderful, big pyramid on Fifty-third Street was assuaged by the emphasis throughout Terry's talk on uses. I think that it is critically important, in preparing for whatever expansion we will achieve, to start from a consideration of how the Museum is used. This has many ramifications, one of which, I think, is provided by history. . . . When the Museum was founded in 1929, it was under the charter of an educational institution, and Terry quite rightly points out that part of the function of this institution is that of a library. I believe that in the next century a part, not by any means the whole, but a part of the function of the Museum will be as a research and resource center for the study of twentieth-century art and twentieth-century culture, including the Museum itself, which has obviously contributed a great deal to providing the actual identity of what modern art is.

I think the issue of uses is a broader one, even, than this. As museums have become successful, many of the practices that they inherited have become extremely cumbersome, and we see how many museums, and to some extent this Museum, have become victims of their own success. A very important part of our function is to provide comfortable access to original works of art. The more successful the institution, the more difficult, potentially, it is to provide that kind of access.

Clearly, nobody wants to adopt the conveyor-belt method that Terry referred to. But we need to rethink the kind of programs that we are doing, and should do so before we think "architecture"; in this sense, we must do a needs analysis before doing an architectural analysis.

We pride ourselves on having the greatest synthetic collection of modern art anywhere, and in addition to doing the kind of loan exhibitions that we do, I do think that we have a responsibility to both research . . . and make available our collections in a broader way than we've done hitherto. I think this applies most obviously to our contemporary works, which we are able to show too little, but it also applies to our historical works. As we speak, we have an exhibition of some 120 of our works by Matisse in Atlanta.[7] That number of our own Matisse works has not been shown in New York since 1978, and I think that we need to think in terms of flexibility of uses of our spaces, so that the great collections that we have in depth—Matisse, Picasso, Dubuffet, Surrealism, Futurism, and the list goes on and on—can be at least regularly, if not frequently, made available to our audience in New York, and made available in a way which allows the kind of "delay" that Terry referred to. What we need to do is to find ways of allowing people to slow down in museums, allowing different kinds of experiences; in some cases we would call them contemplative, in other cases I think we might call them aggressive—in either case, experiences where viewers are able to confront works of art in a one-to-one way. Lighting is certainly part of this, and it's certainly among my hopes for a new Museum that we can introduce natural light in some form into some of the galleries, despite the difficulties of the site—in any event, to reconsider the way in which works of art are presented and then gradually move from these sorts of considerations to a consideration of the increasingly distant envelopes from these works, which ultimately leads to a consideration of the whole building.

GLENN D. LOWRY: Terry, I wonder if you would consider elaborating upon a couple of points that you touched upon in your lecture and that also grow out of Mary Lea's and John's comments. The first has to do with the notion of the white box, or its opposite, the black box; that is, what has come to be seen, certainly in some circles, as the need in galleries for—and here I use quotation marks—"neutral spaces," and its implications in terms of the actual experience of looking at art. And as a kind of corollary to that, could you discuss the notion of intimacy and what structures intimacy—that is, what are the experiential components that intimacy demands. I think it is one of the issues that is of great importance for this Museum, as we have come to be appreciated as an institution that has created and sustained an intimate relationship between those who look at art, and the objects themselves.

TERENCE RILEY: Actually, discussions have been going on for decades now about the idea of a "white box," a purportedly completely neutral space. They have to be inflected, because, on the one hand, there is an ideological aspect to the white box, which, indeed, as the environment gets less and less formal—as it gets to the point where it has no characteristics whatsoever—the formal characteristics of the work of art are heightened or underlined, perhaps in ways that allow a specific work of art to be experienced as never before. But the artist's studio isn't a white box, the collector's house isn't a white box, etcetera. We must also realize that the converted industrial space is not a neutral space either; it has its own characteristics and inflections that are not neutral.

What I find interesting and that I think is probably important for a museum to think about, vis-à-vis the *black* box, is that part of the evolution of the white box was not just ideological; part of it was purely pragmatic. Despite the fact that this Museum has expanded almost every ten or twenty years since the day it was founded, the institution has never been as big as its program. This institution, if you compare it in terms of square footage to its peer institutions around the world, is minute. The way that the Museum has always achieved its program is by reprogramming the galleries—that is, by having very little that was ever permanent, and by continuously rotating material, taking down the permanent collection, tearing down walls, building new walls, putting up new art, taking that down—a kind of "dumpster architecture." Quite frankly, if the art weren't so fabulous and wonderful, nobody would ever want to come into this building.

A black box—this room—achieves its distinction, not because it has a permanent showing of one film, but because it is, like the white box, endlessly reprogrammable. I think this was evident very early in the Museum's history. In the late '50s, Philip Johnson designed a multistory addition to the Museum at the eastern edge of the garden, and when discussing it amongst his peers he actually apologized, saying, "There's no architecture to it."[8] He made the explicit equation that flexibility means no architecture, and that's a purely economic equation. If you're going to tear down the architecture continuously to reprogram the space, of course the architecture can't have much distinction. The point is, I think there's a difference between the "dumpster architecture" white box, and a kind of a space that upholds the contract that I feel The Museum of Modern Art has with the artists it represents, which is that we will show their works of art to their best advantage. While these works will always be seen in a context that a curator defines, to the extent that it is possible, there will be the moment where that work of art can be seen as the artist invented it. I think that's something we want to continue. There's a second part to your question?

GLENN D. LOWRY: What structures the experience of intimacy?

TERENCE RILEY: Intimacy is a big word here, and its meaning depends, I suppose, on the point at which you became familiar with the institution. Certain people can remember the Museum at a certain point. I think when those people speak of intimacy, they are referring to a culture that grew up around this institution that was more personable, where people knew each other more. There certainly weren't escalators and those sorts of things. But obviously, as John Elderfield noted in one of our many discussions about intimacy, being in a small room with two dozen people all trying to see the same painting isn't necessarily intimate. Making small spaces isn't necessarily going to guarantee intimacy.

I started to try to theorize the word, if you will. When we talk about intimacy, we talk about being touched, about being moved—"It was a touching experience"—and I think what that refers to is the occasion where an experience impresses upon someone the fact of that experience; that is being touched. I think that you would all be challenged to try to describe a space where one is being touched. What would that physically look like? What would that feel like? But I do think that this is the goal that needs to be striven for. I think we have to come up with a Museum where moving through it is not akin to being on a moving sidewalk, a conveyor belt, past works of art. Who could be touched by that experience? They actually do it in the Tower of London. You're just there in the dark, moving past the crown jewels, and you're out before you know it—and there's the souvenir stand.

GLENN D. LOWRY: What I'd like to do now is, having heard a little bit from some of us and a considerable amount from Terry, open the floor to you to respond to your questions, thoughts, comments, observations.

AUDIENCE MEMBER 1: By a "white box," do you mean the space of the artist's studio, or the artist's intention—the way the artist conceived the work, to be displayed as it was displayed in the studio?

TERENCE RILEY: No. The white box is frequently bandied about as an absolute ideal. The odd thing is that, until a work of art arrives in the museum, into the white box, it's never been seen in that context before. It was never created in that context, it was never displayed, if it was owned by an individual, in that context. So I was actually saying the opposite: The artist's studio is indeed usually a different environment from the museum environment.

AUDIENCE MEMBER 2: You mentioned "black box" and "neutral box." I wonder if you could go into what that actually means a little bit more. The movie theater, is that a black box, because it's dark? Is that what a black box is?

TERENCE RILEY: Yes, in a certain sense.

AUDIENCE MEMBER 2: How can an art gallery be a black box?

TERENCE RILEY: We consider films to be works of art, so this, the theater we're now in, is an art gallery. This is one of our types of art galleries.

AUDIENCE MEMBER 2: But you wouldn't have a black box for paintings.

TERENCE RILEY: No, but that's the point. If you think that art comes in different varieties other than paintings, you can't say that the whole experience of the Museum is a gallery. That's been a premise of this institution from day one. The garden is not just a garden, it's a sculpture garden, and it was imagined as an environment to put sculpture in. The white box, the neutral box, was perceived as the most ideal space, in an ideological sense, to put a painting, where there's no distraction, and this space was considered the most ideal form for another art form that we show, which is video. So the point that I was trying to make is that any museum in the future is going to have, necessarily, many types of spaces to show art. Art is changing—that's not a headline—and if the original spaces in the Museum reflected both the kind of small-scale intimacy of the bourgeois apartment and to a certain extent the artist's studio, a lot of the works of art that we collect today were never designed to be in anyone's apartment or in their house. I think that obviously means there will be different kinds of spaces in the future for showing art.

On top of that, some artworks aren't just artworks, they're spaces of their own. We have works that are not objects, they are spaces, they are experiences. Imagine that, just as a concept, a gallery isn't an art environment but a gallery is a *mega* art environment in which completely different art environments exist. What's interesting to me about this concept is that it suggests that the whole notion of *a* building by *one* architect, or one giver of a formed spatial experience, is eroding. Even if we have one architect redesign the whole thing, we actually have five architects: we have Goodwin, Stone, Philip Johnson, Pelli, and then on top of that we have all these artists who don't really want to participate in that space, they want to create their own space. I think that's great. I look forward to the time where we could imagine a building that embraces those things.

MARY LEA BANDY: Terry, could I say one thing? I don't really like to think of this theater as a black box, but I'll deal with that at another time. I don't know if any of you have been to the Gulbenkian Foundation in Lisbon, but they have a film theater that's quite remarkable. It's long and not terribly wide, and one wall of it is solid glass, floor to ceiling, the whole side wall, and it opens onto the gardens. The Gulbenkian is a series of pavilions; you go in and look at the art in a pavilion, then you go out in the garden and you go to another pavilion. And this is one of the most creative "black boxes" I've ever seen, because you can have a relationship with the sculpture garden, can be opened up, it can be part of, it can have that courtyard experience the theater. I like to think that we're going to play around, as Glenn knows, with the many different theaters I'm hoping we'll have in the new Museum. One of them may be as imaginative as that.

AUDIENCE MEMBER 3: Is the concept of the Museum as it now exists a tabula rasa? Is demolition being considered?

GLENN D. LOWRY: I think it's not so much that the concept is a tabula rasa, but that we are in the process of studying what the various options are. One of the things that I've learned in my short time in New York is that building in New York City is not quite like building anywhere else in the world. So part of the needs analysis that John Elderfield was referring to has been to try and quantify what it is we want to achieve and what kinds of spaces—how many of them, their relationships to each other—are going to be required. Unpacking some of these ideas and seeing how they actually work out spatially has made it very clear to us that we're going to have to spend a good deal of time studying the site and understanding what the implications are of converting the Dorset, keeping it as it exactly is, demolishing it, playing around with internal arrangements within it. From my point of view, flexibility, at this point, is vital because we have to deal with both the complexities of New York City zoning regulations and the need to fit our jigsaw puzzle into the spaces we have. So I think the most important element here is that this is just a process that we've begun to look at intensively, and we're a long way from knowing what action we're going to take.

AUDIENCE MEMBER 3: Did John Elderfield suggest earlier that the Museum owns too much art and intends to show some of it elsewhere in New York?

JOHN ELDERFIELD: I wasn't, in fact, intending to suggest moving art in the collection to other areas of the city, but rather to suggest that, as part of our planning for the building, we have to think about options other than the one that we have about how we show our collections. We may end up deciding that the way we presently show them is the way we want to continue to show them, but there are large numbers of works which we can't show, and I think that, even if we can double our space, there will still be a significant number of things that we can't show. So it raises the question: Should we have a certain specified number of works which are more or less always on view, or should we rather have a smaller number of works which are always on view and other groups of works circulating? The possibility of making works of art available to other areas of the city, or to other cities, is, I think, something that we have talked about and continue to talk about. In its early days, the Museum had a very active national circulating program, and if there are important things or less important things that we can't show here, I think that we have a responsibility to find some way of making them available. The point about a white box is not the fact that it's neutral, because obviously no space is neutral, but that one of its ideological foundations was the idea of constancy, that one provides a constant environment for works of art. I think that what you've been hearing tonight is that there is a strong feeling that, in fact, what we should be providing are different kinds of spaces for different kinds of experiences. I think part of this is something which is owing to broad cultural changes, but I think also, and more particularly, to change within the reception of twentieth-century art. I think that, in many respects, some of the battles have been won—not all of them, but some of them. I think we can allow ourselves more varied ways of approaching the works in our collection. I'm not saying that we should abandon ourselves to an absolute relativism, but I do think that it's possible to have different stories being told, both at the same time and at different times, and some of the stories will be of interest to a few people and some of the stories will be of interest to a large number of people, and that the kind of programs that we offer should be responsive to small numbers of people as well as large numbers of people.

TERENCE RILEY: There's one idea that's always appealed to me about this project, and maybe not even just about this project but about museums in general or spaces in general. As someone who looks at a lot of architecture, what I really admire is when somebody comes up with an incredibly beautifully worked-out system of spaces that tells a whole story and is adaptable to many different circumstances. The other thing that I really admire is someone who makes exceptions. It's sort of an opposite feeling. Once you get used to the notion of the kind of systematized thing, the exception turns out to be the thing that makes you most interested. In our building, the space where the Monet *Water Lilies* is becomes an exceptional space. It's got a huge glass window— one whole wall is glass onto the garden—and its exceptional quality makes it extraordinarily special, and I'd like to think it might even be possible to build in to a new building exceptional experiences, carefully calibrated. Why couldn't certain works of art enjoy a certain kind of environment that was indeed that exceptional?

GLENN D. LOWRY: May we have last words from John Elderfield, Mary Lea Bandy, and Terry Riley?

JOHN ELDERFIELD: One thing we're certainly talking about is the audience of the institution. Should we be operating on the assumption that a museum that gets bigger and bigger and bigger should be aggressively trying to increase its audience all the time or, is there, in effect, a sort of normative audience which is appropriate for a particular kind of space? We've had recent "touching" experiences where, say, with *Picasso and Portraiture,* everybody was crammed in, but you could walk in other galleries of the Museum that were not crowded at all. It seems to me at the moment we can have about five thousand people in this building, and if they're dispersed you can have very good relations with the work of art, but if three thousand of them are pushed into a very small gallery this isn't going to work. I think one of the things is to make clear the extent of what we will program at any particular time. Another thing is probably as much curatorial as architectural, although it has an architectural component, which is that I think we have to provide more space for doing presentations of the same number of works that we now are showing, so that an exhibition of a hundred works probably needs twice the amount of space that we're devoting to it now, simply to allow more space for people. We've seen exhibitions where in fact it's impossible to see over people's shoulders to see pictures, and I think this is something that we have to pay attention to, both architecturally and also through curatorial responsibility, so that if we have larger spaces it doesn't mean we put twice as many pictures on the walls.

MARY LEA BANDY: If I may say one quick thing about the history of the cinema. The cinema was invented in many different countries simultaneously in the 1890s, but the French claimed credit for the invention of the medium because film was considered to begin when it is seen in a theater with a group of people, when it is shown publicly to a crowd, many of whom of course touch each other during the experience. But the film in this country evolved from the individual experience of someone looking into a nickelodeon box and seeing the film individually—and of course that type of film continues to be shown in pornographic theaters—to the major experience of big theaters as epitomized by Radio City Music Hall at Rockefeller Center, which is considered perhaps the greatest film theater built in this country. So of course we are very committed to making sure that there will be a variety of experiences where people can see film as a shared experience, championing that precisely because we feel that the individual experience of looking at a film on your VCR, while it is very important and part of our daily lives, is not the real experience. We are contemplating how to do this in the best way possible, recognizing, of course, that individual access to the works is essential for study and research. It's a very big problem for us, and an interesting one.

TERENCE RILEY: Anybody who cares about museums is frequently worried that the hoopla diminishes the experience of everybody involved. I actually think that when you think about the future in this regard it's actually brighter than it has been. At the Pocantico conference that we spoke of with artists and architects and critics, Bill Viola, the video artist, gave a very interesting rendition of a model of growth in a kind of cyberworld. (Believe it or not, this is the first of these events we've had for a year where nobody's talked about new technology.) I'm not talking about videos in the gallery or cyber-technology in the gallery in this instance. What Bill Viola was talking about was what in the modern world, in the twentieth century, were mass movements, and the way that one perceived of growth in the twentieth century was through those kinds of movements, with loudspeakers and banners—you get the whole thing moving. That's the kind of hoopla that I think everyone's afraid of. But he talked about the impact of the World Wide Web, the Internet: how you no longer could talk about mass movements per se. I'm probably misquoting him, but he said that the Internet becomes a sort of connection of desires; in other words, that people who want the same thing can find it more naturally than they ever could before, and that the whole means of disseminating information and building a community— and again, not talking about museums on the Web, but how the museum finds its audience—could actually be so much easier and so much more interesting than it was in the past. I don't think—and I'm repeating what other people have said from the very beginning, principally Glenn, about what drives this expansion—this is not based on the notion of getting more people into the building; it's based on improving the experience that people have when they're here. There is a major distinction in different types of expansion. It's fundamentally to improve the experience. Beyond that, when I think of how the Museum could grow, I love the idea that, with technology, growth could become more benevolent than it has been in the past.

GLENN D. LOWRY: Let me just add that, if the Museum is an inherently heterotopic environment, it's also an inherently heterogeneous environment. There is no single audience for this Museum. There are many different audiences that come to the Museum with very different interests and concerns, and I think if it's going to be a successful museum it's going to be an institution that can create an environment that allows those different audiences to both feel comfortable and engage with each other—that is, to intersect with each other—in a stimulating way. Terry also highlighted what I think is an essential component of this, which is the way in which, to a very large degree, one can rationalize these two competing impulses, to promote the institution and have an ever-increasing audience, and the obvious recognition that looking at and thinking about works of art requires an environment of contemplation. I think that anyone knows that there's a curve. It's not like a movie theater, where each viewer will have the same experience of the film, whether there are 450 people in the theater or only one. When you look at works of art in a public gallery, it's one kind of experience if it's crowded and shoulder-to-shoulder, and another if you are relatively alone. But there is a reality: We are a museum, and museums are public institutions. They are about a public engagement with art, not a purely private engagement with art, and I think the challenge is balancing those competing needs but always recognizing that what creates the possibility of a museum of modern art is precisely its engagement with the public. With that, I'd like to thank John Elderfield, Mary Lea Bandy, and, above all, Terry Riley for this evening, and you for joining us.

Notes

1.   Intertitle, *L'Architecture d'aujourd'hui* (1931), directed by Pierre Chenal. Circulating Film and Video Library, The Museum of Modern Art, New York.

2.   Frances Fitzgerald, *Cities on a Hill: A Journey Through Contemporary American Cultures* (New York: Simon and Schuster, 1981; reprinted 1983, 1986), p. 232.

3.   Octavio Paz, *Marcel Duchamp: Appearance Stripped Bare,* translated by Rachel Phillips and Donald Gardner (New York: Viking Press, 1978), p. 2.

4.   Ibid.

5.   Paul Nelson, "New Use of Space Determines Design of Proposed House," *Architectural Record* 13/14 (December 1938), p. 39.

6.   Philip Johnson in conversation with the author.

7.   A reference to *Henri Matisse: Masterworks from The Museum of Modern Art, New York,* shown at the High Museum of Art, Atlanta, November 2, 1996– January 19, 1997.

8.   Philip Johnson Oral History, interview conducted by Sharon Zane, 1991; transcript, p. 137. The Museum of Modern Art Archives, New York: The Museum of Modern Art Oral History Project.

1. Aerial view of The Museum of Modern Art site, 1996

The Charette

Introduction
Terence Riley

In January 1997, the ten selected architects were invited to participate in the next phase of the Architect Selection Process, the Charette, a problem-solving design exercise in which the fundamental philosophical issues guiding the future expansion of The Museum of Modern Art would be explored through the lens of architecture and urbanism.

From February 17 to 19, 1997, the Charette participants met at the Museum to familiarize themselves with its urban, spatial, and physical characteristics, as well as to engage in a dialogue with the trustees, chief curators, and senior staff about the conceptual and programmatic nature of the new Museum. Existing zoning regulations were outlined by representatives of Cooper, Robertson and Partners, and detailed drawings and plans of the site were provided to each of the participants.

After that meeting, the Charette phase provided four and one-half weeks for the development and presentation of the architects' ideas. The participants were asked to consider the nature and range of options for planning the new Museum and to document their thinking in both written and graphic form. The essence of the design exercise was the exploration of basic urbanistic and conceptual strategies for the redevelopment of the entire Museum. As the Charette was not a formal design competition, the architects were not asked to develop, refine, and present a single, optimized scheme. Rather, the goal was to generate multiple responses to the site conditions and to the Museum's preliminary conceptual and programmatic needs. It was intended that the Charette results would play a significant role in the Museum's discussions on these issues as well as have an impact on the final drafts of the Needs Analysis and overall Architectural Program.

Issues Addressed by Charette Participants
The following questions and problems were of particular interest to the Museum. The architects were asked to respond to any and all of the issues they felt were relevant.

1. After its first two and one-half years in rented commercial space, in 1932 The Museum of Modern Art moved to a partially renovated townhouse, the typical mid-block building type before the commercial development of Midtown Manhattan, on Fifty-third Street. In 1939, construction was completed on a new structure designed by Philip Goodwin and Edward Durell Stone. The urban conditions that influenced the Goodwin and Stone design have changed drastically in the subsequent fifty-eight years (see appendix, figs. II–1 and II–2,

pp. 155–156). What are the most critical new urban conditions in the immediate area? How can the current assemblage of buildings and spaces be rethought in light of these changed urban circumstances?

2. The essence of the Goodwin–Stone *parti* was the interrelationship between the Museum building and the garden. Through many subsequent additions this interrelationship has been maintained, although it could be argued that it is now stretched to its ultimate configuration (see appendix, fig. II–3, p. 157). The addition of the Dorset Hotel site extends the Museum's ground plan far to the west and suggests that the garden will no longer be the central experience that it once was. Toward reconceiving a new building, what new design concepts might guarantee as coherent an experience as that of the Goodwin–Stone *parti*? What opportunities exist that might include additional open space in the new Museum's configuration?

3. From the time the Goodwin–Stone building opened, the Museum has been characterized as a place of many places: art galleries, sculpture garden, film theater, library, restaurant, etc. The perception of the new Museum of Modern Art will depend largely on the arrangement, in plan and in section, of its various public areas and the quality of the connective spaces between them. How can the arrangement of the public spaces address the fundamental issues described in the Museum's Mission and Executive statements? How can these arrangements reflect the changing uses of the Museum throughout the day and evening?

4. While the public may judge its experience of the Museum on the basis of these public spaces, the Museum is also a place where some five hundred people work each day. Many work spaces and offices are by necessity situated below-grade. How can these and other work spaces be made more dignified? Some public spaces may also need to be located below grade. What planning strategies can be used to make these spaces feel more integrated with the above-grade public spaces?

5. A large part of the unique character of The Museum of Modern Art is derived from its Midtown Manhattan location, perhaps most obviously, its verticality. Part of the paradox of Manhattan is the recognition that the vitality of its culture is maintained within a rigid series of zoning and building codes. Accepting the New York City Zoning Resolution as a given, in what ways can the new Museum of Modern Art express this paradoxical situation? Furthermore, how can the opposing needs for controlled interior spaces, on the one hand, and orientation within the Museum and the larger urban context, on the other, be balanced (see fig. 1, p. 142; and appendix, fig. II–4, p. 158)?

6. The Museum of Modern Art can be said to be the work of various architects: Goodwin and Stone, Philip Johnson (East Wing, North Wing, interior renovations, sculpture garden), Cesar Pelli (Museum Tower expansion, Garden Hall, interior renovations), and others. Despite this "campuslike" composition,

the tendency has been to make the interior experience a seamless one in order to maximize continuity between old and new spaces. What are the identifiable drawbacks of a seamless interior experience within the Museum? Is is possible or advisable to maintain distinctly different environments within a single institution? Where would the critical junctures be within the overall campus of buildings, and how can these be treated? Is it possible or advisable to make some of the Museum's new spaces distinct environments involving more than one architect? What sort of model for this kind of multiple authorship might be appropriate?

Charette Submission Requirements

As the purpose of the Charette was to elicit architectural and urban concepts rather than designs for specific architectural solutions, the traditional bound sketchbook, with its flexibility and familiarity was suggested as an ideal medium for documentation and presentation. However, recognizing the diversity of contemporary practice, the Charette requirements allowed for a variety of formats in addition to the bound sketchbook, including loose-leaf and spiral-bound sketches.

Beyond emphasizing the conceptual nature of the Charette, the sketchbook format was suggested to discourage elaborate presentation techniques and materials. To further discourage extensive presentation efforts, the size of the submission formats was limited and all the materials were required to be submitted in a green clothbound box measuring 11 by 17 by 3 inches, provided to each of the architects.

The architects were asked to include a plan that documented their urban analysis and a summary statement of between 500 and 1,000 words. Other than these cursory requirements, the architects were free to submit any material, written or graphic, they felt was relevant. Similarly, there were no limits on the type of graphic material submitted: freehand, hard-line, or computer-generated sketches, diagrams, and drawings were allowed. Submissions were to be received by March 24 (with an additional two and four days allotted to European and Japanese participants, respectively).

Charette Program

While the architects were not asked to provide detailed architectural proposals, a schematic statement of the space needs of the Museum was provided in the form of an abbreviated Architectural Program, the Charette Brief. This document (see appendix, pp. 152–159) reflected the in-progress Needs Analysis being developed by the program architects and was intended to enable the architects participating in the Charette to anticipate the overall programmatic needs of the Museum in projecting their architectural concepts. In addition to square footages for assignable and non-assignable spaces (see appendix, figs. I–1 and I–2, respectively, p. 152), the schematic program included various requirements as to adjacencies, street-level and below-ground uses, and overall organization.

Charette Site

The Charette participants were required to carry out their explorations for the new Museum within a set of site constraints defined by the New York City Zoning Resolution and certain legal agreements with adjoining properties. The relevant aspects of the restrictions were summarized in the Charette Brief (see appendix, fig. II–5, p. 158). Furthermore, certain limited waivers or variances were assumed to be obtainable and were incorporated into the Charette guidelines.

The Charette site consisted of two properties: the existing Museum site (also containing the separately-owned Museum Tower residential building) and the expansion site (see appendix, fig. II–6, p. 159). Because of zoning restrictions, the two properties were not to be merged into one lot. This imposed a number of constraints, described below, on massing, location of floor area, and connections between the two portions of the site. Nevertheless, it was the task of the architects to explore during the Charette ways in which a comprehensive and integrated plan for the entire project site can be developed.

Charette Submissions

The participating architects were also asked to make presentations of their various concepts and positions to the Architect Selection Committee during the week of March 31 through April 4, 1997. As the Charette participants were not expected to make final conclusions but explore a variety of urban and architectural approaches, each hour-and-a-half presentation was followed by discussion between the architect and the committee regarding the relative merits and drawbacks of the submitted schemes. The diverse architectural and urban positions of the Charette submissions succeeded in broadening the Museum's awareness of the complex issues involved in designing a museum for the twentieth century in a dense urban environment as well as the potential for exciting solutions.

The urban and architectural implications of each Charette submission were then briefly summarized for the Board of Trustees, as follows:

WEIL ARETS, like a number of the architects, recognized the potential for a through-block entrance hall, afforded by the consolidation of the existing Museum site and the newly acquired property. Extending from Fifty-third Street to Fifty-fourth Street, the entry sequence continues up a monumental flight of stairs (which passes over the Museum Tower's loading dock; see p. 162 bottom) toward a second-story overlook of the garden (p. 162 top). As with the proposed entry sequence, the upper floors of the consolidated site take full advantage of the potential for continuous floor plates in the north-to-south direction. Arets illustrated his conception of the Museum's public spaces with a reproduction of Piet Mondrian's *Broadway Boogie Woogie* (p. 169), the broad fields of white representing the openness of the galleries, the bands of color representing movement between the galleries, and the dense concentrations of saturated colors representing movement and spatial expansion in the vertical dimension. He also presented a series of small sketches that capture, like storyboards, his conception of the experience of the Museum to be a series of experiences that unfold through movement (pp. 167–169). Just as he created a sequence of open light wells reaching down into the gallery spaces, Arets projected a succession of volumes upward from the mass of the Museum, like small towers, to house the curatorial offices (p. 165). His proposal not only assures proper daylight for the working spaces of the Museum, but also imparts a distinct urban image to the massing of the Museum, as if the block had become, in itself, a mirror of the dense profile of Manhattan's skyline.

JACQUES HERZOG AND PIERRE DE MEURON's analysis of the site provides two distinct urban strategies, referred to as "Agglomerate" and "Conglomerate," respectively. In the former, the architects noted the possibility of continuing the existing pattern of expansion; that is, each incremental growth of the Museum is represented by the addition of a new, discrete wing (p. 233). Also referred to as the "still life" strategy, this approach implies that the new extension would, like those that preceded it, retain its own formal identity. The second strategy implies a more synthetic approach. Rather than retaining its image as a succession of discrete additions, the "Conglomerate" approach suggests that the new Museum should be created by interventions throughout the entire site—a "horizontal" rather than "vertical" strategy (p. 235). The architects also identified various ways of transforming the architectural fabric of the Museum: recladding, excavation, and demolition, as well as new construction. In two speculative schemes, they demonstrated some of the implications of the various architectural and urban strategies. In one instance, they proposed an agglomerate scheme that included a vertically-organized extension, extending upward into the sky-exposure plane, and the relocation of the sculpture garden to the west, so as to retain its central location within the overall site plan (p. 234 top). In a second scheme, the architects reconfigured the Museum by relocating the sculpture garden to the roof and replacing that public space with two diagonally related urban courtyards for large-scale contemporary sculpture (p. 237).

STEVEN HOLL outlined two schemes, one of which was called "Cutting" and the other called "Bracketing." The two strategies outlined by Holl, illustrated in his series of illuminating sketches, clearly define many of the issues addressed by others and reflect, perhaps, the shared concerns of contemporary architects. Opposing verticality and horizontality, involution and evolution, discrete addition and synthetic transformation, the architect developed schemes in sufficient detail to explore not only their urbanistic and architectural implications, but also the spatial implications of these approaches. In the "Cutting" scheme, which implies verticality, Holl pursued the potential in the concept of a multistory building. The mass of the new structure, rendered in red, extends upward into the sky-exposure plane, reflected in its angular form (p. 172). Openings cut into the sloping surfaces provide daylight into all of the vertically-arranged galleries. In other studies, the architect projected the relationship between the art exhibited and the quality of the light present (p. 172 bottom). In the "Bracketing" scheme, the architect reconciled the various floor levels of the existing construction and the proposed new construction with sloped, moving ramps that bridge an atrium space that organizes and defines the spatial sequence of visiting the Museum (p. 176 top). In this scheme, the architect also studied the possible relocation of the garden, shifting it to the west to maintain its centrality in the overall plan and raising it a half-level to create a large space for contemporary art installations and performances below (pp. 176–77).

TOYO ITO's studies synthesize observations on the Museum, the urban culture of Manhattan, and the past and future of modern culture. Despite being presented in the traditional form of architectural drawings (plans, sections, and elevations), Ito's project is, nonetheless, characterized more by its metaphorical quality rather than by any pragmatic concerns. Reflecting the historic Midtown urban pattern, the architect proposed parallel blocks of construction along Fifty-third and Fifty-fourth streets, separated by a central, linear circulation space in much the same way that the rear yards formerly separated the brownstones on opposite sides of the block (p. 186, p. 188 top). Ito also referred to the proposed construction along Fifty-fourth Street as a "horizontal skyscraper," noting the fact that the northern property line of the new Museum site was as long as the Museum Tower was high. In yet another allusion to the urban culture of Manhattan, the architect diagrammed the complex and random activity patterns that might take place in a typical visit to the Museum: Against a background of a rationalized architectural plan, a dotted line takes a bumble-bee path from viewing works of art, to eating, to buying a catalogue, to resting, etc. (p.186). The elevations proposed by the architect have a similar metaphorical quality—a collage of materials with encoded cultural messages that speak to the past and future of the Museum (p. 184). Green Tinian marble, a hallmark of Ludwig Mies van der Rohe's heroic modern work of the twentieth century, is overlayed with the striped patterns of the international bar code, a new symbol of the dematerialized cyber world of the coming century.

REM KOOLHAAS's single proposal interweaves urban and architectural concepts, reflecting both the specific conditions of Manhattan and global issues. In a series of bold operations, he proposed lowering the sculpture garden to one level below street level as well as eliminating all of the enclosed space at ground level with the exception of entryways and service functions. The result is a continuous sidewalk-level public space that extends under the existing and expanded Museum and overlooks the relocated garden, recalling aspects of major Manhattan civic spaces such as Rockefeller Center Gardens and the Lever House plaza (p. 198 top). Incorporating and extending the existing floor slabs beneath the Museum Tower, the architect projected a 200-foot-by-200-foot block representing the gallery spaces (p. 192). Staff functions are similarly reorganized and streamlined. A slender golden tower extends upward from the East Wing housing "MoMA, Inc.," the Museum's fundraising and administrative offices; below the tower, curatorial offices are relocated in the 1939 building, acting as a conduit between MoMA, Inc. and the galleries (p. 195). At the juncture between the curatorial offices and the galleries, the architect proposed a computerized study center where visitors might retrieve works of art from storage via an automated retrieval system (p. 193). The technological ethos of the proposal is further evident in the public circulation system, a tramlike conveyance that travels horizontally through the lower levels, diagonally through the gallery block, and, finally, vertically through the upper floors of the Museum, which reflect the triangular form of the sky-exposure plane (p. 198 bottom, p. 199 left).

DOMINIQUE PERRAULT's investigations focused on the grand urban gesture, the search for an overall *parti* diagram that would best represent a reconstituted Museum. All of the architect's explorations derive from an analysis of the Museum's public space using a tree as a metaphor, the trunk representing the principal circulation spaces and the branches and sub-branches representing the myriad of different destinations within the Museum. As did a number of architects, Perrault projected a central "spine" of public spaces and circulation dividing the site and running in an east-to-west direction (p. 202 bottom). Based on this metaphorical conception, the architect projected three *partis,* which he described as "Aside," "Along," and "Above." The first concentrates the new construction principally on the site of the existing Dorset Hotel, treating the project more like an expanded wing of the Museum rather than a synthetic restructuring (p. 202 top). The second proposal, "Along," projects a long, narrow extension of the Museum running the entire length of the site from east to west, with a reconfigured sculpture garden running parallel to it along Fifty-fourth Street (p. 204 top). The final scheme, "Above," envisions a vast horizontal plane hovering above the existing and new sites at approximately the seventh-floor level; containing the gallery spaces, the scheme includes an open ground level that would provide for a greatly expanded sculpture garden (p. 207 top). In essence, the organizational structure of the Museum would reflect the overall structure of the expanded Museum: a north-to-south striation and a vertical striation, in the "Along" and "Above" schemes, respectively.

YOSHIO TANIGUCHI's submission reflects a series of sketch investigations of the architectural possibilities of various aspects of the existing structures, combined with an urban analysis of the immediate Midtown site. Working through a developed architectural scheme, the architect envisaged an east-to-west spine of circulation and public space connecting the various components of the Museum. His urban analysis embraces the notion of a Fifty-third Street façade of collaged historical styles and a unified synthetic façade running along Fifty-fourth Street (p. 247 top, p. 246 bottom). The two façades would be tied together by a through-block north-to-south entranceway, with the new principal entrance on Fifty-fourth Street. Reconstituting the sculpture garden as the center, both physically and historically, of the Museum, the architect envisioned symmetrical pavilions to the east and west, creating a frame of classically balanced composition for the garden that reflects the assemblage of neoclassical buildings clustered to the north of the site (p. 246 bottom). Working in sufficient detail to allow for the investigation of the spatial qualities of the site, he projected a series of serene, multiple-height volumes of space surrounding the garden for the principal public areas, suffused with daylight and providing flowing, continuous circulation (p. 248). The organization of the Museum's principal spaces is seen as a vertical arrangement, with the principal circulation spaces at ground level, the galleries immediately above, and the administrative and curatorial offices rising above the principal, six-story mass of the building in a slender, glazed slab positioned midblock (p. 246 top).

BERNARD TSCHUMI devoted considerable effort to developing a conceptual plan that recognizes the interior experience of the Museum as a spatial sequence that can reinforce its curatorial mission. Beginning with a through-block entrance hall running between Fifty-third and Fifty-fourth streets (p. 257 top, p. 261 top), this sequence of spaces consists of a continuous forward path through the Museum, comprising vertical circulation as well as a series of periodic courts and terraces for the display of sculpture and other uses (pp. 259–260). Retaining the current location of the garden as well as Philip Johnson's North Wing, the architect's scheme attempts to create the maximum transformation by reconceiving the existing spaces rather than creating altogether new ones. With a gallery for contemporary art cantilevered above it, the roof of the North Wing is reprogrammed as a distinctive space for sculpture and special events and becomes a significant element of the series of new spaces unfolding within the Museum's fabric (p. 258 bottom). The architect developed various schemes to the point where an exploration of the nature of the gallery spaces was possible. For the core works of the permanent collection, the scheme envisions a series of more fixed galleries around the perimeter of the structure, with a series of more flexible galleries in the center—an architectonic arrangement that corresponds to a logical sequence of construction types from exterior to interior (p. 257 bottom, p. 261 bottom). Whereas various schemes by various architects projected a horizontal or vertical method of organizing the principal spaces of the Museum, Tschumi has proposed a hybrid, wherein the principal spaces of the Museum interlock in section reflecting the complex and varied nature of how the institution operates.

RAFAEL VIÑOLY generated a broad study of the fundamental urban and architectural issues facing the Museum. In ten different schemes, the architect investigated the relationship of the structure to the surrounding neighborhood, exploring the implications of placing the entrance on Fifty-fourth Street (p. 212 bottom, p. 213), retaining the existing entrance, and creating multiple entrances. The sculpture garden was reconceived as a public space accessible from the street; it was further studied as a space that could be principally public in nature but could also be periodically covered over by means of a retractable roof and palisade-like enclosures along Fifty-fourth Street (p. 217 top and bottom left). In another instance, an expansion of the Museum's exterior spaces is achieved by extending the sculpture garden upward in the form of terraces, mirroring the principal circulation system (p. 212 top). The architect also considered the possibility of a major east-to-west circulation spine located on the level above street level on the south side of the building as well as a centrally-located spine that serves as a grand stairway connecting all of the public spaces of the Museum (p. 214). The architect also studied variations on the Museum's current pattern of exhibition galleries, including large north-south floor plates connected by a vertical circulation system in the form of a double helix (p. 216 top). Other gallery types include a series of open spaces that are negotiated by means of wandering ramps and a loftlike system of spaces with movable wall panels attached to the structural columns, extended throughout the Museum in the 25-foot-square grid pattern of the original 1939 building (p. 218).

TOD WILLIAMS AND BILLIE TSIEN focused in their investigations on a broad spectrum of issues. In addition to exploring many of the themes that were of common interest among all the Charette participants, Williams and Tsien's sought to address more directly the fundamental questions of ambiance and subjective experience in their proposals. Recognizing that the successful experience of the Museum depends on a multitude of factors, the architects sought to reinforce the notion of individual experience as a prerequisite. As a way of orienting the observer within the increasingly complex interior environment of the Museum, various strategies were adopted to insure continuity with the overall urban context. This was accomplished in a variety of ways. Discrete sources of light were deftly inserted into the fabric of the structure to provide reorientation (p. 224 bottom). Double-height spaces connect below-grade spaces with the principal public spaces of the Museum, with a bridge spanning the north edge of the garden, connecting the new galleries envi-sioned on the site of the Dorset Hotel as well as those proposed for the current site of the restaurants, thereby ensuring a continuity of experience (p. 222). From various perspectives, views out onto the city activate the interior of the expanded Museum. A courtyard, open to the environment but substantially controlled by various cli-mactic devices, is shown as a way of connecting the experience of viewing art to the greater experience of everyday life (p. 225 bottom). The importance of scale was fur-ther addressed in the architects' suggestion that the Museum not exceed the histori-cal six-story height of the existing structures, insuring a distinctive and intimate profile in the increasingly overbuilt context of Midtown Manhattan.

Appendix

This Appendix includes extracts, tables, and diagrams drawn from the brief provided in February 1997 to the architects participating in the Charette.

I. Charette Program

The Charette Program is intended to represent a schematic statement of the space needs of the Museum. It defines the conditions and design requirements to be met by the Charette participants by identifying all Museum spaces by use and size, and by functional adjacency requirements.

The Program is divided into two categories of spaces: Assignable and Non-assignable. The Assignable Spaces represent those Museum needs that can be quantified and are expressed as specific uses with a required area in square feet. In most cases, for the purposes of this Charette, they are described as blocks of space having a similar use rather than individual rooms. The assigned area for these blocks of space includes their internal circulation.

The Non-assignable Spaces represent those that are also required but cannot be quantified until a design is developed. These spaces typically include circulation, mechanical rooms and shafts, elevator cores with toilet rooms and stairs, and service and loading areas. For the purposes of this Charette, the participants should assume that the total Non-assignable Spaces will account for a minimum of 40 percent of the total building area.

I–1. ASSIGNABLE SPACES

Space	Area in Square Feet
1. Gallery Space	
1.1 Collections Galleries	82,500
1.2 Temporary Exhibitions Galleries	40,000
2. Theaters and Assembly	
2.1 Titus 1 (Existing)	5,170
2.2 Titus 2 (Existing—see note below)	3,630
2.3 120-seat Theater with Projection Booth	2,500
2.4 Performance/Meeting/Entertaining Space	3,200
3. Library and Archives	21,600
4. Education Department	8,000
5. Curatorial Departments	
5.1 Painting and Sculpture	6,500
5.2 Drawings	6,500
5.3 Prints and Illustrated Books	6,500
5.4 Architecture and Design	6,500
5.5 Photography	6,500
5.6 Film and Video	6,500
5.7 Chief Curator at Large	1,000
6. Conservation	10,800
7. Office and Other Workspace	60,200
8. Art Storage	43,200
9. Food Service	
9.1 Staff Cafeteria with Support	2,500
9.2 Public Restaurant with Support	4,200
9.3 Public Cafeteria with Support	8,500
9.4 Main Kitchen	2,000
9.5 Storage and Service Areas	2,800
10. Design and Book Store with Support	15,000
Total Assignable Space	**355,800**

Note: For the purposes of improved planning, Titus 2 may be replaced with a new theater of similar size (220 seats) in a different location.

I–2. NON-ASSIGNABLE SPACES

Space	
1. Main Public Lobby	To include 1,800 square-foot coat check.
2. Public Circulation	As required.
3. Public Restrooms	As required.
4. Staff Entrance	Includes small lobby for security.
5. Staff Circulation	Must be separate from public for security.
6. Staff Restrooms	As required.
7. Loading Docks	Two required. Each to accommodate a truck 48 feet (ft.) long. Minimum dimensions including staging areas: 23 ft. wide by 76 ft. long by 14 ft. clear height.
8. Service Circulation	Must be separate from public for security.
9. Mechanical Space	Includes equipment rooms and shaft space. Assume size to be 8 percent of total building area. Can be distributed.
10. Theater Lobby(s)	Can be either one large shared lobby for two or more theaters, or individual lobbies for each theater. Requires separate street entrance.
11. Lobby for Group Visits	To accommodate 120 visitors. Also for shared use by Education Department for school groups. Includes coat storage.
12. Elevators	One freight elevator dedicated for artworks. Dimensions: 18 ft. wide by 12 ft. deep by 12 ft. high. One freight elevator for non-art uses. Passenger elevator(s) for visitors—as needed. Passenger elevator(s) for staff—as needed.
13. Stairs and Other Vertical Circulation	As required for fire exiting and internal circulation. Staff and visitors' vertical circulation must be separate for security. The original 1939 Goodwin–Stone open stairway presently connecting the second- and third-floor galleries may be incorporated into the new Museum design.

II. Charette Site

EXISTING MUSEUM SITE

Current plans for each floor, typical cross-sections, and elevations of the existing Museum are included in the drawing package provided to each Charette participant. The plans indicate current uses, entry locations, circulation patterns, and structure.

The building massing on the existing Museum site may be reconfigured within certain constraints, given below.

Regardless of changes to building massing, no additional above-grade floor area may be created beyond the 264,000 gross square feet (GSF) which is currently on the existing Museum site.

If building massing is modified, it must conform to the yard, height, and setback constraints described below.

Below-grade floor area may be increased beyond the current 113,000 GSF, but sub-strata rock will be encountered at approximately 30 feet below sidewalk level, so cellar levels should not extend deeper than that.

Alterations to use and circulation can be made within the existing building. There are two specific elements of the original 1939 Goodwin–Stone building that Charette participants should consider incorporating into the new Museum: the large film theater ("Titus 1") and the open stairway, which presently connects the second- and third-floor galleries.

Alterations to structure can be made within the existing building. In the areas beneath the Museum Tower, columns may not be altered, although changes may be made to the floor slabs.

The elevator stair shafts and entry lobby for the Museum Tower must remain as shown on the plans, as must the shear-wall structure adjacent to the main elevator shaft.

The exterior envelope of retained portions of the existing Museum building may be clad in new materials, but the portion of the Fifty-third Street frontage designated as the "Goodwin and Stone Façade" (see fig. II–5) should be retained with its current appearance from the second floor up.

Access and egress locations for pedestrians can be repositioned from current locations, and loading berths can be relocated as described under "Parking and Loading" below.

The Garden should retain its current location and configuration.

Contiguous floor areas on the existing Museum site and the expansion site must be separated by a fire-division wall. Openings are permitted through this wall (with appropriate fire-rated doors or other closure devices). The maximum size of an opening is 120 square feet, with a maximum dimension of 12 feet. At each floor level, the aggregate width of openings cannot exceed 25 percent of the length of the wall.

FLOOR AREA ON THE EXPANSION SITE

All additional above-ground floor area on the project site must be located within the boundaries of the expansion-site portion of the project site.

The expansion site has, by zoning, a maximum above-grade capacity of approximately 216,000 GSF. There is no limit on below-grade site capacity; however, the sub-strata rock imposes the same limitation as on the existing Museum site. Two full basement levels would add approximately 51,000 GSF to the site capacity.

The Museum does not anticipate that the program of Assignable Spaces given for the Charette, when augmented with Non-assignable Spaces (circulation, mechanical space, elevator cores, stairs, toilet rooms, and loading areas), will require that the expansion site be built out to its maximum capacity. If participants do not choose to retain all of the floor area currently on the existing Museum site, any deficiency in the needed floor area would need to be made up on the expansion site within the overall capacity constraint described above.

YARDS

There are no front or side yards required for new construction on either the existing Museum site or the expansion site. There are, however, requirements for rear yards on both sites (see fig. II–5).

A rear yard 20 feet deep is required on the expansion site where it backs onto the Fifty-third Street properties west of the expansion site. Cellars, and no more than one other story, up to 23 feet above curb level, are permitted to extend into the rear yard.

Rear yards 20 feet deep are required on both the expansion site and the existing Museum site where the two sites abut at mid-block. These rear yards are only required on the upper floors of the building, above an elevation of 110 feet above the sidewalk level.

A 20-foot rear yard is also required on the existing Museum site where it backs onto St. Thomas' Church at the east end of the site. This rear yard was the subject of variances obtained in the past, so the height and floor area of the structure within the yard cannot be increased.

HEIGHT AND SETBACK

New construction on both the expansion site and the existing Museum site is subject to height and setback requirements.

The street wall of all new construction must be built at the street line for its full length, and to a minimum of 72 feet in height, or the full height of the building, whichever is less.

Above a height of 85 feet, the building must set back at least 15 feet from the street line, and then fit within the defined maximum bulk envelopes (see fig. II–7).

On the existing Museum site, an additional limitation on height is imposed. Within a distance of 50 feet from the face of the Museum Tower, all new building mass must be below a height of 110 feet above curb level (see fig. II–5).

PARKING AND LOADING

Automobile parking spaces are not included in the program for the Museum. Off-street loading berths are required.

The Charette program calls for the provision of two loading berths for the Museum on the project site. The Museum Tower also requires a single loading berth.

Loading berths may be located on either the expansion site or the existing Museum site. The loading berth that serves the Museum Tower may be relocated and may be housed in the combined facility serving both the Museum and the Museum Tower, but it must be a dedicated separate berth in any combined facility and must provide both appropriate connection to the Museum Tower service elevator and appropriate configuration to permit garbage containers to be stored and then rolled by hand to the curb for pickup.

The size of the loading berth for the Museum Tower must match that of the current berth. The loading berths for the Museum must accommodate 48-foot trucks and each be at least 23 feet by 76 feet and 14 feet high (including staging areas).

Curb cuts for loading areas cannot be located on Fifty-third Street. The width of curb cuts on Fifty-fourth Street cannot exceed 15 feet for one-way traffic and 25 feet for two-way traffic.

II–1. Midtown location plan

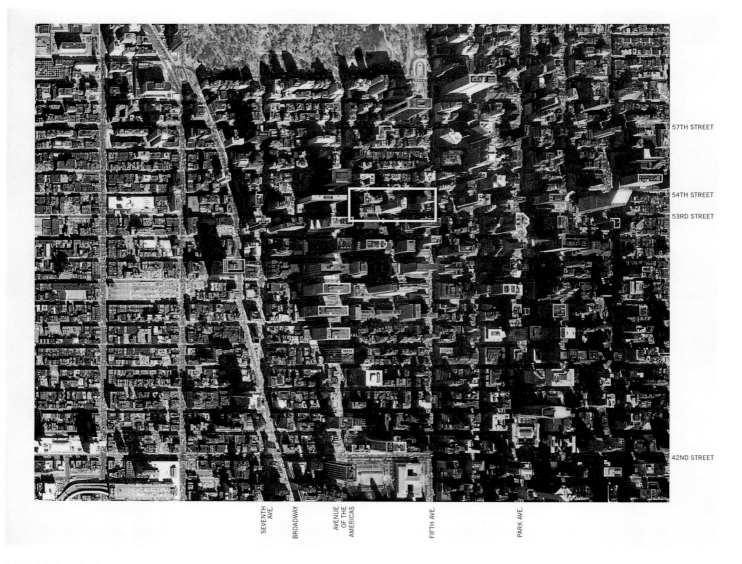

II–2. Aerial view of Midtown Manhattan, 1996

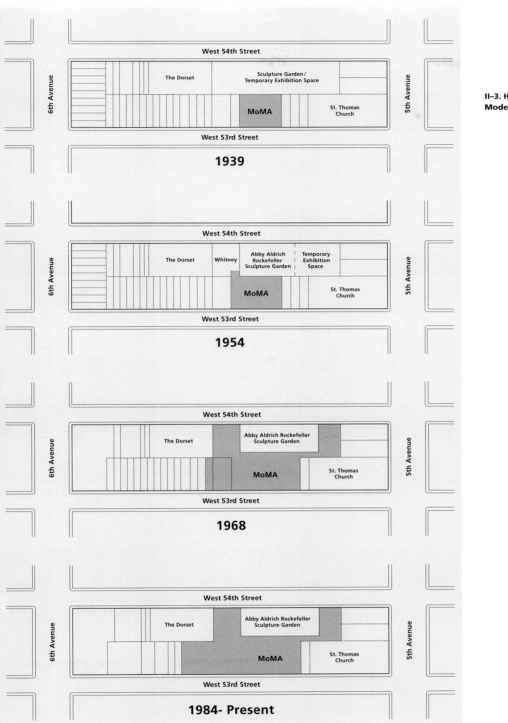

II–3. Historical development of The Museum of
Modern Art site, 1939–present

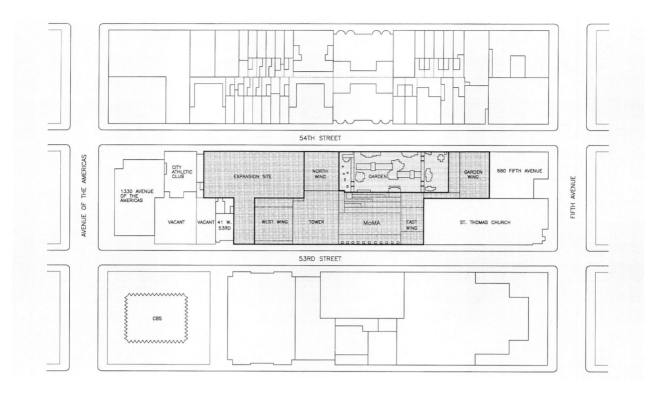

II–4. Block plan

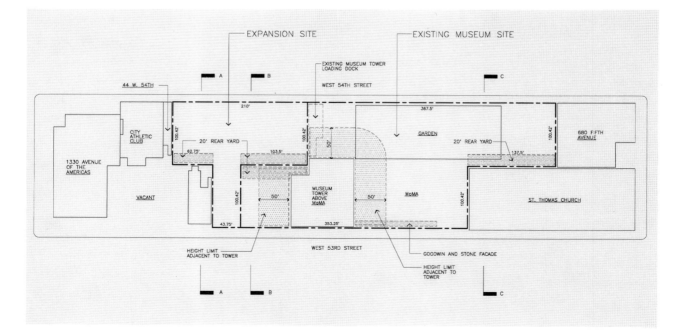

II–5. Site constraints diagram

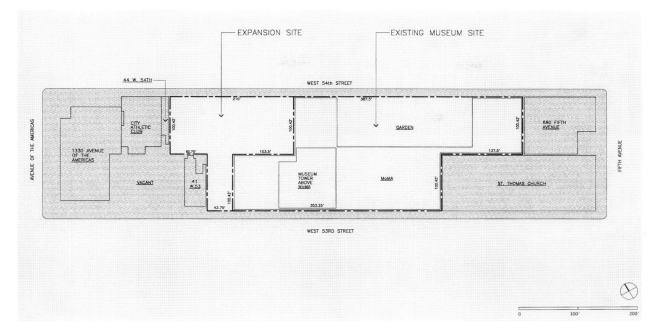

II–6. Project site plan

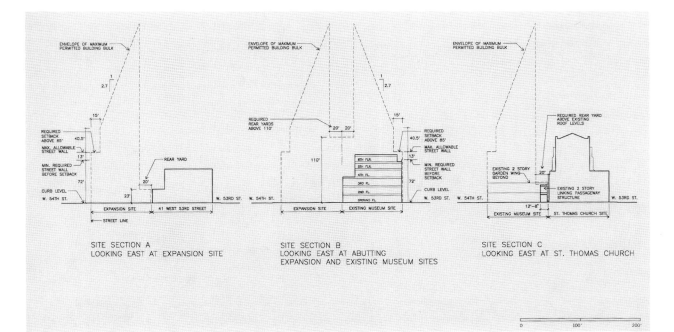

II–7. Site sections A, B, C

Wiel Arets

Born in Heerlen, The Netherlands, 1955
Education: Doctorate in Architecture, Technical University, Eindhoven,
The Netherlands, 1983
Selected Recent Projects: Academy of Arts and Architecture, Maastricht,
The Netherlands, 1989–93; AZL Pension Fund Headquarters, Heerlen, The
Netherlands, 1990–95; Police Station, Vaals, The Netherlands, 1993–95

FROM THE ARCHITECT'S STATEMENT

In our era the world seems to become increasingly more immaterial; because of this, the relationship with the object is changing. Our perception has been changed by the way electronics play an important role in our daily life, and this has undeniably influenced our way of thinking. Ours is a global age in which the world seems to have become an image.

The grid and zoning codes of Manhattan are rigid, but the vitality of its culture is maintained. Any application of mathematics to our view of the world brings with it the challenge of the grid.

The history of MoMA is shown literally by the development of the site and the contributions by different authors. It is this assemblage of different impressions transforming into a new idea that Paul Valéry based his thoughts upon when he wrote about the combination of seemingly random impressions into a new reality. It is not only the juxtaposition of different programmatical devices and architects' handwritings in the building we are talking about, but it could also be a strategy to show art.

Whereas modern architecture is primarily an architecture of the hygienic, the pure, the unblemished, and the imperturbable, we, on the other hand, accept imperfection, noise, and disorder as essential elements of the processes of modern technology. Our ideas are not upset, but (quite the reverse) are stimulated by collisions with information and concepts; these are interpretable not simply as opposition, but also as an accelerating or a condensing of our ideas.

At present, most architecture does nothing other than attract and titillate its spectators in every way possible. It tries to create the most powerful image at the most conducive place. This project breaks with the code of imagery so that, instead of using architecture to endear a place to the public, people are relieved of their obligation to respond to that architecture.

The double-high entrance hall, connecting Fifty-third and Fifty-fourth streets, can be seen as a transitional space; it is a space in which to slow down. One could enter the complex and leave quickly, yet pass slowly so as to be able to make one's choice where to go.

MoMA is an urban museum; it is a place to meet people and to study art. The entrance hall is connected to a café, a bookshop and design shop, and education center. In the lobby one experiences the galleries already through the structural shaft, through which light from the very top penetrates the complex. The four theaters are situated directly after ticket control, where the theater lobby is a void connecting Fifty-third Street with the sculpture garden. From the main public lobby, ramps bring people down to the temporary exhibition spaces and up to the different collection galleries.

The galleries are positioned between the public entrance area and the office towers, with their roof garden for the 600 employees. It is the structural voids between the towers that allow filtered natural light to enter the galleries and continue down to the lobby. These voids visually connect the floors vertically and create an atmosphere of intimacy. These voids are sometimes bridged and reading rooms are positioned in them.

The different proposals are dealing with the issue of circulation through the void. An opening in the skin of the city allows art, employees, and visitors to be brought in and encouraged to construct their own itineraries as they move from site to site within the complex. Public circulation, staff, scholars, and art are not anonymous; all these form part of the life of the Museum and the city of Manhattan, the life that takes place between dream and reality.

Project Credits
Wiel Arets; Dominic Papa, Henrik Vuust, Ivo Daniels, Bettina Kraus, Janneke Wessels, Jeroen Storm, Martine Nederend

Above:
Conceptual model. Wood, 5⅛ x 9 x 1¾" (13 x 22.9 x 4.4 cm)

Left:
Interior perspective sketch of lobby. Ink on tracing paper, 11 x 11⅜"
(27.9 x 28.9 cm)

Left, top to bottom:
Interior perspective sketch of lobby with grand staircase. Ink on tracing paper, 11 x 11⅜" (27.9 x 28.9 cm)

Interior perspective sketch of lobby with grand staircase. Ink on tracing paper, 11 x 11⅜" (27.9 x 28.9 cm)

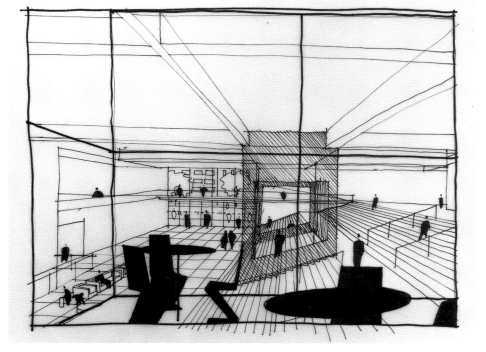

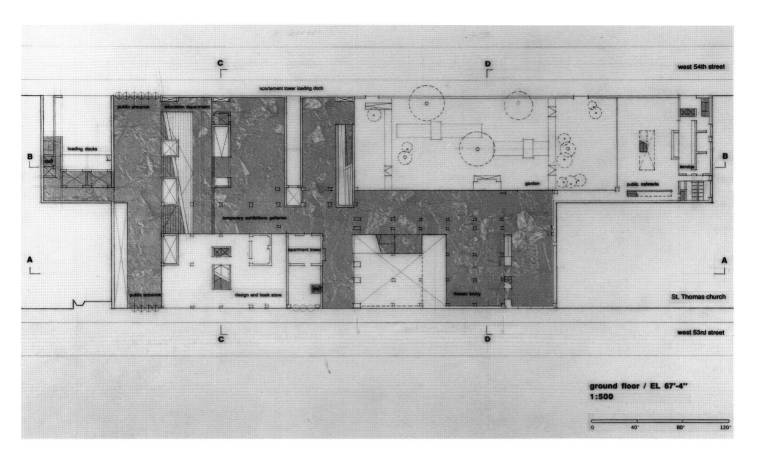

Above:
Ground floor plan. Pencil, colored pencil, and collage on tracing paper, 11 x 15½" (27.9 x 39.4 cm)

Left:
Interior perspective sketch of gallery. Ink on tracing paper, 11 x 11⅜" (27.9 x 28.9 cm)

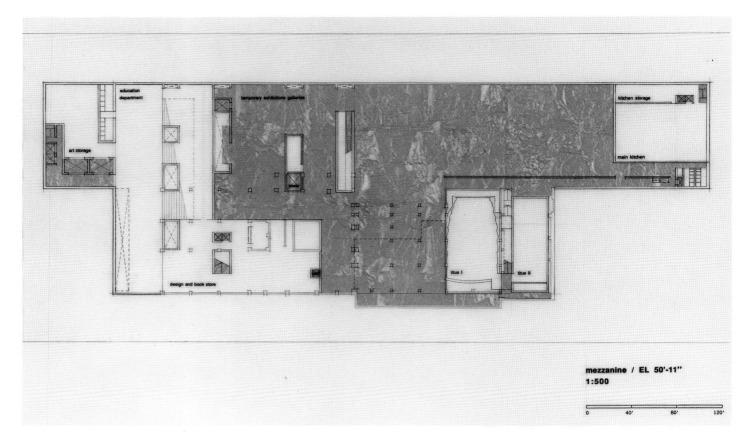

mezzanine / EL 50'-11"
1:500

0   40'   80'   120'

Above:
Mezzanine floor plan. Pencil, colored pencil, and collage on tracing paper, 11 x 15½" (27.9 x 39.4 cm)

Right:
Interior perspective sketch of theater. Ink on tracing paper, 11 x 11⅜" (27.9 x 28.9 cm)

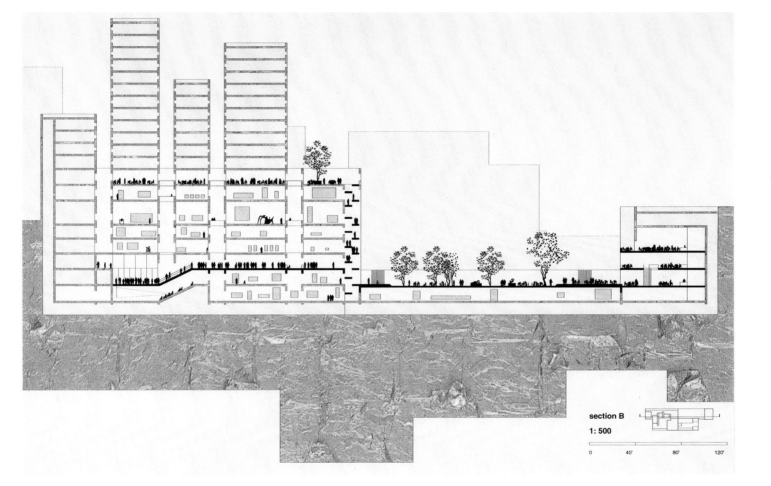

section B
1 : 500

0   40'   80'   120'

**Section B. Computer-generated print on paper,
11 x 15½" (27.9 x 39.4 cm)**

Interior perspective sketch of reinstated Members' Lounge.
Ink on tracing paper, 11 x 11⅜" (27.9 x 28.9 cm)

**Sketches of circulation patterns. Pencil and ink
on paper, 11½ x 10⅞" (29.2 x 26.6 cm)**

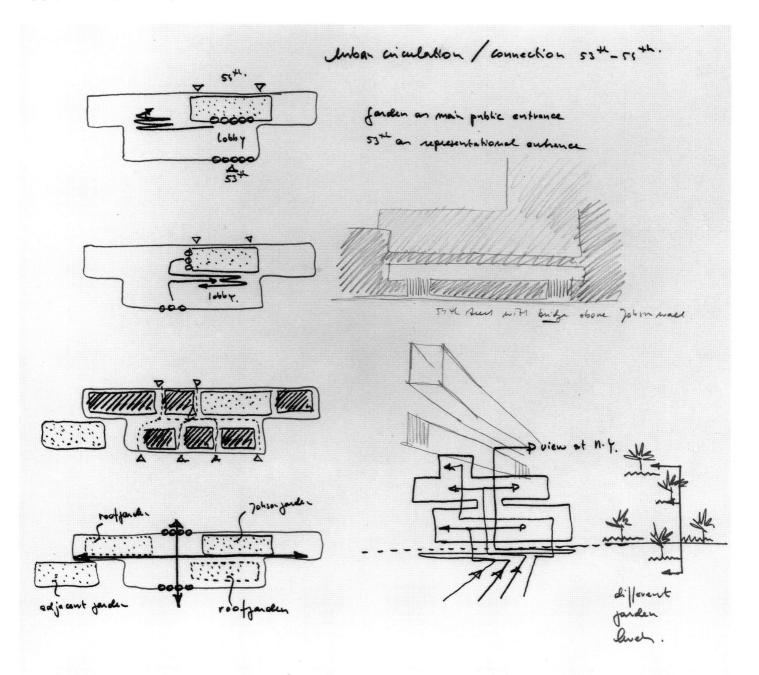

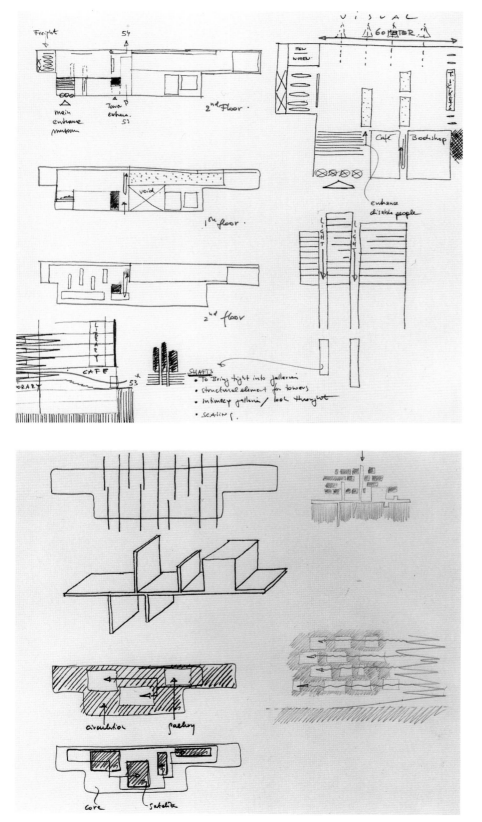

Left, top to bottom:
Diagrams of light shafts. Pencil and ink on paper,
11½ x 10⅞" (29.2 x 26.6 cm)

Diagrams of core and satellite gallery circulation.
Pencil and ink on paper, 11½ x 10⅞" (29.2 x 26.6 cm)

**Diagrams of circulation. Postcard, pencil, and ink
on paper, 11½ x 10⅞" (29.2 x 26.6 cm)**

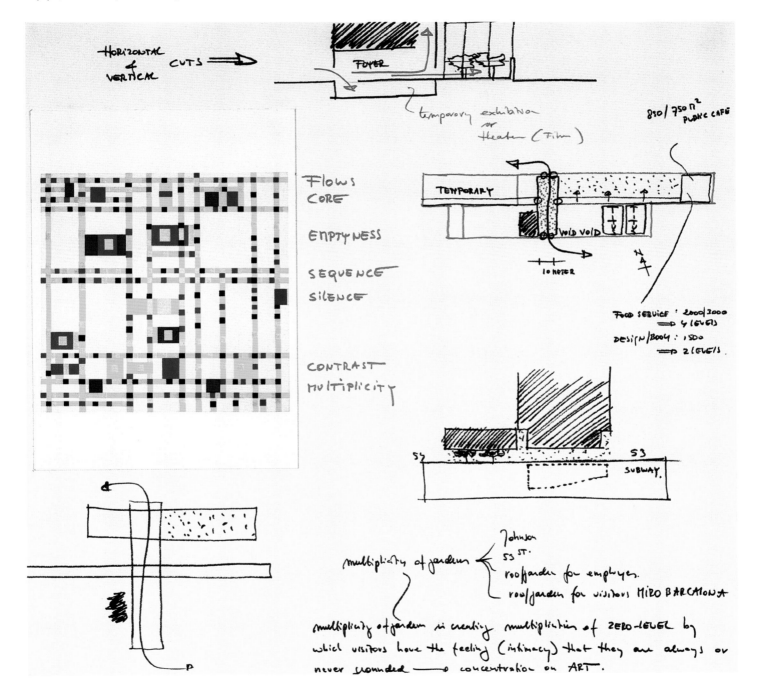

Steven Holl

Born in Bremerton, Washington, 1947
Education: Architecture studies in Rome, Italy, 1970; Bachelor of Architecture, University of Washington, Seattle, 1971; postgraduate studies, The Architectural Association, London, England, 1976
Selected Recent Projects: Fukuoka Housing, Kiyushu, Japan, 1989–91; Stretto House, Dallas, Texas, 1990–91; Kiasma, Museum of Contemporary Art, Helsinki, Finland, 1993–98 (projected completion date)

FROM THE ARCHITECT'S STATEMENT

The origin of *museum* as a room of the muse, a place to think and consider deeply and at length, is an idea to contemplate as we are faced with a major transformation of The Museum of Modern Art.

Architectural concepts at this stage in MoMA's redefinition provoke rather than resolve many questions. We have adopted a comparative method, proposing two concepts as heuristic devices enabling a better understanding of the potentials for MoMA's next expansion. These two concepts are dialectical. Concept A, *Cutting*, is vertically organized, while Concept B, *Bracketing*, is horizontally organized. Concept A adopts an evolutional, architectural, and urban form, while Concept B brackets the entire campus into a unified whole.

Questions of the Institution

EVOLUTION VS. INVOLUTION: Is the growth of MoMA evolutional or involutional? If each successive building addition attempts to swallow the earlier buildings, isn't the expression turning inward? To roll up or wrap in a new envelope is to decline the evolutional expression of a succession. If a strategy for an overall envelope is adopted, what about the potential of further additions? On the other hand, if we allow a reworking of past elements now, can it yield new dimensions?

ECLIPSE OF THE MODERN: Has there been an eclipse of the idea of the institution or does a transformed version continue? Has there been a break between the historical explanation of "modern" and subsequent interpretations? Can we locate this epistemological break in time: 1960? 1964? 1966? 1970? Is this period analogous to a natural eclipse—a partial darkening with transformation and recurrence?

ART IN OUR TIME: . . . As the much-expanded institution prepares for the next century of art, it must balance its commitment to its historic collection with its original mission statement. Alfred Barr's metaphor of "the collection as a torpedo moving through time" may today be seen as an overweight torpedo carrying a large burden.

MULTIDEPARTMENTAL STRUCTURE: Is the present multidepartmental structure actually contradictory to the original mission of "art in our time," given the present challenges to distinct and traditional art categories? Should the structure be extended to more departments?

Could a revolutionary closure of the present categories give birth to a cross-department hybrid?

ROOMS VS. FLEXIBLE SPACE: Rooms, which were the gallery character of museums in the eighteenth and nineteenth centuries, were supplanted by flexible space and movable partitions in the twentieth century. On the cusp of the twenty-first century, the new diversity of contemporary art media requires the acoustic and spatial separation of a gallery of rooms.

Art as Fundamental

THE COLLECTION, SPACE TO PLACE: . . . New galleries for the collection could be formed specially for individual masterworks, providing "a place in which they belong." To recognize the place of a masterpiece in a museum is to keep the museum with you wherever you go. Special rooms for Picasso's *Les Demoiselles d'Avignon*, Brancusi's *Bird in Space*, *Fish*, *Magic Bird*, and *Socrates*, or for Giacometti's works, would be great spaces of contemplation to which one could always return. The materiality of the walls and ceiling could be plaster, for example, reinforcing the fundamental solidity and quality of these spaces. Details where the wall meets the ceiling and the floor are essential in a contemplative gallery. These subtle conditions come to the foreground and intertwine with the experience of the art, establishing an important role for architecture, the subtle realm of touch, the haptic realm.

NEW ART, TOWARD AN UNKNOWN: Evolutional or experimental galleries in which any form of media could be presented would be offered. These spaces would be wired and equipped for projection devices from ceilings, walls, and floors. Ceiling structure would have the capacity for suspension of various screens and platforms. Artificial illumination would be adjustable, reaching a theatrical nature if necessary. These evolutional spaces (or nonspaces) could be fused into one another or, alternately, closed off.

Concept A: Cutting

The new site's zoning envelope is taken as a ready-made form, which is cut for natural light. A major cut is made for the main lobby, connecting Fifty-third Street, Fifty-fourth Street, and the garden. This is a large public space with a ramp down to the cinemas and up to the galleries. In raising the issue of the evolutional nature of MoMA's campus, Concept A accepts each building phase as evolution expressed. The zoning envelope, itself a consequence of building density and light, is incised, creating internal light.

The volume is built out to the allowed floor area of 216,000 square feet, offering some loft galleries with exceptionally high volumes. This expanded area could concentrate all the galleries; one could move from the new collection galleries below to "evolutional," or experimental, galleries above. Staff offices are relocated in the former gallery floors. All work spaces receive natural light from the original façade and a few selective cuts from above. In the upper levels, truss space on sloped exteriors double-functions as light-baffle zones and mechanical-duct space. The deep cuts could contain all intake air, exhaust grilles, etc.

URBANISM: The public lobby connecting garden views with Fifty-third and Fifty-fourth streets has true urban proportions. A through-block connection between Fifty-fourth and Fifth-third streets would be a neighborhood contribution. . . . The vertical character of Concept A affords a public roof garden at the top of the building with fine urban views.

LIGHT: . . . In the cutting concept, the potential of natural light is introduced into many of the galleries. This would be a nonglaring, diffused natural light, bounced off ceilings through the use of specially shaped baffles. All galleries with natural light have black-out screens, which are electrically operated and allow the light to be individually adjusted for particular works.

CIRCULATION: The through-block public lobby opens a free flow of public circulation to all main areas. A direct ramp down to the cinemas prevents backup in the lobby and facilitates changing programs between day and evening. Elevators carry the public to upper galleries, with open stairs and ramps allowing a walk down. The staff entrance is through a reconstruction of the original 1939 MoMA entry. Stairs interconnect staff offices and allow natural light to enter from above.

The current escalators are replaced by a new "hall of reverie" running transversely the length of the garden. Here the view of the garden is enhanced along its full length. . . . This would be a special hall for receptions, open to the garden in summer.

CONSTRUCTABILITY ISSUES: . . .The main construction would go on while the Museum remains open. Once the new galleries and public lobby areas are completed, selective parts of the existing MoMA can be renovated in phases. . . .

ALTERNATE STUDIES: Certain aspects of Concept A could be developed differently. For example, a horizontal gallery organization would connect to existing gallery floors. The upper floors of the ready-made zoning envelope might be staff office lofts.

Concept B: Bracketing

A maximum of connectivity of gallery circuits is envisioned within an outer bracket, with the garden as the main focus at its center. This horizontally-organized concept proposes lifting the garden 11 feet and shifting it ±70 feet west. This affords a more central position for the original 1939 building as well as two new below-garden experimental exhibition areas of 21,000 square feet each. Access is enhanced from all sides. The garden is perfectly rebuilt with the addition of glass bottoms in the pools and water year-round (dissolving snow from skylight to below).

Staff offices are located in the thin floor plates of the upper levels of the bracketing scheme, providing light and air to all offices. The staff café would have a roof garden.

URBANISM: The reconfigured site provides an overall identity for the Museum within the city. Lobby and through-block connections are offered as in Concept A. Public view windows along Fifty-fourth Street to the lobby gallery would enliven the currently blank street wall. The public roof area would be larger—however, lower in elevation— than in Concept A. The proposed moving rubber ramps would connect to this upper garden directly.

ART UNDERGROUND: The underground, or "Orpheum," space gained in Concept B is an experimental space of vast proportions. This 21,000-square-foot, below-ground volume corresponds to an underground focus on art of any and all media. This space, added to the given program, provides the volumetric equivalent of a prediction for a very active "art of our time" in the future.

DARKNESS: The mysteries of darkness and the unknown are an aspect of Concept B. Natural light plays a much subtler role in the horizontal organization. The horizontal promenade is bracketed by natural light at turning points in the sequence of galleries. The "Orpheum" underground space is characterized by darkness with glowing bits of light. All staff offices are located aboveground with natural light.

CIRCULATION: A through-block lobby contains quiet moving ramps lifting the public to the horizontal gallery floors and finally to the roof garden. . . . The staff (and public library) entrance is east of the garden on Fifty-third Street, with separate elevators. The art and service loading docks are reached at opposite ends on Fifty-fourth Street.

ALTERNATE STUDIES: Studies might consider a version of Concept B that doesn't move the garden. . . .

Project Credits
Steven Holl Architects: Steven Holl, Justin Rüssli, Jan Kinsbergen, Annette Goderbauer, Michael Hofmann, Molly Blieden, Julia Barnes Mandle; Consulting Engineers: Guy Nordenson, Ove Arup and Partners; Code Consultant: Beth Lochtefeld Code Consultant/Expediter, Inc.; Consulting Artists: Solange Fabião, James Holl

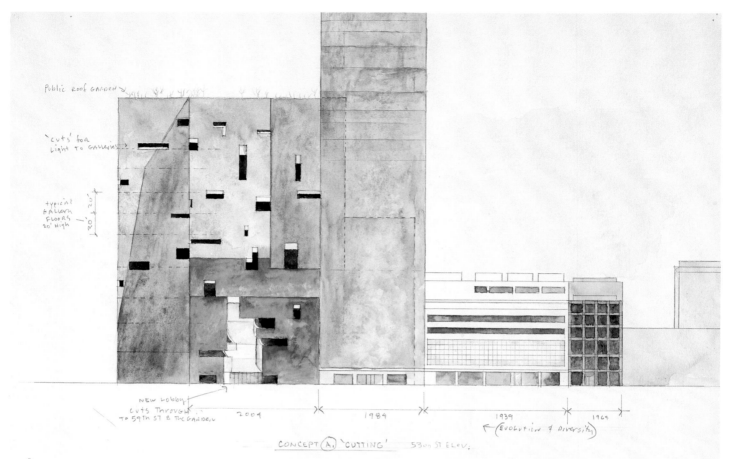

Public ROOF GARDEN

'CUTS' FOR
LIGHT TO GALLERIES

TYPICAL
GALLERY
FLOORS
20' HIGH

NEW LOBBY
CUTS THROUGH
TO 59TH ST & THE GARDEN

2004   1984   1939   1964

← (EVOLUTION & DIVERSITY)

CONCEPT (A) 'CUTTING'   53RD ST ELEV.

CUTTING SCHEME:

① NATURAL LIGHT IN
EVERY GALLERY
- A CUTTING, SLICING,
PIERCING OF THE
MAXIMUM ZONING
ENVELOPE

② A SLICE OR POT
OF NATURAL LIGHT
IN EACH GALLERY
ALLOWS
- SENSE OF
TIME, DAY
& SEASON
- ORIENTATION
- DIFFERENTIATION

③ SERVICE &
HVAC IN
RESIDUE
SPACE

SOLID
MARKING
PLASTER
WALLS

SLICE OF
NATURAL LIGHT
IN VIDEO &
ED. GALLERY

53

Above:
Concept A: Cutting. Fifty-third Street elevation.
Watercolor and pencil on paper, 11 x 16¾" (27.9 x 42.5 cm)

Left:
Concept A: Cutting. Section and interior perspectives. Watercolor and pencil on paper, 11 x 16¾" (27.9 x 42.5 cm)

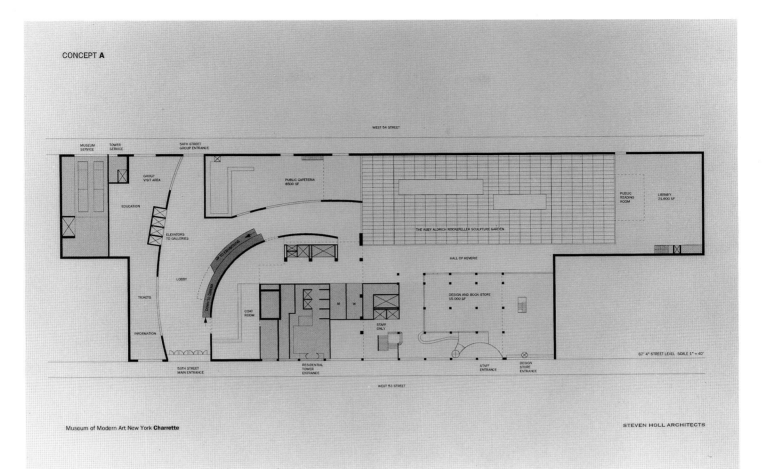

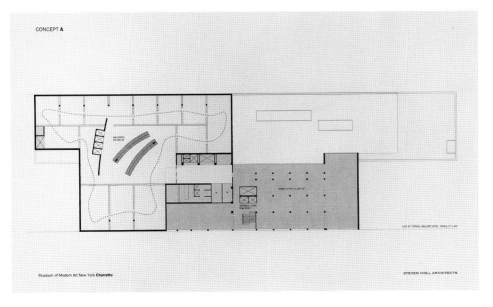

Above:
Concept A: Cutting. First floor plan. Computer-generated print, 11 x 17" (27.9 x 43.2 cm)

Left:
Concept A: Cutting. Gallery floor plan. Computer-generated print, 11 x 17" (27.9 x 43.2 cm)

Concept A: Cutting. Three views of model. Color laser copy on paper, 11 x 17" (27.9 x 43.2 cm)

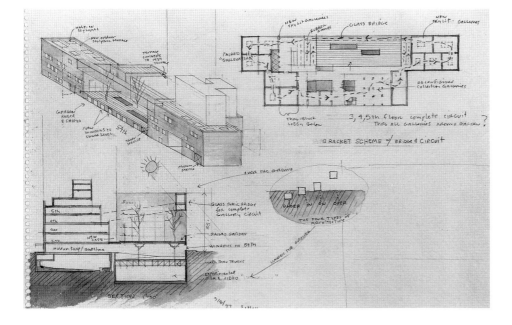

Concept B: Bracketing. Section, plan, and perspective. Watercolor and pencil on paper, 11 x 16¾" (27.9 x 42.5 cm)

Above:
Concept B: Bracketing. Exterior perspective. Watercolor and pencil on paper, 11 x 16¾" (27.9 x 42.5 cm)

Left:
Concept B: Bracketing. View of model. Color laser copy on paper, 11 x 17" (27.9 x 43.2 cm)

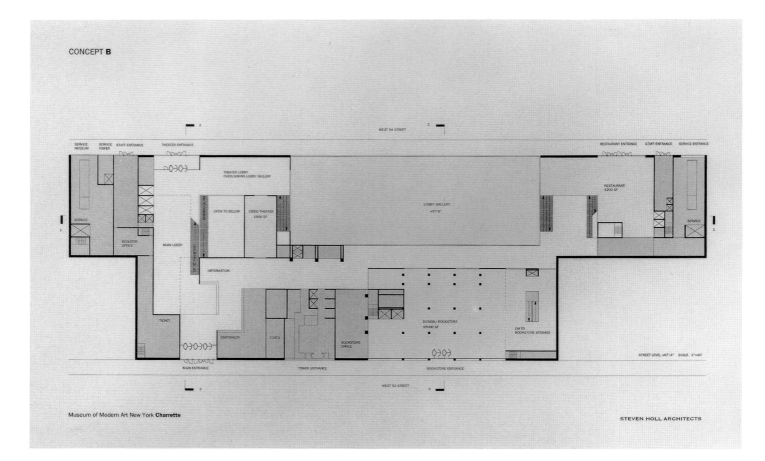

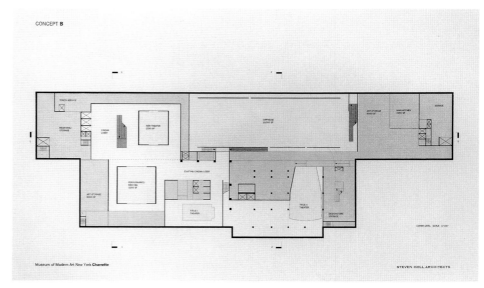

Above:
Concept B: Bracketing. First floor plan. Computer-generated print on paper, 11 x 17" (27.9 x 43.2 cm)

Right:
Concept B: Bracketing. Mezzanine floor plan. Computer-generated print on paper, 11 x 17" (27.9 x 43.2 cm)

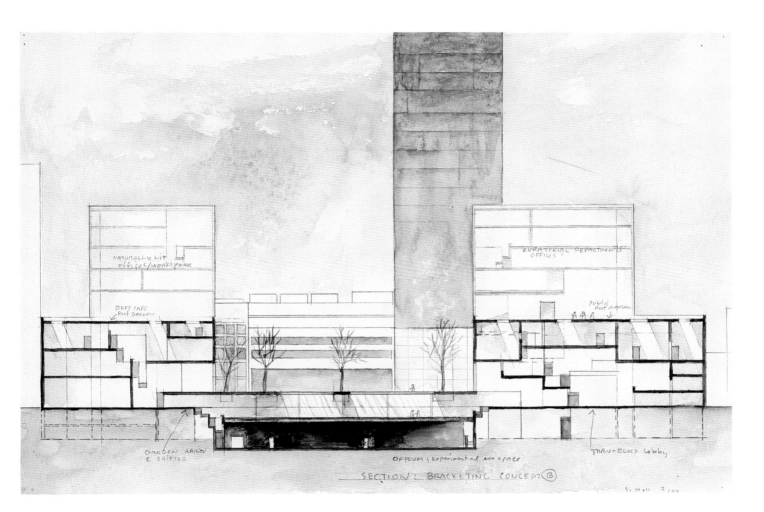

**Concept B: Bracketing. Section. Watercolor
and pencil on paper, 11 x 16¾" (27.9 x 42.5 cm)**

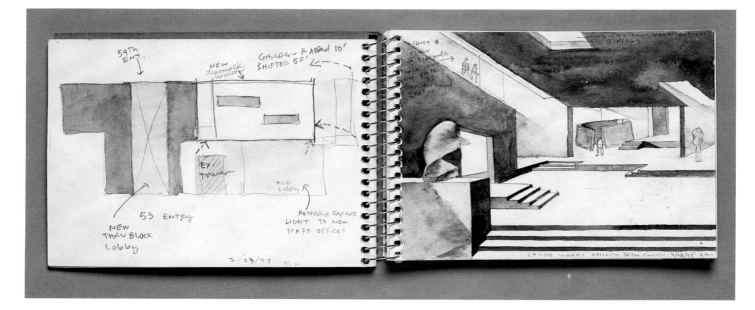

Above:
Sketchbook: First floor plan and interior perspective of gallery. Watercolor on paper, 5 x 14⅛" (12.7 x 35.9 cm) overall

Right:
Sketchbook: "MoMA's Centennial Wing" (detail). Watercolor on paper, 5 x 14⅛" (12.7 x 35.9 cm) overall

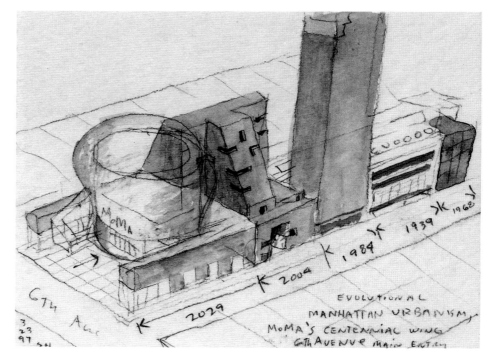

Above:
Sketchbook: "Evolutional or Involutional." Watercolor on paper, 5 x 14⅛" (12.7 x 35.9 cm) overall

Left:
Sketchbook: "Catatonic problem of categories" (detail). Watercolor on paper, 5 x 14⅛" (12.7 x 35.9 cm) overall

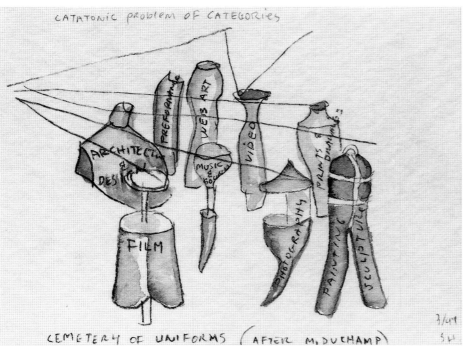

Toyo Ito

Born in Tokyo, Japan, 1941
Education: Bachelor of Architecture, Tokyo University, 1965
Selected projects: Tower of the Winds, Yokohama, Japan, 1986; ITM Building,
Matsuyama, Ehime, Japan, 1990–93; Shimosuwa Municipal Museum, Nagano,
Japan, 1990–93

FROM THE ARCHITECT'S STATEMENT

When I leave Tokyo and visit New York, I visit MoMA. This is where the sense of being in Manhattan becomes real to me. It is always a somewhat mysterious experience. While I am expecting a sense of speed, and the experience of hard-edged as well as transparent space in New York, I find a sense of ease and comfort in the space of MoMA, which is completely different from the surrounding space of New York. When I linger in front of the paintings by Mondrian, or feel the presence of Oldenburg's sculptures, I feel a kind of certainty that is hard to describe. It even appears that just being in MoMA gives me a supportive sense of conviction in what I am trying to do in my own work.

This kind of experience I know I can never have in museums in Tokyo. That is a totally unique quality, which I think is completely founded on MoMA's sense of place, a place one can perhaps describe as a Manhattan within Manhattan. In MoMA, various objects create their own spaces around them, together forming many "places," not unlike the condition in a city. I visit and wander among those "places," as if I were island-hopping, and those islands connect themselves with me, which in turn become another Manhattan for me.

Main Concepts

1. MOMA 21 IS ANOTHER TOWER (LYING SKYSCRAPER): Many historical places where art and space coexist are scattered around MoMA. The new MoMA must integrate these fragmented places and create a strong image as a whole through the expansion. We propose to design a skyscraper that lies horizontally on Fifty-fourth Street, connecting The Abby Aldrich Rockefeller Sculpture Garden and the expansion site.

2. MOMA 21 CONCEIVED OF AS A BAR(R) CODE: Town houses in Manhattan are laid out in a bar-code manner along the streets. MoMA, which has been expanded over time, also conforms to this bar-code-like spatial structure. We propose to enhance this bar-code spatial structure through the expansion. Specifically, we propose to enhance the bar code of time (history) along Fifty-third Street, and the bar code of space along Fifty-fourth Street. The bar-code system, in our definition, juxtaposes all the components as parallel, without any center, and creates a kind of abstract space, which enables free expansion. This is exactly the code we feel that most closely aligns with the spirit of MoMA's founding director, Alfred Barr.

3. MOMA 21 EMBODIES . . . ANOTHER MANHATTAN WITHIN MANHATTAN: These two parallel bar codes create a rather ambiguous space between them, and that is where a junctionlike traffic space is provided, connecting the two bar codes. This space is not to be a simple linear route, but rather a kind of changeover, instrument-like space that enables visitors to choose their own different routes. This space is also a highly fluid and multidimensional urban space. This space enables visitors to develop a poetic sensibility by making their own free choices.

Proposal

1. PRESERVATION AND RENOVATION: We propose to preserve the existing buildings in principle, except that the ground floor of the north wing will be reconstructed, in order to enhance the relationship between the sculpture garden and the new expansion site.

2. NEW GALLERY SPACE: We propose to maintain the existing collection gallery spaces as they are for the most part. There will be nine gallery space units (one unit = approximately 6,500 to 8,000 square feet, from mezzanine level to fourth floor) on the expansion site. While six of them will be temporary exhibition spaces, all the gallery spaces will be interchangeable and have the freedom of being able to change their use.

3. ENTRANCE: In principle, Fifty-third Street provides the entrance for the general visitors, members, and staff, and Fifty-fourth Street for service. We propose to maintain the existing main entrance as it is and provide a new entrance on the western end of Fifty-third Street for visitors to the theaters, library, and education center, and for visitors, members, and staff. There will be a new, second loading dock on the western end of Fifty-fourth Street. Other entrances will remain as they are.

4. CONNECTION SPACE: The connection among the different functions, horizontally as well as vertically, will be provided at the center through a devicelike space, which we propose to call "Manhattan." It consists of various elevators (ten in total), escalators (eleven in total), stairs, and void spaces, which give junction space the impression of a three-dimensional electric-circuit panel.

5. GARDENS AND TERRACES: These variously characterized spaces and a complex spatial organization will be integrated by a series of gardens and terraces. Other than the existing sculpture garden at the ground floor, we propose a new performance space on the second floor of the north wing, which could be used as an interior as well as exterior space, a new rooftop garden on the third floor of the garden wing, and another new rooftop garden on the fourth floor that spans between the west wing and the expansion site. In addition, we propose to renovate the terraces that are adjacent to existing spaces. These gardens and terraces will not only clarify the positional relationships among the different spaces for the visitors, but also provide a space for the comfort and relaxation of visitors and staff.

6. MEZZANINE LEVEL: We propose to make various openings on the ground floor in order to create a visual connection between the ground floor and the mezzanine, and thus endorse the spatial value of the mezzanine. By renovating the lobby space to serve the three theaters, as well as connecting it to a new entrance on the western end on the ground floor, we propose to create a spatially festive atmosphere not unlike the theater district at night.

7. IMPROVEMENT OF SPACES FOR THE CURATORIAL DEPARTMENTS: The six curatorial departments will be situated on the fourth to sixth floors along the Fifty-third Street side, two departments on each floor. Each department will have a clear and comprehensive layout which consists of different spaces, such as a study center, storage space, and individual office spaces for the curators. We also propose to renovate and provide the gardens, terraces, and staff lounge, in order to guarantee a comfortable environment for the staff. The new curatorial department design will also make use by outside researchers easier and more accessible.

8. CONSTRUCTION STRATEGY: This proposal retains all of the existing buildings except for the north wing, and thus makes it possible to keep the Museum open as it is now during construction. The construction can be assumed to be phased into the following three stages: 1) New construction of the expansion site; 2) Demolition of the north wing, renovation of the connecting part between the expansion and the existing wings, renovation of the sculpture garden and the garden wing; 3) Renovation of the spaces along the Fifty-third Street side.

Project Credits
Toyo Ito; Takeo Higashi, Sinichi Takeuchi, Nobuhiro Tsukada, Akihisa Hirata, Hironori Matsubara, Mikko Summanen

MoMA 21 = LYING SKYSCRAPER

MoMA 21 = another Tower (Lying Skyscraper).
Many historical places, where art and space are coexisting are scattered around MoMA. The new MoMA(MoMA 21) must integrate these fragmented places and create a strong image as a whole through the expansion.
We propose to design a skyscraper that lies horizontally on 54th street, connecting the Abby Aldrich Rockefeller Sculpture Garden and the expansion site.

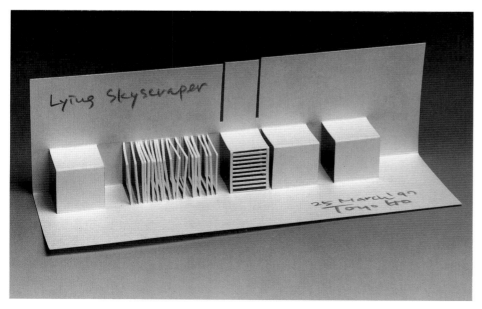

Above:
"MoMA 21 = Lying Skyscraper": View of conceptual model. Computer-generated print on paper, 11 x 16½" (27.9 x 41.9 cm)

Left:
Conceptual model. Paper, 2⅛ x 6¾ x 2⅛" (5.4 x 17.1 x 5.4 cm), variable

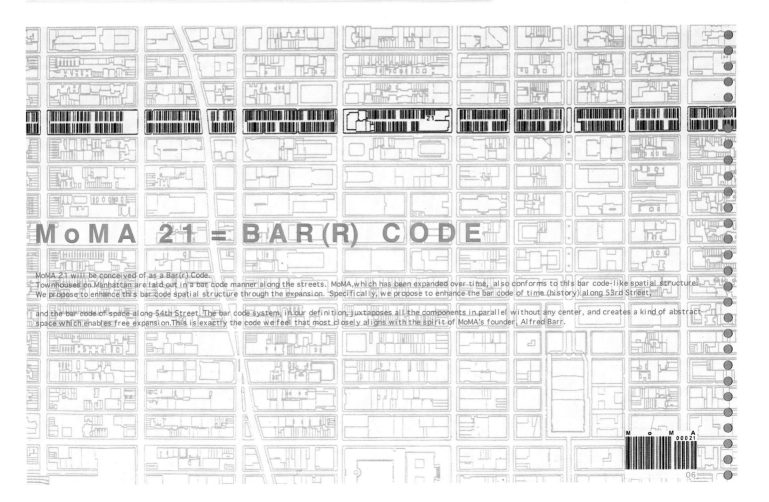

SITEPLAN 1"=100'

Left:
Expansion site plan. Computer-generated print on paper, 11 x 16½" (27.9 x 41.9 cm)

Below:
"MoMA 21 = Bar(r) Code." Computer-generated print on paper, 11 x 16½" (27.9 x 41.9 cm)

MoMA 21 = BAR(R) CODE

MoMA 21 will be conceived of as a Bar(r) Code.
Townhouses on Manhattan are laid out in a bar code manner along the streets. MoMA, which has been expanded over time, also conforms to this bar code-like spatial structure.
We propose to enhance this bar code spatial structure through the expansion. Specifically, we propose to enhance the bar code of time (history) along 53rd Street,

and the bar code of space along 54th Street. The bar code system, in our definition, juxtaposes all the components in parallel without any center, and creates a kind of abstract space which enables free expansion. This is exactly the code we feel that most closely aligns with the spirit of MoMA's founder, Alfred Barr.

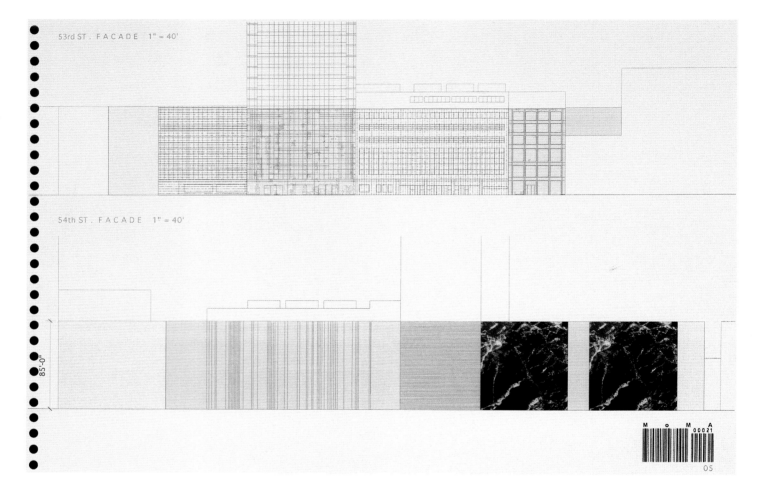

53rd ST. FACADE 1" = 40'

54th ST. FACADE 1" = 40'

85'-0"

Elevations. Computer-generated print on paper,
11 x 16½" (27.9 x 41.9 cm)

MoMA 21 = ANOTHER MANHATTAN

MoMA 21 embodies the discovery of another Manhattan within Manhattan.
These two parallel bar codes create a rather ambiguous space between them, and that is where a junction-like traffic space is provided, connecting the two bar codes. This space is not to be a simple linear route, but rather a kind of changeover instrument-like space that enables the visitors to choose their own different routes. This space is also a highly fluid and multi-dimensional urban space. This space enables the visitors to develop poetic sensibility by making their own free choices.

**"MoMA 21 = Another Manhattan": Site plan.
Computer-generated print on paper, 11 x 16½"
(27.9 x 41.9 cm)**

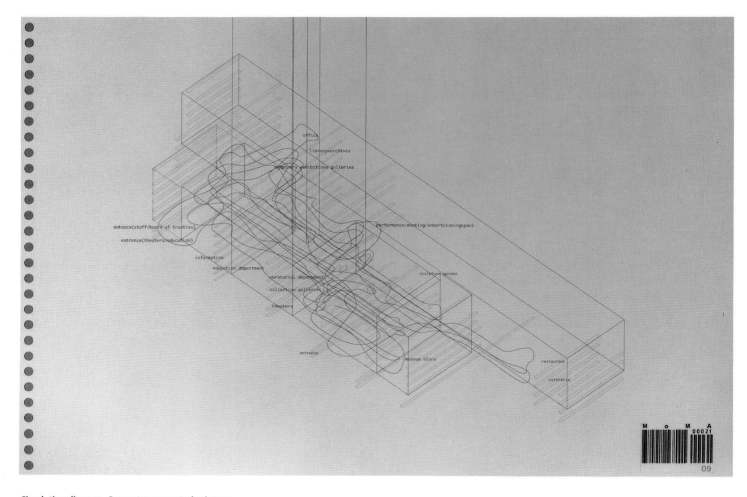

**Circulation diagram. Computer-generated print on
paper, 11 x 16½" (27.9 x 41.9 cm)**

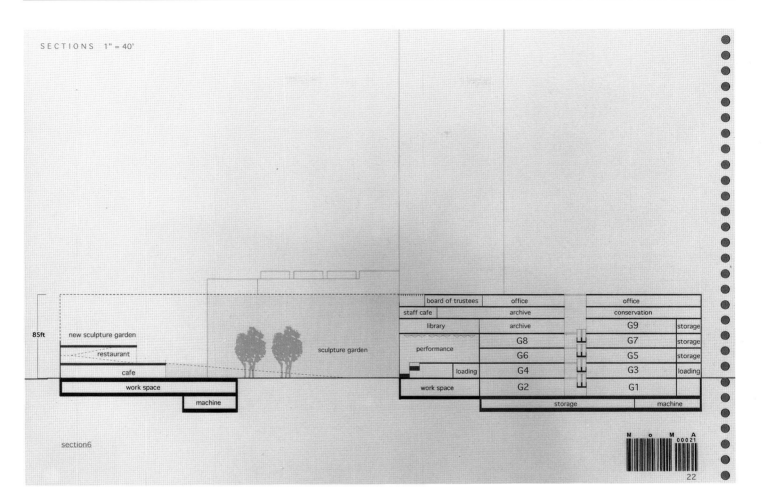

SECTIONS 1" = 40'

	board of trustees	office		office	
staff cafe	archive		conservation		
library	archive		G9	storage	
performance	G8		G7	storage	
	G6		G5	storage	
	loading	G4		G3	loading
work space	G2		G1		
		storage		machine	

85ft

new sculpture garden

restaurant

cafe

work space

machine

sculpture garden

section6

M o M A 00021

22

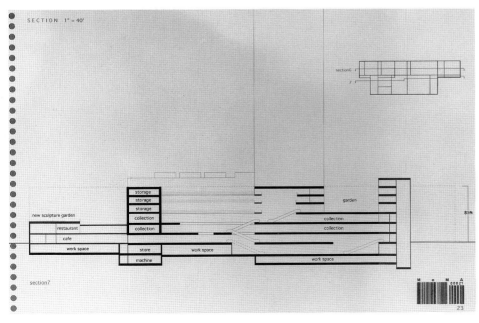

SECTION 1" = 40'

section6

new sculpture garden

restaurant

cafe

work space

machine

store

work space

storage
storage
storage
collection
collection
collection

collection

garden

work space

85ft

section7

M o M A 00021

23

Above:
Section. Computer-generated print on paper,
11 x 16½" (27.9 x 41.9 cm)

Left:
Section. Computer-generated print on paper,
11 x 16½" (27.9 x 41.9 cm)

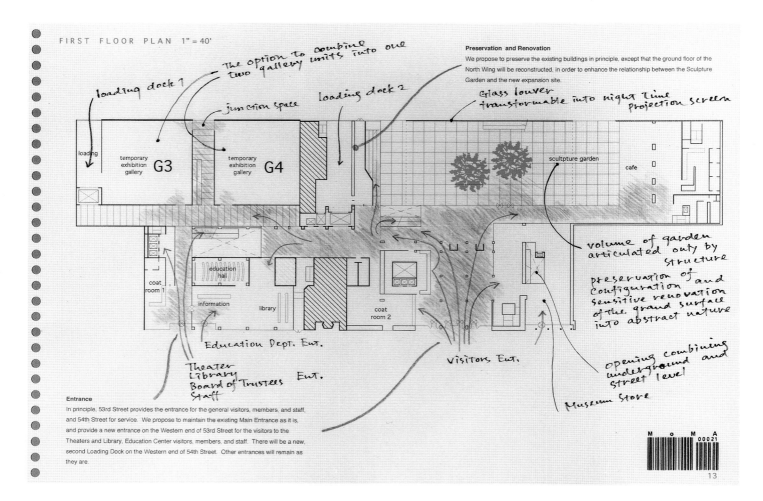

FIRST FLOOR PLAN 1" = 40'

loading dock 1

The option to combine two gallery units into one

junction space   *loading dock 2*

Preservation and Renovation
We propose to preserve the existing buildings in principle, except that the ground floor of the North Wing will be reconstructed, in order to enhance the relationship between the Sculpture Garden and the new expansion site.

Glass louver transformable into night time projection screen

loading

temporary exhibition gallery **G3**

temporary exhibition gallery **G4**

sculpture garden   cafe

volume of garden articulated out by structure

coat room 1

education hall

preservation of configuration and sensitive renovation of the grand surface into abstract nature

information   library   coat room 2

Education Dept. Ent.

Theater Library Board of Trustees Ent. Staff

Visitors Ent.

opening combining underground and street level

Museum Store

Entrance
In principle, 53rd Street provides the entrance for the general visitors, members, and staff, and 54th Street for service. We propose to maintain the existing Main Entrance as it is, and provide a new entrance on the Western end of 53rd Street for the visitors to the Theaters and Library, Education Center visitors, members, and staff. There will be a new, second Loading Dock on the Western end of 54th Street. Other entrances will remain as they are.

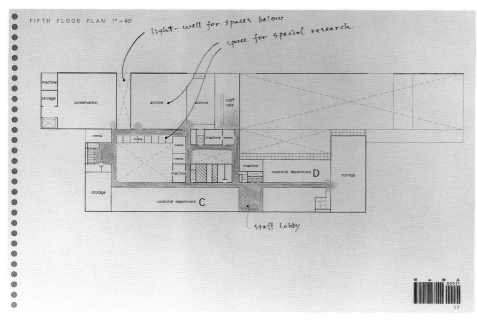

FIFTH FLOOR PLAN 1" = 40'

light-well for spaces below

space for special research

machine

storage   conservation   archive   archive   staff cafe

meeting   meeting   machine   meeting

meeting

meeting

machine   curatorial department **D**   storage

storage

storage   curatorial department **C**

staff Lobby

Above:
First floor plan. Ink on computer-generated print on paper, 11 x 16½" (27.9 x 41.9 cm)

Left:
Fifth floor plan. Ink on computer-generated print on paper, 11 x 16½" (27.9 x 41.9 cm)

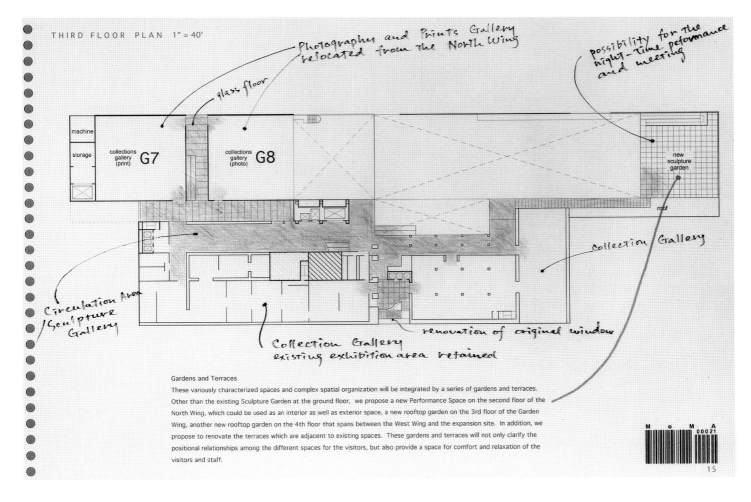

THIRD FLOOR PLAN 1" = 40'

Photography and Prints Gallery relocated from the North Wing

possibility for the night-time performance and meeting

glass floor

machine

storage

collections gallery (print)   **G7**

collections gallery (photo)   **G8**

new sculpture garden

roof

Collection Gallery

Circulation Area / Sculpture Gallery

Collection Gallery existing exhibition area retained

renovation of original window

Gardens and Terraces

These variously characterized spaces and complex spatial organization will be integrated by a series of gardens and terraces. Other than the existing Sculpture Garden at the ground floor, we propose a new Performance Space on the second floor of the North Wing, which could be used as an interior as well as exterior space, a new rooftop garden on the 3rd floor of the Garden Wing, another new rooftop garden on the 4th floor that spans between the West Wing and the expansion site. In addition, we propose to renovate the terraces which are adjacent to existing spaces. These gardens and terraces will not only clarify the positional relationships among the different spaces for the visitors, but also provide a space for comfort and relaxation of the visitors and staff.

15

Third floor plan. Ink on computer-generated print on paper, 11 x 16½" (27.9 x 41.9 cm)

Rem Koolhaas

Born: Rotterdam, The Netherlands, 1944
Education: The Architectural Association, London, England, 1968–73
Selected Recent Projects: Kunsthall, Rotterdam, The Netherlands, 1987–92;
Fukuoka Housing, Kiyushu, Japan, 1989–91; Congrexpo, Lille, France, 1990–94

FROM THE ARCHITECT'S STATEMENT

. . . Theoretically, MoMA is about newness. Newness is ambiguous. It cannot last; it cannot have a tradition. . . .

The splendor and uniqueness of MoMA's history complicates its relationship with the present. The expectation of continuity penalizes what is "other," what does not "fit," or the "merely" contemporary. Beyond its power to intimidate, to set standards, to consecrate, an entire domain of exploration, experimentation has become problematic: its investment in a master narrative and the abundant evidence to support "the line" make certain new shows seem like mere tokenism or simply impossible. What can you challenge in a temple? . . .

In this project, we have interpreted the extension as a single operation that maintains what is good, undoes what is dysfunctional, creates new potentials, and leaves open what is undecidable. . . .

The creation of a single display building—a new MoMA— implies that it can be fully equipped to generate unique conditions for each segment of the collections and any of the exhibitions. It will have to accommodate drastically different scales. . . . Because a . . . new building will contain the entire Museum program, it will have the advantages of bigness. . . .

Day and Night

Contemporary art needs spaces equipped for the interaction of human beings and technological implements, people and apparatus. Somehow, daylight is not conducive to this kind of interaction. . . . Whereas painting and sculpture are best revealed in conditions of (simulated) daylight, new arts need a darker, more artificial accommodation, an American night, illuminated by electronic haze, glowing and flickering. There is no escaping the inherent artificiality of the Museum. . . .

Individual vs. Collective

It is a truism that museums are for the masses, the public. . . . Their spaces, their circulations, their diagrams insist on the group, an abstract, undifferentiated client. Yet, more and more technologies provoke the splintering of the collective into an infinite number of individuals, each with his own interest. . . . Such a shift implies that an extension should not only contain new, bigger rooms, but begin to accommodate the individual visitor with a highly specific aim, and also offer cellular accommodation. . . .

Storage vs. Viewing

A museum is an ambiguous treasure house of collections: part is on view and accessible, an often larger part is hidden in storage, aggressively inaccessible. . . . The museum is the only institution that systematically freezes its assets away. Within the extension, the notion of storage should be emancipated. New forms of automated storage, visible storage, and robotic retrieval eliminate arguments of difficult access, unwieldy logistics, and impossibility. Combined with the appeal for a more customized, individual museum experience, the rethinking of storage initiates a new way of conceptualizing the collection. . . .

The Project(s)

URBANISM 2: . . . The city should be admitted to the Museum. The ground floor is reconsidered as a single urban surface. The sculpture garden is lowered, so that its perimeter can inject daylight into the former basement. Because the sculpture garden is sunken, the wall that now surrounds it disappears. This creates a direct visual transparency between Fifty-third and Fifty-fourth streets. The two streets acquire a potential equivalence that allows a large variety of entry and exit points and the orchestration of the different flows of visitors. The new level of the sculpture garden is extended as a garden/moat around the entire perimeter of the ground floor, which becomes in its entirety a metropolitan island. . . . This island has become the new lobby. Technically, these spaces—as an explosion of the notion of the present bookshop, used as a café, urban living room, and introductory platform to MoMA's adjunct activities, such as education—could even be entirely open-air in the summer. Daylight now surrounds the former basement on all sides. This new garden level becomes the formal entrance. Previously unfindable elements such as the theaters benefit from a new exposure.

The site of the present restaurant is liberated. As an interior extension of the sculpture garden we project a MoMA forum: a space designed to enable MoMA to organize a wide variety of events, from conferences to parties. . . . A large balcony—partly inside, partly outside—hovers on street level to create a potential autonomy. It has an independent entrance off the revalued Fifty-fourth Street. Loading bays for both the Museum and the tower are organized on the west, against the Athletic Club building. The site to the west of the Museum of American Folk Art site is used as a temporary MoMA store. Its roof, accessible from the new Museum, is used as an outdoor exhibition area.

TECHNOLOGY: . . . There are two areas in which recent inventions can make a radical difference: control and transport. . . . Miniaturized technologies offer literally infinite variety, choice, differentiation, and individualization in otherwise stable structures. Robotics replace laborious, unwieldy processes of storage, retrieval, sorting, and reshuffling with smooth movements of frenzied ease that force us to rethink entire systems of classification and categorization. Electronic wiring enables the coexistence of authentic and virtual worlds. . . .

The second innovation is in transport. As more and more architecture is finally unmasked as the mere organization of flow—shopping centers, airports—it is evident that circulation is what makes or breaks public architecture. . . . Two simple, almost primitive, inventions have driven modernization toward mass occupancy of previously unattainable heights: the elevator and the escalator. . . . One moves only up and down, one only diagonally. . . .

At the dawn of the twenty-first century, a number of advances in vertical transportation are being made, from cableless self-propelled elevator systems to Otis's . . . Odyssey, a small train, platform, or large box that moves horizontally, vertically, and diagonally—literally opening up new architectural potential: to extend the urban condition itself from the ground floor to strategic points inside a building in a continuous trajectory. . . . We have investigated Odyssey's potential of vertical movement in the context of the new MoMA. The program of MoMA is so enormous that it inevitably organizes the public on at least ten levels or more, and the Dorset site extends the length of MoMA to over 600 feet. The escalator cannot deal with those heights, the elevator cannot deal with the length: the Odyssey offers . . . hybrid movements up to the challenge. Beginning above the sculpture garden, its trajectory perforates the new Museum with a diagonal courtyard to ascend to the top of the triangle in a single, fluid movement.

THE BOX: . . . By projecting the front of the Pelli construction to the north, across the Dorset site to Fifty-fourth Street, a square is generated that accommodates the entire exhibition program in six layers. Instead of a logic of consecutive extensions that are more-or-less noticeably connected, this strategy would clearly establish a center of gravity on the site. Since all displays would take place in this building, all of its technical equipment and innovation would benefit the entire collection. . . . Such an operation consolidates circulation, services, and adjunct facilities. It creates the greatest possible potentials and freedoms for all imaginable conditions of display and exhibition.

Four typologies have been developed for this charette. . . . We propose two versions of the ultimate box. In the first, the Pelli extension is completely dismantled around the Museum Tower, so that an entirely new condition can be constructed. In the second, the façades of Pelli's buildings are stripped and the floors remain, so that with the addition of a new building the whole would create a differentiation of spaces, ceiling heights, floor levels, and other conditions.

TRIANGLE/PENTHOUSE: The remaining program fits exactly in that section of the zoning envelope that forms a single triangular volume spanning between Fifty-third and Fifty-fourth streets. . . . The triangle contains a restaurant at the roof of the exhibition building, public storage accommodation, research facilities, individual viewing cabins for contemplation or study, offices, a library, conservation studios, ateliers, a members' room, and, at the apex, a special-events center.

OLD MoMA: The concentration of the entire exhibition program in a new building liberates the old MoMA for a new role. It accommodates, in a self-evident way, the six departments, one per floor. On each floor, storage would be organized on the west side, as a buffer or connector between the departments and the new Museum. The old personnel core connects this storage silo with the larger horizontal storage underneath the new exhibition building. By using the old MoMA for the departments, we can also reduce the height of the second floor and so add another 6 feet to the height of the ground floor.

MoMA, INC.: On the east side, the individual departments are connected to MoMA, Inc.: a tower using Philip Johnson's 1970s building as a base, dedicated to administration, membership, publishing, and other activities of dissemination and aura-enhancement. Plans are made and funds raised in the MoMA, Inc., tower, which filter down to the curatorial departments; the "thinking" and "knowledge" then activate the idle treasures in their respective storages, which are then propelled to the exhibition surfaces. . . . The Museum's chain of fundraising, "curating," storage, artifact selection, and public display would correspond to the diagram of the new buildings. The chain is also, literally, an ambulatory that runs along Fifty-third Street on the level of the original balcony to connect tower, box, and triangle.

Project Credits
Rem Koolhaas, Dan Wood with Vincent Coste, Isabelle Da Silva, Rojier van Est, Wilfried Hackenbroich, Matthias Hollwich, Joshua Ramus, Ole Scheeren, Kohei Kashimoto; Graphic Design 2x4: Michael Rock, Susan Sellers with David Israel, Chin-Lien Chen, William Morrisey, Hitomi Murai; Vincent DeRijk; Steven Ahlgren; Hans Werlemann with Frans Parthesius; Stijn Rademakers, Jeff Hardwick; Bill Price, Eric Schotte

Conceptual models. Acrylic resin, paint, and mixed metals, larger model: 8½ x
8¾ x 2⅞" (21.6 x 22.2 x 7.3 cm), variable, on base measuring 1¾ x 17¼ x 11½"
(4.4 x 43.8 x 29.1 cm); smaller models, each 1⅜ x 3 x 3" (3.5 x 7.6 x 7.6 cm)

**Charette book: Perspective view of automated study
center. 10½ x 23" (26.7 x 58.4 cm) overall**

For the charrette we have explored four versions of the new museum building. In order to accumulate per-mutations that demonstrate the essential versatility of the concept, each has different qualities and advantages. The versions are not intended to be mutually exclusive. In a further elaboration, aspects of each could be incorporated in more definitive research.

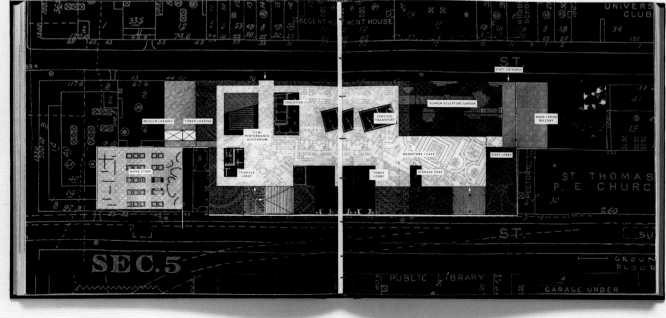

Above:
Charette book: Perspective. 10½ x 23" (26.7 x 58.4 cm)
overall

Opposite:
Charette book. Top: Plan variations for curatorial
block. Bottom: Ground floor plan. Each, 10½ x 23"
(26.7 x 58.4 cm) overall

Above:
View of relocated sculpture garden from lower-level gallery. Collage on paper, 8½ x 14⅛" (21.6 x 35.9 cm)

Left:
Exterior perspective of Fifty-third Street façade. Collage on paper, 8¾ x 13¼" (22.2 x 33.7 cm)

Left:
"MoMA Forum." Collage on paper, 11¾ x 16½"
(29.8 x 41.9 cm)

Below:
View of lower-level gallery. Collage on paper, 11¾ x
16½" (29.8 x 41.9 cm)

Above:
**View of open plaza, ground level. Collage on paper,
11¾ x 16½" (29.8 x 41.9 cm)**

Right:
**Charette book: East-west section showing path of
the "Odyssey" transportation system. 10½ x 23"
(26.7 x 58.4 cm) overall**

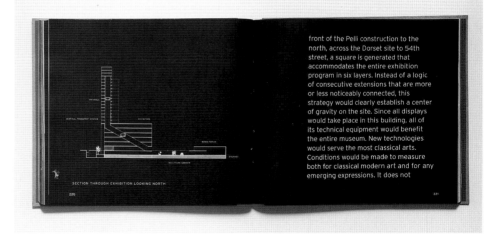

front of the Pelli construction to the
north, across the Dorset site to 54th
street, a square is generated that
accommodates the entire exhibition
program in six layers. Instead of a logic
of consecutive extensions that are more
or less noticeably connected, this
strategy would clearly establish a center
of gravity on the site. Since all displays
would take place in this building, all of
its technical equipment would benefit
the entire museum. New technologies
would serve the most classical arts.
Conditions would be made to measure
both for classical modern art and for any
emerging expressions. It does not

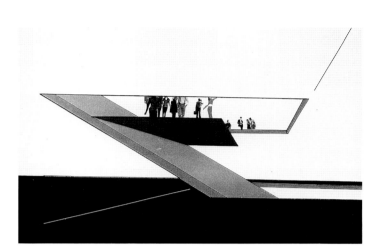

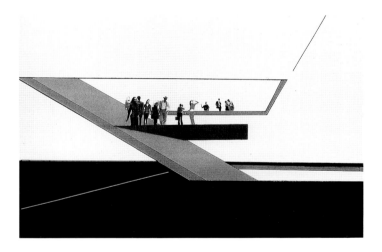

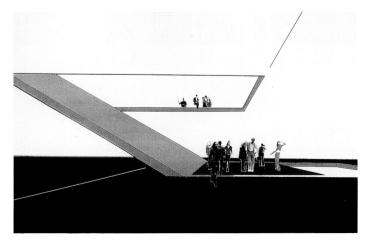

Above:
View of relocated sculpture garden. Collage on paper, 11¾ x 16½" (29.8 x 41.9 cm)

Left:
"Odyssey: A new transportation system." Collages on paper, each 5⅞ x 8⅛"
(14.9 x 20.6 cm)

Dominique Perrault

Born in Clermont-Ferrand, France, 1953
Education: Architect's Diplomas, École Nationale Supérieure des Beaux-Arts, Paris,
France, 1978; Certificate of Advanced Studies in Town Planning, École Nationale des
Ponts et Chaussées, Paris, 1979; Master in Historical Studies, École des Hautes Études
en Sciences Sociales, Paris, 1980
Selected Recent Projects: École Supérieure, Marne-la-Vallée, France, 1984–87; Biblio-
thèque Nationale, Paris, 1989–95; Olympic Velodrome, Berlin, Germany, 1992–98
(projected completion date)

FROM THE ARCHITECT'S STATEMENT

The work presented results from the quest for several architectural solutions. It is not simply a catalogue of projects; following analysis of a given context, our diagnosis . . . clearly identifies the elements to be protected and those to be created. The former constitute the system's common core; the latter reveal the Museum's future evolution and metamorphoses. These variations on a single theme form the basis of our architectural responses.

Our design approach eschews aesthetic bias and calls for the intellectual participation of all. Flexibility, interactivity, and an open mind put quality at the heart of the architectural work.

A priori reflections as to what a great modern art museum of today "ought to be," though doubtless interesting, seem to me to be of the order of a purely intellectual pleasure. . . . The "reality principle" is the bedrock on which the idea of the new Museum will emerge, and not vice versa.

All our work is based on a pragmatic approach to working with what exists . . . but without preconceived notions. The new MoMA will germinate, emerge, and acquire conviction *on the basis of its true situation*; far from rejecting its past, the Museum will assimilate its novel geography, constituting both a pole of identity within the neighborhood, and a landmark for the city of New York.

What are the positive aspects of the existing situation? The range and quality of the Museum's collection, the MoMA team's commitment to the communication and conservation of modern art, a 1930s façade, and a garden—all facets of the *genius loci*.

What are its negative elements? Uncomfortable, ill-adapted workplaces; cramped, inflexible exhibition spaces; and above all, the absence of natural lighting and a lack of visual or physical relations with the Museum's urban surroundings.

Initial analysis reveals differences in character and function between Fifty-third and Fifty-fourth streets. The former is predominantly pedestrian, with public or private access to the Museum and proximity to a branch of the New York Public Library, the Museum design store, and other activities in the vicinity. The latter is primarily a thoroughfare furnishing access to service vehicles, but more impor-

tantly, it is the site of a patch of nature, the garden. The opposition constitutes MoMA's specific identity within the city street (Fifty-third Street) and garden (Fifty-fourth Street).

This ambivalence sums up the whole history of MoMA; its specific geography forms the basis of our design solutions. The resulting diagnosis privileges two avenues of development: extension of the Goodwin and Stone front, in order to create a homogeneous street front and highlight Cesar Pelli's soaring tower; extension of the garden in two directions toward Fifth Avenue and on the site of the Dorset Hotel.

This reading clarifies the urban situation by dividing the block lengthwise into two distinct parts—built façade overlooking Fifty-third Street; open façade overlooking Fifty-fourth Street. And yet one cannot speak of a "front" and a "back"; rather, there is a street Museum front, and a garden Museum front.

The public or private entrances, like so many addresses along a street, punctuate Fifty-third Street while preserving the beautiful main entrance, which guarantees direct visual access to the garden. The idea of further access on Fifty-fourth, via part of the garden, is in no way incompatible with this. Our transversal configuration "opens up" the Museum to the life of the neighborhood. The stroller, attracted by the "open space" of the garden, will be able to enter the Museum without having to walk around it.

The entrances situated on either side lead into MoMA itself, whose organizational structure can be compared to that of a tree. It extends into the ground as if in search of "life force"; an elongated main body forms a sturdy "trunk," while its "branches" and foliage extend "aside," "along," or "above." To crown it all, Pelli's tower soars skyward in concert with its neighbors.

Whatever these roots and branches, the trunk is our initial concern. It constitutes the heart of the project. Architectural and functional analyses of the existing building show that the exhibition spaces are not in their "rightful" place.

By installing the library and conservation departments on floors currently given over to the exhibitions, we optimize the existing building, both functionally and in terms of the quality of its workplaces. Extended office spaces occupy the top of the building and are lit naturally. Our clarification "puts things back in place" without requiring costly restructuring—we privilege efficiency, quality, and economy of means.

Extension of the garden hall throughout the length and height of the edifice creates a living space bathed in natural light, furnishing access to all levels via a system of vertical and horizontal distributions. This artery constitutes MoMA's spinal cord.

The garden hall becomes a promenade within the Museum. Leading directly off to the entrance halls, overlooking the garden throughout its length, and bringing light to the Titus theaters and the temporary exhibition gallery below, this ambulatory space intersects with the library and reading room at the second level, brings the public into contact with the departments, and leads into the Museum's treasure—the collection galleries. . . .

Thus the "trunk"—the beating heart of MoMA—is constituted without causing major disruptions, and develops and amplifies the morphology of the existing building. From there, three possible configurations are imagined for the Museum's exhibition spaces: aside, along, and above.

Aside

In the "tradition" of MoMA's extensions to date, this variant constructs a new building termed "large gallery" on an adjacent site earmarked for this.

A structure overlooking Fifty-fourth Street, equivalent in volume to that of the garden (void equals solid), sits above the temporary gallery. Accessible from both streets, a vast entrance hall leads off to all the functions open to the public. A flooring system consisting of freely organized plateaus constitutes the Museum's museographic spaces. Carefully filtered and modulated natural light penetrates to the inner recesses of the building. This translucent glass case makes for a considerable degree of flexibility in its organization. One might even envisage sliding floors or partitions, allowing for easy modulation of the exhibition spaces.

The garden front, visible from Fifth Avenue, forms a grand window onto the city, in particular the skyscraper group culminating in Philip Johnson's AT&T Building.

Along

This tribute to the modern movement takes the form of an elongated block running the whole length of the existing building. Especially noteworthy are the precise geometrical relations between vertical (the Pelli tower) and horizontal (the low-rise block itself). The length of the garden on Fifty-fourth Street is equal to the height of the tower. . . .

The global morphology of MoMA can be thought of as a musical stave, a series of parallel lines punctuated with various events (or "notes"). The first of these lines is the trunk or common core along Fifty-third Street, as previously described; the second is the garden hall, a vast promenade bathed in natural light; the third is the horizontal line of collection galleries and their peristyle, or colonnade, which in turn liberates a fourth line, the garden, running the whole length of the Museum on Fifty-fourth Street.

The temporary exhibition spaces are deployed beneath the garden, alongside the "theaters" and their common foyer. . . . The space divides up into several exhibition spaces, from the "cabinet" to a vast plateau for works that are "monumental," whether in size or in significance.

We thus imagine a "line of light"—a translucent structure filtering direct natural light by day, which becomes opalescent when artificially lit at night. Careful geometrical treatment confers a large degree of architectural unity on the Museum as a whole.

The tower no longer overwhelms the Museum, but rather crowns it in the manner of a campanile, highlighting the purity of the building, the generous dimensions of the garden, and the soaring tower. . . .

Above

Our search for possible architectural developments of the exhibition galleries from the common core or trunk led us to envisage a third possibility, that of a hanging extension.

This technically more intricate variant liberates generous open spaces (garden and garden hall) and protected spaces (temporary exhibition and collection galleries): An inhabited roof floating above the garden covers the existing building; a large roof resembling a thin foil or leaf federates the various buildings in the manner of a shelter—a mythical "first dwelling" protecting the human group and its culture against a hostile world; a spacious, well-lit roof that lets in light and water at given points and thus enables the garden to "breathe" naturally; a roof caught between earth and sky that borders Fifty-fourth Street without walling it off or shutting out light; a roof crowns the Fifty-third Street group of buildings, forming an attic story of free-standing glass; a roof whose breadth affords diverse possibilities of development so as to adapt to the management and growth of the collections; a roof within which the museographic promenade is free and flexible; a roof that hallmarks MoMA's identity as a cultural institution open to the public at large; a roof reflecting the sensibility and vision of modern art as an "installation," conferring "another" meaning on the site and effecting a metamorphosis, perhaps even a transfiguration; a roof conferring identity on the site while preserving the diversity of its component parts, in the manner of de Tocqueville's conception of democracy; a roof suggesting an architecture freed from the constraints of gravity—a "certain idea" of immateriality.

Project Credits
Dominique Perrault; Aude Perrault, Gabriel Choukroun, Maxime Gasperini, Gaëlle Lauriot-Prevost, Anne Kaplan, Guy Morisseau, Georges Fessy, Didier Ghislain

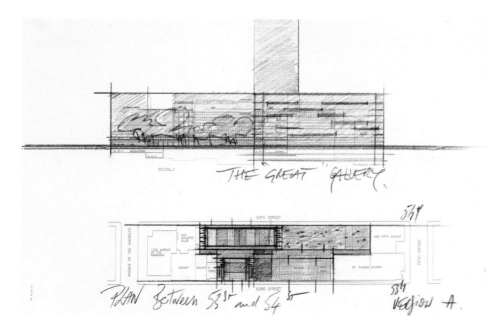

Above:
Conceptual model for "Aside." Plexiglass, plastic, and foamcore, 6 x 11⅛ x 5½" (15.2 x 28.3 x 14 cm), variable, on homosote platform: ½ x 12 x 6¾" (1.3 x 30.5 x 17.1 cm)

Left:
"Project 1: Aside." Section and site plan. Colored pencil on mylar overlay, 11 x 16½" (27.9 x 41.9 cm)

Left:
"Project 1: Aside." Section. Colored pencil on mylar overlay, 11 x 16½" (27.9 x 41.9 cm)

Below:
"Project 1: Aside." Exterior perspective, Fifty-fourth Street. Pencil on paper, 11 x 16½" (27.9 x 41.9 cm)

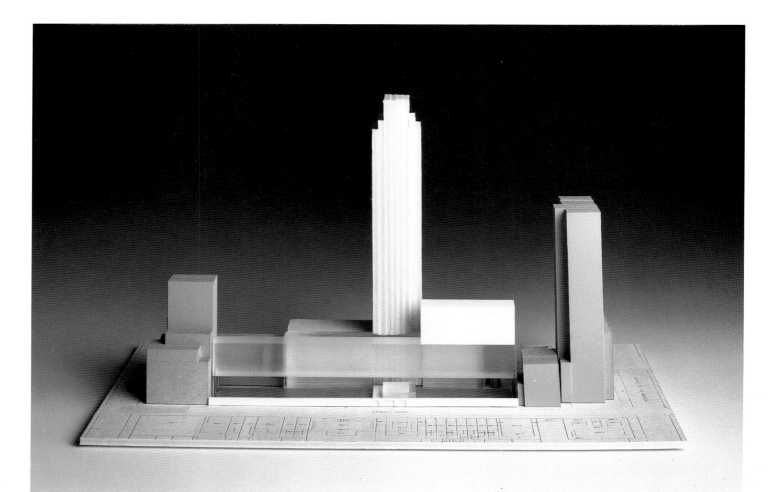

Above:
Conceptual model for "Along." Plexiglass, plastic, and foamcore, 6 x 11⅛ x 5½" (15.2 x 28.3 x 14 cm), variable, on homosote platform: ½ x 12 x 6¾" (1.3 x 30.5 x 17.1 cm)

Right:
"Project 2: Along." Galleries plan. Colored pencil on mylar overlay, 11 x 16½" (27.9 x 41.9 cm)

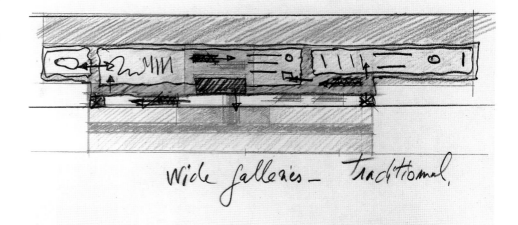

"Project 2: Along." Section. Colored pencil on mylar
overlay, 11 x 16½" (27.9 x 41.9 cm)

"Project 2: Along." Exterior perspective, Fifty-fourth
Street. Pencil on paper, 11 x 16½" (27.9 x 41.9 cm)

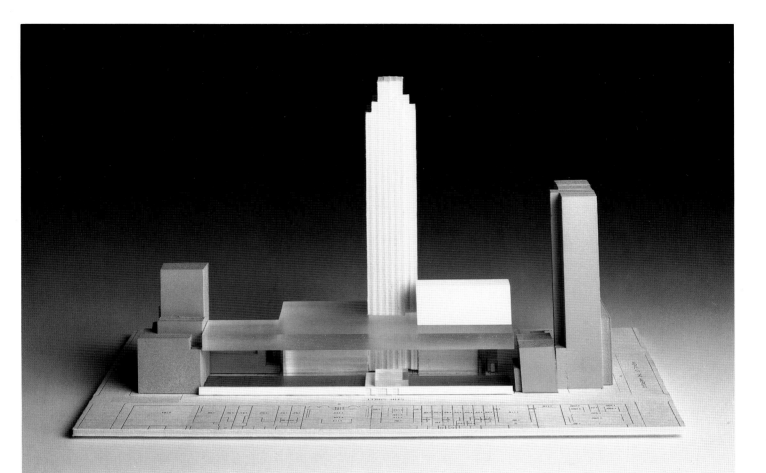

Above:
Conceptual model for "Above." Plexiglass, plastic, and foamcore, 6 x 11⅛ x 5½" (15.2 x 28.3 x 14 cm), variable, on homosote platform: ½ x 12 x 6¾" (1.3 x 30.5 x 17.1 cm)

Left:
"Project 3: Above." Site plan. Colored pencil on mylar overlay, 11 x 16½" (27.9 x 41.9 cm)

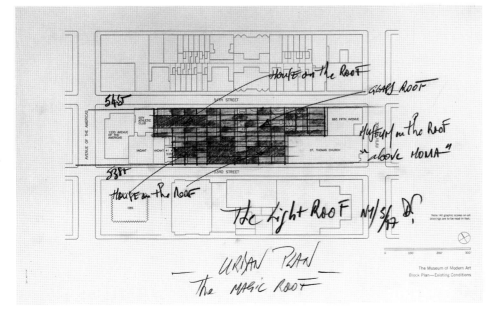

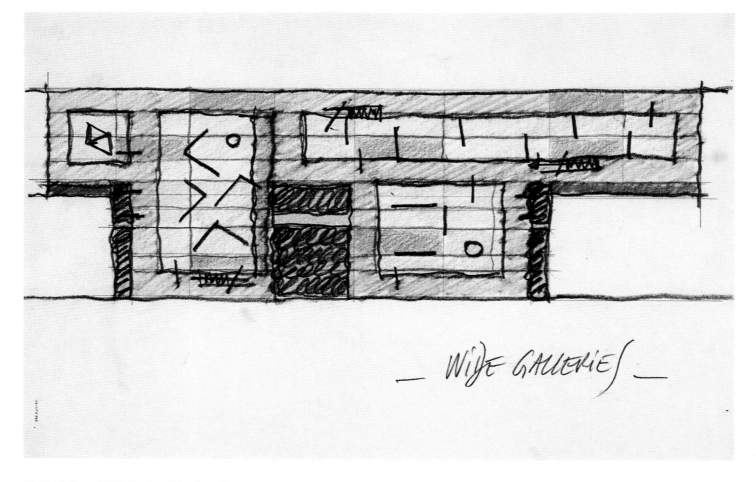

"Project 3: Above." Galleries plan. Colored pencil on
mylar overlay, 11 x 16½" (27.9 x 41.9 cm)

Rafael Viñoly

Born in Montevideo, Uruguay, 1944
Education: Master in Architecture and Urban Design, University of Buenos Aires,
Argentina, 1969
Selected Recent Projects: Tokyo International Forum, Japan, 1992–96; Physical Edu-
cation Facility, Herbert H. Lehman College, New York City, 1989–94; Baltimore Per-
forming Arts Center, Maryland 1995–99 (projected completion date)

FROM THE ARCHITECT'S STATEMENT

The ideas in this box represent a range of alternatives which, although they seem to have reached some finality, are only impressions from an intuitive process tested directly in drawings and models. They were useful to understand the potentials of the program and the limitations of the site. . . . They also map the evolution of my thinking. . . .

These sketches are *partis*. . . . The *parti* coordinates the multiple narratives that we call a design. A *parti* is not a master diagram providing a universal solution for all problems, but a thread that allows different solutions to work together. Some of these ideas could be partially or metaphorically useful in a further phase of development. . . .

Of the many issues discussed . . . two things remained in my mind as being crucial: one, the idea that the experience of art should be decelerated; and two, the complex layers of this midblock midtown urban condition are rich with potential. Deceleration is generated by friction, and in this case that friction should be produced by increasing attention. An assemblage of disparate functions and identifiable spaces could provide the opportunities for multiple arrests in the journey through the Museum. As far as the second, the site's uniqueness, its sense of openness in this dense urban fabric, promotes an architecture of exposure, a building which could relate to the uniformity of the zoning envelope by establishing a dialogue between itself and the city, creating a place from which to contemplate the city also as a work of art.

For me, the primary challenge is how to make the building public while maintaining its various degrees of privacy, that is, how to make the transition between the social act of participation and the private act of contemplation without going from monumentality to alienation. In these sketches, I have investigated . . . the possibilities of that transition. I think now that the key is in the legibility of the choices and the curiosity that could be generated by the articulation of the spaces. The gallery is the place of resolution between the collective and the individual; the procession to it should simultaneously expose (to see and be seen) and orient the viewer. . . .

The building becomes a stage for multiple interpretations, which are initiated by the curatorial staff and iterated by the public. . . . The degree to which space may promote inquiry or "skepticism," its capacity to affirm or question social conventions, is in its capacity to make us reflect on the normative aspects of life. . . . This inquiry would not be created in the neutrality of a flexible box, but through juxta-

posing multiple viewpoints suggested by the opportunities to deviate from a canonized sequence.

This project . . . has important design limitations . . . that may suggest that it is about micro-managing several compromises. For me, the purpose of architectural work is to establish a unique relationship between reality and images, a connection between facts and imagination. The link that makes that relationship possible is the condition of "making." Artistic content in buildings (wonder) comes from the meaning we attribute to that relationship and the intelligence with which this condition is met.

Sketchbooks

1: This sketch explores the idea of attributing to the garden the original reading that defined the scale and character of the midblock condition. It produces an intimate, quasi-residential building . . . with a series of terraces. The image is of a new Museum, . . . with an atmosphere of "protected intimacy," versus a monumental public gathering space. . . .

2: In opposition to the idea of a residential garden, there is the possibility of transforming the garden into a public forecourt to the building. By opening a gap between the Goodwin and Stone building and the church rectory, the entry to the garden would be visible from Fifty-third Street and hinted at from Fifth Avenue. The entry would be from both Fifty-third and Fifty-fourth, giving equal importance to each street, creating a through-block condition. The lobby can now be refocused to the west side of the site, where new, larger-scaled galleries . . . can be located. The existing buildings now become located around an urban court. . . .

3: The *scala regia* takes advantage of the site's strongest dimensional characteristic, its length, and creates a space of encounter and circulation, . . . connecting the basement-level public theaters and working spaces with a rooftop garden. This diagonal perspective from some points would be 600 feet long. . . . There is no straight passage under the tower, and fire walls do not allow for a clear connection between the expansion site and the existing building. The "grand" circulation route is a device to link the disparate building elements.

4: These sketches investigate . . . the Museum's present "architectural collection" of buildings. We suggest a subdivision of the site into four blocks: two renovation projects and two new structures. . . . From the west, a new building for public galleries provides a variety of gallery spaces. The next volume is where the visitors interact with the curatorial staff in study centers and art storage areas. Renovating the Goodwin and Stone building provides a structure dedicated to the curatorial staff of the Museum. A new performing/video arts wing can be located at the east end of the garden. Each project would be designed by a different architect within discrete sites, as the elements are relatively independent from each other. . . .

5: Using the idea of a campus of buildings, an alternative form of circulation is a double helix of grand stairs, where the public circulation is always focused on exterior views, utilizing the light to provide orientation within the building. The alignment of the route is in the north-south axis of the site, reinforcing the street views. . . .

6: This proposal investigates the idea of consolidating all of the gallery spaces on three levels utilizing the entire site area. The double-height window of the Goodwin and Stone building is extended and corresponds to an "elevated sidewalk." This double-height circulation system is reached through a reconstruction of the original stair of the Goodwin and Stone building. It encircles the site, surrounding the galleries. . . .

7: This diagram explores the idea of creating an extrusion building on Fifty-fourth Street, much like a "horizontal tower." The garden becomes an open room, architecturally defined. A sliding roof and wall panels run on a frame that can temporarily enclose the garden for special events. The wall of the garden at grade is replaced by a glass partition that allows public viewing. The residential tower is also "extruded" vertically with an open framework, creating a structure that gives the Museum a place in the skyline of the city. This frame supports a movie screen in the sky that is helium supported. . . . The gallery spaces are based on a module: . . . through the simple device of sliding floor panels, a variety of spatial arrangements can be created within the gallery spaces.

8: The eighth scheme accepts the perimeter of the building as defined by the zoning envelope and the existence of a sequence of discrete interior spaces enclosed by the fire-separation walls. This interior space is shaped by a "network" that links all the public components of the building. This "path of glass and light" provides a web of orientation within the building envelope. . . . The space-making is focused on incidents and elaborations along the internal path rather than on monumental internal volumes. Views to the city are revealed; programmatic elements become destinations. . . . The destination for this route is a new type of gallery, a *Kunsthalle* filled with light and surrounded by the city.

9: This scheme adopts a planning grid to organize the gallery spaces. . . . A 25-by-25-foot grid supports a movable panel system, which can be used to define gallery walls, providing a flexible display system and eliminating the need to constantly rebuild the galleries.

The grid also allows an organization of the new and existing construction. A series of buildings is located on Fifty-fourth Street, linked by an urban-scaled canopy that can announce Museum events. . . .

10: The investigation of the size of the galleries for each department led to the generation of several schemes that respond to the requirements of the specific departments. . . . Each . . . is housed in a separate volume, the most transformable space being that of the temporary galleries. The volumes themselves form the links between departments; the galleries . . . form a route for the viewing of the art. The nature of the galleries is defined as static or linear; an ascending spiral of walkways carries the path through the special galleries. This approach implies an intimate knowledge of the extent and specific nature of the collection, a collaborative approach intimately relating the space to the program.

Project Credits
Rafael Viñoly; Maria Aviles, Jay Bargmann, Carolina Buzzetti, Lauren Crahan, David Crandall, Todd Davis, Ryo Fukai, Manuel Glas, Joseph Levechi, Amanda Levi, Sandra McKee, Takeshi Miyakawa, Gonzalo Negrete, Bora Yin; Richard Sennett

SECTION

1-6

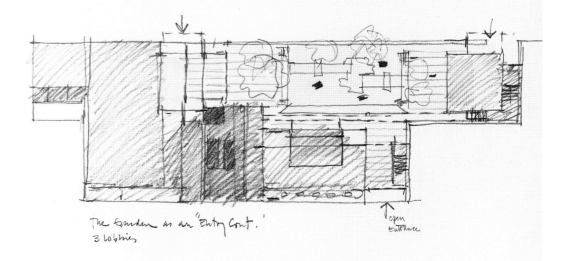

The Garden as an "Entry Court."
3 Lobbies

open
entrance

2-2

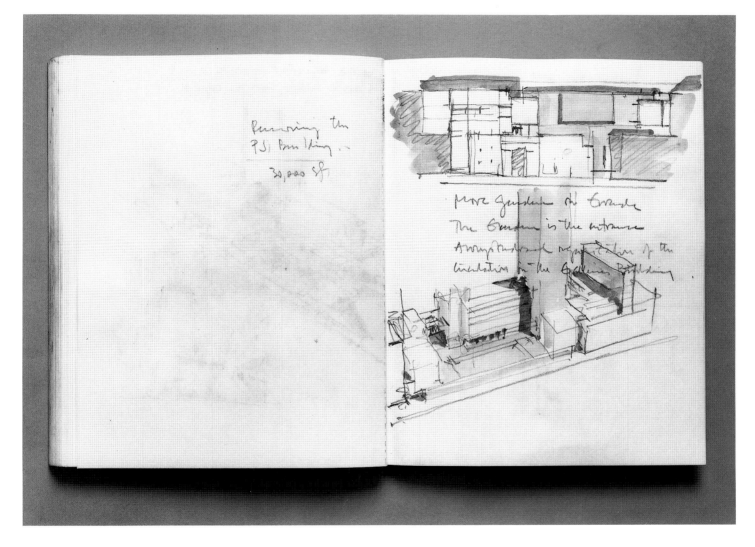

Opposite, top to bottom:
Sketchbook #1: Terraced gardens. Section.
Watercolor on paper, 11 x 16⅞" (27.9 x 42.9 cm)

Sketchbook #2: "The Garden as an 'Entry Court.'"
Plan. Watercolor on paper, 11 x 16⅞" (27.9 x 42.9 cm)

Sketchbook #2: "The Garden as an 'Entry Court.'"
Plan and perspective. Watercolor on paper, 11 x
16½" (27.9 x 42 cm) overall

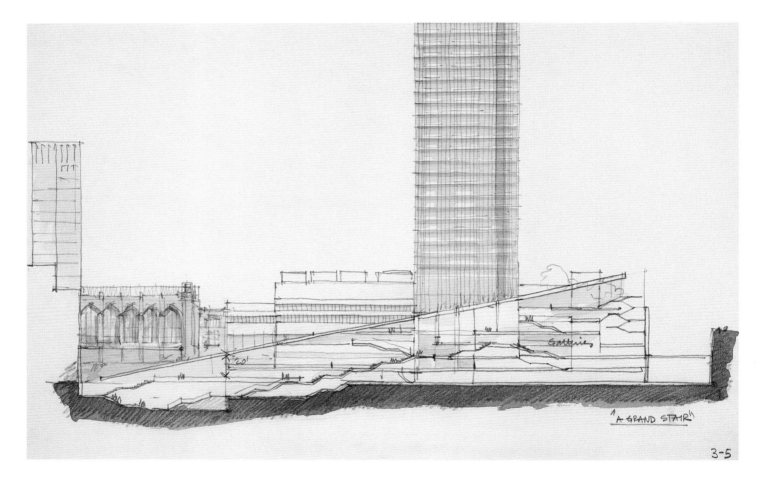

**Sketchbook #3: "A Grand Stair." Section. Watercolor
on paper, 11 x 16⅞" (27.9 x 42.9 cm)**

Sketchbook #4: Two renovation projects and two
new structures. Three views of conceptual model.
Color laser copy on paper, 11 x 17" (27.9 x 43.2 cm)

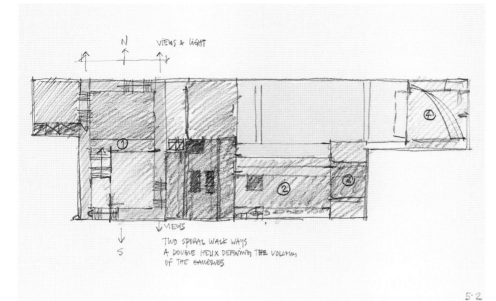

5·2

Left:
Sketchbook #5: Double helix of grand stairs. Plan. Watercolor on paper, 11 x 16⅞" (27.9 x 42.9 cm)

Below:
Sketchbook #6: Consolidation of galleries on three levels. Second floor plan. Watercolor and pencil on paper, 11 x 16⅞" (27.9 x 42.9 cm)

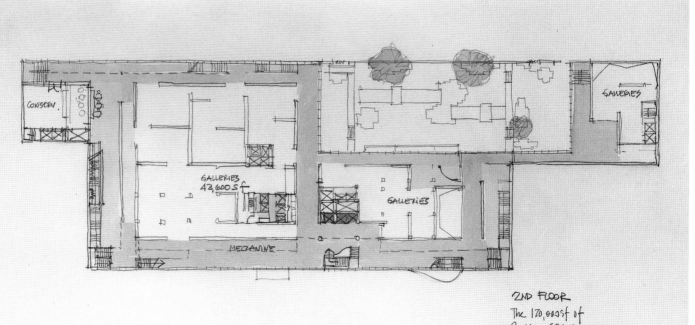

6·5

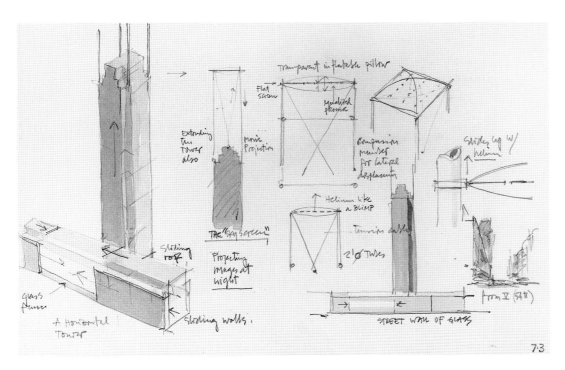

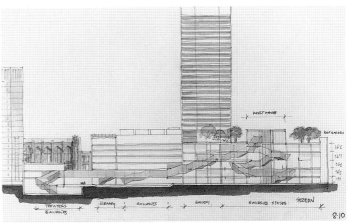

Top:
Sketchbook #7: Sliding roof and wall panels creating a garden room. Perspectives and elevations. Watercolor and pencil on paper, 11 x 16⅞" (27.9 x 42.9 cm)

Above:
Sketchbook #8: Path of glass and light. Section. Watercolor and pencil on paper, 11 x 16⅞" (27.9 x 42.9 cm)

Left:
Sketchbook #7: Sliding roof and wall panels creating a garden room. Perspective. Watercolor and pencil on paper, 11 x 8¼" (27.9 x 21 cm)

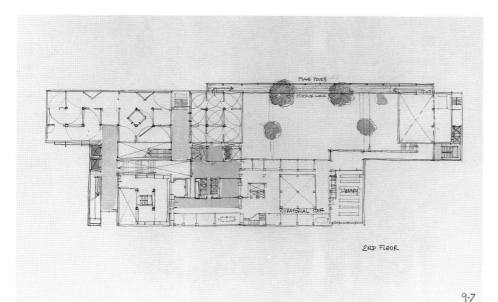

Left:
Sketchbook #9: Organizational planning grid. Second floor plan. Watercolor and pencil on paper, 11 x 16⅞" (27.9 x 42.9 cm)

Below:
Sketchbook #9: Organizational planning grid. Details of movable partitions. Watercolor and pencil on paper, 11 x 16⅞" (27.9 x 42.9 cm)

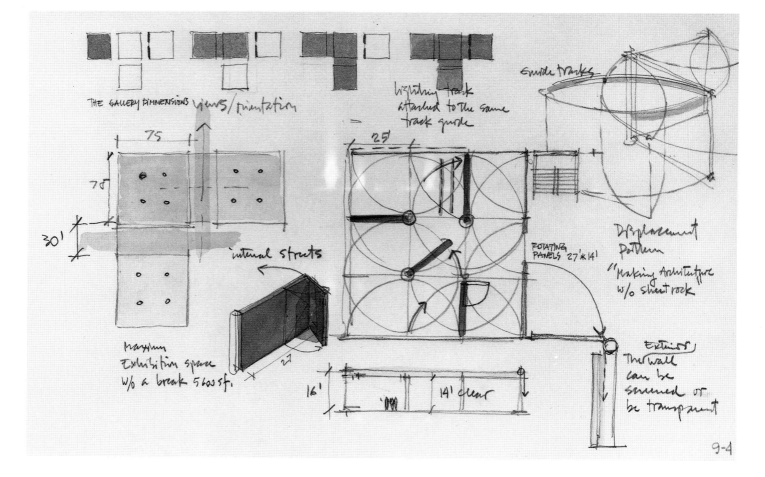

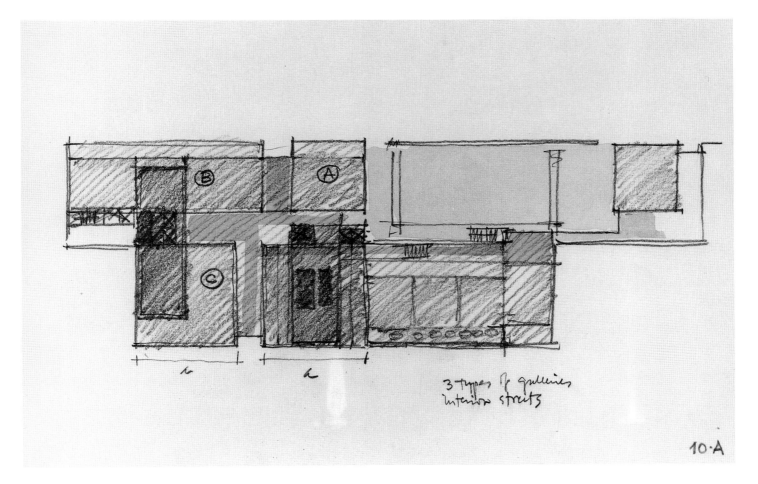

Sketchbook #10: "3 Types of Galleries." Second floor plan.
Watercolor and pencil on paper, 11 x 16⅞" (27.9 x 42.9 cm)

Tod Williams/Billie Tsien

Tod Williams
Born in Detroit, Michigan, 1943
Education: Bachelor of Arts, Princeton University, New Jersey, 1965; graduate studies, Cambridge
University, England, 1966; Master of Fine Arts and Architecture, Princeton University, 1967

Billie Tsien
Born in Ithaca, New York, 1949
Education: Bachelor of Arts, Yale University, New Haven, Connecticut, 1971; Master of Fine Arts
and Architecture, University of California at Los Angeles, 1977

Selected Recent Projects: Hereford College, University of Virginia, Charlottesville, 1989–92;
Phoenix Art Museum/Phoenix Little Theatre, Arizona, 1990–96 (completion of Phase I); The Neuro-
sciences Institute, La Jolla, California, 1992–95

FROM THE ARCHITECTS' STATEMENT

. . . We believe in a relatively low horizontal building that encourages the exploration of the Museum by foot at an appropriate pace. Traveling as much as possible by nonmotorized means . . . gives the eye time to see and the mind time to experience, think, and understand. While providing elevator access to all levels, we place primary importance on walking circulation paths. . . .

Moreover, by keeping the building below the level of the 50-foot setback from the Museum Tower, we are better able to provide galleries of potentially grand proportion while avoiding the constriction that occurs above 110 feet that pushes possible connections between the existing and new buildings to the Fifty-fourth Street edge.

By accepting and embracing the presence of the two-hour fire wall, we have traded FAR (floor-area ratio) on the existing site to reconfigure volumes. The fire wall, rather than being a hindrance, acts as an ally to help define the great vertical sky court.

While sharing the same premises we have formulated two directions, which focus on the presence or lack of an elevated connection along the north boundary of the Rockefeller garden.

The bridge scheme is based on the desire to put galleries in a new structure built above the current Sette MoMA location and to find a way for people to move through them in a natural and interesting manner. These galleries would occur on the second, third, fourth, and fifth floors. Sette MoMA would move to the sixth and top floor. Connection between these galleries would happen vertically with stairs and elevators, and a horizontal connection to the permanent collection galleries would be made by an enclosed bridge at the fourth and fifth floors. The bridge would leave open space from above the garden wall to about 50 feet above the ground. . . . The wall of the bridge would visually connect the complete MoMA site, making a coherent statement on Fifty-fourth Street. Thus, Fifty-fourth Street would provide the unifying façade of the Museum. . . .

Views of the garden would be framed by the top of the existing wall and bottom of the bridge. The bridge, by being high above the garden and to the north, would not create a shadow but would have a presence. Taming and quieting that presence would be essential to its success. . . .

In this scheme the Goodwin and Stone building is used for staff and curatorial offices on the second through the sixth floors. Galleries are in the new addition. The store remains in the Philip Johnson building and uses the second and third floors.

The second scheme, or nonbridge scheme, uses the space above the existing Sette MoMA to make a building to house staff offices. This will allow the majority of the office and support staff to work in spaces with light and air. It will be a freestanding building with connection to the rest of the Museum and staff entry and circulation occurring at the lobby and basement floors. The Goodwin and Stone building remains as permanent collection gallery space on the second and third floors while the fourth through sixth floors are devoted to curatorial space. . . .

We believe that the Museum must find its identity and the *integrity* of its identity from the inside out. In this way it is always interesting because it is both fixed and changing. Rather like the *Book of Sand* in the short story by Jorge Luis Borges, the insides keep shifting while the cover contains them and stays the same. . . .

Quiet

We think of the garden as the quiet heart of the Museum. The new addition needs to develop other places of quiet focus and delight. . . . We have thought about a great light court, a glass-enclosed space open to the sky that would serve no other purpose than to give the Museum a quiet light from top to bottom. Another scheme proposes a large pool of water at the level of the existing lobby, extending the feeling of the garden. . . .

We propose a vertical excavation of the Museum Tower's space surrounding its elevator cores. By cutting openings through from floor to floor, we believe that this space can be "mined" to create dramatic vertical shafts of space between the old museum and the addition. . . .

Interior streets moving east-west will structure movement of visitors and staff, and these paths will . . . be punctuated by a "necklace" of large and small light courts and vertical floor-through connections that provide visual orientation and memorable experiences.

Façades

. . . We believe that all significant structures should be perceived externally and internally. We believe that each existing building should stand on its own. Its clear expression should come down to the street. . . .

FIFTY-THIRD STREET: The Goodwin and Stone and Philip Johnson façades should be preserved. The translucent panels in the Goodwin and Stone façade should be restored to bring light to the stairway or to public space and offices. The Johnson building . . . will, as originally intended, provide useful and distinct space for the Design Store and the curatorial staff. The long horizontal line and canopy trying to link the Museum Tower and the Pelli addition to the Goodwin and Stone façade should be removed. We believe that the Pelli clad museum addition should be demolished and rebuilt. This would leave the Museum Tower coming down as a clear shaft to the ground. . . . The new addition should develop its own façade as a fourth building. . . .

FIFTY-FOURTH STREET: The addition of the Dorset site gives the Museum a chance to develop a coherent and powerful façade. . . . This . . . will stand in marked contrast to the multiple presence on Fifty-third Street.

Entrance

. . . Fifty-third Street is the historical front door and . . . remains the front door for the Museum and the Museum's education entrance. We propose a second entrance at Fifty-fourth Street. These both occur at approximately midblock. There will be no back door.

The Fifty-third Street lobby now feels busy and impersonal. . . . If it were possible to pay for admission prior to entering the Museum, the lobby could become more serene. . . .

The Fifty-fourth Street entrance is through a garden court adjacent to but shielded from The Abby Aldrich Rockefeller Sculpture Garden. One will be able to have views through to it, but the quiet of the garden will be protected.

Circulation

A central circulation spine runs midblock parallel to Fifty-third and Fifty-fourth streets. It can be extended east and west in future expansions. The primary vertical circulation of the new Museum occurs at the middle of the site, with secondary stairs and elevators at the far east and west extremes of the site. At the subcellar level, the spine is private circulation for staff use only.

Garden(s)

The Abby Aldrich Rockefeller Sculpture Garden would remain intact. More importantly, we believe that it can be enhanced. The removal of the old Whitney to create a new garden court entrance could increase the sense of openness to the west. And a new sculpture terrace above this entry could be connected by a stair to the existing garden, recalling the connection to an upper garden before the Pelli addition. . . .

Galleries

. . . We believe that what we are trying to do is provide a place that is a balance between the container and the contained. . . . The curators should be able to create a variety of spaces within the same space. We propose changing exhibit galleries on the ground floor and the third floor, with 20-foot-high ceilings. On the top floor is a temporary gallery for experimental works, with a 40-foot-high ceiling. Ceiling lighting grids could raise and lower so that the sense of space can vary from intimate to grand. At the top westernmost portion of the building would be a 30-by-30-foot room open to the sky. The ground-floor gallery could have a monumental garage-type door so that very large pieces of sculpture could be installed with direct access from Fifty-fourth Street. . . . All new galleries would be structured so that they would be column-free spaces.

The speculation that artwork will continue to grow in size relies on a linear progression. . . . Certainly the reduction of huge amounts of visual information to the size of a CD-ROM is a portent of the future. . . . But it is important to speculate on how the Museum can dignify the viewing of digital information, not just for research or as additional curatorial information, but as art. So that even as we plan for the possibility of larger work, we plan for the possibility of smaller work. . . .

In considering the issue of core and satellite spaces, we believe that if the containing volumes of the galleries can convey a sense of wholeness without being obtrusive, then satellite spaces could be configured freely anywhere within the container. . . . This would allow curators the freedom to construct and design the relationships as they occur. . . .

What Is Being Kept

. . . The stair will be restored in one scheme as a public stair linking the permanent collection galleries on the second and third floors with the lobby at grade. In a second proposal the stair is restored as a staff stair, connecting staff offices on the second and third floors.

Having reviewed a number of options, we feel it will be least disruptive and expensive to keep the Museum Tower loading dock in place. We are also keeping Titus 1 and Titus 2 intact, although surface renovations/restorations may be required. . . .

Project Credits
Tod Williams/Billie Tsien; Betty Chen, Matthew Baird

Bridge concept: Exterior perspective. Colored pencil, pencil, and white paint on photocopy, 11 x 17" (27.9 x 43.2 cm)

Illuminated light court and skylights running east/west

Left:
Bridge concept: View of model. Color laser copy on paper, 11 x 17" (27.9 x 43.2 cm)

Below:
Bridge concept: Interior perspective of entrance lobby. Ink, colored pencil, and white paint on tracing paper overlay, 11 x 17" (27.9 x 43.2 cm)

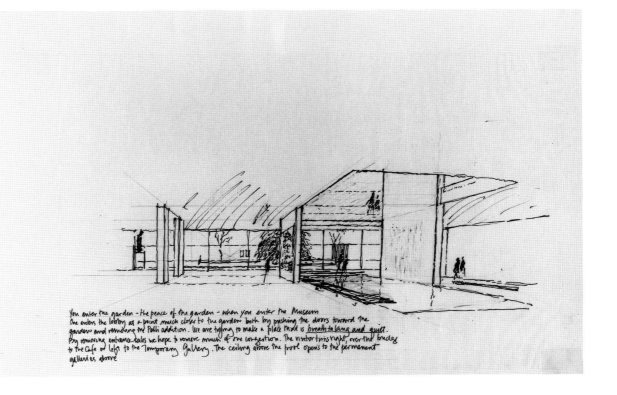

You enter the garden - the peace of the garden - when you enter the Museum
One enters the lobby at a point much closer to the garden both by pushing the doors toward the garden and removing the Pelli addition. We are trying to make a place that is _breathtaking and quiet_. By removing entrance sales we hope to remove much of the congestion. The visitor turns right, over the bridge to the Cafe or left to the Temporary Gallery. The ceiling above the pool opens to the permanent galleries above

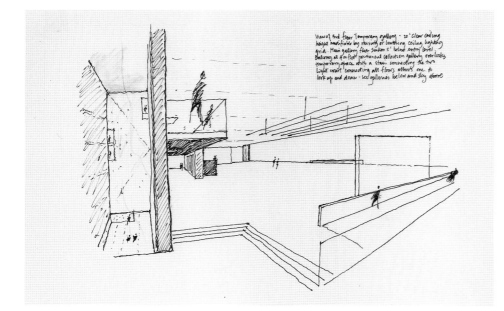

Left:
Bridge concept: Interior perspective of gallery, Ink and colored pencil on tracing paper overlay, 11 x 17" (27.9 x 43.2 cm)

Below:
Bridge concept: Section. Ink and pencil on paper, 11 x 17" (27.9 x 43.2 cm)

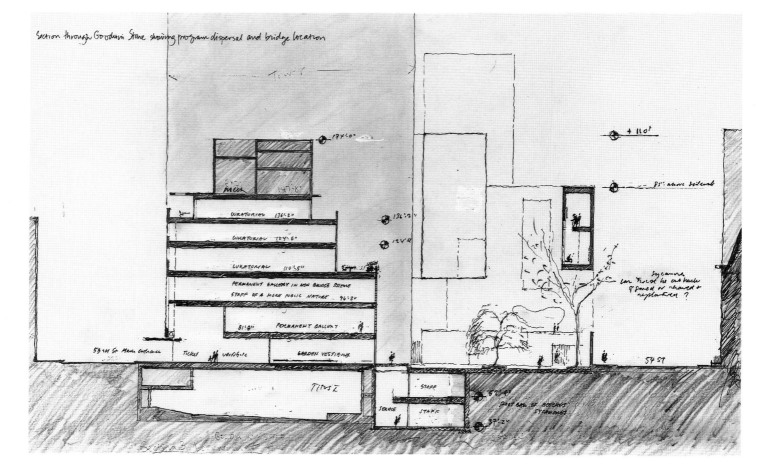

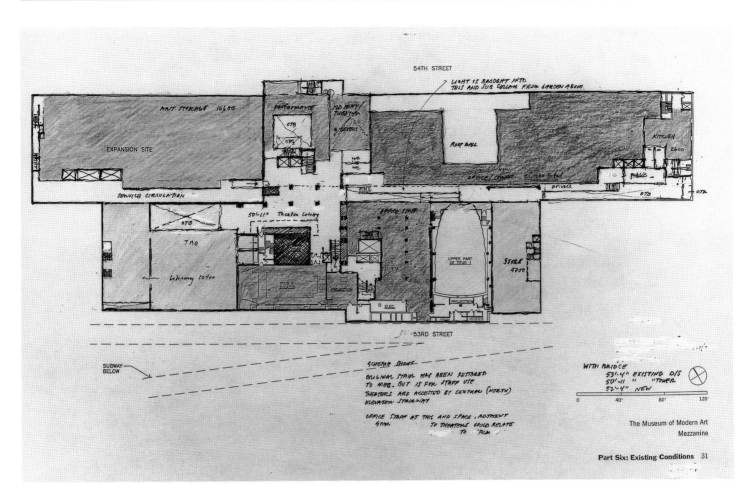

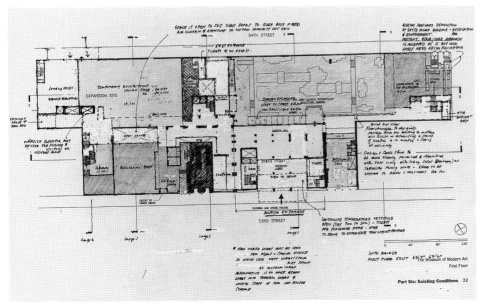

Above:
Bridge concept: Plan. Ink and colored pencil on paper, 11 x 17" (27.9 x 43.2 cm)

Left:
Bridge concept: First floor plan. Ink, colored pencil, and white paint on paper, 11 x 17" (27.9 x 43.2 cm)

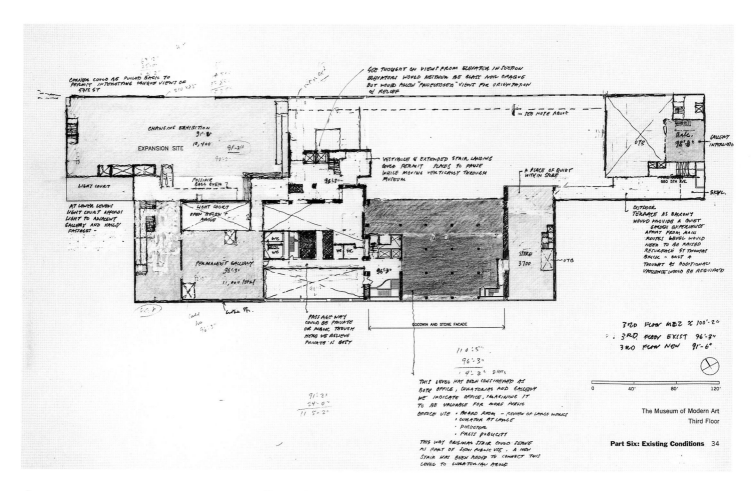

The Museum of Modern Art
Third Floor

Part Six: Existing Conditions 34

Above:
Bridge concept: Third floor plan. Ink, colored pencil, and white paint on paper, 11 x 17" (27.9 x 43.2 cm)

Right:
Bridge concept: Floor plan with movement pattern. Ink and colored pencil on tracing paper overlay, 11 x 17" (27.9 x 43.2 cm)

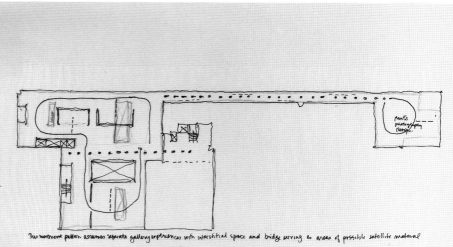

Non-bridge concept: Exterior perspective of garden.
Colored pencil, pencil, and white paint on photocopy,
11 x 17" (27.9 x 43.2 cm)

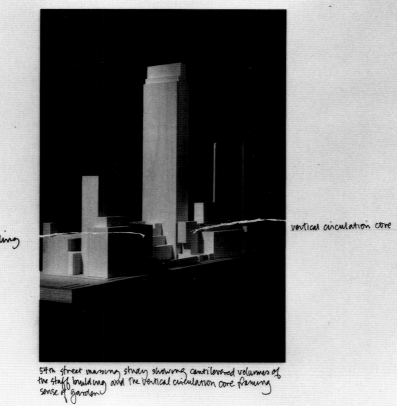

Staff Building

vertical circulation core

54th street massing study showing cantilevered volumes of
the staff building and the vertical circulation core framing
sense of garden

Left:
**Non-bridge concept: View of model. Color laser copy,
11 x 17" (27.9 x 43.2 cm)**

Below:
**Non-bridge concept: Floor plan. Ink and colored
pencil on photocopy, 11 x 17" (27.9 x 43.2 cm)**

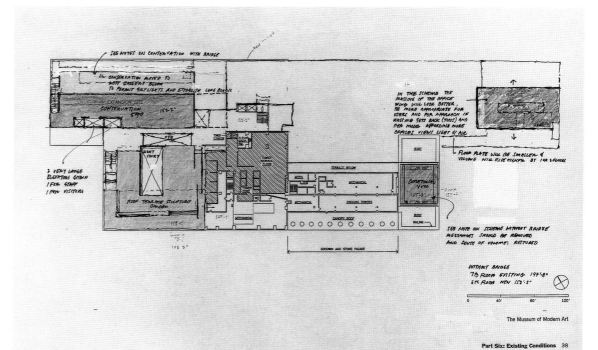

The Museum of Modern Art

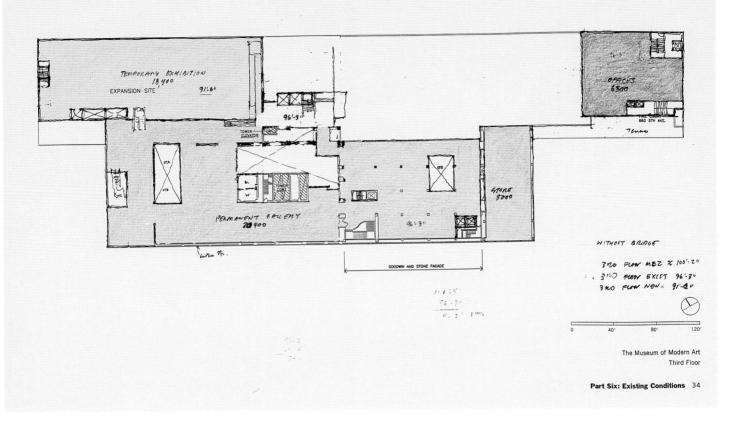

The Museum of Modern Art
Third Floor

Part Six: Existing Conditions 34

Non-bridge concept: Third floor plan. Ink and colored pencil on photocopy, 11 x 17" (27.9 x 43.2 cm)

Jacques Herzog and Pierre de Meuron

Jacques Herzog and Pierre de Meuron were born in 1950 in Basel, Switzerland. They studied at the Federal Institute of Technology (ETH), Zurich, Switzerland, where each received a degree in architecture in 1975. They have been partners of Herzog & de Meuron Architekten in Basel since 1978, and visiting professors at Harvard, Cornell, and Tulane universities. In 1994, they won an international competition for the Tate Gallery of Modern Art, Bankside, London, England.

FROM THE ARCHITECTS' STATEMENT

. . . The new Museum complex will need to focus on the encounter between works of art and people. An art museum is a place for art and people: it is not Disneyworld; it is not a shopping mall; it is not a media center. It is a place where the world of art can express itself in the most direct and radical way—in spaces that find the approval not only of architects and critics but of artists and visitors, spaces that stimulate people to concentrate on the perception of art. . . .

Unlike other great Manhattan museums, MoMA does not border on an avenue. Urban strategies for the new MoMA site will therefore need to enhance the fact that the complex is located between two streets. . . . Public space could be one space or a suite of open and closed spaces. Open courtyards could alternate with covered or enclosed lobby spaces. . . .

Flatness means to accept the allowable street wall height of 85 feet and to turn this height into a kind of overall horizon of the new building complex. This . . . continuous façade height helps to integrate existing buildings along Fifty-third Street. Even on Fifty-fourth Street the former Whitney building could become part of the new complex if this turns out to be desirable in the further planning process. . . . This landscape-like building with courtyards and gardens inside and on top of the roof would have a very complex spatial structure, with different transparencies generated by the layering of spaces, courtyards, and surfaces. . . .

The flatness of the building complex could be interrupted and accentuated by some individual buildings which would stick out from roof gardens. These buildings could be a group of roof galleries, perhaps the library or the restaurant. . . . The MoMA roof garden fitted out with modern and contemporary art—including the possibility to relocate and remodel Philip Johnson's sculpture garden—will be a thoroughly genuine Manhattan experience. An artificial natural space . . . will extend between Fifty-third and Fifty-fourth Streets in courtyards at street level, in patios on higher levels, and all over the roof of the new building complex. . . .

The Sculpture Garden

. . . To us the garden is an exhibition space in a living museum and not a petrified monument of the 1960s. . . . To a certain extent there is a conflict between the wish to keep the garden as the wonderful and quiet oasis that it is now and the needs of a lively museum which wants to use it more as a *terrain vague*. Options for the new site should therefore try to include both or to combine both—a sculpture garden as a quiet oasis as well as a *terrain vague*. . . .

With the Dorset Hotel site becoming part of the MoMA site, the garden wing will be even more off-center. One option will be to move the whole garden farther west, thus creating a stronger and larger garden wing that can host galleries and other facilities and become a more integrated part of the new site. . . .

Moving the garden farther down into the site toward the south would improve the connection between the different wings on the site. This option would transform the sculpture garden into an enclosed courtyard—it would become more of a museum space itself and less of an idyllic garden. . . .

The longer we worked on the scheme, the more we became aware of the necessity to reconsider and rethink the garden as it is now. . . . An interesting option would be to create new courtyards or gardens on street level, courtyards that could work as entrance areas where a first encounter with art would be possible. These courtyards could have temporary art installations and would be used in a more experimental way than the sculpture garden is being used today. . . .

Museum and Building Types . . .

AGGLOMERATE TYPE: This . . . clearly identifies the different *partis*, such as the Goodwin and Stone building, the new garden wing, the sculpture garden, and the new Dorset wing, which could become a new landmark in Manhattan. . . . This option would allow for different architects to work on the scheme in a clearly separate way. . . . The separate buildings in the agglomerate type might be compared to a still life. Such a "still life" concept has the advantage that pieces can be taken away and added to, according to the willingness to grow or change. . . .

CONGLOMERATE TYPE: Another . . . option takes inspiration from the homogeneous building types with continuous façade heights. An even height of all surrounding façades of 85 feet would allow . . . a continuous roof level, which could be shaped and landscaped in many interesting ways. The landscaped roof could . . . express the richness and diversity of the new site: some spaces, such as roof galleries, the library, or the restaurant would stick out of the various gardens on the rooftop— some of them penetrating through the whole building complex. . . .

Individual pieces of architecture within the conglomerate could be a new entrance courtyard on Fifty-third Street (possibly the Goodwin and Stone building transformed into a courtyard) and another courtyard on Fifty-fourth Street (possibly Philip Johnson's Whitney wing transformed into a courtyard). Other new spaces such as the library, the galleries, or the restaurant could be designed by different architects. . . .

Circulation and Orientation . . .

The new enlarged site should have more than one entrance. . . . The new entrance will need to run from Fifty-third to Fifty-fourth street. . . . People will be walking through the new site, which could be designed like an artificial landscape of art, nature, and architecture, with existing and new buildings done by different architects. . . . People can sit down and look at art on display in these public zones and visit one of the cafeterias, shops, or restaurants. . . .

A linear concept is an obvious option considering the given shape of the site. A central spine would be the logical consequence of such a concept. There are any number of interesting architectural and structural strategies to make a rich spatial experiment and to avoid the "airport" character of such a long axis. . . .

CENTRAL CONCEPT: The individual departments are too big, and the shape of the site would not allow for such a "classicist" concept. Some kind of a central area or a "center of gravity" is, however, needed in order to provide a good orientation and a simple organization to control the ticketed areas of the site. . . .

In a *Raumplan* concept, spaces would be connected with other spaces in a kind of a continuous spatial flow. . . . A kind of spatial matrix will be required to connect different areas in the building, not only through the main circulation spaces, but also through smaller and more intimate paths, stairs, or bridges. . . .

MULTIPLE CHOICE: . . . We see a strong potential for architecture in the combination and new interpretation of simple elements such as stairs, courtyards, solid walls, light walls, and the perception of seasons, of weather, of day and night. . . .

Galleries

. . . If we imagine how artists conceived their own studios in the early twentieth century . . . we discover that these spaces were very different from the official museum spaces at that time. Only much later did the museums change and shift away from the bourgeois living-room style. . . . What we can learn from this is that we should trust the artists . . . and not try to invent "futuristic" spaces for some art to come in the next millennium. . . .

Gallery spaces need a solid floor, solid walls, and a ceiling that provides daylight and artificial light. This sounds very simple but it is very difficult to achieve in a straightforward and bold way, especially faced with an increasing number of technical requirements for services, security, lighting, fire, etc. We think the new MoMA building will need to offer a wide range of materials, a variety of room sizes, room heights, and lighting concepts. . . .

In recent constructions, wall-height side light has provided very pleasant daylight and worked well with painting, sculpture, and people, who can find better orientation within the building. Wall-height windows are more generous than "ordinary windows" cut into the walls, and they don't compete with the format (classical, modern) of paintings. . . .

The core and satellite principle works best when some gallery spaces—not necessarily singled out architecturally but with a strategic "topographic" position within the building complex—are selected for a more permanent installation of outstanding masterpieces. . . . If such installations . . . are not changed for long periods, the whole gallery space could become like a core . . . within the whole Museum complex. Around these "cores," which would work like islands of memory, the installations could change more often and could be seen in changing relationships. . . . We see the "cores" as islands of stability within constantly changing installation concepts in the Museum. They should be easy to find and to access from the main circulation areas. We also see them as a help for orientation, both geographically and historically. . . .

Architectural Strategies for the New Parts of the Site . . .

COURTYARDS: They are interesting spaces for temporary and permanent art installations, spaces where a collaboration between architect and artist can provide unexpected solutions.

ROOF GARDENS: Partition-like galleries could act as spatial dividers in the roof gardens. Pavilions and other artworks are for people to use. Stone walls and glass walls could enhance the artificiality and the sheltering quality of the roof gardens.

FACADES AND INTERIORS: These could act together to enhance the depth of the building complex, which would be built in multiple spatial layers. Different materials and surface treatments can achieve such multiple and changing transparencies.

STAIRS: A kind of "ceremonial staircase" where people are not moved by escalators or lifts but consciously walk through the building complex. Each major *parti* could have its own set of stairs, for example, the Dorset stairs, the Goodwin and Stone stairs, or the garden stairs.

Project Credits
Jacques Herzog and Pierre de Meuron; Christine Binswanger, Jean-Frédéric Kuscher, Andrea Saemann, Lukas Kupfer; Models: Bela Berec, Lukas Huggenberger

Sketchbook: "Art and People in the 21st Century."
Agglomerate concept: sections. Pencil on paper,
8 x 6" (20.3 x 15.2 cm) overall

Agglomerate Concept (Still Life)

40

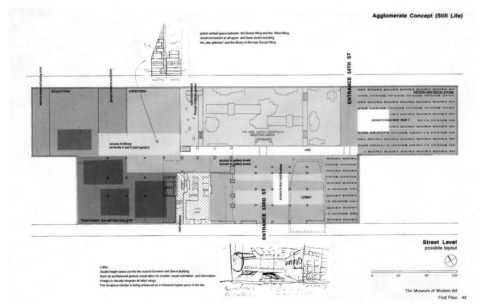

Above:
"Agglomerate Concept (Still Life)": View of model.
Color laser copy on paper, 11¼ x 16½" (28.6 x 41.9 cm)

Left:
"Agglomerate Concept (Still Life)": First floor plan.
Computer-generated print mounted on mylar, 11¼ x 16½" (28.6 x 41.9 cm)

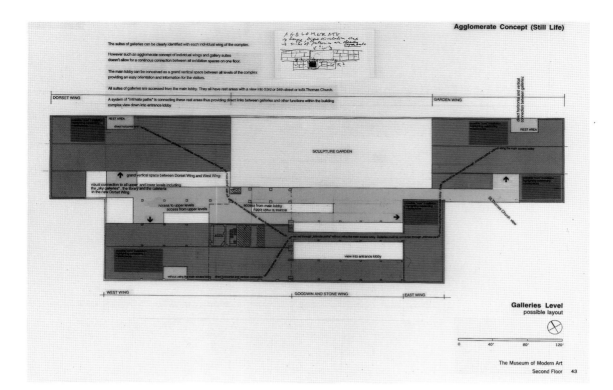

Above:
"Agglomerate Concept (Still Life)": Galleries plan.
Computer-generated print mounted on mylar, 11¼ x
16½" (28.6 x 41.9 cm)

Right:
"Agglomerate Concept (Still Life)": Cross-section
through Dorset Hotel site and West Wing. Photocopy
and computer-generated print mounted on mylar, 11¼ x
16½" (28.6 x 41.9 cm)

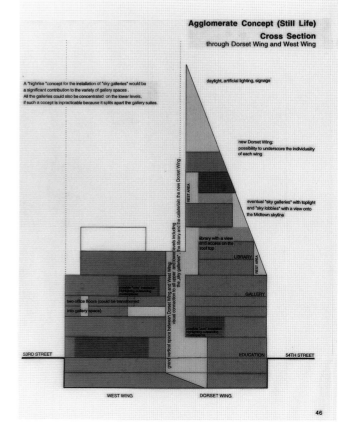

Conglomerate Concept

47

"Conglomerate Concept": Views of model. Color
laser copy on paper, 11¼ x 16½" (28.6 x 41.9 cm)

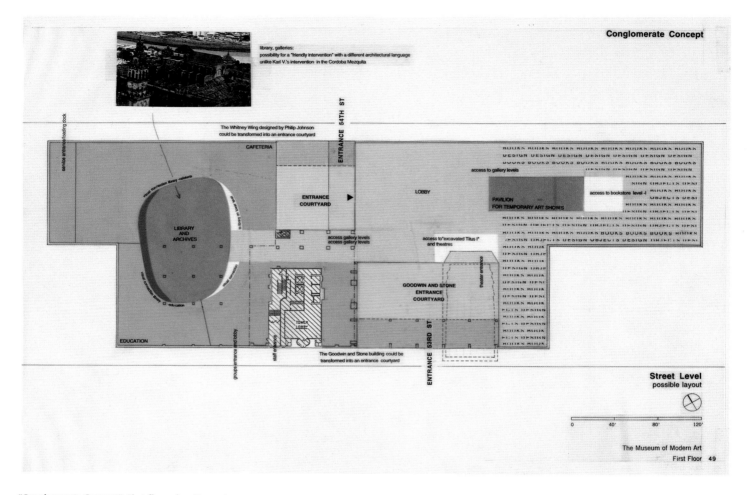

"Conglomerate Concept": First floor plan. Computer-
generated print on mylar, 11¼ x 16½" (28.6 x 41.9 cm)

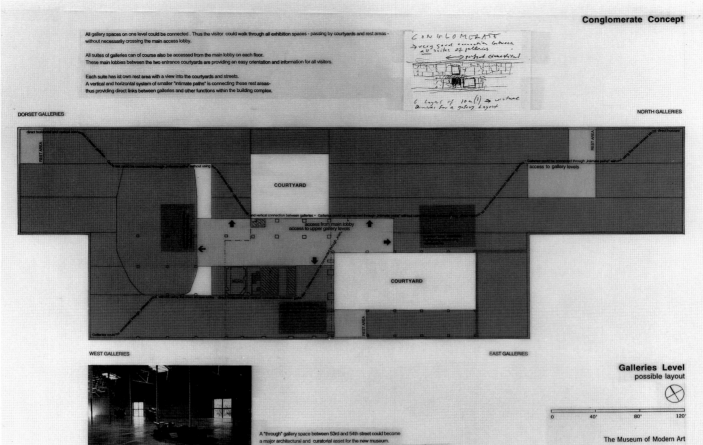

Conglomerate Concept

All gallery spaces on one level could be connected . Thus the visitor could walk through all exhibition spaces - passing by courtyards and rest areas - without necessarily crossing the main access lobby.

All suites of galleries can of course also be accessed from the main lobby on each floor.
These main lobbies between the two entrance courtyards are providing an easy orientation and information for all visitors.

Each suite has ist own rest area with a view into the courtyards and streets.
A vertical and horizontal system of smaller "intimate paths" is connecting these rest areas-
thus providing direct links between galleries and other functions within the building complex.

DORSET GALLERIES

NORTH GALLERIES

COURTYARD

COURTYARD

WEST GALLERIES

EAST GALLERIES

Galleries Level
possible layout

A "through" gallery space between 53rd and 54th street could become
a major architectural and curatorial asset for the new museum.
The unexpected dimension of such a space would echo the generosity of industrial spaces .

The Museum of Modern Art
Second Floor 50

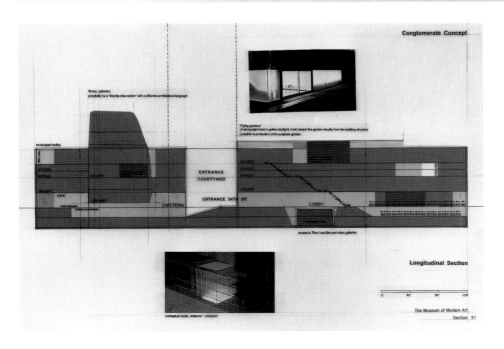

Conglomerate Concept

ENTRANCE
COURTYARD

ENTRANCE 54TH ST

Longitudinal Section

The Museum of Modern Art
Section 51

Above:
"Conglomerate Concept": Galleries floor plan.
Computer-generated print on mylar, 11¼ x 16½"
(28.6 x 41.9 cm)

Left:
"Conglomerate Concept": Section. Computer-
generated print on mylar, 11¼ x 16½" (28.6 x 41.9 cm)

Urbanistic Thoughts

Between two streets

Unlike other great Manhattan museums the MoMA does not border on an avenue. Urban strategies for the new MoMA site will therefore need to enhance the fact that the complex is located between two streets. The options we are developing all emphasize the specific character of this site between 53rd and 54th Streets in Manhattan. Entering the new MoMA site from two streets instead of only one is a chance to transform the museum into an even more genuine Manhattan place.

Incorporating the Dorset site within the new scheme offers the opportunity to enter the new building complex from two sides. Such an entrance concept would be based on creating a through entrance area between 53rd and 54th Streets which could then become a very attractive space, a condensed mixture of art, architecture and information that would literally attract people.

Courtyards—slowing down the daily rhythm

This through public space could be one space or a suite of open and closed spaces. Open courtyards could alternate with covered or enclosed lobby spaces. Certainly the creation of entrance courtyards would be a very strong urbanistic statement in Manhattan. The courtyards can be seen within the tradition of great New York public spaces but also as a strategy to prepare the visitors for a world which is different from the hectic rhythm of their daily urban lives. This strategy of slowing down the daily rhythm is probably vital to a future in which the survival of art museums will depend on offering an atmosphere that is different from the mass media <u>without</u> competing with them.

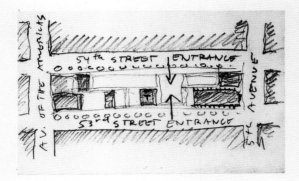

The new site: ....through entrance area between 53rd and 54th Streets....

Courtyards:.....a strategy of slowing down the daily rhythm.....
Daniel Buren, place royale, Paris ?

6

Sculpture Garden

Roof gardens

Finally we explored options where <u>the sculpture garden would be removed from its current position on street level</u>. All of a sudden the spatial and logistic options on street level as well as on the other levels were becoming richer and also architecturally more interesting.

<u>Entrance courtyards on both 53rd and 54th Streets</u> would welcome people in a very attractive way before entering the museum lobby. These courtyards would help to create a very good orientation within the whole building complex: they would be setting up a spatial rhythm creating visual links to other "holes" and other "bodies" in the building complex, such as Titus I, the new library, or the roof galleries. Such courtyards would be very attractive architectural connections between all levels—underground and overground—including the roof which could become a park-like extension of the courtyards.

As we worked on different options for the new MoMA site, the whole roof of the building complex became more and more interesting. It promises to become a fantastic place for gardens: extending along 54th Street and crossing on to 53rd Street, small groups of buildings could be installed on that landscaped roof. They could be temporary pavilions or permanent installations, e.g. a group of galleries ("roof garden galleries") or other public spaces such as the library or the restaurant.

This landscaped roof could be subdivided into different garden areas and even designed by different architects. A very special and attractive garden option on this landscaped roof <u>could be a re-produced, adapted, or entirely remodeled sculpture garden!</u>

...The roof could become a landscape built with artworks, architecture and plants....
Courtyard landscape in Northern China
Pavilion in the park: Sonsbeek Arnhem, Netherlands.

Entrance courtyards on street level on 53rd and 54th Streets - landscaped roof top

Above:
"Urbanistic Thoughts." Photocopies on paper, 11¼ x 16½" (28.6 x 41.9 cm)

Left:
"Sculpture Garden": Concepts for a roof garden. Photocopies on paper, 11¼ x 16½" (28.6 x 41.9 cm)

Architectural Strategies rather than a homogeneous architectural Language

The fact that the reconfiguration of the whole site will include old and existing parts as well as new buildings requires the development of architectural strategies rather than a homogeneous architectural language

Strategies for the existing parts of the site

The integration of old and existing parts in the scheme is an opportunity to rethink the multiple relations between conservation/reconstruction and destruction.

Conservation/Reconstruction

Whole partis (Titus I, eventually Philip Johnson's East wing) could highlight their original beauty or enhance their individuality within the whole complex.

Transforming buildings into courtyards

The Goodwin & Stone building and the north wing of the Philip Johnson section could be reconfigured to create entrance courtyards in the building complex. Especially for the G+S building this could be an interesting architectural gesture that would highlight this first MoMA building in a new, unexpected and contemporary way.

Facades by Goodwin & Stone and Philip Johnson

Excavating

Titus I and other underground spaces would bring them to public consciousness.

Remodeling, relocating

The sculpture garden, part of a new and spectacular artificial landscape on top of the roofs of the new site, could become an all-embracing symbol for both the old and the new MoMA.

Viviendas subterraneas, Valencia , Spain

33

Jacques Herzog and Pierre de Meuron:
Selected Recent Projects

Among the projects Herzog and de Meuron have completed recently is a gallery for the Goetz collection of contemporary art, completed 1992, a freestanding volume that can be used as both a public and a private gallery. The architectural conception for the building reflects the contemporary collection that it houses of works dating from the 1960s to the present. Situated in a parklike area of birches and conifers, the gallery is composed of birch plywood, matte glass, and untreated aluminum. It appears as a simple, flush-detailed form, yet, on closer inspection, reveals itself as a complex compositional study.

The Ricola-Europe SA production and storage building in Mulhouse-Brunnstatt, France, completed 1993, also has distinctive exterior walls: translucent polycarbonate façade panels, a common industrial building material that allows light to filter through. Using a silkscreen process, these panels were printed with a repetitive plant motif (based on a photograph by Karl Blossfeldt) that becomes less visible as daylight diminishes, assuming the character of a material more substantial than polycarbonate.

The Signal box Auf dem Wolf in Basel, completed in 1995, contains the electronic equipment for a railway engine depot. The six-story building consists of a concrete shell insulated on the exterior and wrapped with approximately 8-inch-wide copper strips that are twisted at certain places in order to admit daylight. While the copper creates a dynamic architectural skin, its functional role is to provide an electrostatic shield.

Above, top and bottom:
Gallery for a private collection of contemporary art,
Oberföhringerstrasse, Munich, Germany. 1989–92.
Photographs above and on facing page by
Margherita Spiluttini

Left and above:
Ricola-Europe SA, production and storage building,
Mulhouse-Brunnstatt, France. 1992–93

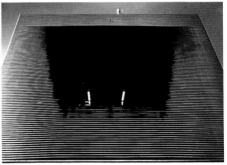

Left and above:
Signal box Auf dem Wolf, Basel, Switzerland.
1988–95

CHARETTE FINALIST
Yoshio Taniguchi

Yoshio Taniguchi was born in 1937 in Tokyo, Japan. He received a Bachelor of Mechanical Engineering degree at Keio University in 1960, followed by a Master of Architecture degree from Harvard University's Graduate School of Design, Cambridge, Massachussetts, in 1964. He was a visiting critic at Harvard in 1978 and 1987, and since 1979 has been president of Taniguchi and Associates.

FROM THE ARCHITECT'S STATEMENT

. . . The primary objective in the design of a museum is to create an ideal environment for the interaction of people and art. Galleries and public spaces are the core elements in a museum. A variety of gallery spaces appropriate to MoMA's collection of twentieth-century masterworks as well as new galleries for the yet-unknown works of contemporary art is the first requirement for an expanded Museum. Renovation and reuse of the intimately-scaled existing galleries, along with the addition of multiuse new galleries with high ceilings and long continuous walls, would provide a diversity of exhibition spaces while creating an interlocking dialogue of space, art, and architecture. . . .

Ancillary to the galleries and public spaces of the Museum are the areas for support services and staff. Services, including loading, workshops, storage, archives, mechanical support, and kitchen, are located in the basement levels with a separate entrance and a new service yard. . . . Offices for trustees and executive staff, curatorial departments, conservation, and administration should be concentrated above the public zone . . . of the Museum. These spaces should be made pleasant and livable, . . . with an abundance of light, air, and views.

In addition to the issues common to all museums, The Museum of Modern Art poses certain unique challenges. Part of MoMA's distinction as the world's premier museum for the collection of contemporary art is its unique history and context. MoMA has in the past used the design of its built form as an opportunity to regenerate itself and to express what is current in the arena of modernism. As an integral part of the Museum's history, this record of regeneration should not be destroyed, but should be preserved and celebrated in the juxtaposition of past and present, the new or experimental contrasted to the known or established.

As a distinctive cultural institution, the Museum must engage the city. The immediate physical environment of the Museum is markedly different on its north and south periphery, and those differences should be reflected in the character of the Museum itself by concentrating the commercial elements of the Museum on the Fifty-third Street side, and by placing the cultural uses and main Museum entrances on the quieter Fifty-fourth Street side. The dual missions of the Museum in the twenty-first century—exhibition of the collection and education of the public—are best given their own symbolic identities. These two realms are housed in separate structures facing the garden. One provides for the viewing of real objects and the other, their representations: the

virtual museum as counterpoint to the actual one. As an architectural composition, however, the two structures work together to define the new public façade of the Museum. A seamless architectural expression of simple geometric volumes will create a powerful horizontal presence on Fifty-fourth Street, in stark contrast to the random verticality of Manhattan, establishing the Museum as a new urban landmark, clearly visible from Fifth Avenue.

Growth and change are integral to MoMA's mission, precluding a static or finished Museum. Structuring the Museum to anticipate the next phase of growth is an essential concept for the expansion plan. While a scheme of galleries and offices structured on a central core is a promising concept, it does injustice to the natural character of this site if it does not accommodate the site's potential for expansion. Being a "street" not an "avenue" museum, the direction of future growth is linear. The circulation spine which unites all portions of the site, and which can also extend to subsequent sites to the east and west, can—at the same time—define a core zone within the Museum about which galleries and offices will be configured. . . .

Organization of Gallery and Public Spaces

ACHIEVING DIVERSITY THROUGH TWO TYPES OF SPACES: The principles underlying the design of gallery spaces are to achieve to the fullest extent possible, . . . the protection of the artworks, . . . and the provision of spaces that facilitate viewing those works by visitors to the Museum.

To provide maximum diversity of gallery spaces, I will use a combination of remodeled existing galleries and newly-built galleries located on the expansion site. The former will undergo major renovation in order to create a visual relationship between elements that symbolize modernism (including the existing windows and the Bauhaus staircase, which will be preserved) and the representative artworks of the twentieth century. The new galleries will be universal spaces with long, continuous wall surfaces and high ceilings capable of accommodating every possible exhibition. The interior will be imbued with a sense of scale solely by a row of columns supporting the upper structure. . . .

A new, generous entrance lobby with all the requisite amenities is to be located on the expansion site, entered from Fifty-fourth Street. Vertical circulation is best provided by a system of quiet, fast, and convenient elevators, which can allow visitors to begin their exploration from any level. . . . A supplementary system of gentle stairways will restore the contemplative mood appropriate to a museum and allow visitors to set their own pace while moving through the galleries.

Functionally Distinct Blocks

THE SYSTEMATIC ARRANGEMENT OF EFFICIENT MAINTENANCE, MANAGEMENT, AND ADMINISTRATION: . . . The organizational intent of the present proposal is to provide efficiency . . . by creating distinct functional blocks. The first floor consists mainly of public spaces, and the galleries all begin on the second level. The library and education areas are approached through their own lobby, which will also accommodate group admissions. The cellar of the garden provides a potential future expansion capability.

The Museum Book Store, Design Store, cafeteria, and restaurant entrances are all deployed along the Fifty-third Street side, at ground level, and can be serviced from below. Curatorial departments and skylit conservation areas are collectively located above the new expansion-site galleries. Linked to these are other office areas, which are arranged above the renovated existing gallery spaces. These work areas will be environments of optimum liveability, and are "accessed" by elevators from their own newly-created entrance on Fifty-third Street. Access to the two theaters on the lower levels will be from a separate Fifty-third Street lobby, which will also be connected at cellar level to a new 120-seat lecture hall.

Respect for History

MAINTAINING THE CENTRALITY OF THE GARDEN AND CONCEIVING OF THE FAÇADE AS A COLLAGE OF HISTORICAL ARCHITECTURE: The Museum of Modern Art is distinguished by its unique history, and by the diversity and abundance of what has accumulated there culturally, socially, artistically. . . . It is meaningless, therefore, to ignore or destroy the historical context in order to create in the design of the expanded and renovated Museum a work of architecture that is merely new. . . . The Museum's garden is, and should remain, central to MoMA's identity. The architecture of the Museum has, throughout its history, developed around the garden, and that space is perhaps the most distinctive single element of the Museum today. While the relationship between the original MoMA buildings and the garden was a cross-axial one, the development of the expansion site offers an opportunity to realign the primary axial relationship to one that is lengthwise, paralleling Fifty-fourth Street. This will enhance the relationship between the garden and expansion site and reorient the force of the entire complex in a new direction of growth. New architectural elements flanking the garden at its east and west ends will exploit this new axis, while closing off the upper floors of the Goodwin and Stone building from the garden will de-emphasize the old axis. These new elements, in combination with the historical landmark buildings on the north side of Fifty-fourth Street, will reinforce the core role of the garden. . . .

Relationship to the City

THE ARRANGEMENT OF CULTURAL AND COMMERCIAL SPACES: . . . One of architecture's most critical tasks is to establish a relationship between a particular site and its environment. In the redesign of the Museum, my principle has been to strengthen the relationship between urbanism, architecture, and art. . . . I propose to relocate the main entrances of the Museum to the Fifty-fourth Street side, where a quiet, more reflective atmosphere, suitable for an art museum, prevails. The commercial spaces of the Museum will be arranged on the more active Fifty-third Street side.

Along Fifty-fourth Street, flanking the garden at either end are two new architectural elements. On the west side of the garden is a building containing the main entrance to the Museum, the lobby, and the new gallery spaces. The building to the east of the garden will house the library and education department. . . .

Architecture for Growth

THE CIRCULATION SPINE AND FUTURE SITES: The history of MoMA has already demonstrated that . . . the architecture for MoMA should not be completed and finished, but should be an expression of a system that is flexible enough to accommodate change.

The circulation zone at the rear of the existing buildings (at present equipped with escalators) will be redesigned and extended eastward and westward to form a spine that connects the entire expanded Museum block. It is here that all principal circulation routes—both horizontal and vertical—will converge, linking the many varied functions of the Museum. This space will function as the backbone of the entire vital organism. Light will pour down from above, and the long horizontal arcade will express the extended development of the Museum. Symbolically, it also has long-term implications relating to a block-long Museum space between Fifth Avenue and the Avenue of the Americas.

Project Credits
Taniguchi and Associates: Yoshio Taniguchi, Shinsuke Takamiya, Brian Aamoth

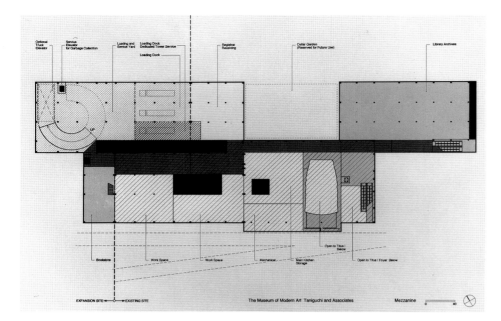

Left:
Mezzanine plan. Computer-generated print on paper,
11 x 16½" (27.9 x 41.9 cm)

Below:
First floor plan. Computer-generated print on paper,
11 x 16½" (27.9 x 41.9 cm)

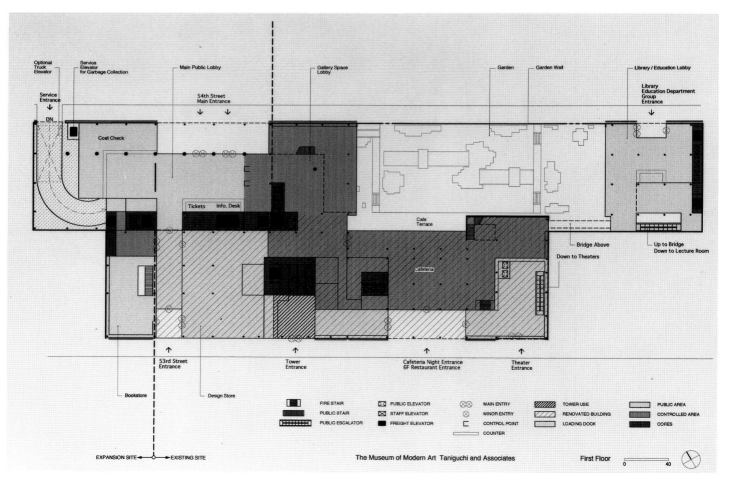

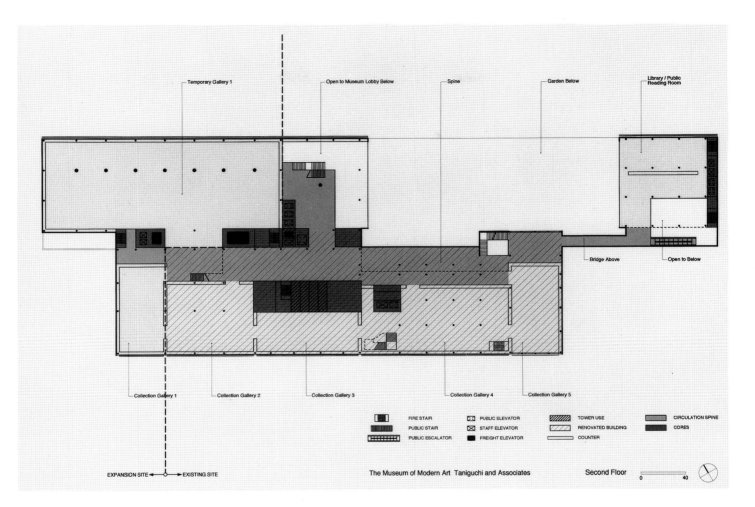

Above:
Second floor plan. Computer-generated print on paper, 11 x 16½" (27.9 x 41.9 cm)

Left:
Seventh floor plan. Computer-generated print on paper, 11 x 16½" (27.9 x 41.9 cm)

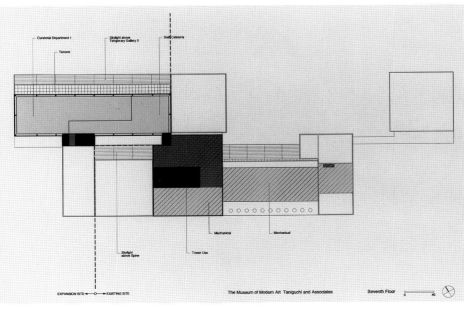

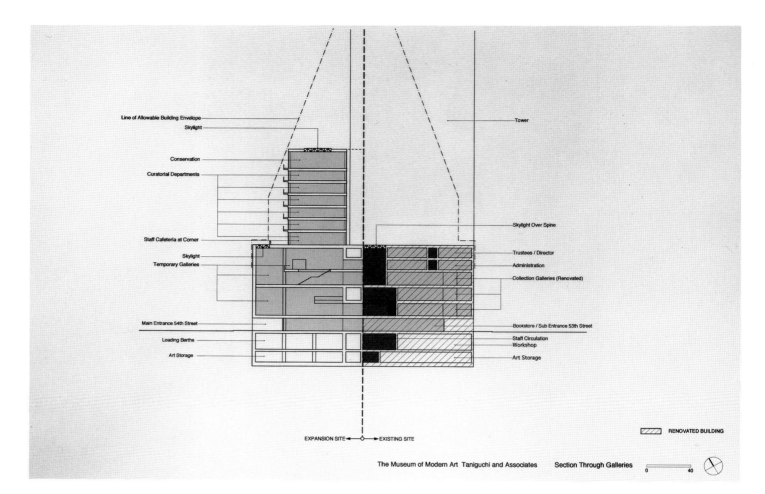

Line of Allowable Building Envelope
Skylight
Conservation
Curatorial Departments
Staff Cafeteria at Corner
Skylight
Temporary Galleries
Main Entrance 54th Street
Loading Berths
Art Storage

Tower
Skylight Over Spine
Trustees / Director
Administration
Collection Galleries (Renovated)
Bookstore / Sub Entrance 53th Street
Staff Circulation
Workshop
Art Storage

EXPANSION SITE ← ○ → EXISTING SITE

RENOVATED BUILDING

The Museum of Modern Art Taniguchi and Associates   Section Through Galleries   0   40

Above:
Transverse section through galleries. Computer-generated print on paper, 11 x 16½" (27.9 x 41.9 cm)

Right:
Site plan and elevation. Computer-generated print on paper, 11 x 16½" (27.9 x 41.9 cm)

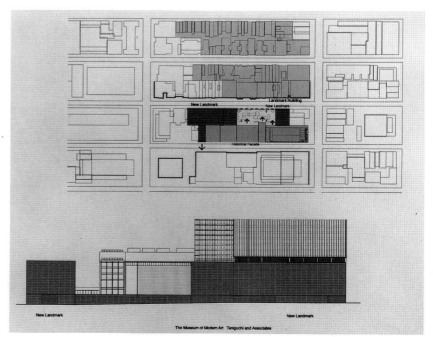

Landmark Building
New Landmark
New Landmark
Historical Facade

New Landmark   New Landmark

The Museum of Modern Art Taniguchi and Associates

Right, top to bottom:
**Diagrammatic plan, elevation, and axonometric.
Computer-generated print on paper, 11 x 16½" (27.9 x
41.9 cm)**

**Axonometric diagrams. Computer-generated print on
paper, 11 x 16½" (27.9 x 41.9 cm)**

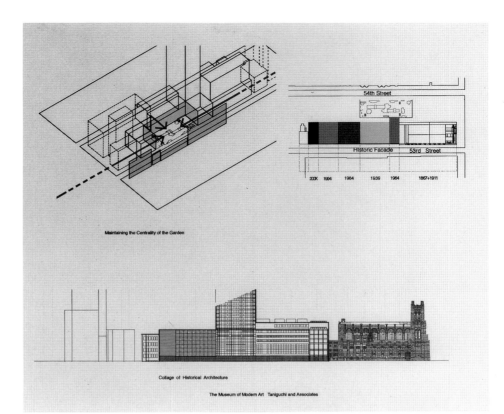

Maintaining the Centrality of the Garden

Collage of Historical Architecture

The Museum of Modern Art Taniguchi and Associates

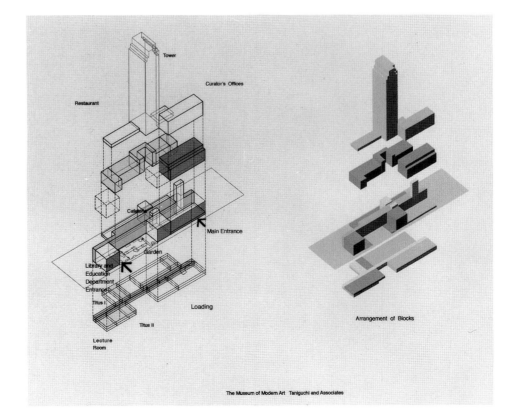

The Museum of Modern Art Taniguchi and Associates

Top to bottom:
Longitudinal section. Computer-generated print on paper, 11 x 16½" (27.9 x 41.9 cm)

Interior perspective sketches and main floor diagram. Colored pencil on computer-generated print on paper, 10⅞ x 10¾" (27.6 x 27.3 cm)

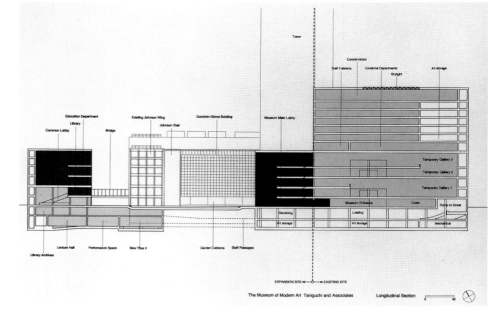

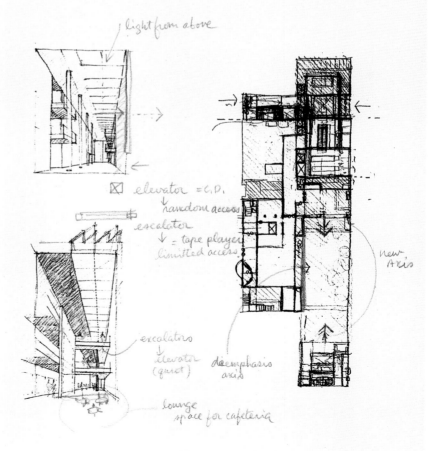

Exterior perspective sketches. Colored pencil on computer-
generated print on paper, 10⅞ x 10¾" (27.6 x 27.3 cm)

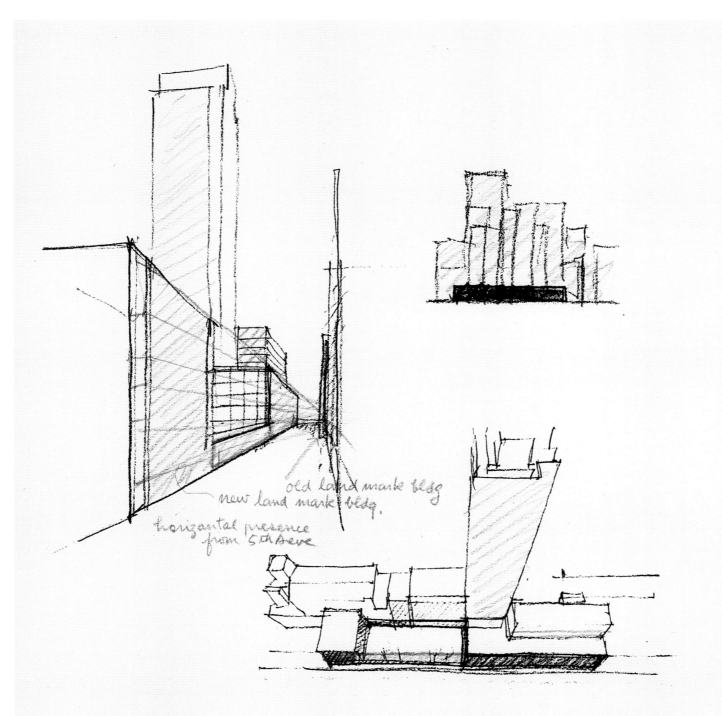

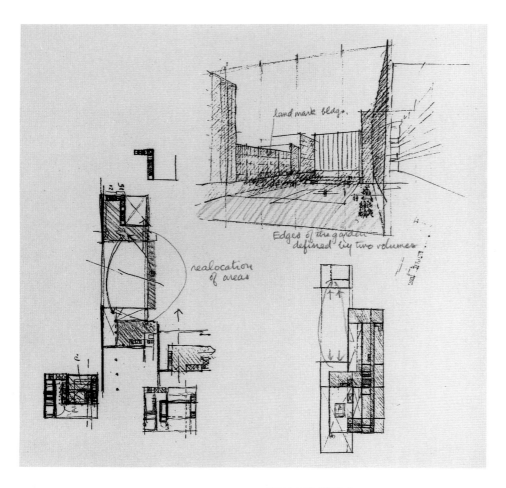

Left:
Perspective sketches and plan diagrams. Colored pencil on print, 10⅞ x 10¾" (27.6 x 27.3 cm)

Below:
Perspective sketches and plan diagrams. Colored pencil on print, 10⅞ x 10¾" (27.6 x 27.3 cm)

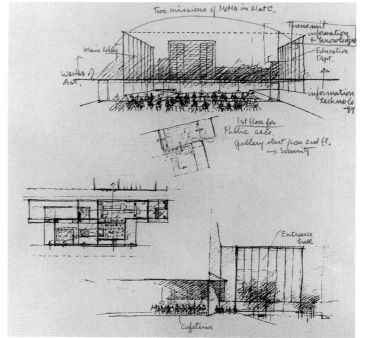

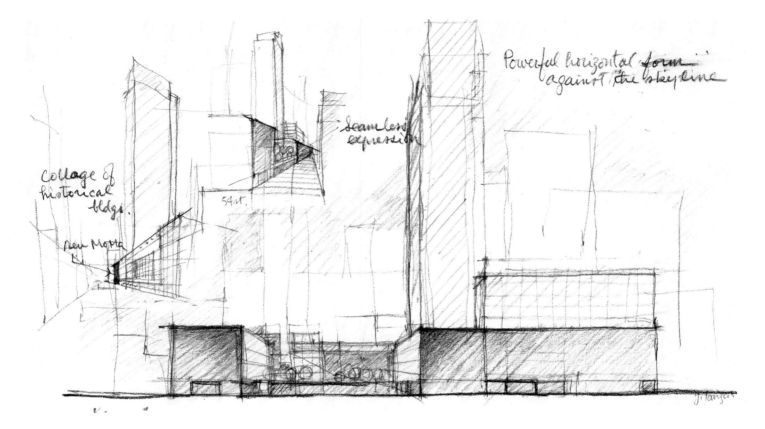

Powerful horizontal form
against the skyline

seamless
expression

collage of
historical
bldgs.

New MoMA

54st.

**Perspective sketches. Crayon and pencil on tracing
paper, 10⅞ x 16½" (27.6 x 41.9 cm)**

Yoshio Taniguchi:
Selected Recent Projects

Well-known in Japan as a designer of museums, Taniguchi has completed several in recent years, beginning in 1990 with the Higashiyama Kaii Gallery, adjacent to the Nagano Prefectural Shinano Art Museum in Nagano City. Designed to display the artist Kaii Higashiyama's paintings of nature, the individual galleries were conceived as larger frames for the pictures within. Situated next to a reflecting pool within a park, the Gallery complements the display of Higashiyama's art, and allows the visitor to contemplate the works while viewing the mountains of Nagano beyond.

Taniguchi was also commissioned to build a museum to house the works that the artist Genichiro Inokuma donated to the city of Marugame. Situated across from the city's railway station, the Marugame Genichiro-Inokuma Museum of Contemporary Art, completed in 1991, harmoniously unites architecture, art, and its urban site. The museum consists of spacious public areas and a large, skylit temporary exhibition gallery on the top floor, as well as an auditorium, an art library, a crafts studio, a restaurant, and offices.

In his design for the Toyota Municipal Museum of Art, completed in 1995 on the site of the old castle of Komoro City (now Toyota City), Taniguchi wanted to express the history and distinct nature of the site by affording views from within the museum, and rebuilt portions of the castle, to the new city. Various museum functions were separated into three levels: the administration and delivery entrances on the lowest, the visitor's entrance on the middle, and the sculpture terrace and garden on the top. While the area around the museum was redesigned as a plaza and park, plans exist to extend the garden to create a cultural and recreational facility for Toyota City residents.

Above, top and bottom:
Higashiyama Kaii Gallery, Nagano Prefectural Shinano Art Museum, Nagano City, Japan. 1988–90. Photographs by Taisuke Ogawa (top) and Toshiharu Kitajima (bottom)

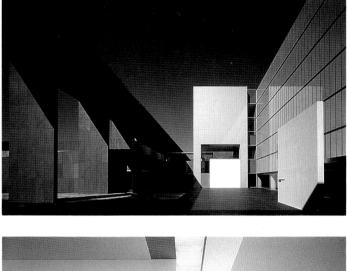

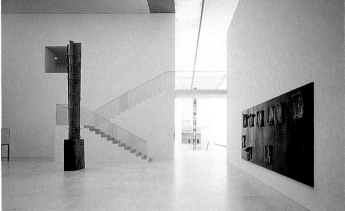

Above, top and bottom:
Toyota Municipal Museum of Art, Toyota City, Japan.
1991–95. Photographs by Toshiharu Kitajima

Above, top and bottom:
Marugame Genichiro-Inokuma Museum of Contemporary Art, Marugame, Japan.
1988–91. Photographs by Hiroshi Ueda (top) and Kazuo Natori (bottom)

CHARETTE FINALIST
Bernard Tschumi

Bernard Tschumi was born in 1944 in Lausanne, Switzerland. He studied at the Federal Institute of Technology (ETH), Zurich, Switzerland, where he received a degree in architecture in 1969. He is principal of Bernard Tschumi Architects, New York and Paris, and Dean of Columbia University's Graduate School of Architecture, Planning, and Preservation in New York City.

FROM THE ARCHITECT'S STATEMENT
Sketchbook

The possibility of a major expansion of The Museum of Modern Art into a twenty-first-century museum requires the imbrication of urbanistic, architectural, and aesthetic strategies. In keeping with the complexity of this endeavor and with the spirit of a sketchbook, we have proposed a series of points that act as conceptual vectors for the development of the project. . . . Our aim was . . . to propose a conceptual armature in which the new Museum could develop. This is the concept of garden and courts, interlocking the old and the new. We subsequently tested this conceptual structure through a series of computer plans and section diagrams of a potential Museum program.

Ten Points for MoMA

1. A DUAL-STREET MUSEUM: Heterogeneity on Fifty-third Street, calm and continuity on Fifty-fourth Street is our hypothesis. This is expressed architecturally, through a variety of façades on Fifty-third Street and a material theme (the beige glazed brick of the garden wall) on Fifty-fourth Street, as well as programmatically: book and design stores, café, restaurant, and film theater access are on Fifty-third Street. We offer two main entrance options: a new dual Fifty-third/Fifty-fourth "entrance court" and the historical entrance in the 1939 building.

    While MoMA remains a street Museum, a new presence will be visible from Fifth Avenue at Fifty-fourth Street in a quiet but spectacular architectural event located above the north wing—a new covered upper garden. . . .

2. A SEQUENCE OF MAJOR INTERIOR SPACES OR COURTS: This allows a unique route through the Museum, a sequential loop of courts that permits a spatially differentiated experience that alternates between art space and social space. . . . The new MoMA is like a city with an interlocking sequence of spaces. . . .

3. A STUNNING ROOF GARDEN: . . . The upper part of the garden and the new building literally interlock. The upper garden unfolds not only into the new building, but into a new reading of the project. Several scenarios are suggested, from a roof high above the north wing to a cantilevered space containing galleries or a performance room.

4. A . . . CONTINUOUS RELATION BETWEEN PUBLIC AND STAFF SPACE: We envision not only the continuity and clarity of the public sequence,

but also the continuity of the office layout, with one single core of elevators allowing for administrative and curatorial environments with their dedicated conference rooms and study centers. This relationship also applies to a group of individuals who belong somewhere between the general public and the curatorial staff, namely, scholars. The library has been relocated to a symbolical space in the Museum, behind the double-height translucent windows of the Goodwin and Stone building.

5. THE INVERSION OF CORE AND SATELLITE GALLERIES: . . . By placing the core at the edges, we secure the best rooms and the best light; by placing the satellites at the center, we get the most flexibility and the most tension. Hence, a reversal of the traditional concept of the Museum, in which certainty is at the core and peripheral values are located at the edges. This is another example in which the programmatic concept becomes the spatial concept of the project. At the "seam" between core and satellite, we also can locate either small permanent or temporary education spaces.

6. SHORT CUTS WITHIN THE MAIN GALLERIES' TWO LEVELS: We have tried to suggest that although the Museum's curators will articulate the story of modern art . . . viewers will be able to construct their own shortcuts in this trajectory. We have suggested replicating the Goodwin and Stone stair at multiple points to perform such linkages. . . .

7. THE INVISIBLE INTIMACY GRID: The conceptual armature that gives scale to the Museum (the expandable 25 feet of the brownstone) . . . may be articulated into small spaces located along the outer limits of the galleries, providing for a quiet critical space of viewing (a form of interactivity).

8. THE POSSIBILITY OF MULTIPLE OPTIONS: The concept allows keeping the historical entrance on Fifty-third Street or creating a new entrance from Fifty-third to Fifty-fourth in the new expansion. Having a simple, new, beautiful roof above the upper garden or having a full cantilevered space. Keeping the existing north wing building or building a new one. The concept also permits options for the future: If the Museum were ever to expand further to the west, the continuity and clarity of both staff and public spaces could be extended while keeping the same organization and spatial logic.

9. GO ALONG WITH HISTORY: Maintain those parts of the existing MoMA that reinforce the new concept; alter the others. This includes only moderate revision of the existing construction of the current buildings. Our aim has been to find the interlocking between the old and new, so that the ... institution is regenerated into a new urban and spatial type.

10. INTERLOCKING IS THE NAME OF THE GAME: ... Each of the major interior spaces is the place of interlocking: between the old and the new, between the permanent and the temporary, between the painting and sculpture collections and the other departments, between the public area and the curatorial offices or the education areas, between the galleries and the film theater spaces, etc. This interlocking is both structural—a spatial diagram—and conceptual. ...

The interstitial spaces between the old and the new are reprogrammed to arrive at ... a sequence of interlinked courts: tower court, upper court, garden court, entry court.

Simultaneous Scenarios for a New MoMA (Homage à Italo Calvino's *Invisible Cities*)

THE MODEM MODERN (OR THE MUSEUM OF MODEM ART): For a nominal site-entrance fee, the Museum offers on-line exhibitions capable of allowing thousands more visitors (in the form of "hits" or virtual visits) per day than any physical museum structure could comfortably accommodate. The permanent collection is shown in its entirety at all times of day and night. ... Special exhibitions are mounted and can remain available to the public for much longer time periods than traditional temporary exhibitions. Contemporary artworks can be displayed real-time in their native media—the digital realm.

Catalogues, monographs, and design-store items are sold in the virtual bookstore and virtual design store. Bulletin boards on the current exhibitions and on a wide variety of art subjects stimulate intellectual discussion and social interaction. The Museum library catalogue and books are available on-line. Special members-only chat rooms foster networking. *Without the need to physically accommodate visitors, the Museum staff moves into several floors of any generic office building equipped to handle extensive computer cabling in any city in the world with sufficient computer hardware support services.*

MOMALL: The design store, bookstore, and eateries (Modern Meals) serve as the anchor stores in a new theme mall; they use the importance of the unparalleled collection of modern art to appeal to the throngs of people who already come to the Fifth Avenue area to shop. ... The exhibition galleries are scattered throughout the mall behind retail storefronts; each is "accessed" and paid for independently as one more commodity in the mall. In this fashion, the exhibitions are able to draw a much larger diversity of visitors. Filled with picnic tables, the garden becomes the obligatory food court.

THE MODERN CLUB: Permanent Club: In addition to the usual public galleries, special Museum galleries contain exhibitions reserved for contributing members. The members' restaurant becomes a social hub/club space from which the members' galleries can be "accessed" or in which the artworks are actually located. While advertised within the public section, these exclusive rooftop spaces are visually severed from the rest of the Museum and remain invisible to the public.

Temporal Club: Certain sections of the Museum accommodate social gatherings for openings or special celebrations. Spaces normally designated for other programs (lobby, hall, temporary exhibitions, library reading room, performance, etc.) are designed to accommodate banquets, parties, or formal dances when necessary.

MORE MODERN THAN MODERN: CONTEMPORARY ARTISTS' WORKSHOP: Actively promoting an artists-in-residence program, the Museum commissions, exhibits, and collects works of contemporary art. Several large, unfinished spaces with rough, industrial detailing and layered traces of their own history provide unique environments in which artists can not only act but react to create site-specific installations. Extensive video and multimedia editing equipment, computer facilities with state-of-the-art graphics, and more traditional machine shops are placed at the disposition of contemporary artists for the creation of new works and are explained to the public to demystify contemporary art. ...

MODERN MULTIPLEX: To allow the Museum to show its film collection to the ever-increasing art-film public, four cinemas are built underneath the sculpture garden. Screenings of modern classics from the MoMA archives are joined by contemporary art films and films on loan from other archives. Themed film festivals are accompanied by lectures, debates, and scholarly publications. ...

THE MODERN PRESERVATION ARCHIVE: Given the extraordinary technical difficulties involved in preserving twentieth-century works of art, several large loft spaces are used as laboratories for experimentation. The fragility of many of the artistic techniques developed during the last century demands immediate attention; the diversity of the techniques requires that multiple scientific possibilities be explored simultaneously. ...

MODERN ART WAREHOUSE/STOCKYARDS: The Museum accumulates artwork from the nineteenth and twentieth centuries, but their exhibition is chronological, encyclopedic public storage. While the artworks are on display to the public, no curatorial efforts are made to contextualize or historicize the art. All of the art is hung in an identical manner. ...

Project Credits
Bernard Tschumi with Kevin Collins, Gregory Merryweather, Peter Cornell, assisted by Rhett Russo, Frederick Norman, Anthony Manzo, Jimmy Miyoshi, Ruth Berktold; art consultant: Kate Linker

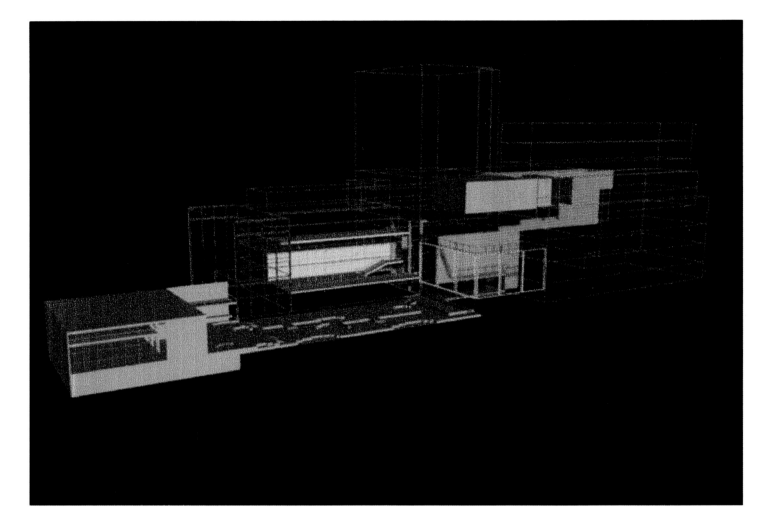

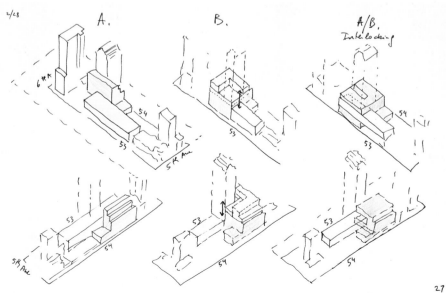

Above:
"Interlocking spaces—A revolving sequence of interconnected courts." Computer-generated print on paper, 11 x 17" (27.9 x 43.2 cm)

Left:
Diagrams of interlocking concept. Ink and crayon on paper, 11 x 17" (27.9 x 43.2 cm)

27

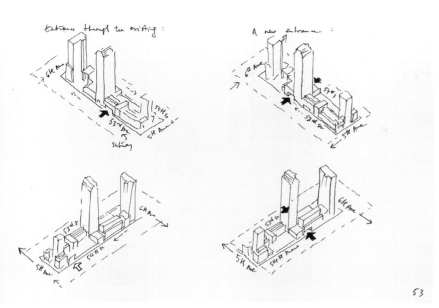

Left:
Diagrams of entrance options. Ink on paper, 11 x 17"
(27.9 x 43.2 cm)

Below:
Conceptual sketches of core and satellite galleries.
Ink and crayon on paper, 11 x 17" (27.9 x 43.2 cm)

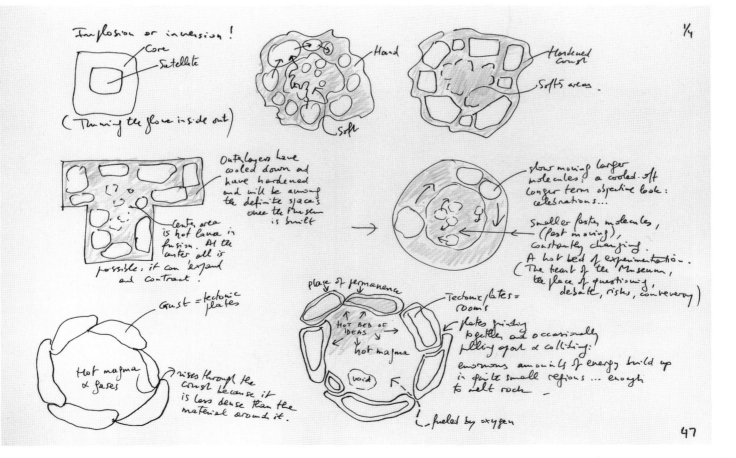

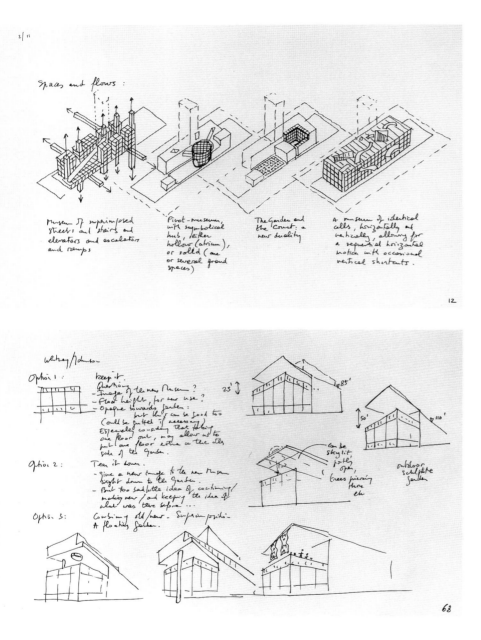

Left, top to bottom:
Diagrammatic sketches of "spaces and flows." Ink on paper, 11 x 17" (27.9 x 43.2 cm)

Options for the old Whitney wing: Exterior perspective sketches. Ink on paper, 11 x 17" (27.9 x 43.2 cm)

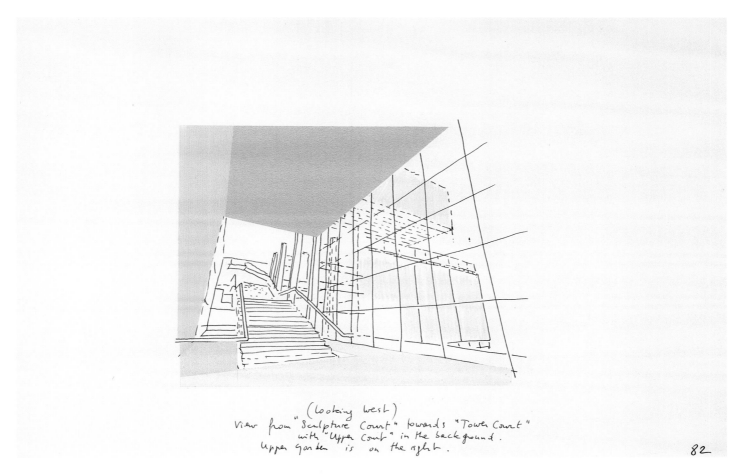

(looking west)

View from "Sculpture Court" towards "Tower Court" with "Upper Court" in the background. Upper garden is on the right.

82

Interior perspective looking from "Sculpture Court" toward "Tower Court." Computer-generated print on paper, 11 x 17" (27.9 x 43.2 cm)

(Looking East)
View from "Upper Court", through "Tower Court",
into "Sculpture Court". The interstice between
the new and the old —

83

"(Looking East) View from 'Upper Court' through
'Tower Court' into 'Sculpture Court.'" Computer-
generated print on paper, 11 x 17" (27.9 x 43.2 cm)

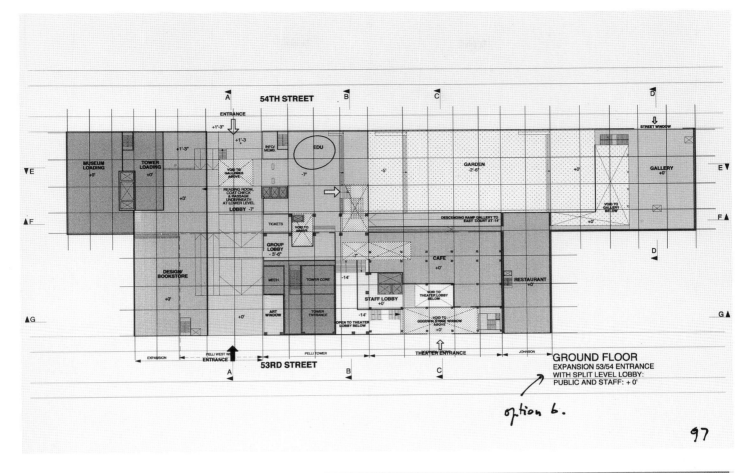

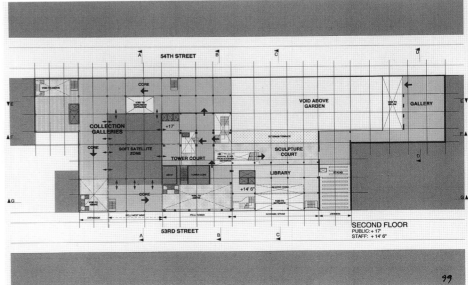

Above:
"Option B": Ground floor plan. Computer-generated print on paper, 11 x 17" (27.9 x 43.2 cm)

Right:
Second floor plan. Computer-generated print on paper, 11 x 17" (27.9 x 43.2 cm)

Right:
Longitudinal section. Computer-generated print on paper, 11 x 17" (27.9 x 43.2 cm)

Below:
Transverse section. Computer-generated print on paper, 11 x 17" (27.9 x 43.2 cm)

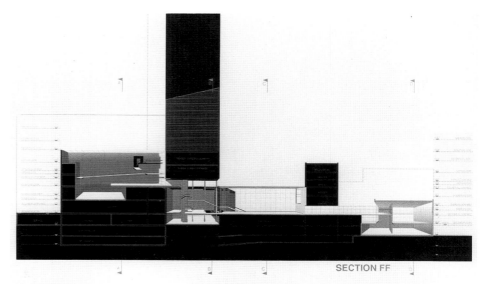

SECTION FF

92

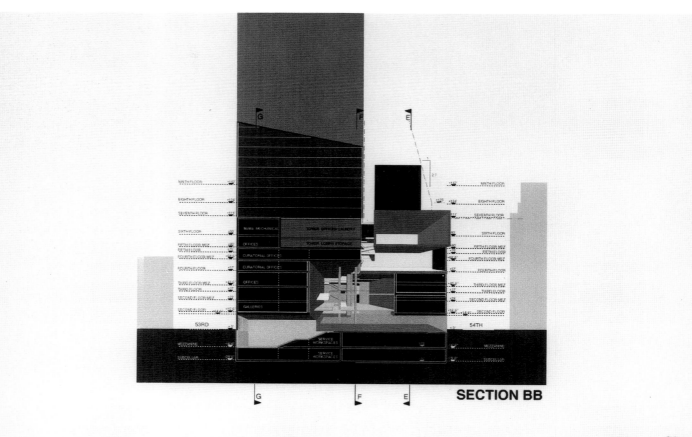

SECTION BB

89

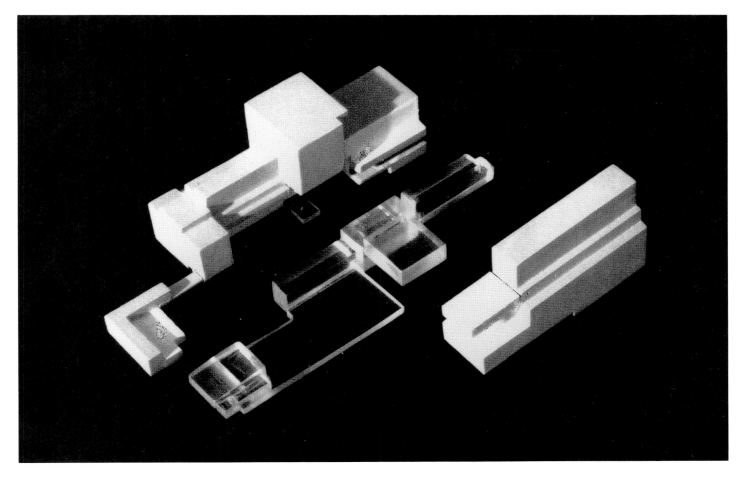

Above:
Conceptual model. Color laser copy on paper, 7½ x 10¾" (19.1 x 27.3 cm) overall

Left:
Conceptual model. Plexiglass and plastic, 1½ x 5¼ x 1⅝" (3.8 x 13.3 x 4.13 cm) overall

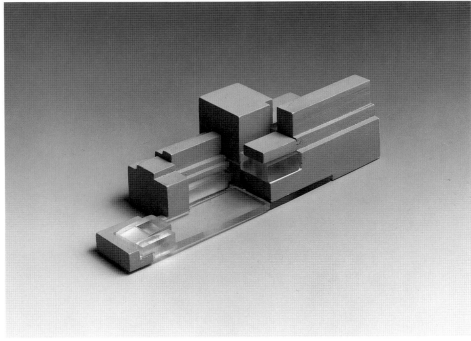

Bernard Tschumi:

Selected Recent Projects

Since winning the competition in 1983 for the Parc de la Villette in Paris, Tschumi, as chief architect, has been responsible for creating the master plan for the 125-acre site, and for coordinating a team of fifty designers, planners, landscape architects, and engineers. The complex includes a museum of sciences and industry, a "City of Music," a grand hall for exhibitions, a rock-concert hall, a movie theater, and an information center. In addition, thirty follies—small pavilions that house restaurants, day-care centers, and computer galleries—exist onsite, with new pavilions presently being built.

In 1991, Tschumi won an international competition for Le Fresnoy, Studio National des Arts Contemporains, in Tourcoing, France, a facility whose main purpose will be to provide postgraduate training in filmmaking. While incorporating an early-nineteenth-century building, this "school of the twenty-first century" will contain a multimedia resource center, two cinemas, an auditorium, photographic and sound studios, a great hall for live performances and exhibitions, a media library, administrative facilities, a restaurant, and workshops for research and production in sound, electronic imaging, film, and video.

Currently under construction is the Lerner Student Center, a student-activity center at Columbia University in New York. Designed in association with Gruzen Samton Architects, the Center is a multipurpose facility with an auditorium, a cinema, theater, clubs, meetings rooms, dining facilities, administration facilities, and a radio station.

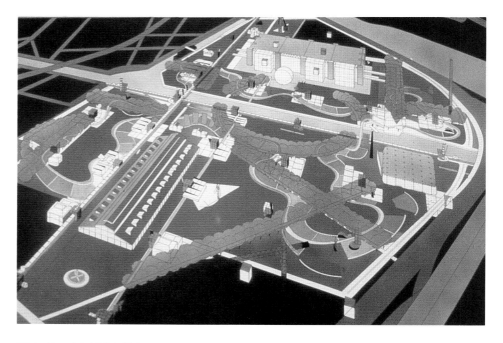

Top:
Parc de la Villette, Paris, France. Conceptual Model. 1982–95. Photograph © Bernard Tschumi Architects

Above:
Parc de la Villette, Paris, France. 1982–95. Photograph © Peter Mauss/Esto

Above and right:
Le Fresnoy Studio National des Arts Contemporains,
Tourcoing, France. 1991–97. Photographs © Dan Cor-
nish (above) and Peter Mauss/Esto (right)

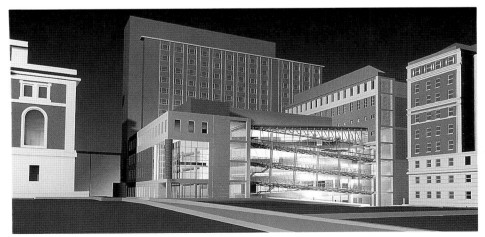

Above and left:
Lerner Student Center, Columbia University, New
York City. 1994–99 (projected completion date).
Photographs © Bernard Tschumi Architects with
Gruzen Samton Associated Architects

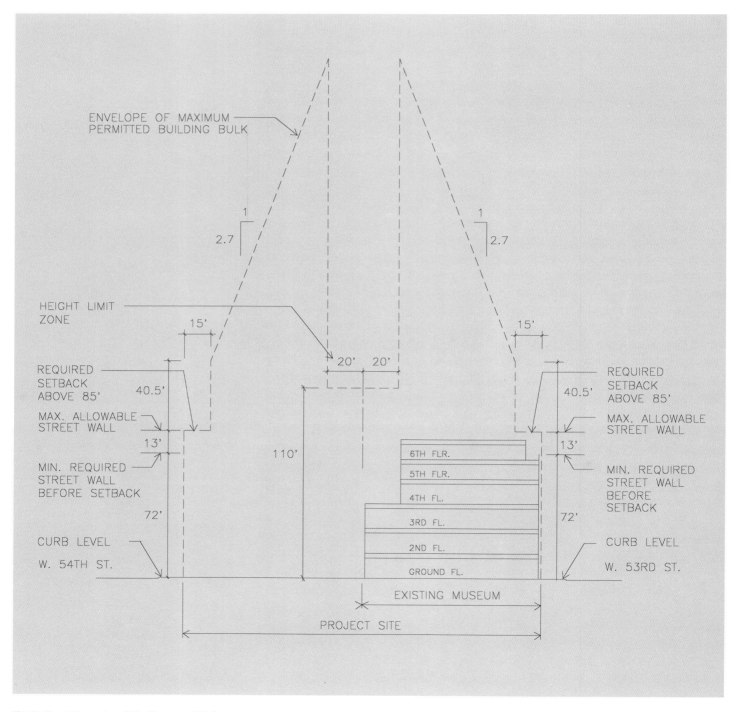

ENVELOPE OF MAXIMUM
PERMITTED BUILDING BULK

HEIGHT LIMIT
ZONE

REQUIRED
SETBACK
ABOVE 85'

MAX. ALLOWABLE
STREET WALL

MIN. REQUIRED
STREET WALL
BEFORE SETBACK

CURB LEVEL

W. 54TH ST.

REQUIRED
SETBACK
ABOVE 85'

MAX. ALLOWABLE
STREET WALL

MIN. REQUIRED
STREET WALL
BEFORE
SETBACK

CURB LEVEL

W. 53RD ST.

15'
40.5'
13'
72'
20' 20'
110'
15'
40.5'
13'
72'

6TH FLR.
5TH FLR.
4TH FL.
3RD FL.
2ND FL.
GROUND FL.

EXISTING MUSEUM

PROJECT SITE

**Site Section A, Expansion of The Museum of Modern
Art, New York, zoning restrictions**

The Architectural Competition

Introduction
Terence Riley

In June 1997, the three selected finalists—Jacques Herzog and Pierre de Meuron, Yoshio Taniguchi, and Bernard Tschumi—returned to the Museum for further consultations with an expanded number of staff and trustees as well as further briefings on the Museum's existing conditions. During this time, the Architectural Competition Brief was presented for discussion (see appendix, pp. 283–97, for excerpts from this document). This document, described below, was formulated as an expansion of the Charette Brief and reflected, in many ways, the urbanistic and architectural ideas put forth in the Charette submissions. However, the single greatest difference between these two briefs can be seen in their requirements for submission. While the former sought multiple, open-ended investigations, the latter emphasized the necessity of focusing on a single, optimized solution:

The ultimate purpose of this Architectural Competition is to elicit proposals for a new Museum of Modern Art that are boldly conceived and creatively define an aesthetic vision above and beyond programmatic, technical, and financial requirements. The Museum seeks proposals that provide a coherent and integrated plan for its existing and new structures, and that anticipate the opportunities and challenges of the twenty-first century.

Throughout the year-long process of defining the goals of the Museum for the next century, the question of architecture has been approached in many different ways. In the Architectural Competition, the challenge will be to render more precisely in the specific language of space, light, and material the important aesthetic, philosophical, and pragmatic issues that face the Museum today.

Because certain aspects of the architectural program will remain undetermined until an architect has been selected, the architectural proposals solicited are to be considered a "concept design." For the purposes of this Competition, a concept design is defined as a single architectural proposal that provides for undefined aspects of the program by means of alternate or optional components. The participants are not expected to provide multiple proposals; the alternate or optional components should constitute variations on a single proposal.

To enable the architects to fully develop a concept scheme, the Competition Brief included much more detailed information than was provided previously. Documentation of the existing conditions included a survey of properties fronting on the Museum site (see appendix, fig. II-1, p. 292), more thorough descriptions of below-grade conditions, access and transportation issues, quantification of existing floor areas and uses, etcetera. The brief also included a detailed survey of the Museum's structural and other technical systems—mechanical, security, audio-visual, and voice/data infrastructure—and expanded on the requirements of the New York City Zoning Resolution and various legal restrictions that affect the site.

In addition to these more detailed analyses, the Architectural Competition Brief differed from the Charette Brief in three significant ways. First, the expansion site was reduced. The westernmost parcel of land was isolated and designated for future expansion, although the architects were encouraged to consider temporary uses for this parcel (see fig. II-1, p. 292). Second, the architects were directed to consider the entire site, which currently is divided into two separate zoning lots, as one. Unlike the Charette, where the aggregate maximum allowable square footage was apportioned according to the different restrictions of each of the two zoning lots, the Architectural Competition Brief directed the architects to redistribute, as they saw fit, the same aggregate maximum square footage over the entire site. The intended result of this relaxation of the restrictions was not to increase the overall bulk of the expansion, but to allow the architects to consider more aesthetically unified schemes. As in the Charette, the participants were forewarned that any variances from the Zoning Resolution would have to be approved as required by city ordinance.

The third instance wherein the brief for the Competition differed from that of the Charette was in respect to The Abby Aldrich Rockefeller Sculpture Garden; it was said that the garden "should retain its current location and configuration." In consultation with the architects, it was clarified that the word "should" was to be considered less prohibitive than "must"; in other words, the architects had to demonstrate an overwhelmingly positive benefit to the relocation or reconfiguration of the garden. In a further clarification, it was determined that the condition referred to the garden as it was originally designed, and that the easternmost terrace (a remnant of a later addition to the garden, most of which was altered in the 1984 expansion) was not subject to the same restriction. Additionally, other important restrictions, mandated by structural, legal, and other concerns, were highlighted:

• Alterations to use, circulation, and structure may be made within the existing building, and portions of the existing building may be demolished as part of the proposed concept design. Note that in areas beneath the Museum Tower, columns may not be altered, although changes may be made to the floor slabs.
• Participants should consider incorporating two specific elements of the original 1939 Goodwin–Stone building into the new Museum: the large film theater ("Titus I") and the open stairway, which presently connects the second- and third-floor galleries.
• The elevator and stair shafts, and the entry lobby for the Museum Tower, must remain as shown on the plans, as must the shear-wall structure adjacent to the elevator shaft.
• The exterior envelope of retained portions of the existing Museum building may be clad in new materials, except that the portion of the Fifty-third Street frontage designated as the "Goodwin and Stone" façade (fig. II-3, p. 294) should be retained with its current appearance from the second floor up. Participants should also include in their concept designs alternatives for the Fifty-third Street façade that

leave the portions of the façade at the base of the Museum Tower and on the Museum to the west of the tower untouched.

• Access and egress location for pedestrians can be repositioned from the current location, and loading berths can be relocated as described under Parking and Loading below.

• The garden should retain its current location and configuration. Proposals that include relocation of the garden should be discussed with the Competition Office. Participants whose concept designs call for cellar floors to be constructed beneath the garden should plan for the reconstruction of the garden above the new cellars.

In addition to the requirements of the New York City Zoning Resolution and the various legal restrictions on the site, the Architectural Competition Brief incorporated, by reference, the New York City Building Code, the salient points of which were provided in the document itself. The most critical zoning restrictions are noted here:

• The street wall of all new construction must be built at the street line for its full length, and to a minimum of 72 feet in height, or the full height of the building, whichever is less. Above 72 feet in height, the building may be set back from the street.

• Above a height of 85 feet, the building must set back at least 15 feet from the street line, and then fit within the defined maximum bulk envelopes (see fig. II-4, p. 295).

• Adjacent to the Museum Tower, additional limitations on height are imposed. On the existing Museum site, all new building mass within 50 feet from the face of the Museum Tower must be below a height of 110 feet above curb level. In addition, on both the existing Museum site and the new site area, within a 40-foot-wide zone straddling the line between these two portions of the site, the 110-foot height limit on new building mass also applies (see fig. II-3, p.294).

While the Charette Brief focused on a limited number of broad architectural and urban issues, the Architectural Competition Brief presented more detailed Design Guidelines that framed the philosophical and theoretical issues that the trustees and staff felt must be addressed in developing a solution to the unique architectural problem of The Museum of Modern Art (see appendix, pp. 283–284). In conjunction with these guidelines, a set of General Requirements was formulated with more specific criteria developed by the Museum trustees and staff (see appendix, pp. 284–291, 297). Even so, these requirements provided no solutions in themselves; rather, they became the subject of the architects' interpretations.

The most explicit directives given to the architects were contained in the brief's provisional Program of Requirements, which enumerated the square-footage requirements of all the various components of the Museum, as well as their required organizational groupings and, in certain instances, required adjacencies. This program also listed various amenities and functional elements, including an overview of all anticipated needs for the Museum's technical systems (HVAC, electrical, plumbing, audio-visual, voice/data, security, etcetera) that were considered essential to a well-designed museum of art.

Directives were also given as to the minimum requirements for presentation: large-scale drawings of the site plan, architectural floor plans, building sections and elevations, as well as an architectural model, all of which were to be documented in the form of an accompanying bound report. Beyond these requirements, however, the architects were free to submit any other material developed during the 16-week competition period that they deemed important.

Prior to the presentation of the work to the Architect Selection Committee in early December 1997, the architects' submissions underwent a technical review to determine compliance or noncompliance with the New York Building Code, the New York City Zoning Resolution, and the Competition Program, as well as a pre-liminary estimate of probable cost. The technical consultants were not asked to make any specific recommendations, but simply to provide data for the Architect Selection Committee's review.

The Architects' Proposals

The Competition for The Museum of Modern Art expansion yielded three proposals that respond in detail to the needs and requirements laid out in the brief. Moreover, each architect's proposal demonstrates an ability not only to solve the myriad prob-lems defined by the program, but to supersede those issues. The result is three dis-tinct approaches to the history and future direction of the Museum. These projects, both collectively and individually, will no doubt have great impact on the continu-ing debates as to the idea of the contemporary museum and the course of architec-ture in the next century. However, their respective successes are intimately linked to the extent to which they have addressed issues specific to this institution and its dense urban context. In this sense, the three architects have not approached the design of the new Museum simply as the reiteration of a particular building type; nor have they conceived of the urban context as a formulaic adherence to a series of height and setback restrictions. Rather, all three schemes bear out the architects' pro-found understanding of the unique character of this particular architectural problem for this particular institution, fusing historical precedent with pure invention. Each is a reflection upon the nature of urban architecture at a time when, in this country and elsewhere, the practice of architecture is an increasingly suburbanized, and even de-urbanized, occupation that focuses on undeveloped sites, the locations of which are farther and farther away from established urban centers. To the extent that all three proposals so skillfully demonstrate the potential role for the architect in trans-forming the built environment, the Competition results can be seen as a primer of architectural strategies for the next century, strategies that can reaffirm and redefine the urban landscape.

JACQUES HERZOG AND PIERRE DE MEURON's proposal represents a spirited defense of the idea of the art museum as a public place of private encounter. While they have included many new and fundamentally transformative concepts, the underlying premise of the Museum remains the same. In the architects' words: "Why is it that art keeps asserting itself, keeps renewing itself, keeps arousing our curiosity and confronting us with such fundamental questions as: who am I, why am I, where are we going?"

According to the architects, diversity of spaces is critical to the encounter with the multifarious works of art in a museum founded in the twentieth century and looking toward the next. Recognizing the broad spectrum of artistic production in the Museum Collection, from early twentieth-century easel paintings to large contemporary installations in multiple mediums, Herzog and de Meuron's proposal advocates appropriate and distinctly different spaces: "The encounter between art and beholder is not restricted to a specific site; it requires many sites and variations in lighting, intimate spaces and large halls, open courtyards and cultivated gardens, rough and refined materials."

The architects' emphasis on the concept of heterotopic space is not solely a recognition of the nature of the art of this century. It also reflects an awareness that the perception of any single painting, sculpture, or installation is not a universal one, and that a diversity of spaces encourages and embraces the idea of the critical observer: "[Diversity] actually governs the task: a museum with a number of distinctive sites for many, many people with as many different ways of looking at and thinking about art: the museum of the twenty-first century." While their philosophical position rejects the idea of the absolute universality of the "white box," it does not imply a museum of capricious and incomprehensible spaces. Rather, Herzog and de Meuron have proposed a vastly extended repertoire of spaces that are characterized by an intellectual as well as a physical sense of refinement, and by a distinctly urban sensibility.

This urban sensibility is not only evident in the multiple spaces dedicated to exhibiting works of art but is fundamental to the architects' conception of the entire building. The proposal reinforces and revitalizes, at the pedestrian level, the street wall of the Museum's Midtown Manhattan site, insuring both the transformation and the continuity of New York City's most distinguishing urban characteristic. Melding their two Charette analyses, the architects have outlined a composition of vertical diversity along Fifty-third Street (see p. 306) and a synthetic horizontal composition along Fifty-fourth Street (p. 307). The strategy equally recognizes the complexity of the midblock site, the importance of its historical structures along Fifty-third Street, and the opportunity for the creation of a single, unified image along Fifty-fourth Street.

As a striking counterpart to what might be called the "normative" or "contextual" treatment of the street wall, this proposal includes a tower for the Museum's curatorial and support staff rising over the western portion of the site (p. 298, p. 299 top). An extended asymmetrical polygon, its axis, unlike those of traditional Manhattan towers, is neither centroidal nor vertical, but projects at an angle toward Fifty-fourth Street. In contrast to its neighbors adjacent and opposite on Fifty-third Street, Herzog and de Meuron's proposed tower is not conceived as a simple vertical multiplication of floor plates but as a complex volumetric form, part "minimal" and part "mathematical," recalling the eccentric volume of their designs for the architects' Signal Box Auf dem Wolf, constructed in Basel in 1994 (see p. 241). It responds to the existing zoning requirements in that the south façade traces the Midtown setback requirements, with floor plans varying in size from 3,200 square feet at the widest point to 900 square feet at the apex (p. 311 bottom). Similarly, the east face of the tower projects outward from its center to the point where it meets the required fifty-foot setback from the Museum Tower, designed by Cesar Pelli in 1984. Nonetheless, the proposal reflects not only current zoning restrictions and building codes, but the architects' precise and rigorous approach to formmaking. Skillfully creating a distinction between their intentions and "deconstructive, neoexpressive or symbolic" clichés, they cite Alberto Giacometti's *Le Cube* of 1934 as an example of a form that "seesaws between abstraction and figuration."

A consistent skin, referred to as a "glass shell," unifies the orthogonal street-wall block and the contrasting polygonal tower. Beyond its aesthetic implications, this skin has an urban dimension of its own: in the architects' words, "a vitality, a kind of animation that allows the buildings to communicate a variety of impressions." This animation is achieved not only by revealing the interior life of the Museum to the street, but in the composition of the skin as well. As proposed by Herzog and de Meuron, the glass shell would have many aspects: "The surfaces may be transparent, translucent or opaque. Variations in appearance are achieved by printing or etching the glass. So sometimes it doesn't look like glass at all but more like stone."

While many of the conceptual underpinnings of the proposal are universal in significance, they also address the peculiar and specific conditions of The Museum of Modern Art's urban situation. The architects recognized that the Museum represents a unique New York typology, the "street museum" (as opposed to the more ubiquitous "avenue museum"), and have reinforced this typology in several ways. Even so, the tower and the development of the Fifty-fourth Street façade lend a strong, iconic image to the Museum from both Fifth and Sixth avenues (pp. 300–01), extending its visual presence beyond its immediate locale.

In their Charette submission, the architects investigated the potential of a public, through-block passage consisting of two open sculpture courtyards, diagonally arranged, behind the Goodwin–Stone façade to the south and the façade of Philip Johnson's North Wing on Fifty-fourth Street. The architects' notion of extending public space into the Museum was retained in the final proposal in the form of two diagonally-related lobbies that provide, in a double-height space, an appropriate setting for urban-scale public sculpture (p. 302). For the visitor to the Museum, this space is emblematic of an institution in a great city and provides an immediate encounter with the Museum's principal purpose: the display of extraordinary works of art.

The interconnected lobbies also frame and extend the Museum's most important open space, The Abby Aldrich Rockefeller Sculpture Garden. Restored to its original proportions in this proposal, the garden's appropriateness for the relatively modest-size sculptures for which it was designed is enhanced. Furthermore, by incorporating the East Terrace (a remnant of the 1964 extension of the garden) into the East Wing, the architects' proposal situates galleries on three sides of the garden, redefining it as the heart of the Museum (p. 299 bottom). The loss of the East Terrace as the site for larger-scale postwar sculpture is more than offset by the creation of a 6,000-square-foot space at the western end of the site. In the words of the architects, this space will be less refined, a *terrain vague* that could accommodate not only large-scale sculptural works but also such unexpected projects as architectural installations and other events that would benefit from a more specifically urban venue.

As in their Charette submission, Herzog and de Meuron's proposal also includes roof gardens and courts conceived much as The Abby Aldrich Rockefeller Sculpture Garden was conceived: as works of art. The architects have proposed that the roof of the East Wing, as well as a court over the galleries, be designed by artists. The tower rises out of a second roof court, flanked on its five sides by various offices and staff spaces.

As requested in the Competition Program, the architects have provided for temporary exhibition space, departmental galleries, and galleries for the Museum

Collection. The proposed temporary exhibition space is located on the second floor and accessible directly from the lobby (p. 310 top). Wrapping around a circulation core, the 31,000-square-foot space is easily subdividable into larger and smaller spaces with greater and lesser ceiling heights. The central portion of the space has a height of 23 1/2 feet and extends the entire 200-foot distance from Fifty-third to Fifty-fourth Street, allowing for views outward if desirable.

The departmental galleries are dispersed throughout the Museum. The Architecture and Design galleries are sited in the new East Wing at garden level, with the Photography galleries above; the Drawings and Prints and Illustrated Books galleries are adjacent on the fourth floor, above the Museum Collection galleries. The theaters dedicated to film and video, including the existing Titus 1 theater, are grouped in the lower level around a central gallery dedicated to related exhibitions (p. 309 top). As such, the departmental galleries can be experienced either casually, as the visitor navigates his or her way through the Museum, or can be seen as destinations in themselves.

In Herzog and de Meuron's conception, the Museum Collection galleries begin on the new second floor—formerly the third floor—of the original 1939 Goodwin–Stone building and continue upward to the next level. In addition to the proposed creation of a double-height space facing the garden, the architects' scheme calls for the restoration of the original building's translucent glass façade, its black terrazzo floors and, perhaps most importantly, the Bauhaus-inspired stair, which would again directly connect the Museum Collection galleries with the lobby.

The location of the earliest part of the Museum Collection in the new second and third floors of the Goodwin–Stone building insures that those works will have the greatest historical resonance with the restored architectural spaces that originally housed them. From the original galleries on the third floor, the reconceived Museum Collection galleries extend outward to the east and west, wrapping around the garden, to the areas of new construction, which would have higher ceilings to accommodate the increasing scale of postwar and contemporary art (p. 310 bottom). A satellite Collection gallery, along with a space for the Projects gallery, is located on street level to create opportunities for an immediate experience with works of art from the Collection as well as those temporarily on view.

The various circuits through the greatly enlarged space dedicated to the Museum Collection provide for both fixed galleries of a more permanent architectural quality and more flexible changing galleries, as well as ample points of repose and periodic reorientation with the garden and the city beyond. Rather than a seamless "white box" experience, the Herzog and de Meuron proposal provides for a variety of spaces with discreet but palpable architectural presence more suited to specific works of art—the restored Goodwin–Stone galleries, reminiscent of both the bourgeois apartment and the artist's atelier; large galleries with diffuse top-lighting for more contemporary works; and spaces for sculpture with views and natural light. Eschewing the notion of neutral space, the architects have sought the appropriate level of architectural expression to "enhance and guide" one's perception of "the museum's extraordinary collection."

Vertical movement through the Museum is achieved principally by a series of escalators located at the point where the two diagonally placed lobbies meet, at the southwest corner of the garden. On the upper floors, the escalators are sited so that they occupy a semi-enclosed space, limiting their visual intrusiveness and noise from the gallery experience. The architects' decision to use escalators instead of stairways is explained in a forthright manner: "Nobody uses stairs anymore." Despite their argument that only escalators can handle the volume of people expected to visit the Museum, the architects recognize the appeal of incidental uses of more traditional stairways. Visitors can also use the restored Goodwin–Stone stair to circulate through the galleries; a run of stairs through the new East Wing; or a grand circular stair to access the theaters. Another stairway leads directly from the lobby to the new space for large-scale sculpture at the western end of the site.

Threaded throughout the Museum are various proposed amenities. Adjacent to the original Goodwin–Stone lobby is an Infotec, a computerized orientation and information center. Above the lobby on a mezzanine—the former second floor—is a public cafeteria with tables overlooking the lobby and the garden beyond, and a public reading room connected to the Education Center. The MoMA Design Store and Bookstore have a separate entrance to the west of the Museum Tower with a relatively discreet link to the interior, adjacent to the escalators. A restaurant, to be designed, like the upper gardens, by a collaborating architect or artist, is located on the fourth floor of the new East Wing overlooking its own roof terrace and the original sculpture garden. The public spaces of the Museum serve not only visitors' circulation through the building but also provide incidental places where the visitor might pause, have a cup of coffee, or refer to Museum catalogues and other sources of information.

The Museum's principal administrative offices are located on the top two floors of the Goodwin–Stone building (the former sixth and seventh floors) and connect with the staff areas farther west on Fifty-third Street and in the tower above. Some semipublic spaces are also located on these floors: The Works on Paper Study Center wraps the five-sided court from which the tower rises, and the Library and Archives similarly wrap the roof garden on the new fifth floor (p. 311 top).

In Herzog and de Meuron's scheme, dedicated staff elevators connect the staff and administrative offices described above with a ground-level staff entrance at the west end of the site and the tower above, housing curatorial offices and other functions. As some curatorial departments occupy more than one level, the tower contains a number of discreet stairs that connect, when necessary, certain adjoining floors.

The Museum's loading docks for shipping and receiving are located at the westernmost and easternmost parts of the site on Fifty-fourth Street. Art and other goods are then transferred, in segregated elevators, to two lower levels with storage and handling spaces. The principal support functions of the Museum (insulated art storage, frame shop, cabinetry shop, registrar, photography studios, etcetera) are also located on these lower levels. The proposal also consolidates the Museum Tower's shipping and receiving area with the Museum's, providing a belowgrade link to the tower's service elevator. An alternate proposal retains the existing location of the tower loading docks with a greatly reduced Fifty-fourth Street lobby.

YOSHIO TANIGUCHI, in his Competition design submission, states that his goal is "to create an ideal environment for art and people through the imaginative and disciplined use of light, materials and space," proposing "a museum that preserves and reinforces MoMA's unique character as (1) the repository of an incomparable collection of modern and contemporary art; (2) a pioneer of museums of modern art with a unique historical inheritance; (3) an urban institution in a midtown Manhattan location; (4) a comprehensive museum with six curatorial departments; and (5) an organization with a large and diversified staff. . . . By seizing the opportunities presented by these aspects of its character, it is possible to transform MoMA into a bold new museum while maintaining its historical, cultural and social context."

Addressing the first of these five points, the architect points out that the proposed Museum Collection galleries and temporary exhibition galleries have been located in the western part of the site, "assuring spacious floor areas and extensive wall surfaces" (p. 319). Furthermore, there is a continuous vertical axis from the lower levels, where the Museum's collections are stored and handled, through the public space of the ground level, then through four floors of Museum Collection galleries, and two levels of skylit temporary exhibition galleries, to culminate in the conservation studios along the western edge of the uppermost floor. This organization is reflected by the massing of the project, which creates "an impressive volume on the building exterior, sheathed in honed black slate, gray marble, and anondized aluminum panels and readily identifiable as the principal element of the reorganized Museum" (p. 312).

Just as the larger volumes of space devoted to the galleries are concentrated in the western portion of the site, the spaces devoted to education and research are located in the eastern portion. From Fifty-fourth Street, the two volumes are intended to make the Museum's mission explicit: "The two simple geometric forms, one accommodating the galleries and the other the educational facilities, symbolize the dual mission of the museum."

The second point of Taniguchi's proposal addresses the specific historical context in which the Museum is situated. The architect identifies The Abby Aldrich Rockefeller Sculpture Garden and the Fifty-third Street façade as the two principal exterior elements that can and should be revitalized through redesign and reuse. In his scheme, the garden's central position, both spatially and historically, within the Museum is reaffirmed (p. 320 left). The southern terrace, which was part of Philip Johnson's original design for the garden, is reestablished, thereby restoring the diagonal relationship between its principal components that was lost in subsequent expansions and alterations. While the plan of the garden regains its original integrity, the architect's proposal does not seek merely to return it to its original appearance. To the east, west, and south, the open space of the garden is extended into the Museum in a more dramatic fashion than before. At ground level, the garden façades are recessed slightly, creating semi-enclosed spaces between the garden and the interiors all around (p. 315). To the east and west, the structures have a stepping section that draws the light and space of the garden deep inside the interior. From Fifty-fourth Street, the new façades to the east and west of the garden, sheathed principally in honed black slate (p. 314 bottom), are composed to frame it, enhancing the visual perception of its centrality.

The stepping section to the west of the garden envelops the proposed new main lobby. Visitors would proceed from the entrance through the lobby toward the garden in order to reach the ground-floor elevators or the grand switchback stair that leads to the second floor and the escalator system, which serves as the principal circulation through the Collection galleries (p. 317).

Programmatically, Taniguchi's proposal further emphasizes the garden as the central element of the Museum. Virtually all of the public spaces are adjacent to it:

the main lobby on Fifty-fourth Street and the restaurant above; the public cafeteria (on the ground floor of the Goodwin–Stone building); the staff cafeteria (ground floor of the East Wing); and the public reading room and education center (ground floor of the new Garden Wing; p. 324 top).

With respect to the southern façade of the Museum, the proposal states that the building façades on Fifty-third Street "will be preserved as much as possible" (p. 314 top). The architecture of the past is afforded as much respect as the works in the collection, and as a result, the Fifty-third Street façade becomes a fascinating collage of milestones in the history of the museum and, in consequence, an apt expression of MoMA's capacity to redefine and renew itself through a dialogue with the past." The façade of the 1939 Goodwin–Stone building, which defined the character of the institution as a "street museum," is reprogrammed, in keeping with its scale, as the auxiliary entry for the film and video theaters.

The Museum's Midtown Manhattan location is the third issue on which Taniguchi's scheme is based, becoming a referent point for a number of design decisions (p. 320 right). As in his Charette sketchbook, the architect proposes a through-block entry from Fifty-third to Fifty-fourth streets—with the principal entry on the latter street—recalling a number of recent midblock interventions in Midtown (such as the Equitable Building, designed by Edward Larabee Barnes), as well as historic precedents (such as Rockefeller Center, designed by Raymond Hood). Another aspect of the proposal that addresses the architectural culture of Midtown is the verticality of the public spaces, specifically, the arrangement of the galleries as described above. An asymmetrical atrium underscores this vertical organization on the interior of the Museum, and its placement reveals the northeast corner of the Museum Tower (pp. 312, 316). In the architect's words, "This selective exposure is an acknowledgement and expression of the museum's strong ties to Manhattan, a city of skyscrapers." Further reducing the amalgamation of the tower's vertical form with the Museum's overall horizontal composition is a range of windows on the south façade that reveal the point where the two forms meet.

Just as the atrium provides an inward focus to this vertically conceived Museum, ample opportunities exist for outward reorientation with the city as the visitor passes through the building. In addition to the frequent views into the garden, Taniguchi has provided for a number of interstitial spaces—"pauses," in effect, in the long gallery sequences—as were requested in the Program (see appendix, pp. 284–285). The placement of these spaces reinforces the strategy of redefining the forms of the Museum and the tower, since these spaces are principally located in the newly-revealed corner of the tower and behind the range of windows that distinguishes its vertical form from the overall horizontal form of the Museum on Fifty-third Street.

The layout of the five departmental galleries is the focus of Taniguchi's next point. In his words, "The Museum of Modern Art's distinctive character as a comprehensive art museum, collecting and exhibiting works in diverse media, will be emphasized and made more apparent." Toward this goal, the architect's scheme calls for all the departmental galleries to be clustered within, or immediately adjacent to, the renovated Goodwin–Stone building. The Film and Video theaters, including the existing Titus 1 and Titus 2 theaters as well as a new theater, are located on two lower levels, connected by a common lobby and gallery space. The Drawings galleries and the Prints and Illustrated Books galleries are side-by-side on the second floor of the

Goodwin–Stone building, with the Architecture and Design galleries located immediately above them. Adjacent to the Architecture and Design galleries are the Photography galleries, occupying the third floor under the Museum Tower. The "Bauhaus stair" of the original 1939 building is reprogrammed, in keeping with its scale, as a link between the departmental galleries. The extant fragment of the stair would connect the second- and third-floor galleries and a new extension would link the upper galleries with the ground floor and the theaters below. Taniguchi sums up his strategy: "As with the Collection galleries, these [departmental] galleries, though now more closely linked physically, are endowed with their own separate identities within the museum. Each departmental gallery, being a distinctive space, is in the nature of a museum within the museum."

The fifth point that Taniguchi addresses is the needs of a large and diversified staff. In his proposal, he describes the principal elements of his scheme: "Dignified spaces for administrators are primarily located in the renovated East Wing and the upper floors of the Goodwin and Stone building. These are pleasant spaces, facing the garden with north light" (p. 321). In the architect's proposal, the curatorial offices would be located principally in the renovated East Wing between the departmental galleries in the Goodwin–Stone building, with the study centers, collections storage, and research library grouped in the Garden Wing, making these areas "easily accessed by visitors and scholars approaching from the group/education entrance on Fifty-fourth Street." A common stair running through the East Wing to a staff lounge and terrace on the top level would also link the curatorial offices and the education offices. The administrative offices would be located primarily in the upper levels of the Goodwin–Stone building, in effect creating an overlap and interconnection between staff spaces and galleries spaces along Fifty-third Street.

In describing the operational aspects of the museum, the proposal states: "The spaces for goods and services are located in the basement and directly linked to loading docks and service elevators. Uses are clearly divided by zoning, and connections among them are established by a clear and simple network of vertical and horizontal circulation." The efficiency of the proposed horizontal circulation is enhanced by the intention to excavate two levels under the sculpture garden, regularizing the plan of the lower levels and providing new space for exhibition production, art handling, shipping and receiving, photography studios, etcetera.

In addition to the five-point summary, the proposal includes a detailed analysis of the scheme's program, structure, phasing, mechanical systems, and circulation, as well as an in-depth study of the architect's ideas for the galleries that, significantly, reverses the current chronological flow of the Museum Collection galleries. That is, Taniguchi has proposed that the earliest works in the collections be situated in the upper Collection galleries rather than in the lower spaces. The intention is not necessarily to reverse the visitor's experience of the collection but, rather, to take advantage of the fact that each floor can be considered a specific destination, and that the lower, larger floors are more suited to contemporary works. Thus, the large public spaces of the main lobby and atrium flow more seamlessly into the larger Collection galleries devoted to recent work, while they gradually break down in scale as the visitor moves upward. This also creates a situation where the visitor's first exposure to the collection, after arriving at the top of the grand stair, is to contemporary art.

In Taniguchi's scheme, the Collection galleries are laid out on three principal levels, beginning on the second floor (p. 318). Each of these gallery levels extends through the block from Fifty-fourth Street to Fifty-third Street. By removing parts of the floor slabs in the present West Wing, the three principal levels would have heights of 30½ feet, 17 feet, and 14 feet, in ascending order (p. 319). Within the grand space of the second-floor galleries would be inserted an intermediate level, which would divide the space vertically into upper and lower parts and provide additional vantage points from which to view the large-scale works. Adjacent to the large second-floor gallery level is an outdoor sculpture garden situated above the Museum's proposed loading docks at the western end of the site.

As requested in the Competition Program, the Collection galleries are divided into more permanent "fixed" galleries and "variable" galleries that could be reconfigured more often. The relationship between the horizontal circulation through each level of the Collection galleries and the vertical circulation between floors has been outlined by the architect as follows: "There is a normal route of circulation through the fixed galleries on each floor beginning and ending at the main circulation core. The normal route does not necessitate moving through any variable galleries to complete a circuit. Variable galleries have been located so that they have direct access to the service core and can be closed off from the fixed galleries without disturbing the normal route of circulation" (p. 325).

In addition to the relationship between the fixed and variable galleries and the location of the vertical circulation core, incidental ramps and stairs between the three main levels of the Collection galleries allow for a variety of experiences. In the architect's words, "Visitors may view the Collection galleries in chronological sequence by the normal route or may create their own paths. Various opportunities for jumping forward or backward in the chronology through interstitial spaces, variable galleries, and interconnecting stairways are provided."

The temporary exhibitions galleries are located on two levels above the Collection galleries and make a similar circuit that both leads from, and returns to, the main vertical circulation. Both levels are partially skylit, have ceiling heights of 20 feet and extending through the block from Fifty-third to Fifty-fourth Street. Like the Collection galleries, the temporary exhibitions galleries also have the possibility of natural lighting at the north and south perimeters, owing to the stepped-back section of the principal façades. By programming the public elevators, the temporary exhibitions galleries can be accessed even when the rest of the Museum is closed.

Taniguchi's proposal also includes an option for retaining the Museum Tower's loading dock as well as the existing façade of the West Wing.

BERNARD TSCHUMI has provided a summary of his Competition proposal in an overview titled "Ten Points for MoMA." Recalling the emphases of his Charette submission, the first of these points is named "An Urban Museum," and summarizes the principal planning strategies insofar as they reflect the conditions of Midtown Manhattan. The architect has taken the concept of the "street museum" and expanded it to the notion of a "dual street museum," proposing a through-block entrance hall connecting the north and south façades of the Museum on Fifty-fourth and Fifty-third streets, respectively. Even as Tschumi's proposal redefines and expands the urban typology of a "street museum," it also addresses a larger identity, that of the "dual avenue museum." The long, narrow, penthouse structure that rises above the westernmost part of the site is canted on one side, for part of its length, toward Fifth Avenue and on the other side, for part of its length, toward Sixth Avenue. It thus provides a highly visible architectural symbol of the Museum and a space for urban-scale informational signs or even for temporary multimedia installations. Tschumi has expanded on the overview's summary of the proposal's urban conception in a section titled "An Urban Museum Manifesto," in which, among other things, the Museum has been conceived, not "as a sculptural object, but as an interior city."

"A Sequence of Major Interior Spaces," the proposal's second point, describes the extension of the architect's urban concerns into the Museum itself. Referring to these major interior spaces as courts, it states: "While providing a clear structure, the courts permit a number of routes through the building rather than a single linear pathway" (p. 334). Rather than simply providing a way of circulating around the building, this sequence of major spaces also has, in the architect's words, "multiple programmatic capacities," such as the exhibition of art, social activities, etcetera. The first of these multiheight spaces is the through-block entrance hall, which is flanked by the MoMA Design Store and Book Store and leads into what is called the Tower Court, a three-story space that incorporates a lobby, a grand stair hall, and an upper-level café, and which leads in many directions (pp. 329–30). From this three-story space, the visitor can proceed upward to the departmental and Museum Collection galleries, ahead to the garden, and, to the left, for the Department of Education and public reading rooms.

Along the south edge of The Abby Aldrich Rockefeller Sculpture Garden is another series of major spaces, all of which connect with the Tower Court: a lower sculpture gallery on the first level (with a public restaurant and café adjacent), a double-height sculpture gallery on the second level, and an outdoor sculpture terrace above (p. 331). Collectively, these longitudinal spaces (sculpture courts) act simultaneously as an extension of the garden as a venue for sculpture installations, as an east-west promenade, and as a connection to the temporary exhibition galleries, all of which are located in the new East Wing. Branching off the Tower Court and the sculpture courts are other multiheight spaces, which in turn connect to various programmatic elements. The three levels of temporary exhibitions galleries are joined by a series of escalators that occupy a triple-height space facing Fifty-fourth Street. Similarly, the North Court connects the four levels of Museum Collection galleries located between the third and sixth floors.

The architect's third point addresses a new exterior space: the Upper Garden (p. 331 top). Located atop the old North Wing, designed by Philip Johnson and principally retained in the architect's proposal, the Upper Garden "expands the experience of the existing garden to the west at higher level." While this new space is open to the environment, with views toward the midtown skyline, it is covered by a cantilevering structure above, and it is connected with the Museum's spatial flow as the visitor moves upward through the multiheight Tower Court and the North Court. The Upper Garden, as well as a temporary outdoor sculpture garden to the west, adds significantly to the amount of space available to the Museum for large-scale contemporary sculpture as well as for social and urban amenities.

Visitors to the Museum can circulate vertically through the structure a number of ways. From the main entrance, a grand stair ascends to the second level, as do discreetly located elevators and an escalator (p. 337). From the second floor to the fourth floor, stairways run parallel to escalators. From the fourth floor to the sixth floor, escalators, in the main, carry visitors, with discreet stairways placed between gallery levels. Vertical circulation throughout the rest of the Museum is similarly diverse, allowing for the most appropriate means of movement given the specific needs of the space.

Tschumi sees "a precise relationship between four parts"—The Abby Aldrich Rockefeller Sculpture Garden, the departmental galleries, the temporary galleries, and the Museum Collection galleries. It is these four principal elements of the Museum that are interwoven by the sequence of major spaces. Temporary exhibitions galleries are in the far eastern portion of the site (from the ground floor to the third floor). The Museum Collection galleries are in the western portion of the site on four levels (the third through the sixth floors), two of which span the entire depth between Fifty-third and Fifty-fourth streets (p. 336). Lastly, the departmental galleries are principally situated in-between (Photography and Architecture and Design in the renovated Goodwin–Stone building, and Drawings and Prints and Illustrated Books in the renovated North Wing, all on the second and third floors.) The Film and Video theaters remain on the lower level of the Goodwin–Stone building. The Titus 1 and Titus 2 theaters, as well as a new 120-seat theater, have a common multi-height lobby. The four principal interior elements reflect the four major volumetric elements of the exterior of the building, a physical arrangement that "avoids privileging media or disciplines while encouraging viewers to frequent different parts of the Museum." While the distribution of the three major gallery blocks encourages viewers to see all of the Museum's collections and exhibitions, it also insures that the sculpture garden remains part of the experience of all three.

The architect's fifth point of his overview addresses the issue of "varied exhibition spaces," and points out that each type of gallery is designed for its particular needs. The Museum Collection galleries have increasingly high ceilings (14 feet on the first two floors, 18 on the third, and 29 on the top level) to accommodate the increase in scale of postwar works. The last of the Museum Collection's contemporary works would be found in a dramatic gallery that cantilevers out over the new Roof Garden, with views onto the Midtown skyline. The location of the contemporary part of the Museum Collection galleries at the top of the sequence also allows for the use of extensive skylighting. The location of the departmental galleries allows for ceiling heights more appropriately scaled to those works, ranging from 11 feet to 15 feet. The ceiling heights of the temporary exhibitions galleries range from 16 to 18½ feet, with the top level again skylit (p. 333). The previously-mentioned sculpture courts and the new Roof Garden provide new and more appropriate spaces for the specific needs of three-dimensional works, while a "black box" gallery, west penthouse façades, and expanded Film and Video center provide, in the architect's words, for "new media and visual and auditory projection. In addition to the spaces available for public signage on the west penthouse façades, a street gallery is proposed to extend the experience of the Museum into the public realm.

The next point in Tschumi's proposal follows up on the idea of variation in the galleries by describing "an interplay between the fixed and variable galleries and their interstitial spaces"—a reference to the requirements laid out in the Design Guidelines of the Competition Program (see appendix, pp. 285–286). In those guidelines, the architects were asked to respond to specific curatorial needs: "fixed" galleries, which would on an ongoing basis represent the core collection of the Museum from all media, as well as "variable galleries," which would also represent works from the Museum's collection but on a more flexible basis. Additionally, the architects were asked to consider the need for periodic pauses in the gallery sequence, not unlike the interior patios in the West Wing of the National Gallery of Art in Washington, D.C. Referred to as "interstitial" spaces, these spaces can either be used to exhibit works of art, to show them differently than in the fixed and variable galleries, or be used for education, refreshment, or simply reflection. In essence, Tschumi has proposed "to extend the notion of the 'interstitial' space into cultural space: an 'interspace' that acts as a filter and transition to and from the galleries; a space that mingles relations among the multiple functions of museum-going; a place in which (as a metaphor) visitors can be seen playing chess against the distant background of the Duchamps."

As in his Charette proposal, Tschumi has designated that the fixed galleries be placed around the periphery of the Museum, allowing for the best light as well as addressing the logic of construction: The most fixed part of the building is the outer skin. Conversely, the variable galleries are located at the center, where the construction, principally nonstructural partitions, is the most flexible. The proposed scheme also addresses the desire for, not a single method, but multiple ways of experiencing the Museum Collection: "Visitors will also be able to construct their own short-cuts in the story of modern art horizontally (through variable galleries) and vertically (through glass stairs that link one set of interstitial spaces)."

In the architect's "Urban Museum Manifesto," included in his proposal, the new Museum of Modern Art is described not as "a unitary totality, but a heterotopia. It combines three distinct types on its site: a) a received type, the 25-foot-square column grid and doubly bay of the historic MoMA…, 2) a borrowed type, the columnless factory type, for its temporary exhibitions, [and] 3) a new type, our proposal for fixed spaces, variable spaces, and interspaces, for the permanent collection."

In the seventh point of his overview, the architect has proposed a "palette of simple materials," identifying light as the "material expression of the concept of the Museum interiors." This interior concept draws a distinction between the interiors of the major public spaces and the galleries: For the former, "walls of glass and other materials reflect light in a vibrant manner, alternating translucency and transparency," and for the latter, "matte, light-absorbing surfaces provide a non-reflective background for art in the galleries." As proposed by Tschumi, only the walls of the galleries would be painted, and the only paint used would be white. All other materials—glass, wood, concrete, and metal—would retain their own natural appearance.

Just as the four principal external volumes of the Museum reflect the four principal elements of the program, the architect has also proposed a series of exterior materials that would reflect the nature of the spaces beyond, "beige brick of the existing Garden wall for all new construction directly on Fifty-fourth Street, translucent and transparent glass for the external walls of the Courts and precise steel surfaces for the cantilever and the façade on Fifty-third Street" (pp. 326, 327 top).

The need for "a clear and continuous relation between staff and public space" is addressed in the eighth point of Tschumi's summary. The adminstrative and curatorial offices are located, for the most part, along Fifty-fourth Street on the fourth floor, on the fourth-floor mezzanine (the former Goodwin–Stone fifth floor), and on the fifth floor (the former Goodwin–Stone sixth floor), affording the maximum amount of interdepartmental communication, light, and views (p. 339). Additional offices are located in the former Goodwin–Stone penthouse and on the second floor. Those on the second floor are primarily semipublic in nature and visible from the double-height entrance space. Conservation is located in the base of the west penthouse, providing ample light for the laboratories and workshops. Above the Conservation area, the penthouse is used primarily for mechanical equipment.

A loading dock is located on Fifty-fourth Street at the far western end of the property (p. 338). Consolidating the Museum Tower's loading dock, this ground-level facility connects to the lower levels of the Museum, which house the spaces for exhibition production, registrar, art storage, photography studios, mechanical equipment, etcetera. A 12-foot-wide passage throughout the subcellar allows for the easy movement of large-scale works of art and other materials.

The "possibility of multiple options" is discussed in the penultimate point in the architect's ten-point overview. Addressing the various unresolved aspects of the building site, the proposal incorporates options that retain the Goodwin–Stone entrance on Fifty-third Street as well as the new through-block entrance. Additionally, it includes options to retain the Museum's current Fifty-third Street façade and the Museum Tower's current loading dock on Fifty-fourth Street, if necessary. It also includes an expansion plan and a proposal to locate the new 120-seat theater on the second floor, linked to the temporary exhibition galleries, if desired.

The last of the ten points succinctly summarizes the architect's approach to redeveloping the site: "Go along with history, maintain those parts of the existing MoMA that reinforce the new concept, alter the others. This includes only relatively moderate revision of the existing construction of the existing buildings. Our aim has been to find the proper 'interlocking' between the old and the new so that the culture of the institution is regenerated into a new urban and spatial type." The term "interlocking" refers to the architect's Charette submission, and describes the intention to interweave the disparate elements of the Museum: the old and the new, the permanent and the temporary, the public and the private areas.

Tschumi concludes the overview with this statement: "The Garden is the symbolic key to this understanding. The Garden is usually viewed as an oasis of nature within the urban culture of New York. While acknowledging this important perspective, we also call attention to the Garden's other, less acknowledged attribute as a space of remarkable range and flexibility that equally accommodates a variety of art forms and performances (Summergarden) and social events of both a private and public nature. We feel that this quality of *programmatic flexibility and social space* provides places for activities and art forms that are not easily contained within conventional exhibition galleries. Our concept extends this quality throughout the Museum in the form of multiple courts. The inherently public nature of the courts not only offers opportunities for contemporary art practices and performances but also, in proximity to the permanent collections, serves to dynamize and revitalize readings of art's ongoing history."

Appendix

The following is an abridgement of the brief presented to participants in the Architectural Competition in June 1997. All diagrams contained herein were prepared by Cooper, Robertson and Partners.

ARCHITECTURAL COMPETITION BRIEF

I. Design Guidelines

PHILOSOPHY

Since it celebrates a living, growing tradition, a museum of modern art should exist in perpetual, invigorating tension between responsibilities to an ever-longer and ever-richer past and commitments to the creativity of the present and future. Ideally, an historical collection makes recent innovations more intelligible and lends weight to the institution, while engagement with new thought sparks the enterprise and provokes constant reassessment of the tradition—providing the Museum's public with steady points of reference and with provocative challenges.

INSTITUTIONAL IDENTITY

The Museum of Modern Art was the first of its kind and prides itself on being the best in its field, by maintaining and enriching the greatest collection of modern art in the world, and by producing exhibitions and catalogues marked by superior intellectual merit. Populist in its aims to inform and educate a broader public for modern art, the institution is thus elitist in its insistence on upholding rigorous standards of quality—which are constantly debated and evolving—in all that it does. Among institutions devoted to art's history, it has been more contemporary and open-ended, while among institutions focused on the contemporary, it has been more historically grounded and less immediately responsive to fashion or trend. In some regards, the Museum has an identity (as in its sans-serif gray typeface and "classic" stylizations) that mirrors the complex modern traditions into which it was born: fueled by high idealism, it often strives to present an overall façade of clarity and disciplined order as the resolution of the indispensable anxieties, demanding arguments, and critical appetite for new challenges that fuel its interior life.

URBAN CONTEXT

The Museum of Modern Art has always had a distinct character, which derives from its Manhattan location, both in terms of its relationship to the city's orthogonal grid and its unique character as a museum-type: a "midblock" museum without a façade facing a principal avenue (fig. II-1, p. 292). Furthermore, in the Goodwin and Stone building, specific spaces and architectural features ensured that the visitor was constantly aware of the presence of the city beyond the Museum's walls: the translucent façade on Fifty-third Street, the sixth-floor roof terrace, the garden, etc. It is critical that the new Museum of Modern Art reinterpret the presence of the Museum within the city as well as re-establish the presence of the city within the Museum.

INTERIORITY

The goal of achieving greater integration with the urban context should not be seen as incompatible with the parallel goal of achieving a greater sense of interior coherence. The experience of the Museum's interior spaces should be expressive and transformative, even as it is an extension of the life of the city. Natural light should be considered an essential tool in creating both the interior and exterior experiences of the Museum.

HISTORICAL CONTEXT/ARCHITECTURAL DIVERSITY

The Museum's mission mandates that the institution will be a place of many places: theaters, galleries, gardens, terraces, etc. In addition to programmatic differences, certain opportunities exist to create environments of distinctly different ambiences within an overall integrated design. These are of two types: historical and new initiatives. In the first instance, there exist various interior elements of the current Museum that reflect the efforts of previous architects at different points in the Museum's history, such as the Goodwin and Stone stair, Philip Johnson's galleries in his 1964 addition, etc. The architects are asked to consider possibilities for reusing or reprogramming the Museum's historical spaces, with their particular character, within the overall reconfiguration of the Museum, without being overly sentimental. Furthermore, the architects are asked to also consider what opportunities might exist for contemporaneous collaboration with other architects or artists within the Museum's new spaces, such as any proposed new outdoor areas, the restaurants, specific architectural installations of art, etc.

While the foregoing underscores the possibility of exploiting the unique opportunities that characterize the built landscape of the Museum, they must be seen as secondary to the principal goal of achieving a coherent, integrated entity.

QUALITY OF CONSTRUCTION

In its Executive Statement, the Museum has articulated the need "to strive to achieve an environment of excellence and aspire to the highest standards." While these standards apply to all of the activities that take place at the institution, The Museum of Modern Art also has a recognized tradition of placing great importance on the physical environment that provides the setting for those activities. There has been a consistent concern to create an environment and context equal to the quality of the works collected and exhibited. The architecture of the expansion must respond to this commitment by its use of materials, refinement of detailing, and constructibility.

The Museum has also stated that a goal of the expansion is a design that is "subtle yet polemical, substantial and enduring." This suggests that construction materials would not necessarily be valued for their cost, but rather how they are expressed, and that the quality of the construction be judged more by its integrity and permanence.

II. General Requirements

PUBLIC AREAS

The Public Areas of the Museum are those which will most affect the public's image of the Museum and must be approached with great sensitivity.

MAIN ENTRANCE

The main entrance, lobby, and other public spaces of the new Museum of Modern Art will greatly affect the public's sense of the institution and its mission. First and foremost, these spaces should convey the identity of the Museum as an institution dedicated to the enjoyment and study of art. In particular, the main entrance should signal that the Museum is a place for art, not a place of commercial or business activity.

The main entrance should accommodate the majority of visitors to the Museum, which could number up to 7,000 per day (current attendance is 1.6 million visitors per year, future attendance is anticipated to be 2 to 2.2 million visitors per year). A separate or clearly demarcated adjacent entrance should be provided for the larger organized groups of tourists and school children that visit the Museum.

The Museum already has an active evening program of films, lectures, and receptions and intends to increase the scope and number of these activities in the future. The public should be able to attend these activities when the galleries of the Museum are closed and should enter either through a separate entrance off the street or through the main entrance but in such a way that security for the rest of the Museum is maintained. Ideally, the staff should have a separate entrance that offers 24-hour access but allows for appropriate security.

LOBBY

The lobby of the Museum must accommodate several vital functions. It is the first space the visitor encounters and therefore should be welcoming yet organized in such a way that the visitor is clear about the various functions and their sequence—whether checking coats, buying tickets, or gathering information about exhibitions. The lobby should be arranged to accommodate an orderly flow of crowds, which during peak times might number up to 2,000 people an hour.

The lobby should include a coat check. It should also include ticket booths, an area for information, and a special area for membership queries including (if the education center entrance is remote) information about educational activities.

In addition to the main lobby, another lobby is required for group and/or educational visits. This lobby should be large enough to accommodate 120 visitors and should have a separate coat check. The staff entrance also needs a small lobby with security control.

All entrances and lobbies described above should be located on the street level.

PUBLIC SPACE

Movement through the building should not be seen as the merely functional activity of getting from here to there, nor should the public spaces be strictly seen as circulation spaces in the generic sense: lobbies, corridors, atria, etc. Rather, the sequence of spaces from the entry throughout the Museum should be seen as a powerful metaphor for the unfolding narrative of the Museum, directly supporting the curatorial message developed in the galleries. Given the complexity of the narrative, the flow of the principal public spaces should be apparent but not necessarily obvious. While the principal public spaces should be large enough to comfortably accommodate the Museum's visitors, it is important that they retain a critical aspect and a sense of scale appropriate to the site. Nor should the public spaces enshrine specific works of art in a manner that undercuts the public's ability to see them in a critical and objective way.

As an urban experience, but also as a departure from the bustle of daily midtown life, the experience of the Museum's public spaces should be exciting; their unfolding sequence should also suggest a transformative process.

The public spaces of the Museum should accommodate a variety of activities: circulation, experiencing works of art, contemplation, meeting people, orientation. Additionally, other activities may occur in the public spaces. In addition to looking at works of art, the Museum wishes to provide space for various other ways of learning about art: either reading or using digital equipment, places where group tours can congregate. Given the scale of the Museum, the public spaces also provide a place to rest. Amenities such as refreshments are desirable; far from those spaces dedicated to food service, a place, or places, to rest and have a cup of coffee would enhance the enjoyment of a long visit to the Museum. Restrooms are to be considered an amenity rather than just a functional element. They should be conveniently located (particularly in relation to the principal entrances) and reflect the needs of the Museum's users, including visitors with infants.

Often, the public spaces serve additional purposes other than the circulation of the Museum's visitors. Special events, large and small, such as receptions, openings, and dinners frequently are held at the Museum in both dedicated spaces as well as in spaces regularly used for other purposes. Some large events, such as dinners for between 500 and 700 people need to take place in, what should be perceived as a single space. Other large events, such as major openings with more than 2,000 people can happen in a series of related spaces. It is often necessary that multiple events, which need separate spaces, be held simultaneously. The public spaces of the Museum should be designed so as to occasionally accommodate those events for which there is no dedicated space.

Certain spaces of the Museum provide amenities to visitors as well as income vital to the Museum: design and book stores, the restaurant, cafeteria, etc. The relationship between these spaces and the main public spaces is crucial and requires a delicate balance. Obviously, to function properly these spaces need to be visible and easily accessible. At the same time, they must be located in such a way as not to confuse the visitor about the Museum's primary educational purpose.

Within the Museum's circulation patterns outside the galleries, and above all in its major public reception spaces, we should isolate in advance walls and locales appropriate to the semi-permanent display of large paintings and sculptures. (Questions of load-bearing tolerances of walls and floors, plus code requirements of circulation, will need to be taken into account in this process.) Factors as simple as daylight or as complex as the various demands of special events (crowds, special equipment, temporary decorations or signage, staging zones, etc.) risk compromising the safety of these works, and/or their aesthetic integrity. Foreseeing these factors, we must minimize the need to remove or relocate artworks in public spaces, while assuring both that the art is out of harm's way and that it is not trivialized as mere decor (for example, by being juxtaposed inappropriately with signage or functional furnishings).

VERTICAL CIRCULATION

Given the multistory nature of the building, the need for handicapped access and other factors, elevators are a necessary form of vertical transport. In addition to using closed-cab elevators, visitors should be able to move between the principal floors of the Museum in a manner that reinforces the continuity of the narrative sequence. Careful consideration should be given to the issues related to vertical circulation: efficiency, beauty, and ambience. No single system addresses all these needs. The ideal vertical circulation system will, no doubt, be a hybrid combining various means of moving from floor to floor tailored to the particular activities located throughout the building. The existing escalators are frequently criticized for their location, which provides for no sound isolation in the Museum's principal public space, and for their positioning between the lobby and the garden.

GALLERIES

The Museum's galleries will be of three kinds for three purposes: Museum Collection; Departmental; Temporary Exhibition.

MUSEUM COLLECTION: These galleries, which will occupy 81,100 square feet, will exhibit painting and sculpture as well as works in other mediums, with the aim of providing a synoptic history of modern and contemporary art in all mediums from the beginning of the Museum's collection until the present.

The galleries are to be organized according to a *fixed-and-variable* system (fig. I-1, p. 286). This mode of organization calls for a sequence (divided into sub-sequences) of "fixed" galleries, occupying approximately two-thirds of the space of the Museum Collection galleries, which will afford the possibility of a manageable tour through the entire history, complemented by adjacent "variable" galleries, which will afford the option of examining aspects of that history in more detail.

The desired effect is *not* of more important and less important galleries. The aim, rather, is that the Museum visitor should be able to experience, in effect, multiple histories on single and successive visits through the following means.

The galleries should make their historical narrative accessible either in whole or in part. It should be possible to make, clearly and efficiently, a *full tour of the "fixed" galleries.* But it should also be possible to *enter and exit* each subsequence of "fixed" galleries *separately from public circulation space,* on a frequent but irregular basis, by way of interstitial spaces that provide facilities for relaxation and educational purposes. (The claustrophobic effect of the present sequence

The "variable" galleries will be reinstalled on a more frequent basis. Every "variable" gallery should be capable of being separately isolated for reinstallation without compromising visitors' progress through the sequence of "fixed-and-variable" galleries to which they belong.

The galleries should be of the following specifications:

The first one-third of the "fixed-and-variable" sequence should have a ceiling height of 14 feet, the next one-third a ceiling height of 16 feet, and the remaining one-third of the "fixed-and variable" galleries, a ceiling height of 20 feet.

The "fixed" galleries are intended to be architecturally permanent. Construction of temporary walls, subdivision of individual galleries, and combination of adjacent galleries are not anticipated.

To the extent possible, the galleries should not be interrupted by columns. The sizes of the galleries should be in proportion to their heights.

The layout of the galleries should take full advantage of the possibility of continuous north-to-south floor plates between the existing site and the Dorset Hotel site.

Natural light brings life to the Museum's spaces. It is desirable that works in the galleries can be illuminated by a maximum amount of controllable diffused natural light and that external, urban views be provided periodically from the galleries or from interstitial spaces dividing sequences of "fixed" galleries. However, any galleries that might contain works on paper need ways of protecting these works from natural light. The "fixed" galleries should be given priority over the "variable" galleries in the provision of natural light but, insofar as it is possible, some "variable" galleries should have natural light.

Since the "variable" galleries will be regularly reinstalled, their design should afford the possibility of the construction of temporary walls, subdivision of individual galleries, and combination of adjacent galleries, insofar as this is consistent with maintaining an architectural character for these galleries not inferior to that of the "fixed" galleries, only different. These galleries have a different function than the "fixed" galleries, but not a lesser importance.

In the latter part of the "fixed-and-variable" sequence there should be provided "black box" galleries of an area of approximately 1,500 square feet, and soundproofed from adjacent spaces.

Consideration should be made for the provision of seating in appropriate locations throughout the galleries.

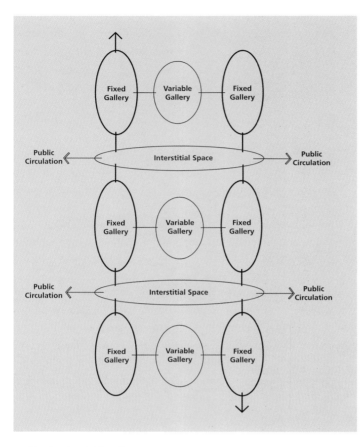

I-1. Fixed-and-variable gallery system

of Painting and Sculpture galleries is to be avoided.) These interstitial spaces should be highly variable.

The galleries should afford the option of both a continuous chronological narrative and proleptic and analeptic jumps (flashforwards and flashbacks) across history. It should be possible, *between* each sub-sequence of galleries, to move not only "along" but also "across" the sequence of "fixed-and-variable" galleries. It should also be possible, *within* each sub-sequence of galleries, to move not only "along" but also "across" this sequence of "fixed" galleries, through the mediation of "variable" galleries.

The galleries should allow parts of the history to be reinstalled at varying intervals. The majority of the "fixed" galleries are intended to be relatively permanent in installation, only changing occasionally when works in these galleries are sent out on loan or substitutions made from the Museum's holdings. However, works on paper in "fixed" galleries (and any "fixed" gallery when devoted exclusively to works on paper) will be reinstalled at least twice every year.

Provision should be made in interstitial spaces for resting, occasional refreshment, and educational functions.

While the fixed and variable galleries may be highly irregular, their overall organization must have clarity, so that the visitor can navigate them without excessive signage.

DEPARTMENTAL: The following indicated galleries should be provided for these departments:

Architecture and Design—Collection galleries of 5,500 square feet with a ceiling height of 14 feet. A thematic collection gallery of 2,800 square feet with a ceiling height of 14 feet. It is anticipated that the helicopter will be permanently installed in public circulation space that is part of the non-assignable area. This space should have a ceiling height of 20 feet. Controllable natural light is desirable.

Drawings—Collection galleries of 3,500 square feet with a ceiling height of 14 feet. It is anticipated that these galleries will be reinstalled at intervals of 4 months. Natural light should not be admitted to these galleries.

Film and Video—A lobby gallery of 3,000 square feet with a ceiling height of 14 feet should be adjacent to the theaters. This is a public non-assignable space.

Painting and Sculpture—While the Museum has collected in many innovative areas, the heart of its collection is modern paintings and sculpture. These seminal works would be the core of the Museum's Collection galleries, which would, in effect, be the principal galleries for this department.

Photography—Collection galleries of 5,000 square feet with a ceiling height of 14 feet. A *temporary exhibition space* of 1,000 square feet with a ceiling height of 14 feet. An educational space of 500 square feet with a ceiling height of 12 feet six inches. It is anticipated that the collection galleries will be relatively permanent in its installation and that the other galleries will be reinstalled an intervals of 4 months. Natural light should not be admitted to these galleries.

Prints and Illustrated Books—Collection galleries of 3,300 square feet with a ceiling height of 12 feet 6 inches, which will be reinstalled three times per year, and an educational area of 300 square feet. Natural light should not be admitted to these galleries.

The departmental galleries are intended to be architecturally permanent. Construction of temporary walls, subdivision of individual galleries, and combination of adjacent galleries is not anticipated.

These galleries may be stacked above or below the Museum Collection galleries and temporary exhibition galleries, or arranged around their periphery, or dispersed throughout the Museum. However, they should not be confusable with the sequence of "fixed-and-variable" galleries or temporary exhibition galleries, but rather, related logically.

TEMPORARY EXHIBITIONS: An area of 30,000 square feet with a ceiling height of 20 feet readily divisible into three parts of 5,000 square feet each, and one part of 20,000 square feet, intended to be used rarely as a whole, more frequently in two parts, and very frequently in three parts. The areas should be designed so that each part may be entered separately from a common interstitial space or public space, in which rest and refreshment facilities, educational facilities, and catalogue sales might be placed, and so that they may be installed and serviced separately. It is desirable that each discrete exhibition have its own entrance separate from its own exit.

These galleries should be placed so that they are not confusable with the sequence of "fixed-and-variable" galleries or departmental galleries, and should be accessible from public spaces even when all other galleries of the Museum are closed.

Suffused natural light is desirable in these galleries but would need to be controlled on occasion.

THEATERS

Recognizing film as one of the key art forms of the twentieth century, a major theater was included in the Museum's first purpose-built structure. Without disregarding the obvious differences in program requirements, the theaters should be considered a particular type of gallery and, to the extent possible, have the same relationship to the Museum's public spaces as the other galleries. However, the theaters, unlike the galleries, are regularly used for multiple purposes: slide lectures, symposia, concerts, performances, meetings, and for private premiers and corporate and institutional events, both during the day and at night when other special events may be occurring at the Museum. As noted above, the theaters should thus have separate evening access (ideally, with connections to food service and the stores) as well as a daytime relationship to the Museum's principal public spaces.

THE GARDEN/OUTDOOR SPACE

The current lack of space for large-scale sculptures can be addressed by the design of the galleries as well as the main public spaces, which could accommodate such works. New exterior spaces should be as inviting and well-designed as the Abby Aldrich Rockefeller Sculpture Garden. Additionally, any new exterior spaces proposed—courtyards, terraces, rooftops—should be considered a potential site for the exhibition of sculpture as well as other uses, such as special events. It should be noted that since the time of the design of the existing garden, the scale of sculpture has increased dramatically. While the existing garden is well-suited to the scale of bronze casts made in the first half of the century, it is somewhat awkward for the larger sculptures made since then.

FUTURE EXPANSION AND POTENTIAL TEMPORARY USES

For the purpose of this Competition, the parcel of land to the west of the Dorset Hotel (see fig. II-1) should be considered as an expansion site which may be programmed for temporary uses. These uses may be exhibition-related, such as a sculpture garden, or more functional in character, such as temporary loading docks which might be relocated westward at a later date.

PUBLIC READING ROOM

The Museum would like to make its library resources more accessible to the general public with the addition of a small reading room on the ground floor, ideally off the lobby or other public space. The new facility would act as a branch affiliate of the main research library, which now primarily serves staff and scholars, and would contain a core collection of books about modern and contemporary art and about the Museum and its collection. The public reading room should be an impressive space, which would make the visitor value the material.

RETAIL

Ideally, the MoMA Book Store and MoMA Design Store, which are now in two locations, should be combined into one retail space. While retail activities provide an important source of income for the Museum, their presence in the Museum is ancillary to its mission and their commercial aspect should not overshadow its primary cultural and educational purpose. In order to make the most judicious use of space, the retail facility can be located on multiple levels of the Museum, including attractively arranged below-grade space.

RESTAURANTS

With an anticipated average of up to 6,500 visitors a day, the Museum needs to provide a cafeteria for light meals and refreshment in a space that is attractive and flexible, yet functional enough to accommodate large volume. The Museum also wants to provide a restaurant that offers more leisurely, "white table cloth" dining for up to 100 people. In addition,

the Museum would like to offer places where visitors can pause, rest and have a cup of coffee or other refreshment; some of these places could be located near the theater or retail spaces and could be available for evening use in conjunction with films or other after-hours activities when the galleries are closed. The cafeteria and restaurant should also be easily accessible to the public after hours.

NON-PUBLIC SPACES
STAFF AREAS

In addition to being an internationally known showcase of modern art, the Museum is also a place where approximately 600 people, including guards and retail-sales staff, work every day (staff levels are projected to increase to 950 when the entire expansion is complete). While in all cases priority should be given to the needs of the galleries and public spaces, it is critical that the operational areas of the Museum be designed to provide a dignified work place for the highly dedicated professional staff employed by the institution. It is desirable that all work places have natural light, or, if this involves compromising other aspects of the concept design, that staff circulation might be arranged to provide ample opportunities for daylight and orientation to the outside as staff moved about the building.

As in the present Museum, staff offices, work areas, and circulation must be separated from public areas open to general visitors. This separation is fundamental for security, since artwork is stored and handled in many staff areas. It is also essential for creating an appropriate and efficient work environment.

Access to staff areas would be through a secured staff lobby. Museum staff should be able to circulate throughout all staff areas without having to pass through any space open to the general public. In areas where staff interact with the public, such as the Education Center and Public Reading Room, controlled access points to staff areas should be carefully considered to prevent unauthorized public access.

It may be desirable to have limited access points for staff to enter gallery floors without having to return to the ground-floor staff lobby. These points must be designed, however, to be thoroughly secured at all times and must not be in or near spaces where art is stored or handled.

Given the vertical nature of the Museum and the necessity that staff will continue to be accommodated on multiple floors in the expanded Museum, providing suitable ways for circulating vertically through staff floors is essential. An appropriate number of elevators should be provided to handle anticipated future staff, in addition to freight and art elevators.

The location of elevators should also be carefully considered as the Museum grows to insure that staff must not walk an inordinate distance.

Interconnecting stairs should be provided in staff areas for use between adjacent floors. Even with sufficient elevator service, many consider using the stairs preferable to an elevator for short trips. Interconnecting staff stairs may be provided in addition to fire stairs required for egress. These stairs could create the potential for vertical porosity and for connections to be established between vertically adjacent areas. They should have a higher level of finish, windows if possible, and be designed to provide opportunities for staff to meet and interact.

CURATORIAL AREAS AND STUDY CENTERS

Although the Museum is most closely identified with its galleries, a very significant aspect of its identity also resides in its curatorial areas with their unseen collection and research centers. Presently, five of the six collecting curatorial departments have study centers. For the most part, the term "study center" should be taken to mean a relatively quiet place in which art objects are brought out from a connected storage area holding related books and archival files. These study centers are used by the public and should be considered an extension of the Museum's public space with specific characteristics: open by appointment only, the study centers are used by student groups, curatorial staff members, independent researchers, and often as a site for acquisition meetings and educational programs which require the presence of works of art.

COLLECTION STORAGE

As described in the Survey of the Museum's Collections, each curatorial department has unique requirements for the location and configuration of its collection storage areas based on the physical characteristics of the mediums stored and on functional requirements. The following collection storage areas are required:

Architecture and Design—4,000 square feet adjacent to the department's study center, 3,500 square feet elsewhere in the building
Drawings—3,700 square feet adjacent to the works-on-paper study center
Photography—3,700 square feet adjacent to the works-on-paper study center
Prints and Illustrated Books—4,100 square feet adjacent to the works-on-paper study center

Film and Video—3,000 square feet adjacent to the department's study center
Registrar (Painting and Sculpture)—8,000 square feet adjacent to or with direct access from registrar preparator areas. More than one space can be utilized to fulfill the total area requirement. Adjacency to the Painting and Sculpture study center is not required.

Collection storage areas adjacent to the shared works-on-paper study center should not be merged as shared storage, but remain distinct department entities, adjacent to respective curatorial office areas.

All collection storage areas have the following shared functional requirements:

High Security—must be fully enclosed, secured, and have controlled access.
Controlled Environmental Conditions—must be fully separated from surrounding areas to maintain required temperature and humidity levels for conservation purposes. Requirements vary by medium (see Part Seven: Survey of the Museum's Collections).
Controlled Light Levels—must have no windows.
No Vibration—locate areas remote from subway if possible.
Minimize Opportunity for Water Damage—No plumbing, mechanical equipment using water, or vertical shafts should be located in, above, or adjacent to collection storage areas.
Collection storage areas may be located below grade if necessary, however additional precautions are necessary to protect the collections. A second full-perimeter foundation wall must be provided at below-grade collection storage areas as well as sump pumps to drain the resulting interstitial space in the event of a city water-main break or other incursion of water from the exterior.

COLLECTION LOADING, CIRCULATION, AND HANDLING

A dedicated loading dock must be provided for shipping and receiving artwork. This dock must be fully separated from the non-art loading dock, have high security, be capable of maintaining climate control, and be able to accommodate a tractor-trailer. The recommended minimum size for this purpose, including area for staging and equipment storage, is 23 feet wide, 76 feet long, and 14 feet high (clearance including lighting, mechanical equipment, and all other obstructions). The exterior door must open to provide a minimum of 14 clear vertical feet. A hydraulic lift should be provided for off-loading from the bed of the truck.

A dedicated art elevator should be provided (18 feet wide x 12 feet deep x 12 feet high minimum interior dimensions; doors 12-foot high minimums) in addition to a non-art freight elevator. The art elevator should be located for direct access to the loading dock, art shipping/receiving areas, and gallery floors. The elevator should not open directly into art storage areas in order to maintain more stable environmental conditions.

Areas where art circulates, such as between preparator areas, the frame shop, photo studios, collection storage areas (containing larger mediums), and galleries, must be properly sized and configured to accommodate handling large-scale work. Corridors must be as direct as possible with no sharp turns. All doors must be at least 12 feet high. Double doors or roll-down doors should be provided to maximize width. In all corridors, staging areas, and other places where art is handled, a minimum of 12 feet of vertical clearance must be provided, including lighting, mechanical equipment, and all other obstructions.

A shipping/receiving area should be provided either adjacent to the loading dock or to the art elevator on another level. A packing/examination/preparation area is required adjacent to this area. Both spaces (registrar preparator areas) should be fully secured. Shop areas where dust is generated must be kept separate from "clean" areas such as the frame shop, photo studios, and collection storage areas.

RESEARCH AREAS

The Museum of Modern Art is a major international research center for the study of modern art. The facilities that support its research function include the library and archives, the conservation department, and the international program, which will expand in the future to include a research program for visiting scholars. Although they need not be adjacent to each other, each of these research areas should be designed to promote scholarly activity and fruitful interaction, especially with the curatorial departments.

USE OF NEW TECHNOLOGIES

With the computerized office, the advent of the Internet, the use of computers for public information and educational purposes, and the proliferation of art forms using video and technological equipment, it is important that any new Museum facility be flexible enough to accommodate the wiring necessary for current technologies as well as any new technology that is developed in the future. All offices should be wired for computers; conference rooms should be able to accommodate the latest audio-visual equipment; theaters should be capable of using the latest technology and certain galleries should be able to accommodate artworks that use high-tech equipment. In addition, the lobby and other public spaces near the galleries should be flexible enough to allow for information kiosks or computers.

CREATION OF NEW MUSEUM-WIDE SUPPORT FUNCTIONS

To support the anticipated increase in its audio-visual needs, the Museum intends to create a new area with staff devoted to maintaining and operating the audio-visual equipment museum-wide. The space allocated for this new support function is described as Audio-visual Services in the Space Program.

The Museum also intends to centralize the shipping and handling of non-art items into one area near the loading dock. This area requires processing space as well as a locked "cage" to store temporarily letters, packages and boxes that are waiting to be shipped out or that have been delivered to the Museum. This area, as part of the Department of Office Services, should be located near the loading dock.

STREET-LEVEL USES

In addition to the entrances, loading docks and lobbies mentioned above and those program elements the Competition participants may determine appropriate for the street level, the following spaces must either be entirely or partially located on the street level:

• a portion of the Library, the Public Reading Room
• a portion of the Education Department
• a portion of Food Service
• a portion of the Design and Book Store with separate entrance

POSSIBLE BELOW-GROUND USES

The following spaces are considered appropriate for location below ground. Since their combined total area exceeds the available below-grade area, the architects are asked to select from this list rather than accommodate all of them:
• up to 11,500 square feet of Art Storage, including Registrar (Painting and Sculpture), and part of Architecture and Design
• theaters
• a portion of Food Service
• a portion of the Library
• a portion of the Design and Book Store
• a portion of the Mechanical Space
• locker rooms
• up to 31,105 net square feet of work areas, including Exhibi-

tion Production Shops, Registrar Art Handling, Photo Studios and Labs, Retail Sales Floor Work Areas, Building Operations and Housekeeping, Purchasing and Telecommunications, Office Services, and Audio-Visual Services/Film Conservation, and Receiving

The location of other office and work areas below-grade is considered a compromise solution. The negative effects of below-grade space for office areas and other spaces not listed above should be, when appropriate, mitigated by design efforts that create spatial continuity with above-grade spaces and that, to the extent possible, bring daylight into the office spaces and/or circulation spaces.

The current below-grade exhibition spaces, the René d'Harnoncourt Galleries, are considered very unappealing and as having a negative impact on the experience of viewing art. Should a compelling reason for locating any gallery space below-grade exist, the drawbacks which currently exist must be decisively addressed: awkward circulation in relationship to the principal flow of circulation, narrow and uninviting access, dead-end circulation, claustrophobic ambience. In any event, only a very small percentage of the total gallery space should be located below-grade.

III. Program of Requirements

The Program of Requirements represents a statement of the space needs and relationships, functional and systems requirements, and constraints for the Competition. It defines the conditions and design requirements to be met by the Competition participant by identifying all Museum spaces by use and size, and by function. It is a provisional program to be superseded by the final program to be completed later this year.

SPACE REQUIREMENTS

The Space Program is divided into two categories of spaces: *assignable and non-assignable* (figs. III-1, III-2). The assignable spaces represent those Museum needs that can be quantified and are expressed as specific uses with a required area in square feet. For the purposes of this Competition, spaces are described by either department or use. The assigned areas for departments represent a block of space including each department's internal rooms and circulation.

The non-assignable spaces represent those that are also required but cannot be quantified until a design is developed. These spaces typically include circulation, mechanical rooms, and shafts, elevator cores with toilet rooms, and stair, service,

and loading areas. For the purposes of this Competition, the participants should assume that the total non-assignable spaces will account for a minimum of 40 percent of the total building area.

ORGANIZATION

The Museum Program of Requirements is generally organized into three groups of spaces:

Public—including galleries and theaters, the cafeteria and restaurant, and the Museum Store. In addition, some parts of the library and education departments are open to visitors.
Staff—primarily office and work space but includes portions of the Library and Education departments as well as those spaces associated with the care and management of the collection. These include conservation, curatorial departments, and art storage.
Service—including those spaces required for the physical operation of the Museum. These are primarily listed as non-assignable spaces.

The design for the new Museum should reflect this programmatic grouping in its organization of the program spaces and internal circulation. There must be a clear separation of high-security areas from public ones, those spaces that are dirty from those that require a clean environment, and between noisy and quiet uses. Access and connection points among those groups must be controlled.

The new Museum must also be able to accommodate both daytime and evening activities in a logical way that does not require opening the entire building for the use of one space. Current evening uses, all of which require clear separation though not necessarily separate entrances, which should be considered for this Competition, are:

• Films, lectures, and performances
• Special events, including large sit-down dinners with dancing
• Operation of the public restaurant
• Evening hours for the Museum stores
• Events in the sculpture garden or other proposed outdoor spaces

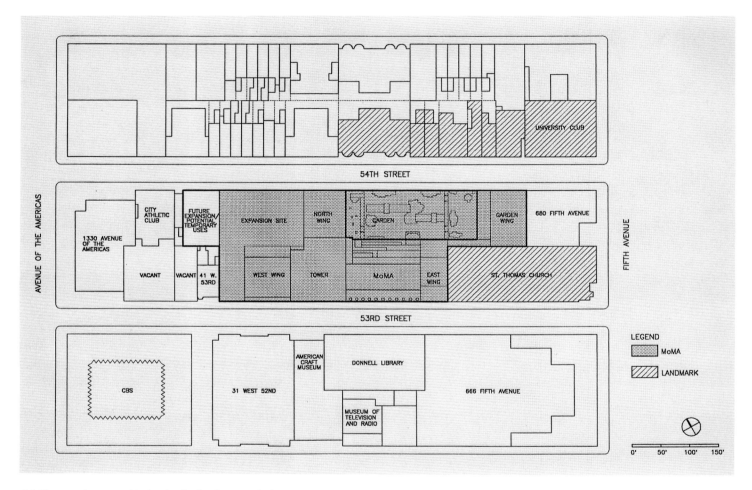

II-1. Diagram of museum site showing landmark status of adjacent and facing properties

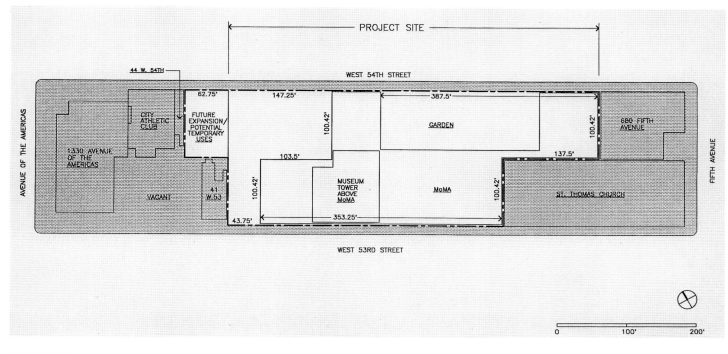

II-2. Project site

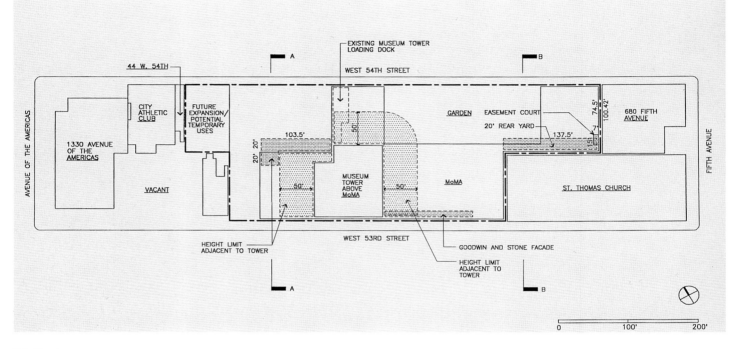

II-3. Site plan

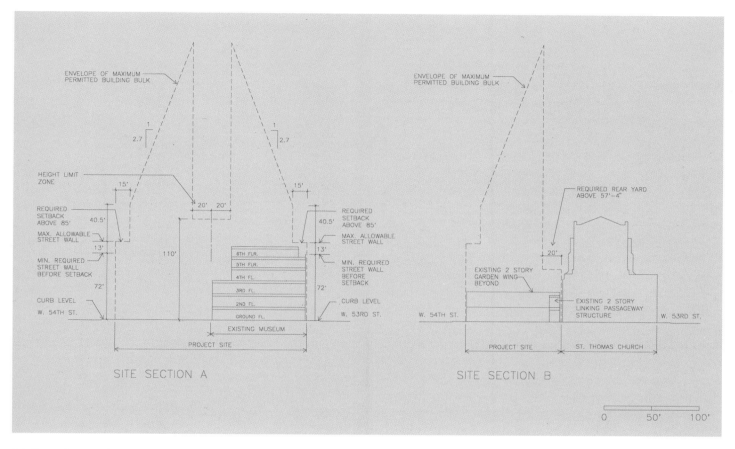

ENVELOPE OF MAXIMUM
PERMITTED BUILDING BULK

ENVELOPE OF MAXIMUM
PERMITTED BUILDING BULK

1
2.7

1
2.7

HEIGHT LIMIT
ZONE

15'

20' 20'

15'

REQUIRED
SETBACK
ABOVE 85'

40.5'

40.5'

REQUIRED
SETBACK
ABOVE 85'

MAX. ALLOWABLE
STREET WALL

13'

110'

13'

MAX. ALLOWABLE
STREET WALL

MIN. REQUIRED
STREET WALL
BEFORE SETBACK

6TH FLR.

5TH FLR.

4TH FL.

MIN. REQUIRED
STREET WALL
BEFORE
SETBACK

72'

3RD FL.

72'

2ND FL.

CURB LEVEL
W. 54TH ST.

GROUND FL.

CURB LEVEL
W. 53RD ST.

EXISTING MUSEUM

PROJECT SITE

SITE SECTION A

REQUIRED REAR YARD
ABOVE 57'-4"

20'

EXISTING 2 STORY
GARDEN WING
BEYOND

EXISTING 2 STORY
LINKING PASSAGEWAY
STRUCTURE

W. 54TH ST.

W. 53RD ST.

PROJECT SITE

ST. THOMAS CHURCH

SITE SECTION B

0   50'   100'

II-4. Site sections A and B, zoning restrictions

III-1. Summary of Assignable Spaces

Department Group Areas	Department	Program Area NSF
Curatorial	Architecture and Design	3,000
	Drawings	2,570
	Photography	3,675
	Prints and Illustrated Books	3,000
	Works on Paper Study Center	3,000
	Film And Video	7,600
	Painting and Sculpture	4,675
	Chief Curator at Large	1,100
	Subtotal Curatorial	**28,620**
Support	Conservation	7,000
	Exhibitions Program	1,125
	Graphics	3,250
	International Council	1,420
	International Program	2,000
	Public Reading Room	1,200
	Research Library	4,500
	Research Library Stacks	4,300
	Archives	2,900
	Exhibition Design	1,900
	Exhibition Production	11,100
	Registrar Offices	2,400
	Registrar Art Handling	5,600
	Photographic Services and Permissions	1,500
	Photographic Studios and Labs.	3,000
	Subtotal Support	**53,195**
Independent	Communications	1,500
	Marketing	1,000
	Contemporary Arts Council/Junior Assoc.	1,000
	Development/Membership	3,000
	Capital Campaign/Planned Giving	1,460
	Education Center	3,500
	Education Offices	2,500
	Publications*	–
	Sales Floor Work Areas	1,750
	Retail Offices*	–
	Special Programming & Events	1,700
	Visitor Services	3,000
	Writing Services	500
	Subtotal Independent	**20,910**
Administrative	Accounting	2,410
	Building Operations/Housekeeping	2,500
	Deputy Directors	2,000
	Director/ Executive Suite	1,500
	Finance and Investments	1,500
	Human Resources*	250
	Information Systems	3,500
	General Counsel/Secretary	1,200
	Office Services	2,000
	Purchasing/Telecommunications	1,000
	Security	1,900
	Trustee	3,000
	Subtotal Administrative	**22,760**
	Subtotal Departmental Space Inventory	**125,485**
Assigned Areas	Gallery Space	133,000
	Titus I Theater / Projection Booth	6,100
	Theater 2 / Projection Booth Shared with Titus I	2,875
	Theater 3 / Projection Booth	2,500
	Theater Lobbies	3,400
	Audio Visual Services / Film Conservation, Receiving	4,155
	Art Storage**	30,000
	Retail Sales Floor / Stock Room	16,250
	Restaurant / Kitchen / Staff Lounge	15,590
	Locker Rooms	3,500
	Coat Check Main Lobby	1,800
	Shared Conference / Lounge	3,345
	Subtotal Assigned Areas	**222,515**
	Total Net Areas	**348,000**

* With offices located at East 54th Street.
** Refer to Part Ten, Collection Storage Areas for individual area requirements.

III-2. Summary of Non-assignable Spaces

Space	Requirements
Main Public Lobby	To include 1,800 square foot coat check.
Public Circulation	
Public Restrooms	Facilities should exceed minimum required by code. Gender parity should be considered.
Staff Entrance	Includes small lobby for security.
Staff Circulation	Must be separate from public for security.
Staff Restrooms	As required by code. Gender parity should be considered.
Loading Docks	Two required. Each to accommodate a truck 48 feet long. Minimum dimensions including staging areas: 23 feet wide x 76 feet long x 14 feet clear height.
Service Circulation	Must be separate from public for security.
Mechanical Space	8% of total building area. Can be distributed.
Lobby for Group Visits	To accommodate 120 visitors. Also for shared use by the Education Department for school groups. Includes coat storage.
Elevators	One freight elevator dedicate to artworks. Dimensions: 18 feet wide x 12 feet deep x 12 feet high. One freight elevator for non-art uses. Passenger elevator(s) for visitors- as needed. Passenger elevator(s) for staff- as needed.
Stairs and other Vertical Circulation	As required for exiting and internal circulation. Staff and visitors' vertical circulation must be separate for security. The original 1939 Goodwin and Stone open stairway presently connecting the second and third floor galleries may be incorporated into the new Museum design.
Telecommunications Closets	Located and stacked on each floor to ensure easy distribution of cables. A minimum of 100 square feet each.

Jacques Herzog and Pierre de Meuron

**Model (detail). Fifty-fourth Street elevation. Acrylic, paint, and photocopy on vinyl foil, 19 x 19 x 6¼"
(48.3 x 48.3 x 15.8 cm)**

Excepting architectural models, the visual materials submitted as part of the Architects' Competition proposals were mounted on boards measuring 30 x 42" (76.2 x 106.7 cm); all images appearing on the following pages were taken from these presentation boards.

Model (detail) of Curatorial Tower. Acrylic, paint, and photocopy on vinyl foil, 19 x 19 x 6¼" (48.3 x 48.3 x 15.8 cm)

Site plan. Computer-generated print mounted on board

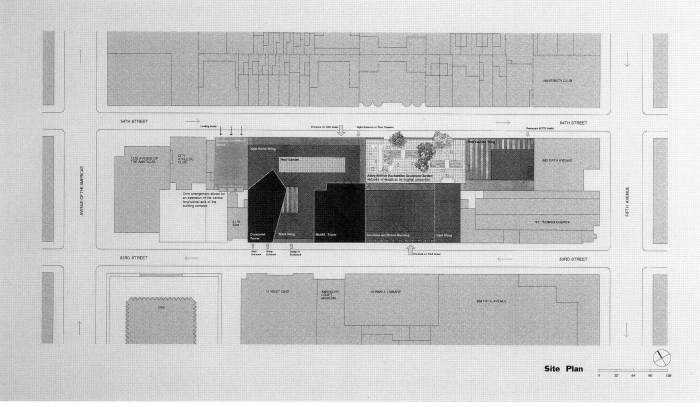

Site Plan

Left:
Photomontage of Curatorial Tower and Museum façade. View from Sixth Avenue and Fifty-third Street, looking east. Computer-generated print mounted on board

Opposite:
Photomontage of Museum façade. View from Fifth Avenue and Fifty-fourth Street, looking west. Computer-generated print mounted on board

Interior view of Goodwin–Stone lobby and Sculpture
Hall, looking north. Computer-generated print
mounted on board

Left:
New Garden Wing gallery. Photograph of model mounted on board

Below:
View of Fifty-fourth Street entrance lobby, looking east. Interior perspective. Computer-generated print mounted on board

Interior view of new Garden Wing gallery. Photograph of model mounted on board

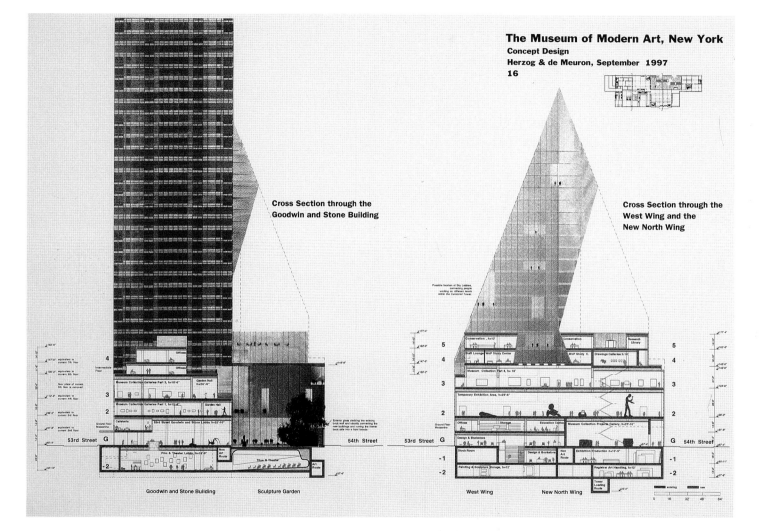

Transverse sections through Goodwin–Stone building
(left) and through west wing, looking west (right).
Computer-generated print mounted on board

The Museum of Modern Art, New York
Concept Design
Herzog & de Meuron, September 1997
17

South Elevation 53rd Street

South elevation, Fifty-third Street. Computer-generated print mounted on board

The Museum of Modern Art, New York
Concept Design
Herzog & de Meuron, September 1997
18

North Elevation 54th Street

North elevation, Fifty-fourth Street. Computer-generated print mounted on board

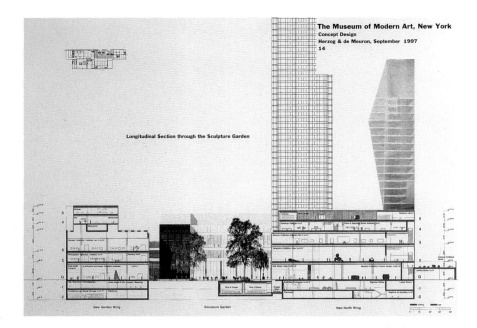

The Museum of Modern Art, New York
Concept Design
Herzog & de Meuron, September 1997
14

Longitudinal Section through the Sculpture Garden

Left:
Longitudinal section through Sculpture Garden, looking south. Computer-generated print mounted on board

Below:
Longitudinal section parallel to Fifty-third Street, looking north. Computer-generated print mounted on board

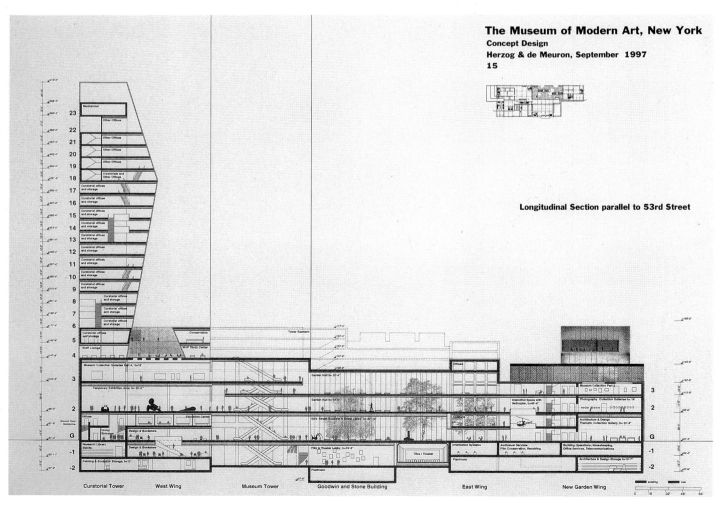

The Museum of Modern Art, New York
Concept Design
Herzog & de Meuron, September 1997
15

Longitudinal Section parallel to 53rd Street

**Floor plan of theater level-2. Computer-generated
print mounted on board**

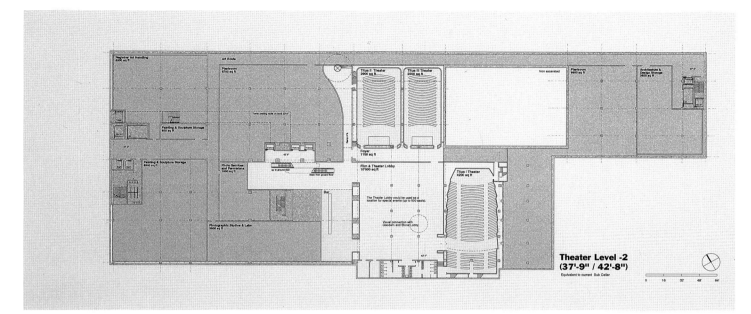

**Ground floor plan. Computer-generated print
mounted on board**

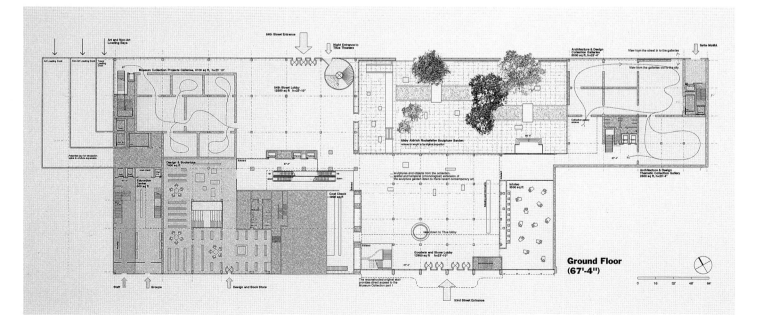

Second floor plan, collection and temporary exhibition galleries. Computer-generated print mounted on board

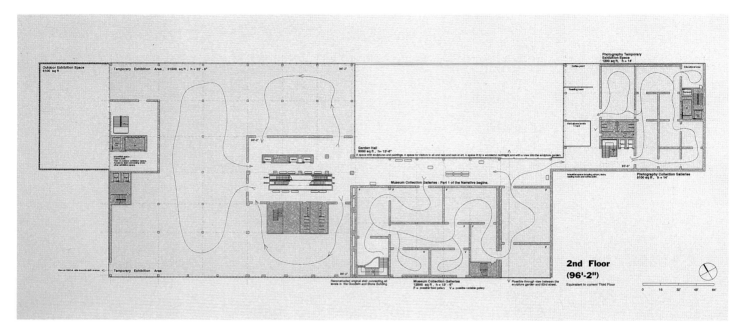

Third floor plan, Museum Collection galleries. Computer-generated print mounted on board

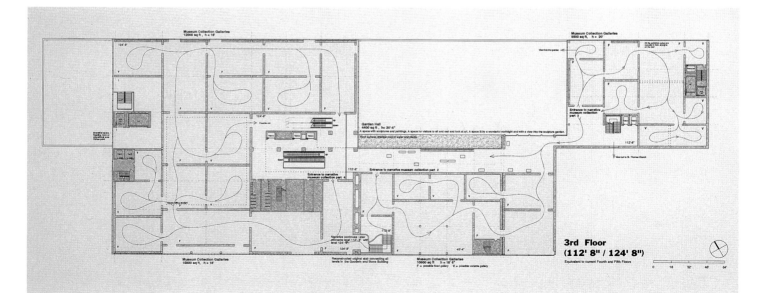

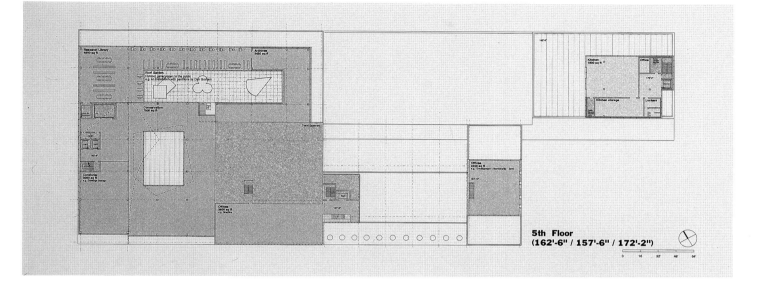

5th Floor
(162'-6" / 157'-6" / 172'-2")

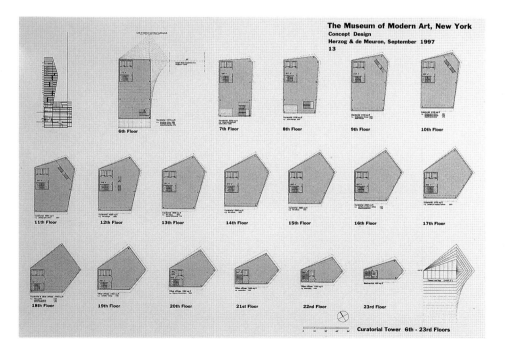

The Museum of Modern Art, New York
Concept Design
Herzog & de Meuron, September 1997
13

Curatorial Tower 6th - 23rd Floors

Above:
Fifth floor plan. Computer-generated print mounted on board

Left:
Plans and section diagram of Curatorial Tower, sixth through twenty-third floors. Computer-generated print mounted on board

Yoshio Taniguchi

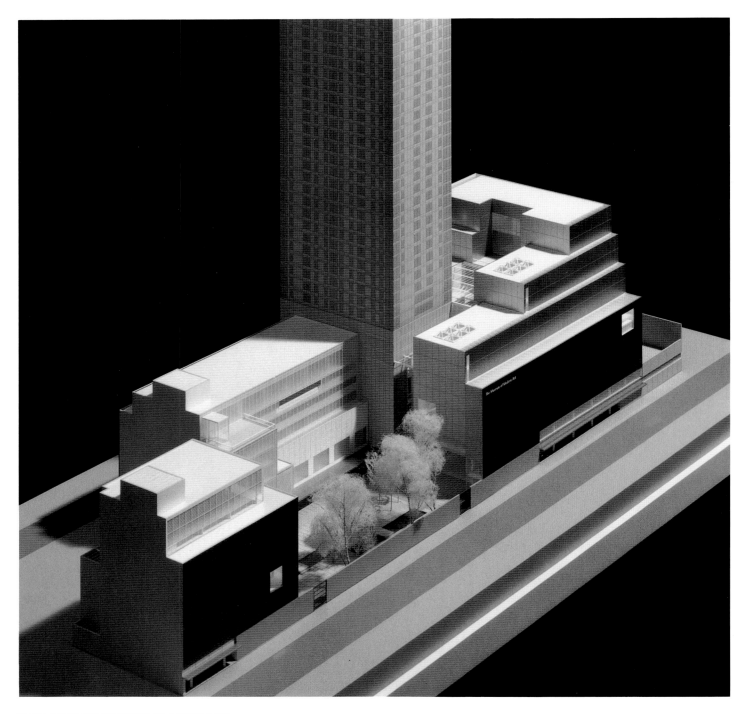

Model. Acrylic, 19⅝ x 24 x 11½" (50 x 61 x 29.2 cm)

Photomontage and aerial view of Museum site. Computer-generated print mounted on foam board

Site plan. Computer-generated print mounted on foam board

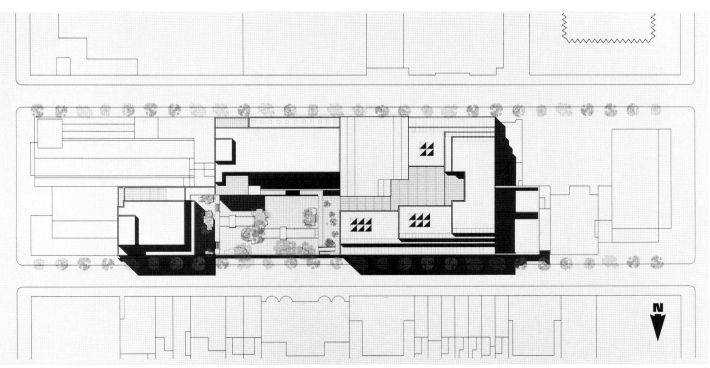

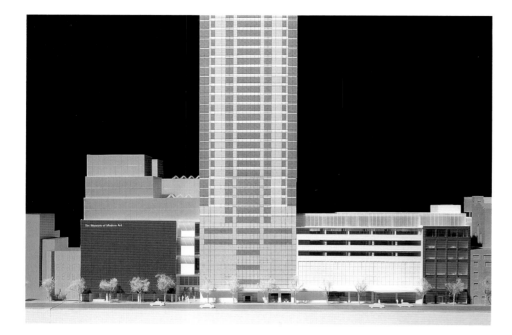

Exterior perspective of sculpture garden and cafeteria. Computer-generated print mounted on foam board, 30 x 42" (76.2 x 106.7 cm)

Opposite:
Two views of model. Top: Fifty-third Street elevation.
Bottom: Fifty-fourth Street elevation. Acrylic

Exterior perspective of sculpture garden with lobby and gallery spaces beyond. Computer-generated print mounted on foam board

Interior perspective of lobby and lobby stairs leading
to galleries above. Computer-generated print
mounted on foam board

01 Incomparable Collection of Modern and Contemporary Art
Collection Galleries Placed Prominently above New Lobby

Spacious and Flexible Galleries

Conservation

Temporary Galleries

Collection Galleries

Main Entrance - 54th Street

Galleries with Ample Natural Light

Conservation

Temporary Galleries

Collection Galleries

54th Street   53rd Street

Entrance Lobby

Axonometric and section diagrams showing Museum Collection galleries above new lobby. Computer-generated print mounted on foam board

Interior perspective of Museum Collection gallery 2. Computer-generated print mounted on foam board

Collection Gallery 3
Various levels within the gallery provide visitors with different vantage points.

Temporary Exhibition Gallery 1
Spacious galleries with extensive wall areas will be provided.

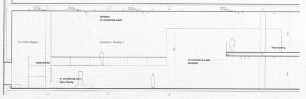

Collection Gallery 3
A variety of ceiling heights creates a gallery appropriate for every kind of contemporary art.

Gallery Space

Temporary Exhibition Gallery 1·2
Linear skylights illuminating walls and localized skylights creating focal points in space suffuse the gallery with natural light.

Elevations and interior perspectives of Museum Collection galleries. Computer-generated print mounted on foam board

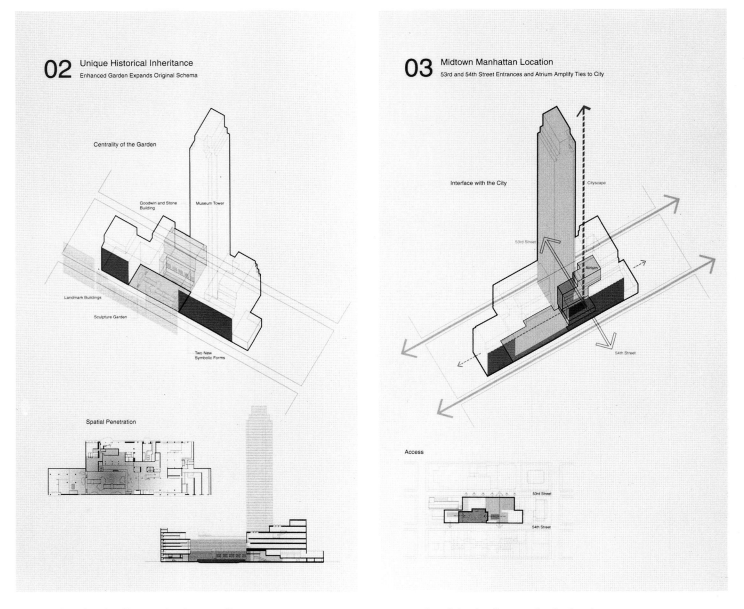

02 Unique Historical Inheritance
Enhanced Garden Expands Original Schema

Centrality of the Garden

Goodwin and Stone Building

Museum Tower

Landmark Buildings

Sculpture Garden

Two New Symbolic Forms

Spatial Penetration

03 Midtown Manhattan Location
53rd and 54th Street Entrances and Atrium Amplify Ties to City

Interface with the City

Cityscape

53rd Street

Atrium

54th Street

Access

53rd Street

54th Street

Axonometric and section diagrams showing centrality of sculpture garden. Computer-generated print mounted on foam board

Axonometric and site plan diagrams showing interface with Midtown location. Computer-generated print mounted on foam board

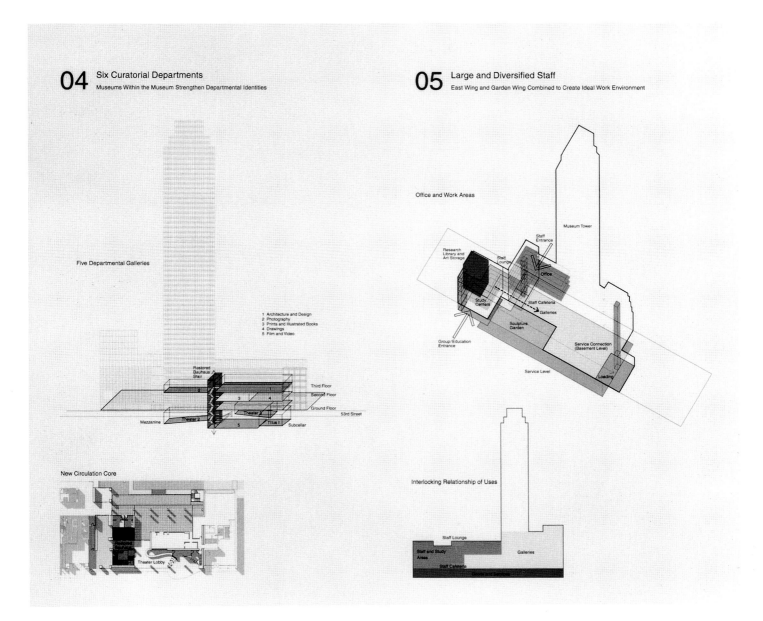

04 Six Curatorial Departments
Museums Within the Museum Strengthen Departmental Identities

Five Departmental Galleries

1 Architecture and Design
2 Photography
3 Prints and Illustrated Books
4 Drawings
5 Film and Video

Restored
Bauhaus
Stair

Third Floor
Second Floor
Ground Floor
53rd Street

Mezzanine   Theater 2   Theater 1   Titus 1   Subcellar

New Circulation Core

Theater Lobby

05 Large and Diversified Staff
East Wing and Garden Wing Combined to Create Ideal Work Environment

Office and Work Areas

Museum Tower

Staff
Entrance

Research
Library and
Art Storage

Staff
Lounge

Office

Study
Centers

Staff Cafeteria

Galleries

Group/Education
Entrance

Sculpture
Garden

Service Connection
(Basement Level)

Service Level

Loading

Interlocking Relationship of Uses

Staff Lounge

Staff and Study
Areas

Galleries

Staff Cafeteria

**Axonometric and section diagrams showing Museum
Collection galleries and staff work spaces. Computer-
generated print mounted on foam board**

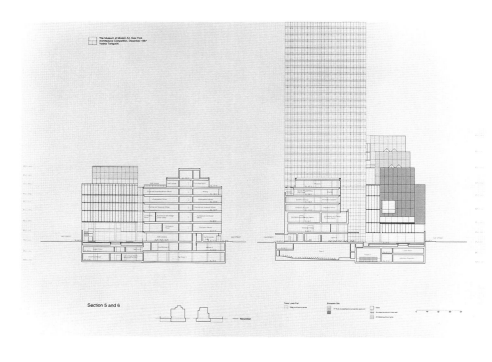

Section 5 and 6

Left
Top: Transverse sections, looking east (left) and west (right).
Bottom: Longitudinal section through public spaces and sculpture garden, looking south. Computer-generated prints mounted on foam board

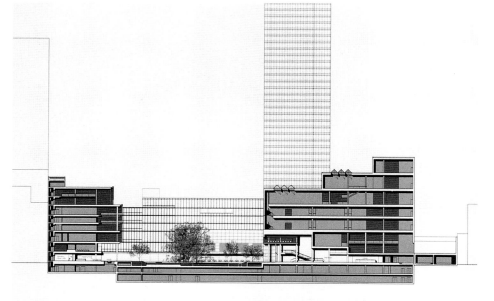

Right:
Top: Transverse section through atrium.
**Bottom: Mezzanine floor plan. Computer-generated
prints mounted on foam board**

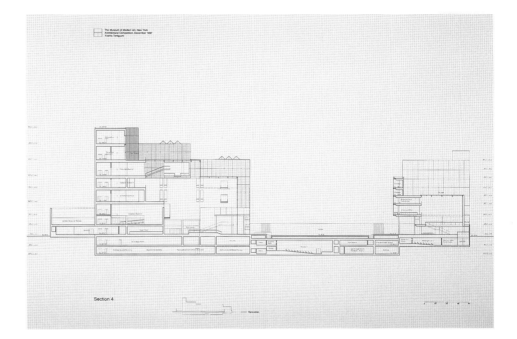

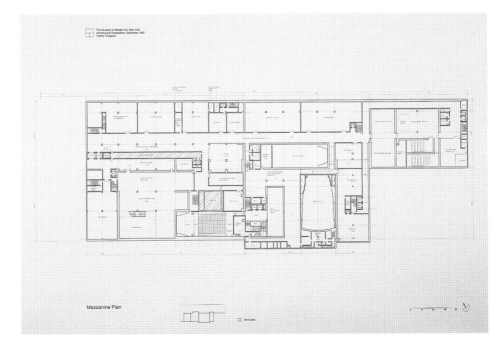

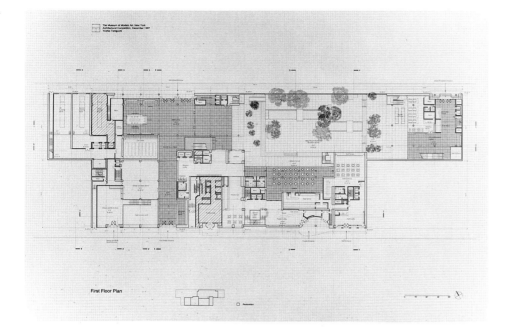

Ground floor plan. Computer-generated print mounted on foam board

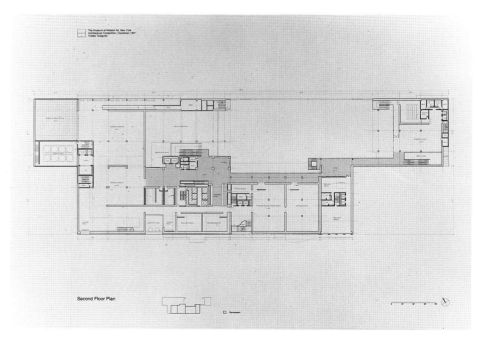

Second floor plan. Computer-generated print mounted on foam board

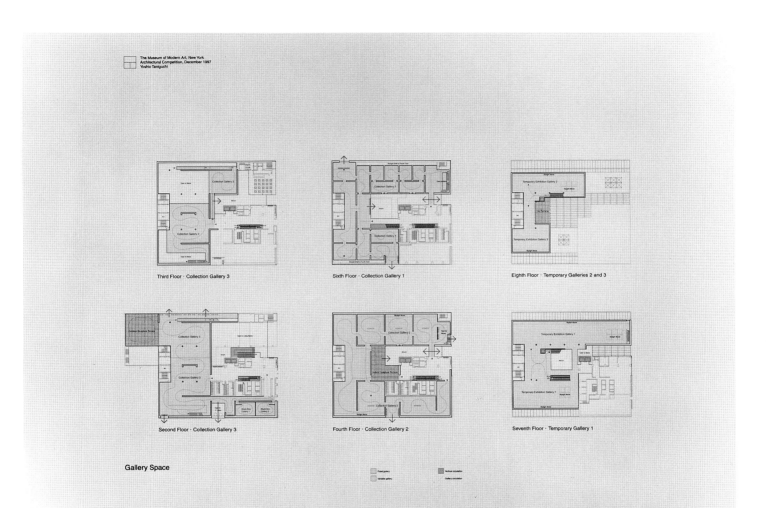

Third Floor · Collection Gallery 3

Sixth Floor · Collection Gallery 1

Eighth Floor · Temporary Galleries 2 and 3

Second Floor · Collection Gallery 3

Fourth Floor · Collection Gallery 2

Seventh Floor · Temporary Gallery 1

Gallery Space

**Plans of gallery spaces. Computer-generated print
mounted on foam board**

Bernard Tschumi

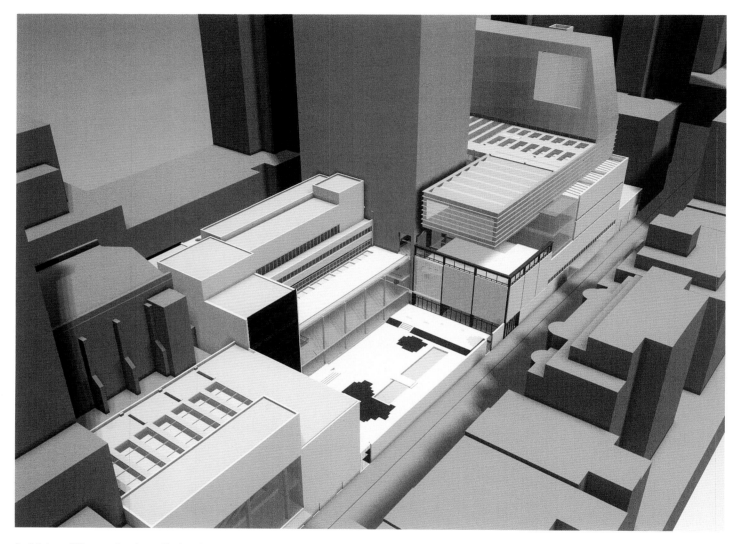

Aerial view of Museum site along Fifty-fourth Street.
Computer-generated print mounted on foam core

Opposite:
Top: Exterior perspective along Fifty-third Street.
Bottom: Site plan. Computer-generated prints
mounted on foam core

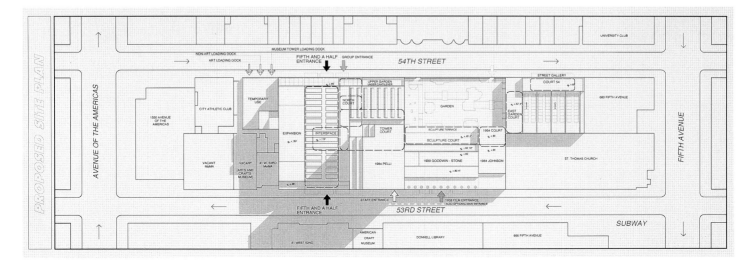

Right:
Diagram showing location of galleries. Computer-generated print mounted on foam core

Below:
Night view along Fifty-fourth Street showing lighted courts. Computer-generated print mounted on foam core

THE MUSEUM COLLECTION GALLERIES AND TEMPORARY EXHIBITIONS GALLERIES LINKED TOGETHER BY THE DEPARTMENTAL GALLERIES, ALL OF WHICH GIVE ONTO THE SCULPTURE GARDEN IN THE CENTER.

DEPARTMENTAL GALLERIES:
PHOTOGRAPHY
ARCHITECTURE AND DESIGN
FILM AND VIDEO

MUSEUM PERMANENT COLLECTION GALLERIES

EAST GARDEN GALLERIES
TEMPORARY EXHIBITIONS

SCULPTURE GARDEN

DEPARTMENTAL GALLERIES:
PRINTS AND ILLUSTRATED BOOKS
DRAWINGS

Left:
Interior perspective of Tower Court, looking east. Computer-generated print mounted on foam core

Below:
Interior perspective of entrance court between Fifty-third and Fifty-fourth streets ("Fifth and a Half"), looking south. Computer-generated print mounted on foam core

Interior perspective of Tower Court from the second
floor, looking west. Computer-generated print
mounted on foam core

Right:
Top: Interior perspective of Upper Garden Court
beneath cantilever. Bottom: Interior perspective of
sculpture court. Computer-generated prints mounted
on foam core

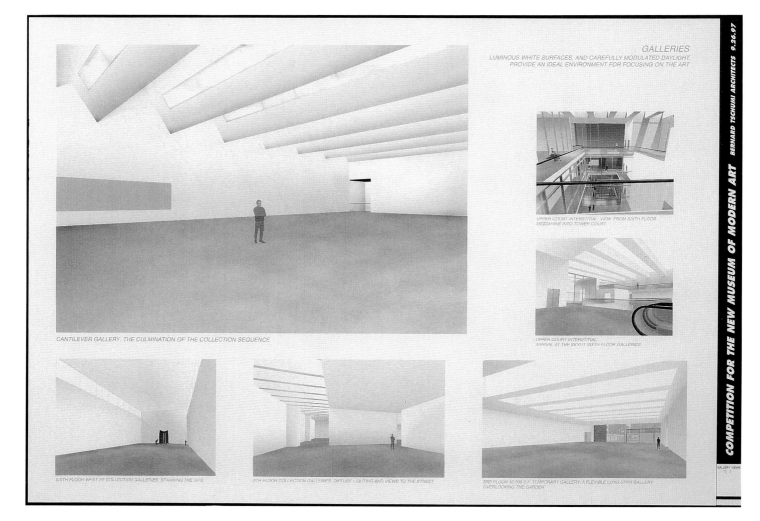

Interior perspective of temporary and Museum Collection galleries. Computer-generated print mounted on foam core

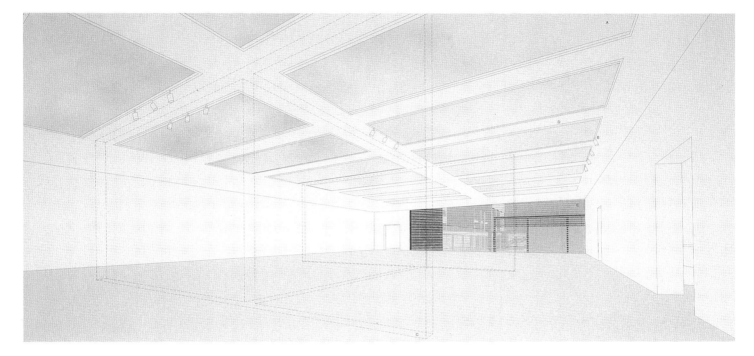

Interior perspective of temporary exhibitions gallery.
Computer-generated print mounted on foam core

Longitudinal section through various courts. Computer-generated print mounted on foam core

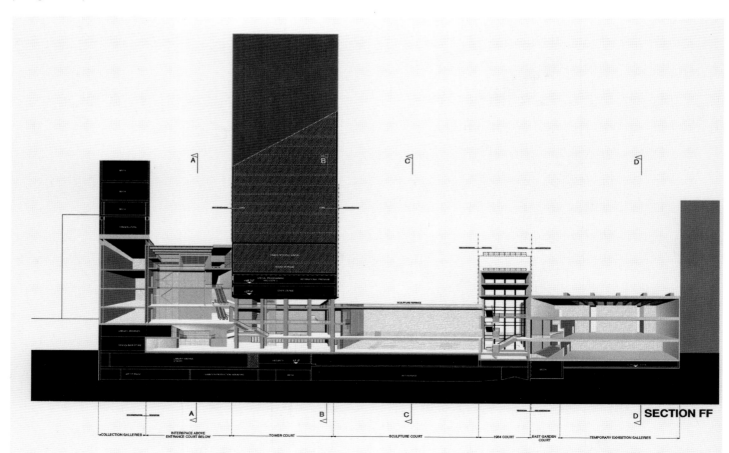

Galleries and Courts: clarity of the spatial sequence.

Conceptual model. Entrance and Tower courts. Computer-generated print mounted on foam core, 5 ½ x 5 ½" (14 x 14 cm)

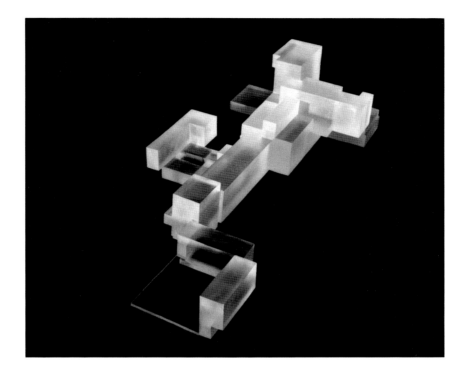

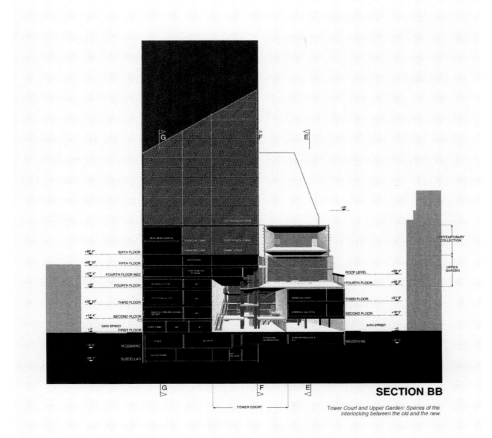

SECTION BB

Tower Court and Upper Garden: Spaces of the interlocking between the old and the new.

Transverse section through Tower Court and Upper Garden. Computer-generated print mounted on foam core

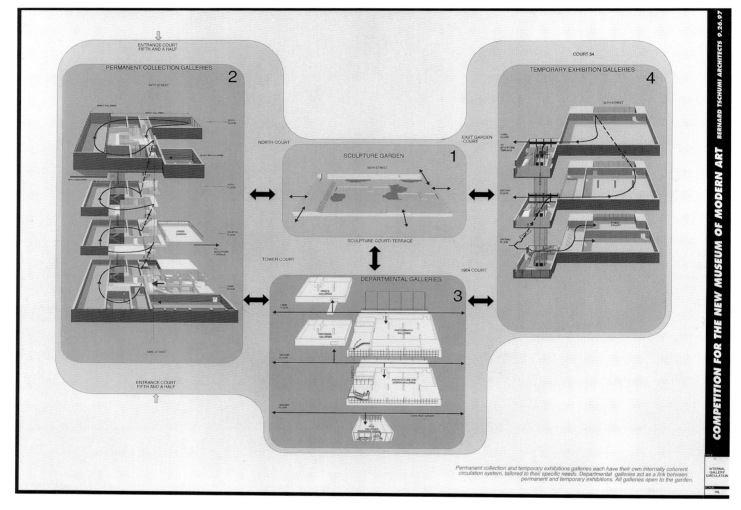

Circulation system diagrams for Museum Collection, departmental, and temporary exhibitions galleries. Computer-generated print mounted on foam core

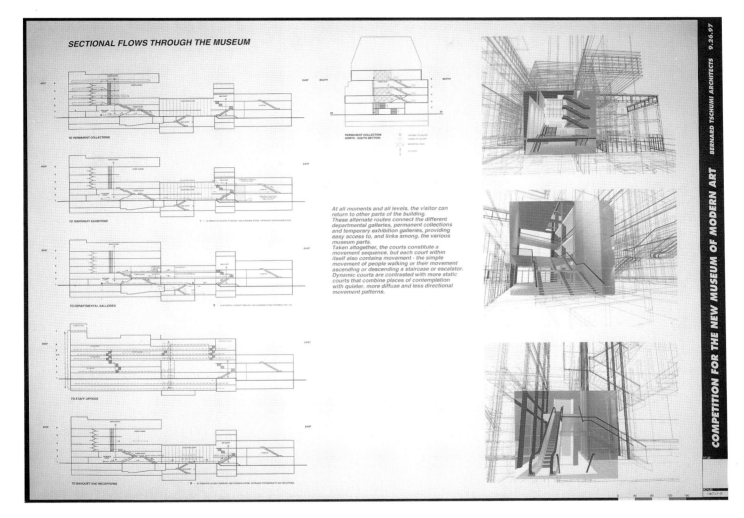

Sections and interior perspectives of circulation
paths through the Museum. Computer-generated
print mounted on foam core

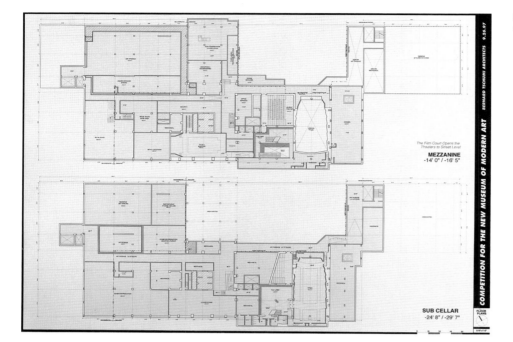

Subcellar and mezzanine floor plans. Computer-generated print mounted on foam core

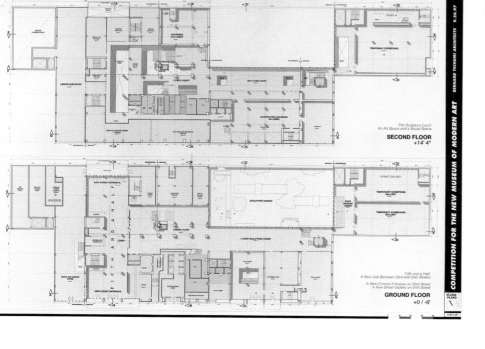

Ground and second floor plans. Computer-generated print mounted on foam core

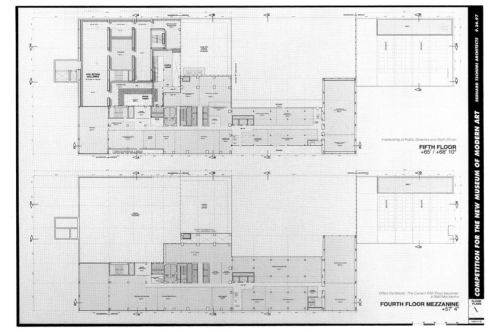

Fourth floor mezzanine and fifth floor plans. Computer-generated print mounted on foam core

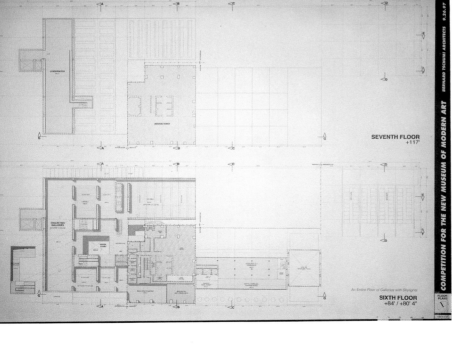

Sixth and seventh floor plans. Computer-generated print mounted on foam core

Photograph Credits

The photographs reproduced in this publication were provided in most cases by The Museum of Modern Art. The following list, keyed to page numbers, applies to photographs for which an additional acknowledgment is due.

Alinari/Art Resource, NY: 126 bottom left, 127 bottom left. David Allison: Cover, Frontispiece, 161–169, 172–179, 182–189, 192–199, 202–209, 212–219, 222–229, 232–239, 244–251, 256–263, 314, 327 bottom, 332, 336–339. James Austin: 124 bottom left. Bamberger Gift, courtesy Graduate School of Architecture, Preservation and Planning, Columbia University: 131 left. Hans–Joachim Bartsch, Berlin, courtesy Stadtmuseum Berlin: 132. Bernard Tschumi Architects: 326, 327 top, 328–331, 333–335. Bernstein Associates, Photographers: 79 right. © Board of Trustees, National Gallery of Art, Washington, D.C.: 79 left. Centre Georges Pompidou, Paris (D.R.): 77 bottom right. Chevojan Frères, courtesy École nationale supérieure des beaux–arts (plan): 119 top. © 1997 The Cleveland Museum of Art: 77 top left. Cooper, Robertson and Partners: 75, 96, 97, 142, 152, 155–159, 266, 286, 292–297. George Cserna, courtesy The Museum of Modern Art, New York: 88 bottom. Thomas Dallal/New York Times Pictures: 74. Robert M. Damora, courtesy The Museum of Modern Art, New York: 87 top left, 120 bottom left and right. Electa Archive (iconographic source): 127 bottom right. © 1998 Estate of Dan Flavin/Artists Rights Society (ARS) New York : 80 top. Foto Marburg/Art Resource, NY: 126 bottom right. Alexandre Georges, courtesy The Museum of Modern Art, New York: 82 top center, 83 top left, 83 bottom right. Ludwig Glaeser: 122 right. Courtesy the Graduate School of Architecture, Preservation and Planning, Columbia University: 124 bottom right, 126 center right. Robert Harrell, courtesy the Freer Gallery of Art, Smithsonian Institution, Washington, D.C.: 77 top right. © 1997 C. Herscovici, Brussels/Artists Rights Society (ARS) New York: 127 top. Herzog & de Meuron: 298–311. © Kotaro Hirano: 313, 315–325. Hirmer Verlag Munchen: 126 top left. Henry Holt & Co. (U.S.) from *The Riddle of the Pyramids* by Kurt Mendelsohn, © 1974 Kurt Mendelssohn; reprinted with permission of Henry Holt and Company: 126 top right. Philip and Frances Huscher, Chicago, Illinois: 130 bottom right. Peter Juley, courtesy The Museum of Modern Art, New York: 86 top left and right. © 1977 Louis I. Kahn Collection, University of Pennsylvania and Pennsylvania Historical and Museum Commission: 125 top right. Kate Keller, courtesy The Museum of Modern Art, New York: 76 bottom. ©Toshiharu Kitajima: 10, 312. *L'Architecture d'aujourd'hui*: 121. James Matthews, courtesy The Museum of Modern Art, New York (section): 119 bottom. Courtesy The Ludwig Mies van der Rohe Archive, The Museum of Modern Art, New York: 131 right. Paolo Monti, courtesy Instituto di Fotografia Paolo Monti: 123 left. Museum of Contemporary Art, Chicago: 110 bottom. Courtesy The Museum of Modern Art, New York: 85 top, 85 bottom left, 120 top, 129 top, 129 bottom left, 129 bottom right. Courtesy The Museum of Modern Art Archives, New York; Archives Pamphlet File: The Museum of Modern Art, Building: 89 left, 89 right, 90 top. Courtesy The Museum of Modern Art Photographic Archive, New York: 83 bottom left, 85 bottom right, 90 bottom left and right. Beaumont Newhall, courtesy The Museum of Modern Art, New York: 86 bottom left and right. Courtesy PaceWildenstein: 130 bottom center, 130 bottom left. Paulhans Peters: 122 left. Courtesy the Philips Exeter Academy: 125 top left, 125 bottom. © 1995 President and Fellows of Harvard College, courtesy Harvard University Art Museums: 77 bottom left. © 1923 W. J. Roege, courtesy The Museum of Modern Art Archives, New York: Slide Collection: 81 top. Lynn Rosenthal, 1992: 124 top. Courtesy the San Francisco Museum of Modern Art: 78 top left. Seattle Art Museum: 110 top. © 1998 Richard Serra/Artists Rights Society (ARS) New York; Tom Powel, courtesy The Museum of Modern Art, New York: 76 top. Skyviews Survey Aerial Photography: 130 top right. Courtesy Sterling and Francine Clark Art Institute: 78 bottom. Soichi Sunami, courtesy The Museum of Modern Art, New York: 81 bottom, 82 right, 86 bottom center, 87 right, 87 bottom left, 88 top left, 88 top right, 118. Thames and Hudson, Ltd. (Europe) From *Egypt to the End of the Old Kingdom* by Cyril Aldred, 1965; reprinted with permission of Thames and Hudson, Ltd.: 126 top right. Courtesy United States Coast and Geodetic Survey: 130 top left. Jacques Vasseur: 128 left. Courtesy Visual Resources Collection, Department of Art History and Archaeology, Columbia University: 126 center left, 126 bottom left, 127 bottom left. Whitney Museum of American Art, New York: 78 top right.

A Note to Contributors

Studies in Modern Art publishes scholarly articles focusing on works of art in the collection of The Museum of Modern Art and on the Museum's programs. It is issued annually, although additional special numbers may be published from time to time. Each number deals with a particular topic. A list of future topics may be obtained from the journal office.

Contributors should submit proposals to the Editorial Committee of the journal by January 1 of the year preceding publication. Proposals should include the title of the article; a 500-word description of the subject; a critical appraisal of the current state of scholarship on the subject; and a list of works in the Museum's collection or details of the Museum's program that will be discussed. A working draft of the article may be submitted as a proposal. The Editorial Committee will evaluate all proposals and invite selected authors to submit finished manuscripts. (Such an invitation will not constitute acceptance of the article for publication.) Authors of articles published in the journal receive an honorarium and complimentary copies of the issue.

Please submit all inquiries to:

Studies in Modern Art
The Museum of Modern Art
11 West 53 Street
New York, New York 10019

Trustees of The Museum of Modern Art